'I dropped the first atomic bomb on Hiroshima. Preparing and planning for that mission took nearly a year. Until now I thought I knew everything that had happened. Then I read this book. Not only did it take me back to that most exciting time leading up to the atomic age, but it opened my eyes on almost every page. As I read it, I kept on saying to myself "that's exactly how it was," and time and again I was jolted by some new fact that the authors had discovered. Their revelations about the Japanese side of things will startle everybody; their factual presentation of all aspects of a momentous event left me filled with admiration. For years now there has been controversy over Hiroshima. Now it can end. This book tells the plain, unvarnished truth.'

—Colonel Paul Tibbets, commander of the 509th Composite Group and aircraft commander of the *Enola Gay* (the bomber that carried the Hiroshima bomb to its target.)

Books by Gordon Thomas and Max Morgan Witts

The Day the World Ended
The San Francisco Earthquake
Shipwreck: The Strange Fate of the Morro Castle
Voyage of the Damned
Enola Gay (expanded as *Ruin From the Air)*
The Day the Bubble Burst
Pontiff
Averting Armageddon

RUIN FROM THE AIR

RUIN FROM THE AIR

The Enola Gay's Atomic Mission to Hiroshima

GORDON THOMAS

AND

MAX MORGAN WITTS

Scarborough House/Publishers

Scarborough House/*Publishers*
Chelsea, MI 48118

FIRST SCARBOROUGH HOUSE PAPERBACK EDITION 1990

Enola Gay was first published in hardcover in the United
States by Stein and Day/Publishers.
Ruin From the Air, an expanded version, dealing with the
same events, was originally published in hardcover in Great
Britain by Hamish Hamilton, Ltd., and is reprinted by
arrangement with the authors and Hamish Hamilton, Ltd.

Library of Congress Cataloging-in-Publication Data

Thomas, Gordon.
    Ruin from the air : the Enola Gay's atomic mission to
Hiroshima / Gordon Thomas and Max Morgan Witts. — 1st
Scarborough House paperback ed.
        p.   cm.
    Reprint. Originally published: London : Hamilton, 1977.
    Includes bibliographical references and index.
    ISBN 0-8128-8509-0
    1. Hiroshima-shi (Japan) – History – Bombardment, 1945. I.
Morgan Witts, Max. II. Title.
D767.25.H6T53 1990
940.54'25–dc20   90-39788
                                                        CIP

The aircraft was above the objective before anyone realised its intentions. From the cockpit of the bi-plane showered oblong shapes attached to parachutes. Caught in the plane's prop-wash, they were scattered far and wide over Miami Beach, Florida. The bombardier was satisfied. He had dumped his promotional cargo of Babe Ruth Candy Bars directly into the target area. He was thirteen years old and this advertising stunt was his first flight. From that moment, he was hooked on flying.

The boy was Paul Tibbets. Later he became a test pilot and one of the first Americans to fight in World War Two. Seventeen years after 'bombing' Miami Beach with chocolate bars, he found himself assigned to a mission more daunting than any he had ever flown in combat.

> I got called in on the bomb job . . . I was told I was going to destroy one city with one bomb. That was quite a thought . . . We had working in my organisation a murderer, three men guilty of manslaughter and several felons; all of them had escaped from prison. The murderer was serving life; the manslaughter guys were doing ten to fifteen years; the felons three to five. After escaping they had enlisted under false names. They were all skilled technicians, primarily tool- and die-makers. They were good, real good at their jobs and we needed 'em. We told them that if they gave us no trouble, they would have no trouble from us. After it was over, we called each of them in and handed them their dossiers and a box of matches, and said, 'Go burn 'em.' You see, I was not running a police department. I was running an outfit that was unique.
>
> —*Excerpt from authors' interviews in 1975–6 with Brigadier-General Paul Warfield Tibbets, 111, USAF Ret., aircraft commander* Enola Gay, *the B-29 bomber used for the Hiroshima A-bomb mission*

CONTENTS

ILLUSTRATIONS

MAPS

drawn by Patrick Leeson

PERSONAE

Some of the persons prominent in the story.

THE EXECUTIVE
United States of America

Franklin Delano Roosevelt	Thirty-second President
Harry S. Truman	Thirty-third President
Henry L. Stimson	Secretary of War
James F. Byrnes	Secretary of State

Japan

Hirohito	Emperor
Kantaro Suzuki	Prime Minister
Shigenori Togo	Foreign Minister
Naotake Sato	Ambassador to Russia

THE SCIENTISTS
United States of America

J. Robert Oppenheimer	Scientific Director, Los Alamos
Enrico Fermi	Director, Advanced Development Division
Niels Bohr	Physicist
Edward B. Doll	Physicist
Norman Ramsey	Physicist

Japan

Tsunesaburo Asada	Physicist, Consultant to Imperial Japanese Navy

THE MILITARY
United States of America

Brigadier General Leslie R. Groves	Director, Manhattan Project (MED)
Captain William 'Deak' Parsons, USN	Director, Ordnance Division, Los Alamos
General Curtis LeMay	Commander 21st Bomber Command, then Chief of Staff, Strategic Air Forces

Colonel Paul Tibbets	Commander, 509th Composite Group
Major Tom Ferebee	509th Group Bombardier
Captain Theodore 'Dutch' van Kirk	509th Group Navigator
Major Charles Sweeney	C.O. 393rd Bombardment Squadron of 509th Composite Group
1st Lieutenant Jacob Beser	393rd Radar counter-measures Officer
2nd Lieutenant Morris Jeppson	1st Ordnance Squadron Electronics Officer
Captain Claude Eatherly	Pilot, aircraft commander *Straight Flush*

and the crew of the *Enola Gay*:

Captain Robert Lewis	Pilot
S/Sgt George 'Bob' Caron	Tail-gunner
S/Sgt Wyatt Duzenbury	Flight Engineer
S/Sgt Joe Stiborik	Radar Operator
Sgt Robert Shumard	Assistant Flight Engineer
Pvt Richard Nelson	Radio Operator

along with some 1,700 others of the 509th Composite Group

Japan

Field Marshal Shunroku Hata	Commander, 2nd General Army, Hiroshima
Major-General Seizo Arisue	Director of Intelligence, Imperial Japanese Army
Lt-Colonel Kakuzo Oya	Chief of American Intelligence Section, Imperial Japanese Army
Lt-Commander Mochitsura Hashimoto	Submarine Commander, Imperial Japanese Navy
2nd Lieutenant Tatsuo Yokoyama	Anti-aircraft Gunnery Officer, Hiroshima
2nd Lieutenant Matsuo Yasuzawa	Pilot, flying instructor, Imperial Japanese Army
Warrant Officer Hiroshi Yanagita	Kempei Tai leader, Hiroshima

along with some 40,000 other military personnel in Hiroshima and:

| Chief Warrant Officer Kizo Imai | Ordnance Officer, Imperial Japanese Navy, Tinian |

along with some 500 others in hiding on Tinian

CIVILIANS

Hiroshima

Senkichi Awaya	Mayor
Kazumasa Maruyama	His chief assistant
Dr. Kaoru Shima	Medical director, Shima Clinic

along with some 280,000 other citizens in the city.

The atomic bomb will never go off, and I speak as an expert on explosives.
> —*Admiral William D. Leahy, Chief of Staff to President Roosevelt, March 1945*

Any brief military advantage the United States might gain with nuclear weapons would be offset by political and psychological losses and damage to American prestige. The United States might even touch off a worldwide armaments race.
> —*Albert Einstein to President Roosevelt, April 1945*

There will be a short intermission while we bomb our target . . . My god . . . !
> —*Captain Robert A. Lewis, USAAF, co-pilot of* Enola Gay, *August 6, 1945*

Hiroshima did not somehow resemble a city destroyed by war, but rather a fragment of a world that was ending. Mankind had destroyed itself and the survivors now felt as though they were suicides who had failed.
> —*Yoko Ohta, Hiroshima poetess*

The Japs well knew—they had been warned / of the Allied might that was being formed / But they chose to die for the Rising Sun / and proudly stuck to their ill-made gun / But a thunderous blast, a blinding light / Brought the 509th atomic might.
> —*Opening verse of poem,* Atomic Might, *composed by Sgt. Harry Barnard, 509th A-bomb Composite Group, on Tinian, August 6, 1945*

If they do not now accept our terms, they may expect a rain of ruin from the air, the like of which has never been seen on this earth.
> —*President Truman, making the official announcement of the A-bomb attack on Hiroshima, August 6, 1945*

A mighty accomplishment. I don't want anything to do with it. I am leaving this world. It will destroy Mankind. Then we will have to start over again.
> —*Reichsmarschall Hermann Goering during interrogation for war crimes, August 7, 1945*

NEW! SENSATIONAL AN-ATOMIC BOMBS! STEP INSIDE!
> —*Sign outside Burlesque theatre in Times Square, New York, August 8, 1945*

There are those who considered that the atomic bomb should never have been used at all . . . that rather than throw this bomb we should have sacrificed a million Americans and a quarter of a million

British in the desperate battles and massacres of the invasion of Japan. The bomb brought peace, but man alone can keep that peace.
    —Winston Churchill, August 16, 1945

That A-bomb, that's dynamite!
    —Sam Goldwyn, film producer and malapropist, Hollywood, August 20, 1945

I have some stumps in my field that I should like to blow out. Have you any atomic bombs the right size for the job? If you have let me know by return mail, and let me know how much they cost. I think I should like them better than dynamite.
    —Letter from farmer in Newport, Arizona, to non-existent Atomic Bomb Corp., Washington DC, August 21, 1945

It did not dawn at once on us that not everybody would look upon us as heroes.
    —Robert Caron, USAAF Ret., tail-gunner on Enola Gay, *in conversation with authors August 20, 1975*

I feel sorry for the citizens of Hiroshima, but the bombing could not be helped, as the war at that time was going on.
    —Emperor Hirohito at a press conference in Tokyo after returning from his American tour, November 1975

Chain Reaction

September 1, 1944 to June 27, 1945

Always before, he had tried to be truthful. If he had lied it was for the sake of others, never himself. Paul Warfield Tibbets guessed that the man facing him in the cloakroom, had asked his question to see whether he would lie now.

The man wore the uniform of a colonel in the United States Army, one rank senior to Tibbets. Minutes before, he had introduced himself as 'Lansdale—Intelligence'.

He had then asked Tibbets to step into the washroom, adjoining the office of General Uzal G. Ent, commanding general of the 2nd Air Force. There Lansdale had posed his question.

Before him, Lansdale saw a stocky, medium-sized figure with the face of a non-practising comedian. A face which gave no clue that here was one of America's most successful bomber pilots; a combat veteran who had flown the first B-17 across the English Channel on a bombing mission in World War Two; who had piloted General Dwight D. Eisenhower and General Mark Clark to Gibraltar to plan the Allied invasion of North Africa; who had taken Clark on to Algiers, landing on a field being bombed and strafed. Tibbets had later led the first American raid on North Africa. Returning to the United States he took charge of flight-testing the new B-29 Super-fortress at a time when the bomber was thought too dangerous to fly; it had killed its first test pilot. Tibbets was courageous, used to command, able to give and execute orders with speed and efficiency.

Some people, though, found Tibbets difficult to work with. He did not suffer fools, and by his own standards there were many fools. Restrained and reticent, Tibbets appeared the paragon of service correctness. Few knew he concealed his sensitivity by steely control, that behind his outward appearance was a shy and cultured man, who had suffered acutely the loss of any of his fliers in action. All that invariably showed on his face was a pleasant non-committal intelligence.

Lansdale waited for an answer to his question.

In these past three hectic days he had found out all he needed to know about Tibbets.

Tibbets was born in Quincy, Illinois in 1915. His father, a whole-sale confectioner, was a strict disciplinarian, who severely punished the slightest infringement of the many rules which hedged in his son's formative years. Paul's mother, Enola Gay, was as gentle as her unusual forenames. She adored her only son, and strongly opposed her husband's decision to send Paul, at the age of thirteen, to the Western Military Academy at Alton, Illinois. Afterwards, it was his mother who first encouraged him to be a doctor and later, against strong family opposition, to join the United States Air Corps; she quietly accepted Paul's wish to abandon medicine in favour of flying. But in those difficult post-Depression days, a military career was not viewed with great favour in the middle-class community in which Paul Tibbets' father was a pillar.

When his son enlisted in 1937, his father's last words on the subject were: 'You're on your own.' His mother had said: 'Son, one day we're going to be real proud of you.' She reminded him always to 'dress neatly', never to promise more than he could do, and always to tell the truth.

Lansdale knew that Tibbets had lived by these maxims throughout his outstanding service career, that they had helped sustain him in his fading marriage, where his frugal eating habits and conservative style in civilian clothes were contributing to the breakdown.

But it was Tibbets' concern for the truth which had enabled Lansdale, in the unlikely surroundings of a washroom, to frame his single question.

Tibbets showed no visible reaction. Nevertheless, he was stunned. How did this stranger know of it, that private event of ten, or was it twelve, years ago; an event of such a passing nature that he himself could not now exactly remember its date? Why had Lansdale been probing something which happened all those years back?

Tibbets tried to keep a sense of detachment about the question. He recognised that this assault upon his privacy, his sense of self-respect, was calculated. But how should he cope with it?

He knew nothing about Lansdale. He did not know he was one of less than a hundred men in the whole world with knowledge of what the Manhattan Project was meant to do: produce the world's first atomic bomb. Many of the scientists involved in the project did not even know they were working on such a weapon.

But soon somebody would be needed to deliver that bomb.

Tibbets did not suspect that this confrontation in the washroom was crucial in deciding his suitability for the task.

He did know that Lansdale's question had nothing directly to do with Military Intelligence. Therefore, he would be perfectly justified in not answering. Then he could walk out, unchallenged, through one of the two doors in the washroom: *that* door would return him to the conventional military world where nobody would dare ask such an intimate question of a much decorated war hero.

4

Tibbets decided to tell the truth.

'Yes. I was once arrested by the police on North Miami Beach.'

'What for?'

'The Chief of Police at Surfside caught me in the back of an automobile . . . with a girl,' confessed Tibbets.

The rest took little telling: his arrest, spell in the cells, the intervention of a family friend, Judge Curry, the indiscretion hushed up.

Lansdale was satisfied.

By admitting the truth about a back-seat dalliance with a girl whose name he now had difficulty in recalling, Paul Tibbets had assured himself of a place in history. Within a year his name would become forever linked with the destruction of Hiroshima, a Japanese city he was yet to hear of.

Until three days earlier on Tuesday, August 29, 1944, Tibbets had not been considered for the task. Then late in the afternoon, General Giles, assistant chief of air staff, decided to replace an earlier nominee with Tibbets. Lansdale immediately supervised the most thorough vetting of Tibbets, staging the cloakroom meeting as the climax.

Lansdale's question about a teenage sexual peccadillo was intended as the final test of Tibbets' character. Tibbets would never understand why it was necessary to conduct the interview in a men's washroom. And nobody would ever tell him.

General Ent was relieved when Lansdale led Tibbets back into his office. He wanted to get this matter over as quickly as possible. Endowed with a simple-hearted sincerity, Ent was not equipped to cope with the wiles of Lansdale.

He looked enquiringly at the intelligence officer.

Lansdale nodded.

Ent then introduced the two men seated beside his desk. One was U.S. Navy Captain William 'Deak' Parsons, whom he described as an 'explosives expert' but who was in fact one of the most influential men in the Manhattan Project; the other was a civilian, Professor Norman Ramsey, a twenty-nine-year-old Harvard physicist.

Tibbets was struck by Ramsey's comparative youth; he had always associated scientists with grey hair and stooped shoulders. Physically, the two men looked fit enough to fly combat, even if Parsons' baldness made him appear older than his forty-four years. And it seemed strange that this naval captain should be involved in what appeared to be an Army Air Force meeting.

'Have you ever heard of atomic energy?' Ramsey had the firm, incisive voice of a natural tutor.

'Yes.'

'How?'

5

'I majored in physics, so I know the atomic scale.'

There was an expectant pause.

'What do you know of the present situation in the field?' asked Parsons.

Tibbets looked at Ent. There was no encouragement there. A few days before, when he had first become aware of the Manhattan Project, Ent himself had been warned he would be court-martialled if any leak of information was traced to him. Tibbets looked to Lansdale, who gave the tiniest of nods.

As confidently as he could, Tibbets began to speak. He understood there had been some experimenting by the Germans to try and make heavy water so that they could split the atom.

'Good.' Ramsey's gentle praise was more suited to the campus than the bleak office of a fighting General. He paused, weighing his words, a mannerism Tibbets would come to recognise.

Ramsey continued.

'The United States has now split an atom. We are making a bomb based on that. The bomb will be so powerful that it will explode with a force of 20,000 tons of conventional high explosive.'

Ent then said that Tibbets was going to drop that bomb.

A letter Albert Einstein had composed five years earlier brought Tibbets to Ent's office to hear of men, places and events so incredible that the twenty-nine-year-old pilot wondered if he had been transported to the world of his favourite Hollywood hero, Buck Rogers.

Einstein signed the letter at his holiday home at Peconic, Long Island, on August 2, 1939. It was a warning to President Roosevelt that research into nuclear fission in Nazi Germany and elsewhere could lead to the stage where 'extremely powerful bombs of a new type may thus be constructed. A single bomb of this type, carried by boat and exploded in a port, might well destroy the whole port together with some of the surrounding territory. However, such bombs might very well be too heavy for transportation by air'.

Alexander Sachs, the financier, agreed to take the letter to the White House. Two months passed before, on October 11, 1939, Sachs saw Roosevelt. The financier insisted on reading aloud Einstein's letter. Roosevelt grew bored; he disliked being read to. He ended the interview by telling Sachs that for the United States to become 'involved at this stage would be premature'.

Sachs was mortified. He begged Roosevelt for another meeting. The President finally agreed to see him again, at breakfast next morning.

The financier spent a sleepless night. Next day the red-eyed Sachs told Roosevelt a story about Robert Fulton, the inventor of the steamship.

'Mr. President, he took it to Napoleon who said it was impractical. Napoleon thus lost for France the vessel which would have allowed him to invade England and claim victory.'

Roosevelt pondered. Then he spun his wheelchair to a drinks cabinet, opened its door and produced a bottle of Napoleon brandy and two glasses. He poured generous snifters, handed the exhausted financier a glass, and said, 'What you are after is to see that the Nazis don't blow us up?'

'Exactly.'

Roosevelt summoned his military aide, General Edwin 'Pa' Watson.

'Pa, I want action on this,' said the President. He thrust Einstein's letter and supporting documents at Watson.

'Pa . . . action!'

Those words were the birth-cry of the Manhattan Project.

In financial terms the first result of Roosevelt's call for action was the expenditure of just $6,000. It bought graphite, essential for one of the many initial experiments in the chain reaction of events which would eventually lead to the atomic bomb. The experiment was a success.

Meanwhile in Britain, perhaps spurred on by the urgency of winning a war America had not yet entered, scientists by the spring of 1941 were certain an atomic bomb was possible. Their confidence carried across the Atlantic. Two American scientists travelled to England to investigate. Their findings, allied to an official British report describing in some detail the men, money, materials and method for building a bomb, provided the final impetus for further American research.

On December 6, 1941 Roosevelt authorised substantial funds to be made available for the specific purpose of producing an atomic bomb.

Next day came Pearl Harbor.

The Japanese attack forced America into what, until then, it did not have: a war as reason for making the bomb. In addition, for many Americans, Pearl Harbor would later provide the justification for using it.

Japan meant to attack Pearl Harbor without officially declaring war. It was a tactic the Japanese had used successfully in the past. Japan had, however, intended to break off diplomatic relations twenty minutes before the raid began, thereby providing in their eyes the equivalent of a declaration of war. They felt this would satisfy the somewhat imprecise rules of the Hague Convention.

Diplomatic relations were not broken in time. What was planned by the Japanese as a 'surprise attack' became in fact a 'sneak attack'.

Roosevelt had vowed vengeance. The Manhattan Project promised it would be awesome and total.

Time and money were key factors in the project. By September 1944 there was plenty of money, never enough time. The galaxy of European scientists working on the project feared that Nazi Germany might produce an atomic bomb before them—and win the war.

They asked for more money, and received it with Presidential blessing. Even so, Roosevelt's own attitude remained surprisingly ambivalent towards the project. His likeable weakness for trusting people, his desire that American research be used for the good of mankind, his folksy, but sincere talk of sharing the 'cake of knowledge' was, in this case, in conflict with another quality in his personality—a passion for secrecy.

Secrecy won.

In 1944, he was still running the project without the knowledge of Congress or the electorate. Funds for the venture were 'hidden' in the Federal budget. Eventually two billion dollars would be spent in financing work in secret sites across America.

Site Y, at Los Alamos in the New Mexico desert, was chosen in October 1942 by Julius Robert Oppenheimer, a former pupil of the Los Alamos Ranch School for Boys. Oppenheimer was the scientific director of the Manhattan Project. His old class-rooms were now filled with world-famous scientists, among them Enrico Fermi, Edward Teller and that other giant of European physics, Niels Bohr.

It was Fermi who had master-minded the key experiment on December 2, 1942 which produced the chain reaction needed to make an atomic bomb. He had conducted his experiment on a bitterly cold day in a disused squash court at the University of Chicago. There had been a momentary fear that the city itself could be endangered by the nuclear energy released. But the chain reaction was controlled. And scientists had demonstrated that when a uranium atom splits, it releases neutrons which can then themselves split more uranium atoms, creating the chain reaction. They formally christened this process 'The K Factor'; among themselves they called it 'The Great God K'.

The next problem to be overcome was a technological one: how to enclose K inside a bomb casing.

That problem was now so close to being solved that Paul Tibbets could be called to General Ent's Office and told he was to command and train a unit capable of delivering atomic strikes on Germany and Japan.

Ramsey and Parsons had given Tibbets a thorough briefing on the history and problems associated with building America's first atomic bomb. Now, in Ent's office, Lansdale took over.

'Colonel, I want you to understand one thing. Security is first, last and always. You will commit as little as possible to paper. You will tell only those who need to know what they must know to do their jobs properly. Understood?'

'Perfectly understood, Colonel.'

Ent concluded the meeting by formally assigning the 393rd Heavy Bombardment Squadron, based in Nebraska, to Tibbets. Its fifteen bomber crews would provide the world's first atomic strike force. Their training base would be at Wendover, Utah. The code name for the Army Air Force's involvement in the project would be *Silverplate*.

Tibbets briefly wondered who had chosen such a homely name for a weapon 'clearly designed to revolutionise war'. Even so he still could not accept that *one* bomb dropped from a single aircraft could equal the force of 20,000 tons of high explosive. Ordinarily, some 2,000 bombers would be required to deliver such a pay-load.

But he had more pressing problems to deal with. He must gather together some of the trusted men who had served with him before; he must inspect Wendover; he must devise a training programme; finally, he must be prepared to work alongside 'a bunch of civilians who would give me a glimpse of Pandora's box'.

As Tibbets was leaving the office, Ent stopped him.

'Colonel, if this is successful, you'll be a hero. But if it fails, you'll be the biggest scapegoat ever. You may even go to prison.'

September 6, 1944
Washington, D.C.

The man with the key to Pandora's box was still furiously angry this Wednesday morning. Eleven days had passed since Brigadier-General Leslie Richard Groves discovered what physicist Niels Bohr had done. Groves' initial disbelief had given way to eruptive anger. The tall, floridly-handsome chief of the Manhattan Project regarded as unforgivable the visit Bohr had made to President Roosevelt at 4 p.m. on August 26.

Bohr had asked Roosevelt to authorise the United States to share its atomic secrets with the world's scientific community.

The scientist made his extraordinary request without consulting Groves, a liberty which made the project chief's Clark Gable moustache quiver with rage.

Groves had still been unable to discover exactly what Bohr had said to Roosevelt. The President made it a rule never to record, or reveal, such private interviews. Bohr had infuriated Groves still further by blandly refusing to tell him.

But Groves suspected that the scientist had been his usual garrulous self. In any event Roosevelt had rejected Bohr's plea.

That did not placate Groves.

At a time when unity was vital to ensure that the project remained on schedule, a deep division was growing within its scientific community. The seeds were sown when some of the scientists learned that American Intelligence had established that the Nazis did not have the resources to produce an atomic weapon in the foreseeable future. The physicists and chemists working on the project began to divide into those who still wanted to build the bomb, and those who were no longer certain it was necessary. Many argued that, as Germany had not yet fallen, Nazi scientists could still be labouring deep in Hitler's shrinking *Festung Europa* on an atomic weapon, and could surprise everyone. Within the American atomic scientific community the claims of both sides were being passionately argued.

Groves tolerated such arguments, though he had no sympathy with the stop-the-bomb brigade. He simply could not understand how they could feel like that now, after all the efforts they had made to produce the weapon and when success was in sight. He had listened impatiently to the argument that in building an atomic bomb they also acquired a moral obligation to mankind. To his military mind, introducing such an issue raised politics and physics to the level of scientific statesmanship. There was no precedent for it, and with a bitter, bloody war still to be won in Europe and the Far East, now was not the time to stop work on the weapon he believed could end that war.

Groves knew exactly which side of the controversy each of the project's scientists supported. His vast number of security agents kept him informed—even though they had failed to anticipate that the bumbling Bohr would go to Roosevelt.

Groves had never experienced such effrontery since taking command of the project on September 17, 1942. It would not happen again. Security was being further tightened at the secret atomic laboratories and townships scattered throughout America. There had been protests. Groves ignored them. He would not be baulked in his mission to deliver an atomic bomb.

When Groves first took command of the Manhattan Project he was answerable only to Secretary of War Henry Stimson and, through him, President Roosevelt.

Both knew more about this man with old-fashioned manners than about any other serving officer. An F.B.I. vetting—the only occasion

10

the agency became involved in the atomic project—turned up Groves' passion for candy, his concern about middle-age spread, his competitive tennis playing, his ability to solve complicated mathematical problems while eating. The probe had revealed that Groves was known as 'Greasy' at West Point, that he had few interests outside his work, was stable and happily married.

Stimson also knew his professional background: an outstanding West Point engineering graduate who had helped build the Pentagon; a man reputed to be the 'best barrack-builder in the Army'.

His service record showed Groves to be a corner-cutter, a dime-saver, and tough, tireless and resilient. He was used to working to time and budget. He got things done. Although he tended both to ruffle the tempers of his equals and inspire fear in his subordinates, Groves seemed to Stimson and Roosevelt the best possible choice to run the world's biggest-ever military project.

From the outset Groves worked a fifteen-hour day, seven days a week. He gave up tennis and put on weight, sustaining himself with pounds of chocolates which he kept locked in the safe where he also stored the project's most important secrets.

But Groves was not just a builder going from site to site with a bag of toffees in his pocket. Even his friends in the project—and they numbered few—believed, in the words of one, that Groves 'not only behaves as if he can walk on water, but as if he actually invented the substance'. Another, less cruel, claimed, 'He has the most impressive ego since Napoleon.'

Forty-eight years old, with a vocabulary capable of blistering a construction worker—though many found more unnerving his deep sigh at a piece of misfortune—Groves came from the same mould as MacArthur and Patton.

Ultimately, nobody could withstand his barrage of orders and demands. Opposition was crushed, and arguments he regarded as pointless ended with a crisp 'enough'. He drafted industrial tycoons as if they were buck privates and drove his work force to exhaustion as he built and ran his empire.

Bullying, cajoling, bruising, buffeting, occasionally praising and rarely apologising, Groves had achieved a feat he himself had once thought impossible. In two momentous years he had brought the atomic bomb from a blue-print to within sight of being tested.

Scientists like Bohr must not be allowed to stop that happening. He would fight them and, if necessary, crush them. There was a war on; this was no time for philosophical discourse; this was a time for action.

His mood lifted at the thought of the special atomic strike force that was about to be formed. Once they began training at their

11

secret base, it would be another step forward. He had approved the choice of Tibbets as their commander because he had all the professional qualities Groves believed were needed for the job.

September 8, 1944
The Pentagon
Washington, D.C.

Working from a temporary office in the complex Groves had helped to erect, Tibbets was coming to realise just how vast his powers were as commander. He could demand anything he wanted merely by quoting the code name *Silverplate*. Using that prefix, he had instituted a search for some of the men who had served with him in Europe, North Africa, and on the B-29 testing and training programme. Some had already been traced and were on their way to Wendover in Utah; others were having their orders cut.

Here, at the Pentagon, General Henry Arnold, chief of the Army Air Force, had said: 'Colonel, if you get any trouble from anybody, you can call on me.'

Arnold had designated two senior officers to liaise with Tibbets when he got to Wendover. Arnold's order to them was simple. 'Just give him anything he wants without delay.'

When Tibbets had inspected Wendover, he found it 'the end of the world, perfect'. It was close enough to Los Alamos by air, an important consideration, for Ramsey had warned him that 'the scientists will be bugging you day and night'. It was only some 500 miles by air from the Salton Sea area in southern California, an ideal bombing range. The location of Wendover would simplify security. The existing facilities on the base were suitable for immediate occupation.

He knew his men would hate the place.

But he planned to work them so hard that they would not have time to dwell on their surroundings.

By now Tibbets had surmised there were only two possible targets for him to bomb: Berlin or Tokyo. He thought the Japanese capital more likely; the war in Europe was already approaching a decisive stage.

If it was to be Japan, then he would need a base within striking distance of the Empire.

He recalled reading recently that the U.S. Marines had captured the Mariana Islands in the Pacific. The newspapers had dubbed one island 'the place where the Seebees are going to build the largest aircraft carrier in the world'. It was just 1,300 miles from Japan. Its name was Tinian.

Tibbets filed it in his memory.

September 9, 1944
Mount Futaba
Hiroshima

The fall of Tinian six weeks before had totally failed to shake 2nd-Lieutenant Tatsuo Yokoyama's belief in the invincibility of the Imperial Japanese Army.

This evening, as usual before gunnery practice, the forty men at the anti-aircraft gun post on Mount Futaba, in the north-eastern outskirts of Hiroshima, were lectured by their young commander on the need to keep faith with the High Command's belief in ultimate victory.

Yokoyama was the classic caricature seen in countless American and British cartoons. He *did* have buck teeth, slanting eyes and a sloping forehead. He *was* a wiry figure in baggy blouse and trousers with sloppy leggings encasing bandy legs.

But his image was deceptive. He was a crack rifle shot at 700 yards. He was capable of carrying 400 rounds of ammunition, double that carried by an American infantryman, and trained to exist on a bowl of rice and fish a day. He regarded surrender as the greatest shame he could inflict upon his family and country.

Deeply religious, hyper-patriotic and totalitarian, he devoutly believed in the divinity of the Emperor and the sacred duty of the Army to protect him. He would spare nothing—neither his family nor his soldiers nor himself—to serve the Emperor.

He told his men this evening that they should look upon the 'withdrawal' from the Marianas—from the islands of Saipan, Tinian and Guam—as a pre-determined action, as part of a carefully prepared plan to draw the enemy closer to Japan.

There, as they all knew, a vast army was waiting, and eager, to deal America and her allies a blow which would send them reeling. The Americans could win a *battle*, he reminded his men, but Japan had never lost a war since 1598. He told them that the Japanese 'departure' from the Marianas meant that the day must be approaching when enemy bombers, launched from those islands against Japan, would at long last come within range of their guns.

13

In anticipation of that moment he drove his gun crews even harder. It was not easy. They were as bored as he was. But the men knew he would severly punish them at the first signs of slackness.

Under his barked commands the guns continued their traverse, moving smoothly on their greased bearings, their long, slim barrels probing the air over Hiroshima.

He passed among the gunners, urging them to imagine they were in action. Suddenly one of the guns jammed. Yokoyama saw that a piece of waste cotton had been left in the mechanism. He halted the practice and furiously ordered the crews to strip, clean and reassemble the guns.

He then returned to his quarters to write up the incident in the Daily Report Book and to think of a suitable punishment for the errant crew. They would expect it.

Harsh to the outsider, Tatsuo Yokoyama knew the Army to be different. It was firm, just in its code of punishments, protective and paternal to those who totally accepted its way of life, its traditions, its authority.

His formative years had been spent watching the Army shape Japan's destiny. He was a spindly-legged eleven-year-old when the Army invaded Manchuria in 1931, in defiance of the Japanese Cabinet. As a teenager he had thrilled to the spirit of militarism, with all its stirring slogans, parades and muscle-flexing.

He was seventeen when the Army invaded China. Three years later, close to his twentieth birthday, in September 1940, Japan signed an agreement with Germany and Italy, binding her to the Axis. A few weeks later he had rejoiced in the Army's occupation of French Indo-China, after France fell to Nazi Germany and was unable to defend her Asian outpost. On December 8, 1941 he had rushed out to buy the Tokyo evening papers, carrying news of the greatest triumph of all—Pearl Harbor. He had revelled in the national mood of chauvinism, aggression and expansionism.

Yokoyama had learned a good deal about the planning behind Pearl Harbour's destruction while at the Army Academy for Officers in Tokyo, which he had entered in 1942. His tutors explained that the young officer largely responsible for the success of the attack had done much of his basic thinking on the subject in London. His name was Minoru Genda, and he had been assistant naval attaché at the Japanese Embassy there during 1939–40. Genda believed that Britain could not win the war against Germany and that eventually Japan must fight America. He was convinced that, to ensure success, 'we had to do something that had not been done before, something that no one had thought of, something that America would not dream of'. After returning to Japan, early in 1941, he convinced the High

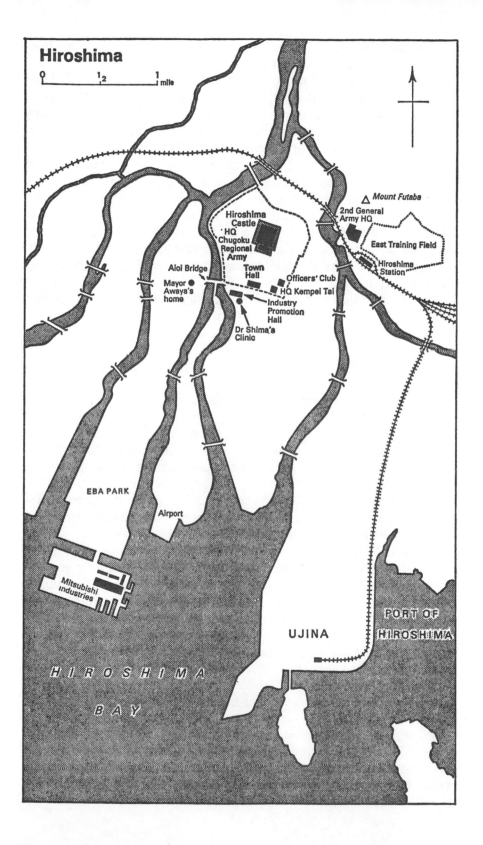

Command that an unexpected carrier-based air attack on Pearl Harbour was both feasible and militarily desirable.

The raid was carried out by 354 planes. Their leader was Captain Mitsuo Fuchida, an outstanding pilot of great daring who was also a close friend of Genda's. It was Fuchida's famous 'Tora—Tora—Tora' signal which had been received by Admiral Yamamoto, waiting aboard a battleship in Hiroshima Harbour for news of the attack.

At the Army Academy, Yokoyama had been taught that the attack on Pearl Harbor was no more than the Americans deserved for trying to strangle Japan economically and deny his country its rightful place in the world by reducing it to the minor power it once had been. His instructors had predicted that the war would be short. Another blow like Pearl Harbor, combined with Russia's defeat by Germany and England's inevitable collapse, would bring America to the negotiating table.

For six months after leaving the Academy events had confirmed the optimism of his tutors. The Army occupied the Pacific. Hong Kong, Malaya, Singapore, Bataan and Corregidor had fallen. Some of his friends died; he envied them. Since boyhood he had accepted that there was no greater glory than dying in battle for the Emperor.

When Yokoyama had been posted to Hiroshima, he had been pleasantly surprised to find that both Genda and Fuchida had close connections with the city. Genda had been born nearby, and many of his relatives resided in Hiroshima. Fuchida sometimes flew into the city's airfield to attend planning conferences and, afterwards, to visit old friends.

Yokoyama yearned to meet these two heroes, to bow and to tell them what a great honour it was for him to stand in their presence.

His other hero was Tojo.

General Hideki Tojo was only five feet three inches in his platform shoes. He was bald, with nicotine-stained moustache and fingers. He wore rimless spectacles. But Tojo exuded charisma for young officers like Yokoyama. They called him 'The Razor', a reference to the ruthless way he slashed through opposition. Tojo had been Japan's architect of war; his presence had been felt in Manchuria and China. In 1940 he had become Minister of War, and then, in 1941, Prime Minister.

Now Tojo was gone.

A little over a month ago, just before Tinian fell, Tojo had been forced to resign.

When he heard the news, Yokoyama had felt 'oddly unmoved'. He concluded that the Army had ousted Tojo, and he knew that the Army had good reasons for everything it did, even if that included sacking the Prime Minister. The Army would still run the country—

and win the war. Yokoyama simply wished he had a more active role in ensuring that victory.

His entry completed in the Daily Report Book, the officer pondered what punishment to give his gunners. He decided on two extra drills.

But first he would enjoy a ritual he performed every evening. Going to the window of his billet, he began to survey the city through binoculars. He knew there would be little change in the past twenty-four hours, but the endless panorama always soothed him.

When he had first surveyed the city from his vantage point close to the crest of Mount Futaba a year before, Yokoyama was struck by an oddity: Hiroshima resembled a human hand. By holding out his right hand, palm down, fingers spread, he reproduced a rough outline of the city. The port was at his fingertips in the south; beyond lay the depths of Hiroshima Bay and the Inland Sea. His wrist corresponded to that area where the River Ota ended its uninterrupted flow from the hills in the north and entered a broad fan-shaped delta. There it broke into six main channels which divided the city into islands. These were linked by eighty-one bridges. The city was mainly flat and only slightly above sea level. Directly under his palm was Hiroshima Castle, the centre of a huge military operation.

Yokoyama amused himself by identifying various installations and placing them in the corresponding positions on the back of his hand. At the tip of his index finger was Hiroshima airport, with its military aircraft. On his thumb he located Toyo Industries; the company made rifles and gun platforms for warships. At the end of his little finger was the Mitsubishi works, with its dockyards and cranes.

The factories, together with the dozens of smaller plants in the city, maintained round-the-clock shifts. A recent edict had inducted schoolchildren of thirteen years into war work; in Hiroshima boys and girls were toiling eight hours a day making weapons. Almost every man, woman and child in the city was actively engaged in the war effort.

Yokoyama stared out at the bay, remembering the first day he had seen it in the high summer of 1943. Then it had been filled with troop ships and merchant ships. Now, by comparison, the bay was almost empty.

Isolated, denied access to any hard information, a tiny cog in the structured command chain of the Army, twenty-three-year-old Yokoyama did not suspect that the Allied sea blockade of Japan was beginning to bite.

Japan began the war with barely enough merchant shipping for her estimated minimum requirements to survive. Acute dependence on importing such basic essentials as oil, iron ore, coal, bauxite and food made Japan's merchant fleet a prime target. Soon, eighty percent of that original fleet would be sunk.

Now, in September 1944, most factories in Hiroshima faced a shortage of materials. The patrol boats used for coastal duty were immobilised for lack of fuel, and training flights from the city's airfield were curtailed.

Yet this evening the war seemed as remote as ever to Yokoyama. The city below him was peaceful, a vast cluster of black-tiled roofs, encased in a natural bowl of reclaimed delta, surrounded by green hills and peaks.

But in Yokoyama's opinion Hiroshima was highly vulnerable to air attack. All a bomber need do was drop its load within the bowl to be almost certain of causing damage. Apart from a single kidney shaped hill in the eastern sector of the city, about half a mile long and two hundred feet high, Hiroshima was uniformly exposed to the spreading energy which big bombs generate.

Structurally, like San Francisco in the earthquake and fire of 1906, Hiroshima was built to burn. Ninety percent of its houses were made of wood. Large groups of dwellings were clustered together. Even the commercial and industrial buildings with reinforced concrete frames showed a striking lack of uniformity in design and in quality of materials. And unlike San Francisco in 1906, Hiroshima in 1944 had antiquated fire-fighting equipment and poorly-trained personnel.

From where he stood, Yokoyama could clearly see the city boundaries; only thirteen of Hiroshima's twenty-seven square miles were built-up, and only seven of these densely. But in that area some 35,000 people were crammed into every square mile. He shuddered to think of their fate in a heavy air attack.

To help prevent that happening his battery was sited on Mount Futaba.

He saw that the gun crews were ready. Another practice began. Yokoyama watched them. The men were stripped to the waist, sweating in the warm evening air. Load, aim, unload. A new traverse. Load, aim, unload, A swift stylistic ritual of crisp commands and grunts.

He was pleased with them now, with the way they responded promptly to his orders. They were the same commands he had given them for every drill since the battery was commissioned as part of the Hiroshima anti-aircraft defence system, in May 1943. Twenty-one ack-ack guns of various calibres now defended the city. They had yet to be fired in anger, in this the third year of the war.

The practice over, the crews were about to relax when Yokoyama ordered the first punishment drill. Immediately that ended, he began the second one, watchful for any signs of slackness. That would earn the crews further punishment.

Satisfied, he stood down the gunners and led them to their quarters. There, as usual, he listened solicitously to their small-talk. It was part of his duty to listen, just as he was expected to eat, drink and sing with his men, to lend them money from his own pocket, to invite them to visit his parents' home in Tokyo. This was traditional behaviour for a Japanese officer, this fostering of a comradely feeling, this encouraging of a relationship in which he was both father-figure and close friend. It was what had helped to make the Imperial Japanese Army so unique and so formidable.

This evening his crews asked him a familiar question: when would they see action?

He understood their desire to fight. It was part of the Samurai tradition, part of the 2,000-year history of Japan. The wish for battle was coupled with a total absence of fear. Japan, more than any other nation, had excised fear from its warriors; death for them was part of living.

Yokoyama told his men to be patient. But he worried whether they would ever have the chance to shoot, to taste that special excitement of which the Samurai soldier-poets wrote, if the story he had heard on his last visit into the city was true. A casual friend had mentioned it to him, a man who worked in local government. Being an officer and well-educated, Yokoyama had at first dismissed the story. But his friend had been so insistent, so specific, claiming 'inside sources' for his information, that Yokoyama wondered if there was any substance in the tale that many people in Hiroshima had relatives in San Francisco and Los Angeles who had petitioned President Roosevelt to spare Hiroshima from attack, and that he had agreed to do so as 'a gesture of goodwill'.

Yokoyama knew that if this was true, then the enemy bombers would never come to Hiroshima, and all his practice would be in vain.

The thought depressed him.

September 12, 1944
USAAF Base
Wendover

Tibbets was right. The officers and men of the 393rd Heavy Bombardment Squadron hated Wendover. They hated the bleaching heat, the inhospitable desert, the primitive accommodation, the dust, the rancid drinking water, the termites, the rats and mice, the sheer remoteness of their position.

19

They hated not knowing why they were there.

On this, their second morning at the base, they awoke to find further cause for hatred. A formidable wire fence now penned them in. Inside its perimeter were warning signs. The largest was beside the exit gate from the base. It read:

WHAT YOU HEAR HERE
WHAT YOU SEE HERE
WHEN YOU LEAVE HERE
LET IT STAY HERE

Sentries were stopping anybody leaving.

Thickly-coiled barbed wire barred the entrance to a number of hangars and workshops. Freshly-painted notices announced that behind the wire lay the Ordnance, Armament, Engineering and Radar shops. Each notice carried the legend:

RESTRICTED AREA

The wire was thickest around hangar Number Six. There a notice announced:

TECH AREA 'C'
MOST RESTRICTED

What was a Tech area? Why 'C'? Where were 'A' and 'B'? Nobody knew.

Those who tried to talk their way past the military policemen guarding the Tech Area were curtly told that they faced arrest if they persisted.

This increased the frustration, uncertainty, anger and hatred the 393rd felt.

A week ago they had been coming to the end of their training in Nebraska; they were intensely proud that their squadron's record was well above average. They expected soon to go overseas. Some of the more enterprising purchased quantities of silk stockings, soap and perfumes to tempt the English and French girls they had heard so much about. One enlisted man packed his record collection of jitterbug seventy-eights, planning to sell them on London's black market.

Instead, the 393rd had travelled to Wendover.

There were no bombers at Wendover. Just a few run-down transport planes. Rumour said they had come to Wendover to pick up factory-fresh B-29's. But where were they? And why here?

Nobody knew.

The brief optimism withered. Other rumours rose, welled and faded. Officers, like their men, had no idea of what was happening. Their commanding officer, Lt-Colonel Thomas Classen, had gone

20

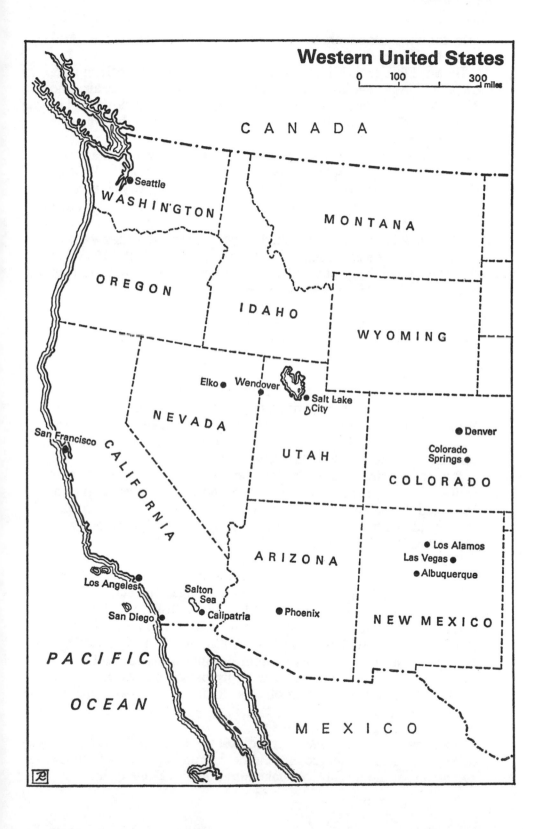

Western United States

0   100   300 miles

CANADA

Seattle

WASHINGTON

MONTANA

OREGON

IDAHO

WYOMING

Elko   Wendover

Salt Lake City

NEVADA

San Francisco

CALIFORNIA

Denver

Colorado Springs

UTAH

COLORADO

Los Alamos

Las Vegas

Albuquerque

ARIZONA

Los Angeles

Salton Sea

San Diego

Calipatria

Phoenix

NEW MEXICO

PACIFIC

OCEAN

MEXICO

into the base headquarters and had hardly been seen since. And when he did appear he stalled all questions.

By breakfast time Military Police were everywhere, their motorcycles and jeeps sending scuds of tangy-tasting dust into the air. The 393rd had never tasted such sand. It permeated their clothes, skin and food. The flavour in their cereals, eggs and hash-browns this morning came from the great salt flats around the airfield.

After the meal, the squadron listened in stunned disbelief as their intelligence officer, Captain Joseph Buscher, tried to make light of their situation. He reminded them that he was a lawyer, used to pleading—and he said he was pleading with them now to 'give the place a chance'.

Buscher admitted that he could not tell them why they were at Wendover, but he could tell them that the base was 'only' 125 miles from Salt Lake City, Utah. Elko in Nevada was 'as close'. Buscher hoped they would find Wendover itself 'fascinating'. The town, with a population of 103, was split down the middle by the Utah–Nevada State Line. Half of Wendover ran their lives according to Utah's Mormon Church. The other side of town took a less staid view of life: there were bars, restaurants and slot machines.

'What about broads?'

The questioner was Captain Claude Eatherly, a tall, wickedly-handsome pilot with a way with girls, cards and a bottle of bourbon. With his little-boy grin, Texas drawl and fund of jokes, Eatherly was the squadron playboy. Nobody suspected there was another, carefully-concealed side to his personality.

Buscher ignored Eatherly's question and launched into a solemn recital of how the flats had been formed, how the pioneer wagons of 1846 had foundered in the salt. For those who liked exploring, Busher said enthusiastically, the tracks of some of the wagons were still embedded in the flats.

'So will our bones be if we stay here!'

The words were spoken by a frustrated 1st-Lieutenant, Jacob Beser, the squadron's radar officer. Beser longed for action. When Britain had gone to war he had tried to join the Royal Air Force. His parents had stopped him, insisting he must complete his engineering studies at Johns Hopkins University, Baltimore. The day after Pearl Harbor, Beser had overcome parental oppositions and enlisted in the Army Air Force. He had eventually passed out as one of the service's highest-marked radar officers. Radar was new and growing in importance. That did not impress Beser—not unless he could use his knowledge 'to kill a few Nazis'.

Beser was a Jew. A small, wiry, quick-witted man, fiercely proud of his middle-class background. He held strong opinions on almost everything. It did not always make him popular. Some of his fellow

22

officers thought him an odd-ball. The enlisted men looked upon him as a 'longhair' because of his university background.

When the squadron was posted to Wendover, Baser had applied for a transfer to a combat unit. His request was turned down.

But now, listening to the urbane Buscher struggling to extol the virtues of Wendover, Beser began to feel excited.

'The place sounded so goddam awful that there just had to be a good reason for my being there,' he later recalled.

Tibbets had reached Wendover three days before. He was glad to see that his old friend, Major Thomas Ferebee, had also now arrived. His formidable combat record in Europe made Ferebee one of the most seasoned and respected bombardiers in the Air Force. He was the perfect choice to train the 393rd's bombardiers in the precision-bombing techniques which Professor Ramsey had told Tibbets would be essential for dropping an atomic bomb.

Unexpected problems had stopped Tibbets from sitting down with Ferebee for a relaxed gossip.

For a start there was the delicate position of Classen. The 393rd's C.O. was a Pacific veteran with a distinguished combat record. His qualities of leadership had made the squadron a cohesive unit. To move him at this stage would be unthinkable. Tibbets had discussed the situation with Classen, explaining that in effect the squadron would have two commanders: Classen would be responsible for its day-to-day running; Tibbets would take all the important policy decisions. He had told Classen he hoped this somewhat unusual arrangement would work. Classen had shown no real reaction.

Tibbets had tried to sweeten matters by giving Classen a briefing on their unique mission. He hoped that would instil a mood of equally-divided responsibility 'in all but a few areas'. But after Classen had gone, Tibbets had grown uncertain as to whether dual command was really possible.

Other matters had soon pushed such thoughts from his mind.

Since breakfast two men had been closeted with him. He knew the older man well. Lt-Colonel Hazen Payette had served with him in England and North Africa as intelligence officer. A shrewd and penetrating questioner, Payette was at Wendover to supervise security at Tibbets' request.

Major William L. 'Bud' Uanna had arrived unannounced. He politely explained that Colonel Lansdale had sent him, plus some thirty agents detached from the main Manhattan Project, to help 'police' the 393rd.

Tibbets liked Uanna's style. He was coolly pleasant and uninterested in anything but his work.

Uanna had arrived with a bulky briefcase. The files it contained were a further reminder to Tibbets of the vast intelligence-gathering resources of the Manhattan Project.

There was a detailed dossier on each member of the 393rd. The information had been collected from their families, friends, school reports, employment records and medical files.

Many thousands of man-hours and dollars had been spent on tapping telephones, secretly opening letters, collecting details of extramarital affairs, homosexual tendencies and political affiliations. The dossiers represented the most thorough investigation to date secretly carried out in the name of the United States Government.

Uanna produced the file on Eatherly. It showed the pilot was an obsessional gambler, with an 'emotional problem'.

Tibbets studied Eatherly's service record. He had logged 107 hours as a ferry pilot flying Lockheed Hudsons to Canada; 103 hours flying LB-30's; a spell on anti-submarine patrol in the Panama Canal; regular transfers from one squadron to another. A normal enough flying record. Eatherly's fitness reports spoke of his 'flamboyance' and of his 'being an extrovert'. Tibbets recognised the type. He had flown with 'wild Texans' like Eatherly in Europe. They frequently got into trouble on the ground. But they were good pilots. Eatherly seemed to be another one of them. Tibbets decided he would let the pilot remain in the 393rd.

He would live to regret that decision.

By late morning the jokers in the 393rd were running out of steam. One of them had been sharply reprimanded by an MP for trying to post a slogan:

WELCOME TO ALCATRAZ

The first letters were being written to loved ones. A number contained the inevitable phrase: Wendover is a good place to be—from.

Uanna's agents had infiltrated the squadron, carrying forged papers which allowed them to pose as clerks, cooks, even a garbage detail. They were not always successful. Captain James Strudwick found a man checking the wiring in his quarters who 'didn't know one end of a socket from another'. Mess Officer Charles Perry discovered two men in the cookhouse 'who had trouble distinguishing a soup ladle from a carving knife'. Executive Officer John King was astonished to see 'a man dressed in a line chief's overalls whose hands had never come near a spanner'.

But not all the newcomers were security men.

Tech/Sgt. George Caron arrived dusty and thirsty from a trans-America journey, with his collar unbuttoned and wearing a flying jacket, a double breach of military regulations.

The MP's at the gate pounced on the diminutive air gunner. They marched him to the orderly room in the headquarters building. There, a policeman began to bellow at Caron 'like a mad bull'.

Suddenly from an adjoining office Caron heard a familiar voice. 'Is that you, Bob?'

'Sure is, Colonel.'

Tibbets was one of the few officers who called Caron 'Bob'. 'Come on in.'

Smiling impishly at the stunned policeman, Caron strolled from the orderly room to see Tibbets. They greeted each other like 'old buddies'.

Caron had been gunnery instructor on Tibbets' B-29 training programme. Feet up on his desk, Tibbets now explained to the gunner why he had sent for him.

'Bob, I need a man who knows what he's doing—and can teach others to do a similar job. And keep their mouths shut.'

'Colonel, I won't even mention I'm here,' said Caron fervently.

Tibbets smiled, re-establishing the easy contact which had marked their previous working relationship. He did not find it unusual to be imparting information to a non-com while senior officers in the 393rd still had no idea of what was happening. It was the way Tibbets preferred to do things, dealing first with the men he knew and trusted, men who had already proved themselves to him. Tibbets believed that the privileges of rank were strictly limited; men had to earn the right to his confidence.

On the B-29 programme, onlookers had spoken scathingly of 'Tibbets' private air force'. Tibbets had shrugged such criticism aside. He meant to adopt the same policy at Wendover, sometimes confiding to enlisted men information he would not entrust to an officer.

He could not foresee that in trying to weld his own hand-picked officers and men into the tightly-knit 393rd he would face not only criticism, but resentment.

After lunch, the squadron was marched to the base parade ground. A truck was parked in the centre. Standing on its tailboard was Tibbets.

This was the first time he had seen his new outfit assembled. He was not over-impressed. They were trying too hard to look nonchalant, 'the way they had seen Alan Ladd do it in the movies'. He thought they looked decidedly inexperienced. He guessed most of the officers were in their early twenties. The enlisted men seemed even younger. He saw that Ferebee and Caron stood out. They know what it's all about, thought Tibbets, the others are trying to pretend they do.

The smartly-dressed officer, standing ramrod stiff, cap squared off —that must be the Exec. Officer, King. He had heard about him from Classen. King was a peacetime professional, Regular Army. Tough

25

but fair, Classen had said. The unit needed such a man, judging by what he had read in Uanna's dossiers.

The 393rd later agreed that, standing there, Tibbets looked tough, mean and moody. One officer put it colourfully.

'He looked as if one mistake from us and he would happily fry us for breakfast and use our remains to stoke his lunch-time stove.'

Beser thought: this is the man I want to go to war with. Feeling Tibbets' stare fall upon him, the radar officer visibly straightened himself; he wished now that he hadn't worn his cap at such a rakish angle.

Command had taught Tibbets a trick—surprise people, shake them by the unexpected.

'I've looked at you. You have looked at me. I'm not going to be stuck with all of you. But those of you who remain are going to be stuck with me.'

This was a new Tibbets to Caron. He shared in the ripple of expectancy around him.

Tibbets continued.

'You have been brought here to work on a very special mission. Those of you who stay will be going overseas.'

A muted cheer came from the rear ranks. Tibbets froze it with one look.

'This is not a football game. You are here to take part in an effort which could end the war.'

This time he allowed the murmur to rise and fall of its own accord. He had them now.

'Don't ask what the job is. That is a sure-fire way to be transferred out. Don't ask any questions. Don't answer any questions from anybody not directly involved in what we will be doing. Do exactly what you are told, when you are told, and you will get along fine.

'I know some of you are curious about all the security. Stop being curious. This is part of the preparation for what is to come. Nobody will be allowed into a fenced-off area without a pass. Lose that pass and you face a court-martial.

'Never mention this base to anybody. That means your wives, girls, sisters, family.'

There was dead silence when he paused. Years ago, when he first became an officer, his mother had given him a piece of advice: sometimes he would have to be tough, but he should always try and temper it by showing the other side of his character, gentleness.

'It's not going to be easy for any of us. But we will succeed by working together. However, all work and no play is no fun. So, as of now, you can all go on two weeks' furlough. Enjoy yourselves.'

Classen was about to dismiss the squadron when Tibbets spoke again.

'If any of you wish to transfer out, that's fine. Just say the word.'
He waited.

Nobody moved.

'I'm glad,' said Tibbets, 'really glad.'

By mid-afternoon, the men were already leaving the base. Many had begun to wonder why, if their assignment was so important in ending the war, they had been given two weeks' leave. Some believed Tibbets had tried too hard to impress them.

2nd-Lieutenant Eugene Grennan, the engineer on Eatherly's crew, decided the talk about security was 'hogwash' after strolling down the flight line. A hangar door had been open. He peered inside, 'and there was this German V-1 rocket'.

A triumphant Grennan decided that the squadron was going to Europe 'to knock down Nazi rockets'.

The rocket was a plywood mock-up and the hangar door had been deliberately left ajar—a trap devised by Uanna. Within minutes an agent reported that Grennan had swallowed the bait. But Uanna was in no hurry to catch the engineer. He had other snares to set.

Navigator Russell Gackenbach reached Salt Lake City and was stopped by an NCO asking if Wendover was the 'headquarters of the Silverplate outfit'. Gackenback had never heard of *Silverplate*. But he suspected a trap and sternly warned his questioner that 'darn-fool questions could get us both in the pen'.

Gackenbach had survived Uanna's obstacle course. Others found themselves enmeshed.

Two NCO's were accosted by an officer in a Salt Lake City hotel. He said he was joining the 393rd; what sort of outfit was it? The men obligingly told him. The officer thanked them. Two hours later, as the talkative NCO's boarded a train for home, MP's stopped them and drove them back to base. In Tibbets' office they were confronted by the officer. He was a Manhattan Project agent. Within an hour both non-coms were posted out of the squadron—to Alaska.

Grennan reached Union Square, Chicago, before his trap sprung. There he ran into a friend from college days. Grennan told him about 'the crazy set-up at Wendover'. His friend listened attentively. They parted company. Grennan arrived home to find a telegram ordering his immediate return to Wendover. There Uanna keel-hauled the young flier for talking. His friend was a project agent. All that saved a crest-fallen Grennan from transfer was his fine flying record. From then on he became one of the most security-conscious men in the squadron.

Five more members of the 393rd were netted by Uanna's agents. They were also swiftly shipped to Alaska. Their records were not good enough to save them.

In the late afternoon Groves telephoned Tibbets, wanting to know why the squadron had gone on furlough. He was told about the security operation now in progress.

The two men had met briefly in Washington. Then, Tibbets had been uncomfortably aware of the immense pressures the project chief was under. Now, Groves appeared to have ample time to talk. He promised new B-29's would be available soon, and reminded Tibbets that 'the world is yours'.

This was Groves at his most cajoling. Now he switched mood. He talked about the scientists who would soon be descending on Wendover. They were 'brilliant men'. But they had little understanding of 'the military side of things'. Therefore, it would be best if Tibbets did not 'inform them unduly' about the training programme.

Tibbets was having his first encounter with the internal arguments which were beginning to bedevil the project.

Groves wanted to restrict news of the Army Air Force's involvement to a few scientists—and then only to those he knew supported his view that the bomb must be produced as soon as possible. He saw those who questioned the validity of what they were doing as befuddled meddlers who were straying out of the scientific and into the political arena. He sensed that if these 'longhairs' were aware that a strike force now existed to drop the bomb their protests would become shriller.

He put it differently to Tibbets.

'Colonel, what people don't know about, they can't talk about. And that is good for security'.

Beser was ordered to remain on base. Tibbets had told him to expect 'important visitors' soon.

When the radar officer attempted to question Tibbets, he 'received the coldest stare any man could give. I just shut up, went to my quarters and waited'.

Tibbets was being hard-nosed 'because I wanted to impress on Beser, and everybody else in the outfit, that I didn't fool around'.

Now, late in the evening, Tibbets and Ferebee finally settled down for their eagerly-awaited reunion.

Ferebee was taller than Tibbets, and raffishly elegant. He could have played the hero in a war movie. He sported a neat R.A.F.-style moustache which made him look older than his twenty-four years.

He had survived sixty-three combat missions, twenty more than Tibbets. They shared the same philosophy about war: it was a rotten business, but it was either kill or be killed.

They had flown together in Europe, been shot up, knew the mean-

28

ing of fear, and become firm friends. It was almost a year since they had last met, but Tibbets was pleased to see the old bonds were still there.

They rambled through the past, remembering English airfields they had flown from, German-occupied French towns they had attacked. They talked about that summer's day in 1942 when they had tangled with Goering's personal squadron of yellow-nosed Messerschmitts. On that occasion one of the gunners in their bomber had his foot shot off, the co-pilot lost a hand, and Tibbets himself had been wounded in the arm. But Ferebee had successfully bombed the German's Abbeville airbase, and in daylight. That evening the B.B.C. had mentioned the raid on their nine o'clock news. They remembered other fliers, men who had died, men who had vanished into German prison camps, men whose fate was uncertain.

Finally Tibbets turned to the present.

'Tom, we are going to need good men for this job. If it works we'll flatten everything within eight miles of the Aiming Point.'

Ferebee considered what he should say.

'That's quite a bang, Paul.'

The bombardier made no other comment. Restraint was one of Ferebee's qualities. He was always prepared to wait and to listen. His friends said the only time he really asserted himself was in combat, at the poker table or when a pretty girl passed.

Tibbets asked him if he could recommend anybody they should bring in for 'the job'.

'What about "Dutch"?'

Theodore 'Dutch' van Kirk had been their navigator in Europe. Quietly professional in the air, he and Ferebee had caroused and gambled off-duty. Occasionally Tibbets had joined them in their whoopee-making, smiling indulgently as his younger companions had staged their own *blitzkrieg* on London's night life. Ferebee explained that van Kirk was back in America, had married, and was now based in Louisiana. Tibbets said he would have the navigator posted to Wendover. Van Kirk could raise the standards of the 393rd's navigators to that required for an atomic strike mission.

'Tom, I want every one of these crews to be Lead Crews, capable of finding their way to a target without having pathfinders up front leading the way and dropping marker bombs.'

Ferebee had two further suggestions for men who could meet Tibbets' requirements. One was a bombardier, Kermit Beahan; the other was a navigator, James van Pelt. Both had previously impressed Ferebee.

Tibbets said they would be recruited. He announced his own choices. They were all men who had served with him on the B-29 testing programme. Three of them were pilots: Robert Lewis, Charles Sweeney and Don Albury.

Lewis, Tibbets explained, 'was a bit of a wild lad, but a natural pilot'; Sweeney was Boston-Irish 'and would fly a B-29 through the Grand Canyon if you asked him'; Albury 'was about the most competent twenty-five-year-old I have ever known'.

He had one other selection, Staff/Sgt. Wyatt Duzenbury, his former flight engineer.

'Tom, Dooz can coax magic out of aero engines, and he's a helluva guy when you're in a corner. Give him an engine fire and he becomes rock steady. Give him two and he becomes even steadier.'

By the end of the evening Tibbets and Ferebee had virtually decided on the men who would fly the first atomic strike. Tibbets' co-pilot would be either Lewis, Sweeney or Albury. Van Kirk would navigate them to the target, Ferebee bomb it, Caron help to protect them from air attack, and Duzenbury give them the engine power to get there and back.

The men of 393rd would only have a minor role to play in completing the composition of the crew. Tibbets did not stop to consider how they would react to that situation.

September 17, 1944
Hiroshima Bay

Lieutenant Command Mochitsura Hashimoto of the Imperial Japanese Navy had ordered a trim dive for 1700 hours. Submarine I.58 was to dive to three hundred feet to test the water-tightness of all hull valves and openings.

I.58 had been commissioned four days earlier; this was the first time she would be submerged. From the day when he had first seen her, back in May, Hashimoto had been impressed by the boat; she was one of the I-Class submarines, larger and faster and better equipped than almost any boat of a comparable class anywhere in the world. Two diesel engines give I.58 a cruising speed of fourteen knots; submerged, her motors drove the submarine at seven knots. She had a range of 15,000 miles and could remain at sea for three months. She had six torpedo-tubes, all forward, and carried nineteen torpedoes. These were the most modern in the world. Oxygen-fuelled and wakeless, they had a speed of fifty-eight knots and a range of 5,500 metres. Each two-foot-diameter torpedo carried a 1,210-pound explosive charge.

Today, for the hull tests, the torpedo room was empty, except for the rats which infested the submarine. Every effort to exterminate them had been unsuccessful. But they were the only problem that Commander Hashimoto had failed to overcome. His endless battles with the Kure Naval Dockyard, the Naval Technical Department and the Naval Research Bureau had paid off. I.58 was equipped in exactly the way he wished.

Standing on the bridge, as the submarine moved through the water of Hiroshima Bay a little over a mile south of the city, Hashimoto looked through his binoculars at the Naval Academy on the island of Eta Jima. Nothing seemed to have changed since he had been a cadet there from 1927 to 1931. Three years later, in 1934, he had been assigned to submarines; he had loved the life. But a spell of duty in destroyers and sub-chasers, operating in the waters off China, had intervened. It was not until 1938 that he was selected to be a full-time member of the submarine service. By then he was married, and in 1940 his wife gave birth to their first child, a son.

Professionally, Hashimoto had found himself caught up in events which stirred him deeply. He was assigned to the Naval Task Force supporting the air attack on Pearl Harbor, a torpedo officer on one of the five submarines which had launched a two-man midget submarine against the American fleet. The midget subs had failed in their mission; all were sunk. But Hashimoto's own craft had made good its escape. Since then he had enjoyed an unspectacular war.

He liked it that way. The first time he had assembled the crew of I.58 he told them he was not expecting 'senseless heroics', but competence.

Many of his 105 officers and men Hashimoto had personally selected. Some of them had been with him on his previous submarine. They thought their thirty-five-year-old captain firm but fair. He was widely experienced and had a reputation for surviving.

A few of the newcomers were young; Hashimoto looked upon this as another sign that the war was demanding a supreme effort. But, like the others, his youngsters were mustard-keen and shaping up well.

I.58 reached its diving station.

Hashimoto climbed down from the bridge to the control room. He watched and listened to the final preparations for diving; the air was filled with quiet orders, reports, the sounds of bell-signals.

The main engines were clutched out, the electric motors began to run at full whine. The outboard exhaust and air induction valves were closed off.

The engine room informed the control room that it was ready to dive. The look-outs came below. The Officer of the Watch spun the handwheel which clamped the flanged lid leading to the conning tower against its seating. The ratings at the ballast tank vent levers reported that all the main vents were clear. The Chief turned to Hashimoto and reported that the boat was ready for diving.

Hashimoto gave the order.

'Dive! Dive! Dive! Thirty feet.'

He watched as the ratings opened the main vent levers. There was a shattering roar of air escaping from the main ballast tanks. I.58 was no longer buoyant. The depth gauge began to move, slowly at first, then with gathering speed. Outside, the sea could be heard slapping against the conning tower. Then the sound died. The bridge was beneath the waves.

The needle of the depth-gauge revolved. The electric motors had taken over.

The Chief reported that the boat was properly trimmed.

Hashimoto ordered the main vents shut. I.58 continued to drop through the water. Suddenly, a vibration ran through the boat. The Chief ordered the submarine to be re-trimmed. At 100 feet, I.58 was suspended on an even keel, held in place by the careful balance of water in the compensating and trimming tanks.

Leakage points and discharge pump capacities were once more tested. There were no defects.

Hashimoto ordered I.58 to be taken deeper. The trouble came, suddenly, and with a gush of water at 200 feet.

A leak had developed in the torpedo room. The area was at once sealed off. The depth gauge began to turn more rapidly.

Hashimoto gave his orders, quickly, with no sign of concern, aware now of the anxious faces around him.

I.58 steadied and then began to climb rapidly towards the surface. There, the diesel motors took over.

Hashimoto quietly cursed the dockyard fitters whose carelessness had nearly caused a disaster. Hiroshima Bay was deep ; there was little chance that grappling crews could have recovered the submarine. The fear that was always at the back of his mind—the dread of being entombed for ever on the sea-bed—made Hashimoto almost physically sick. If he had to die, he wanted the end to come in battle. All but five of his old classmates from the Naval Academy were dead, victims of American destroyers. Nowadays the life expectancy of a submarine crew was measured in weeks, not months, without the slipshod Kure dockyard workers shortening the odds still further.

Hashimoto was not a superstitious man. But he liked to believe that 'anything which begins so badly must only improve'.

It was a comforting, and very necessary, philosophy for a commander who knew that every day the odds of his surviving were lessening. His great hope was that before he succumbed, he would have a chance to sink an enemy ship.

32

On this calm late summer's day, just a few miles from Hiroshima, there was, of course, nothing to show him that he would achieve his wish.

Or that in doing so he would shake the Manhattan Project to its very foundations.

September 19, 1944
Los Alamos

The drab, olive-green sedan stopped on the outskirts of the sleepy town of Santa Fe in New Mexico. Colonel John Lansdale told Tibbets and Beser to remove their Air Force insignia. He handed them Corps of Engineers emblems. In explanation, although it was hardly necessary, he said:

'Security.'

The security chief was glad to be dealing with Tibbets and Beser. They were used to military discipline. Not like the scientists who tormented his agents with their childish games. Lansdale was still smarting from the latest prank. A physicist had somehow opened the secret steel safe in the Los Alamos records office and placed a piece of paper on top of the priceless atomic secrets it contained. Printed on the paper were the words: 'Guess who?'

Beser was too overwhelmed by events to play any games. Yesterday he had been called to Tibbets' office. The radar officer had immediately recognised by name the 'important visitors'; Norman Ramsey and Robert Brode were physicists whose papers he had read as a student. They had questioned him for an hour on his academic background and radar qualifications. Finally Brode had told Beser that he could 'do the job, on the understanding that my life was expendable'.

Nobody had yet explained to Beser what the job was. And Beser now knew better than to ask.

Early this morning he and Tibbets had flown south from Wendover to Albuquerque, New Mexico. Lansdale was driving them on to Santa Fe. He cautioned them again.

'You are nothing to do with the Air Force. You have never heard of Wendover. Don't volunteer anything you know.'

They drove into town, stopping before a wrought-iron gate, centuries old, through which was a small Spanish-style courtyard.

For two years this patio had been the receiving point for some of the world's most distinguished scientists. Here, those men and

33

women were given coffee, doughnuts and comforting words from motherly Dorothy McKibben, who acted as 'front office receptionist' for the Manhattan Project's most secret centre—Site Y, Los Alamos.

Norman Ramsey was waiting on the patio to escort Tibbets and Beser there. He enjoined them never to address anybody they would meet as 'Doctor', or 'Professor'.

'Security,' said Beser solemnly.

Two considerations had influenced the choice of Los Alamos as an atomic laboratory. It was remote enough for security purposes; if one of the experiments conducted there resulted in a premature explosion, there was no sizeable civilian population nearby to be imperilled by the release of radio-activity.

Tibbets' first impression was disappointing. He felt 'the birthplace of the actual bomb should look more factory-like'.

What he saw were clusters of buildings set out on a flat tableland, part of the plateau of the Jemez Mountains. Seven thousand feet above sea level, the site was close to a canyon and scented pinewoods. The abandoned caves of Indians were clearly visible in the sides of the canyon.

Six thousand scientists, technicians, their wives and children now lived within the high-wire fences. Beser thought the place looked like a concentration camp. Inside, this unhappy image persisted. Many of the buildings were of rough construction; speed, not comfort, had been the rule. As at Wendover, there were areas marked 'RESTRICTED' and 'MOST RESTRICTED'.

Waiting for Tibbets and Beser in his office was Robert Oppenheimer, the shy, frail, theoretical physicist who was the scientific director of the Manhattan Project. He greeted them warmly, but was less effusive towards Lansdale.

For months now the security chief had been playing cat and mouse with Oppenheimer, because of the scientist's former association with various Communist organisations, his financial contributions to left-wing groups, his friendship with 'fellow travellers'. Oppenheimer was a product of his academic background where gullible espousal of a Soviet utopia was fashionable. Versed in Oriental literature, an aesthete who abhorred the violence of war, Oppenheimer had been under surveillance since March 15, 1943.

He was followed, his mail was opened, his telephone tapped, and, in Lansdale's later admission, 'all sorts of nasty things were done to keep a watch on him.'

Groves himself had questioned Oppenheimer and was satisfied that his 'closest, most indispensable collaborator' had severed all connections with his offending past.

He had ordered the watch on his scientific director to be lifted.

Lansdale ignored the order. His agents continued to harass the brilliant, although politically naïve, Oppenheimer.

They were watching the wrong man.

This morning, after Beser and Lansdale had left for Ramsey's laboratory, Oppenheimer simply said to Tibbets: 'You had better know everything.'

Pandora's box was finally being opened for the flier.

Here at Los Alamos, Oppenheimer began, men were delving into the unknown world, asking such questions as 'what is matter?' and 'how short can a "short time" be?' Here, they spoke of thousands of tons of energy as if energy could be weighed. They talked of a thousandth and then a millionth of a second as they devised ways to reduce time itself almost to nothing. They argued over the relative merits of the gaseous diffusion and electro-magnetic processes for separating uranium-235 from uranium-238; the U-235 produced could be measured in thimblefuls.

These men were also discovering the special nature of a chain reaction, and studying the unique problem of critical-mass: how to bring together two lumps of uranium-235 of the right potency to cause an atomic explosion at the right time.

Oppenheimer reduced the problem to a few words. 'Time. That's the problem, Colonel. Getting the timing right. If we are successful in solving that, then your problems will begin.'

The scientist looked benignly at Tibbets. 'There will probably be problems right up until the moment when the bomb explodes.'

Sparing Tibbets the mass of details behind the years of research, Oppenheimer explained how they intended to build the uranium bomb. A suitable mechanism had to be devised to bring two hemispheres of uranium-235 into contact quickly so that their combined mass reached the critical point and detonated. The amount of uranium-235 to be used, the size of the two spheres, the speed with which they must collide, the scattering angle, the range of the neutrons to be projected by the chain reaction—those, Oppenheimer said, were just some of the questions to be answered.

He rose to his feet and told Tibbets to follow him. They went into a nearby building, unmarked except for a sign.

POSITIVELY
NO
ADMITTANCE

This was where Captain Parsons and his team were dealing with the problem of how to ensure that the bomb would explode at a pre-determined height above the target.

Oppenheimer said that Parsons would probably be going along on the first mission.

'Good. Then if anything goes wrong, Captain, I can blame you,' said Tibbets lightly.

'If anything goes wrong, Colonel, neither of us will be around to be blamed,' replied Parsons soberly.

He described to Tibbets one of the experimental machines they had built to test the theory of critical mass. It had been nicknamed 'The Guillotine'. A piece of doughnut-shaped uranium was placed in the machine. Then another piece of uranium was dropped through the hole in the doughnut. For a split second the extra uranium plunging through the gap brought *both* pieces *close* to critical mass. It was a dangerous game to play. They called it 'twisting the dragon's tail'.

Parsons explained more about the bomb's mechanism to Tibbets.

'It is designed to ensure that the bringing together of the two "sub-critical" pieces occurs for the first time at the moment of planned detonation over the target. The pieces will then combine in a critical mass, causing the chain reaction explosion. That's the theory. Until that moment we cannot know for sure whether the bomb will work.'

Tibbets was impressed by the calm manner in which Parsons faced possible failure. He was glad, after all, that this soft-spoken naval officer would be on the mission. He asked Parsons how it was planned to bring together the two pieces of U-235.

Parsons described how the heart of the bomb was really just 'a good old gun, a five-inch cannon with a six-foot-long barrel. After the bomb has left the plane and is on its way, a piece of U-235 about the size of a soup tin will be fired down the barrel into a second piece of uranium fixed to the muzzle'.

'And if it doesn't work,' persisted Tibbets.

'We will just make a nice big dent in the target area and will have to go back to the drawing board,' said Parsons.

To avoid that dismal prospect, explained Oppenheimer, in the coming months Tibbets' unit would drop test bombs. These would help the scientists develop the final shape of the atomic bomb casing as well as proving the proximity fuses which governed the height at which the bomb would explode.

So far the proximity fuses were proving troublesome.

Tibbets continued to be astonished by Oppenheimer during his conducted tour of Los Alamos. Late in the afternoon they were walking down another corridor, past identical rooms, whose inner walls were lined with blackboards covered with formulae, and whose occupants pored over slide rules and logarithm tables.

Suddenly, Oppenheimer halted in mid-stride. His head was cocked alert, like a dog scenting its prey. He turned and stalked back to an office.

Inside, a man sat slumped on a straight-back wooden chair, staring fixedly at a blackboard. He was unshaven and dishevelled.

Tibbets wondered if he 'might be the building janitor taking an unauthorised rest after a night out'.

Oppenheimer stood silently behind the man. Together they stared at the blackboard with its jumble of equations.

Oppenheimer moved to the blackboard and rubbed out part of an equation. Still the man on the chair did not move.

Oppenheimer quickly wrote a set of new symbols in the space he had erased.

The man remained transfixed.

Oppenheimer added a final symbol.

The man leapt from his chair, galvanised, shouting, 'I've been looking for that mistake for two days!'

Oppenheimer smiled and walked out of Enrico Fermi's office, leaving one of the founders and greatest geniuses of nuclear physics happily re-starting work.

Beser was enjoying 'the most fantastic day in my life'. He had met and talked to a dozen renowned scientists who were his teenage heroes.

Hans Bethe and Ernest O. Lawrence were among those who gave Beser a glimpse of their work. The scientists told him about the strange kinds of guns they had devised which used atomic bullets. When fired at each other, on impact, the bullets devoured one another. They described how they hoped this phenomenon would be used to produce an atomic explosion. They spoke of temperatures they hoped to create which would make a light 'brighter than a thousand suns'.

Ramsey outlined the role the radar officer would play on the mission. Beser would be taught how to monitor enemy radar to see if it was trying to jam or detonate the intricate mechanism of the bomb. To understand how this could happen, Beser must learn what few of the scientists involved knew—the minute details of the bomb's firing mechanism, including its built-in mini-radar system.

On this first day, nobody seemed concerned about how much they should tell Beser. They poured information over him, 'leaving me sinking in a scientific whirlpool'.

There was possibly another reason why the scientists spoke so freely to this young man with the shiny new Corps of Engineers insignia on his uniform. It was one way of cocking a snook at the security arrangements. One scientist even confided to Beser that, by sharing a secret with him, it was no longer a secret, 'and then what can security say?'

Many of the scientists took an increasing delight in challenging what they regarded as oppressive new security arrangements introduced after Niels Bohr's visit to Roosevelt.

Bohr could be heard complaining almost daily since his abortive visit to the White House, that he was being treated less as a partner in a research project, more as a secret weapon against the enemy. He resented having to continue to use the alias of 'Nicholas Baker'. He objected to having to refer to Enrico Fermi as 'Henry Farmer'. And Bohr thought it positively childish that Groves rejoiced in two cover-names: 'Relief' and '99'.

Bohr, in the exasperated words of one security man, 'was getting to be a bore'.

But his presence was crucial to the project. Groves sent out an order that Bohr's tantrums should be tolerated.

Yet the atmosphere of sweet reasonableness and total co-operation on all sides, which had characterised the pioneer work at Los Alamos, was fading. In its place there were often antagonism and suspicion.

Some of the more radical scientists invented a new game to torment the security men: they would communicate with each other in pidgin Russian, leaving the agents baffled and enraged.

None of them knew that many of the project's secrets were already in the hands of Russian scientists, due to the treachery of trusted workers at Los Alamos. These spies were the most dangerous of all, betraying not for money but for an ideology.

Late in the evening Beser was introduced to a dour young technician, David Greenglass. Nobody yet suspected that Greenglass had just stolen the first of many blueprints. His haul would eventually include schematic drawings of a special lens crucial to detonating the plutonium bomb which was being developed parallel with the uranium bomb. The drawings would be spirited to Russia through the highly-professional espionage ring the Soviets had been able to set up from inside Los Alamos. Greenglass would receive a paltry few hundred dollars for his treachery.

Later, Beser was to believe that, on this very evening, he had interrupted Greenglass in his espionage activities.

When the radar officer left Greenglass it was dark. With difficulty he reached the small guest house assigned to visitors. He opened the front door and stopped dead in his tracks. Sprawled on a couch, sipping a drink, was an attractive brunette, stark naked. She carefully lowered her glass and rose to her feet.

'Can I help you?' The voice had just a trace of a German accent.

It was Katherine Oppenheimer, wife of the scientific director. She had left Germany at fourteen; her relatives included the Nazi General Keitel.

'Ma'am, I'm sorry . . .'

Blushing furiously, Beser stammered into silence. He had never seen a naked woman before.

'Are you looking for someone?'

'Yes, ma'am . . . no, ma'am . . . my . . . bed . . . I mean the guest quarters, ma'am.'

'They are at the back of the house. You have come in the wrong door, but you can go through here.' Mrs. Oppenheimer sat down and resumed sipping her cocktail.

Averting his eyes, Beser stumbled past the languid first lady of Los Alamos.

Her husband was in the process of startling Paul Tibbets. The two men were alone in Oppenheimer's office, reviewing what Tibbets had been shown. The flier felt that in a few hours he had received 'a better scientific education than all my years in school'.

Now Oppenheimer began to question him. Apart from enemy interference, the scientist wanted to know what other risks were involved in a bombing mission. Tibbets explained there was always the chance of bombs jamming in their bays, or a faulty mechanism detonating them prematurely. Oppenheimer was confident that such risks could be eliminated in the atomic bomb.

Then he stared intently at Tibbets. For a moment the scientist did not speak. When he did so, his words astonished Tibbets.

'Colonel, your biggest problem may be after the bomb has left your aircraft. The shock waves from the detonation could crush your plane. I am afraid that I can give you no guarantee that you will survive.'

October 1, 1944
Osaka

The scraping against the stone floor of his *geta*, the Japanese wooden clogs he favoured, was the only sound in the Osaka University Laboratory of Dr. Tsunesaburo Asada, arguably Japan's most imaginative scientist. His staff had come to recognise that this habit of shuffling his feet was a signal that Asada was content.

Putting his weight first on one foot, and then on the other, the white-coated Asada studied his latest creation, a proximity fuse. It was similar in design and purpose to those being perfected at Los Alamos.

Months of work had gone into the fuse's development in Asada's well-equipped laboratory. He rarely left the campus nowadays, working well into the night, cat-napping on a couch in a corner of the laboratory, impatient of any interruptions.

He was still, as he had been when the war began, Chairman of the Physics Department. But since late 1941, he had done no teaching. His brilliance made him one of the scientists crucial to Japan's war effort.

Since 1937, Asada had regularly lectured at the Naval Technical Research Institute in Tokyo and at the Naval Aeronautical Research Institute in Yokosuka. Naval officers were intrigued by his argument that scientific discoveries could be adapted for military purposes. He had described to them his time at the Kaiser Wilhelm Institute in Berlin where he had worked alongside Otto Hahn and Fritz Strassmann, the two Germans whose pioneering experiments had helped reveal the vast potential source of energy residing in uranium. He told them how Niels Bohr had endorsed the conclusion that the Germans had split the atom.

Asada had lost track of these scientists after returning to Japan. He suspected some of them might have perished in the European conflict.

As well as lecturing, Asada worked closely with the military authorities before Japan entered the war. He was particularly proud of the plan he had devised in the autumn of 1941 whereby the secret code being used by the American Consulate in Osaka had been successfully broken. When the war came, he had offered his services unconditionally. And on December 17, 1941, he was one of the scientists selected to work on Project A.

This was the code name for Japan's atomic research. Eleven days after President Roosevelt had authorised the go-ahead for the Manhattan Project, the Japanese had entered the field, determined to develop an atomic bomb.

Asada would always remember the mood of blind patriotism which had gripped the first meeting after Pearl Harbor at the Naval Club in Tokyo. There had been promises of generous funding for the atomic research. His caution about the vast technical problems to be overcome had been brushed aside. Those were the days when the Japanese appeared invincible. A naval officer had said that perhaps their new allies, the Germans, could help. Asada pointed out that many of Germany's leading atomic scientists were Jewish and, if they had not been expelled from the country, were probably dead. Some, he added, might be in the United States. He had expressed the opinion that in all likelihood America had the potential to develop atomic weapons. The naval officer had reprimanded him. 'America— and Japan.'

For a year he and the other scientists involved had studied the question. In December 1942, they had presented their conclusions. It would take them ten years to produce 'some atomic weapons'. Even that was optimistic as Japan did not have the essential raw uranium.

Project A was quietly shelved by the Navy, although development work by the Army on Japan's atomic bomb would continue in a desultory fashion until well into 1945.

Project B was then initiated by the Navy. Asada immediately recognised its potential. It was concerned with developing radar, navigation techniques and the proximity fuse.

In the past eighteen months astonishing progress had been made on all three. Asada often remembered how useful two famous British warships—the *Prince of Wales* and the *Repulse*—had been in the development of Japan's radar. The ships had been sunk off Singapore with heavy loss of life in the high days of 1941. Japanese divers had located them on the sea-bed and performed the herculean feat of dismantling the radar apparatus from both ships. It had been shipped to Japan, reassembled, and provided invaluable information to research workers.

Asada himself had developed the proximity fuse. Soon it would go into full-scale production. His contribution to that aspect of Project B completed, he had joined a small and select band of scientists working on the most staggering of all weapons.

They were building a Death Ray.

It was a machine from the pages of science fiction. It was designed to project an invisible beam which would pluck an aircraft out of the sky either by shattering its propellers or killing its crew.

With such a weapon Asada knew that Japan could still snatch a stunning victory. No plane would be safe against the deadly ray. Carefully-sited batteries of Death Rays could guarantee all Japanese cities immunity from air attack. Other batteries could be deployed against hostile craft approaching by sea. Later, the Navy could have Death Rays mounted on their ships and destroy the enemy far away from the home islands.

The potential was heady and limitless.

So far a prototype had killed a laboratory rat. This modest success gave Asada hope.

The principle had been proven. Killing a rat at six feet was he knew, the first step towards eventually bringing down a bomber from 30,000 feet.

Given the time and the facilities, Professor Asada believed he could present the enemy with 'a very unpleasant surprise'.

The next step Asada planned was to direct the Death Ray at a pig.

Imperial Army GHQ
Tokyo

Surprising the enemy was the abiding concern of Major-General Seizo Arisue. Surprises were his business. He created them, spread them, anticipated them and defused them.

He was head of Imperial Army Intelligence, Japan's acknowledged spy-master.

This bantam-sized man with a formidable intellect and a fearful temper to match his harsh, rasping voice, kept a file on every important Japanese politician and officer. He knew more secrets than any man in the Imperial Army. He often used them to good effect to maintain his own position.

In turn, the file on Arisue kept by the rival Naval Intelligence described him as 'arrogant, supremely confident in his own abilities and dangerously ambitious'. At that moment, the relationship between the two intelligence branches was icy. They were locked in a power struggle over which could provide the most valuable information.

Today Arisue was coming to believe that at last he might have the opportunity to resolve that issue with a striking espionage coup. He had been in his cramped office in a wing of the monolithic headquarters since before breakfast trying to verify an intriguing report. It had been sent by Arisue's contact in Lisbon. Ordinarily the report would not have reached Arisue. But he had given an explicit order that he must see 'everything relating to America'.

For many months now he had been bombarded with material. Much of what he read was dross. Some of it came from the *Abwehr* in Berlin; there were out-of-date snippets from Madrid and Mexico City. The weekly summaries of the American Press were more helpful. Army Intelligence subscribed to 140 American newspapers and magazines. Very often the *New York Times*, *Saturday Evening Post*, *Colliers*, *Time*, and *Newsweek* contained clues of troop movements and battle casualties that helped Arisue piece together a surprisingly accurate mosaic of the United States at war. At first he had been suspicious of the material gleaned from the American Press. He thought it might be a trap laid by enemy intelligence. But repeatedly he had been able to confirm independently the newspaper reports. He grew astonished at the American censors for allowing such important material to be published.

Now, as he studied the Lisbon report, he wondered what the Portuguese censors had made of it. No doubt they had passed copies on to British and American Intelligence; in the past six months he had suspected this was regularly happening.

Arisue had requested more information from Lisbon. He had been told none was immediately available. He had no more to go on than this one tantalising message.

His man in Lisbon had picked up a whisper that the United States had embarked on a huge new war project.

After hours of pondering, Arisue knew there was only one way to verify the truth of this claim. He must slip an agent into the United States.

That would be the most difficult operation he had yet mounted. No native Japanese could hope to remain undetected for long in North America. Arisue could call upon the flourishing German spy network in South America to provide an operative, but it might take months to clear matters through Berlin, especially as the tide was turning against Hitler. The Italians were already in disarray.

Arisue ruled out any help from the Axis.

He considered his own resources. His Lisbon contact was not qualified for such a dangerous mission. His men in Madrid and Mexico City were local recruits, capable of little more than acting as intelligence 'post boxes'.

Brazil: he put a query against his agent there. He was a good man. But where would he begin?

The message from Lisbon had given no clue as to where the new American war project was being carried out, or what it was.

The problems were immense. But they always had been, from that day when Arisue had taken over Army Intelligence in the grim period of post-mortem after the battle of Midway.

Arisue was one of the few men in Japan who knew the full truth about Midway. The facts were hidden from the Japanese people because of the effect they would undoubtedly have had on morale.

Midway had been a calamity.

Even now, two years later, Arisue would wince at the memory of that day in June 1942, when the reborn American fleet had sailed from Pearl Harbor to meet Admiral Yamamoto's force which had sailed from Hiroshima Bay. This time surprise was on the American side; U.S. cryptanalysts had broken the Japanese battle code. Yamamoto's every move was known in advance. He was crushed.

Midway had been the turning point in the war. There were no further Japanese advances. America began slowly but systematically to regain captured territory.

The naval battle had stunned the Imperial High Command. It recognised the weakness: Naval Intelligence. The Army also over-hauled its Intelligence arm, found it wanting and appointed Arisue to take control.

It was a wise choice. Arisue had experience abroad as a military attaché; he was a friend of Mussolini and a confidant of Canaris,

43

head of the *Abwehr*. More important, his pre-war contacts with ranking American officers provided Arisue with an invaluable insight into American thinking. It all helped to give him the whip-hand over Naval Intelligence.

Within a year, Arisue had built up Army Intelligence to its present pre-eminent position. His spy network stretched from Brazil to Spain, Portugal and Sweden. In the Pacific he had dozens of natives spying on his behalf. In Japan he had set up special units to monitor air-to-air conversations between American fliers. So far this source had provided little information; air raids were still sporadic.

But with the fall of the Marianas, Arisue expected an increasing number of bombers to attack Japan. He only wished he had planted more spies in those islands; he had not expected them to fall so quickly.

The Navy had blamed Army Intelligence for the loss of the Marianas, arguing that Arisue should have anticipated the American attack. In a towering rage. Arisue had castigated Naval Intelligence. When he had asked the Navy for a map of the islands' defences, they had been unable to provide one.

And it was the Navy's machinations which had forced Tojo to resign, exerting pressure on the Cabinet to oust him from the premiership. The departure of his old friend had left Arisue deeply troubled. It indicated 'the politicians were thinking of taking a soft line towards America'.

If he could only discover what this new American war project was, it might be enough to stiffen the government's resolve to fight on to the end.

Arisue sent for Oya.

Lt-Colonel Kakuzo Oya was chief of the American Intelligence section at Arisue's headquarters. He had steeped himself in Americana, listening to the broadcasts of Walter Lippmann and reading the newspaper articles of Hanson Baldwin. His intellect and intuition were masked by a bland and deceptively easy-going manner.

Recently Oya had been called in to interrogate an important American prisoner of war, Colonel Richard Carmichael, who had been shot down while leading a bomber raid from China. During the questioning, Oya had 'tried all kinds of things', but he found the flier 'a hard one to get to talk'.

Carmichael was tough. He would survive the war; not all of those Oya later interrogated would be so fortunate.

Lt-Colonel Oya was a man to be feared.

The two intelligence officers spent the rest of the afternoon discussing the prospects of infiltrating a spy into the United States.

44

Hiroshima

That evening, at 7.30 p.m., the local Hiroshima radio station broke into its scheduled programme with an air raid warning.

The anti-aircraft gun batteries were alerted by field telephone.

The battery commanded by 2nd-Lieutenant Tatsuo Yokoyama on Mount Futaba was the first to report to the central control in Hiroshima Castle that its guns were ready for action. They began slowly to traverse in a 360-degree arc.

Yokoyama stood by his hand set awaiting further instructions from central control. He told his men to be ready to fire on his command. He asked them to remember all they had practised. He promised them beer and sake if they scored a hit.

At 8 p.m. the All Clear was announced. It had been a false alarm.

October 21, 1944
USAAF Base
Wendover

The B-29's intercom carried further orders.

'We'll do it by the book. They're all gonna be watching. Nobody's gonna screw it. Right?'

The crew of the huge silvered bomber gave no response to Captain Robert Lewis, the pilot. For the past hour they had been 'doing it by the book'. Strictly following the procedures laid down in the buff-coloured manual in Lewis's possession, they had checked the outside of the bomber, clambered aboard, stowed their parachutes and begun the pre-flight count-down.

Even Duzenbury, the engineer, and Caron, the tail gunner, who had flown with Lewis many times before, were surprised how formal he was this crisp fall morning. They knew Lewis as a jokey twenty-six-year-old who wore a battered peak cap and a stained flying jacket. He looked like a combat veteran, even though he had never seen action.

Lewis was treating this flight, in the words of Caron, 'as if he had on board the President and the Cabinet'.

Squashed in the tiny tail turret, the gunner was tempted to snap on the intercom and tell the pilot to relax.

The impulse passed. The checking continued.

'Equipment secure, navigator?' The intercom emphasised the broad Brooklyn accent of Lewis.

'Secure.'

Captain Theodore 'Dutch' van Kirk, the navigator, settled himself more comfortably in the padded seat with its fitted arm-rests. He wondered who Lewis was trying to impress. In the week he had been at Wendover, van Kirk noticed that Lewis enjoyed an audience.

Tibbets had tried to reassure the navigator. He told van Kirk that Lewis was 'just letting off tension; in the air he's a natural'. Van Kirk had his own ideas about 'naturals'. Too often he had found them to be 'dare-devils trying to prove things to other people'. He hoped Lewis was not like that. In the navigator's view, a B-29 was no place for high-jinks.

Lewis had always thought all navigators a strange breed, with their blind belief that any pilot could steer a course to an absolute degree. Today, though, the pilot intended to follow explicitly the slightest course change van Kirk might indicate. In that way Lewis could not be blamed for any 'foul up'.

Seated in the cockpit, watching the winking lights on the instrument panel, Lewis experienced a familiar feeling of well-being: he had come a long way.

There had been those boyhood days on the streets of New York where a swift pair of fists were better than a classy accent; flying school, where he knew his abrasive manner had told against him. But in the end, even his most demanding instructor had conceded that Lewis was a highly gifted pilot. He'd never forgotten the pride his 'Mom and Pop' showed when they first saw him in officer's uniform, and his own satisfaction while walking through his Brooklyn neighbourhood and being 'greeted as somebody'. Then there had been the day he had taken the legendary Charles Lindbergh up in a B-29. After the flight the record-breaking aviator had bestowed on Lewis rare praise—Lindbergh said he would have been happy to have had Lewis fly with him on his historic flights.

But it was Tibbets who had developed Lewis into one of the most experienced B-29 pilots in the Air Force. That was why the summons to Wendover had not surprised Lewis. He had written to his father in explanation.

'Paul needs me, because I am so good at my job.'

Modesty, as Lewis would admit, was not one of his endearing qualities. But he had others: generosity and a fierce loyalty to his crew, especially the enlisted men. Down on the flight line, mechanics hero-worshipped Lewis because he bent regulations to get them better conditions.

He had come together with his flight crew a few days earlier when the B-29 arrived, the first one to be delivered to Wendover. There had been keen competition among the pilots to fly it. Lewis had been almost schoolboyishly excited when he was chosen to do so. He immediately began to talk of 'my crew' and 'my ship'.

But for this flight van Kirk and Ferebee had taken the places of his usual navigator and bombardier. Tibbets had explained to Lewis that van Kirk and Ferebee would take turns flying with all the crews. Tibbets had added a promise.

'It will be just like the old days, Bob.'

That cheered Lewis. The 'old days' were when he had 'a one-to-one relationship with Paul without other people getting in the way'.

In his ten days at Wendover, it had not been like that. Lewis felt that Tibbets never had time to sit down with him and yarn about those 'old days'. Worse, 'he didn't laugh at my jokes, he wasn't so tolerant if I made a small mistake. I put it down to nerves over a new command'.

Tibbets had heard the jokes before. He was determined nobody would be allowed any slip-ups. It was not nerves, but concern with unique problems which made Tibbets preoccupied.

The last flight checks were ending. Lewis asked van Kirk the estimated flying time to the Initial Point, the map reference from which the bomber would commence its bombing run.

The navigator told him.

From the IP to the AP, the Aiming Point, would be a matter of a few miles. Over that distance Lewis would work with the bombardier, Ferebee.

He had disliked Ferebee from the day they met. He thought the bombardier 'superior'. The way Ferebee talked reminded Lewis of 'a playboy in the movies'.

One night he and Ferebee had played poker. Lewis lost $200, half his month's salary. He could ill afford to do so; a broken marriage had left him short of cash. Half-jokingly, Tibbets told Lewis to stay in his 'own league'.

Tibbets knew Ferebee was one of the best poker players in uniform. He also knew Lewis was a 'poor loser'—an accusation the pilot would always hotly deny—and Tibbets did not 'want card games creating unnecessary problems'.

This morning Ferebee was in his take-off position, seated back-to-back with van Kirk. They hardly spoke to Lewis.

The co-pilot told Lewis that all the pre-flight checks were now complete.

Lewis ran through in his mind the main points of the briefing Tibbets had given. He was to climb to 30,000 feet and fly south to the bombing range, the man-made lake of Salton Sea in Southern California. There Ferebee would aim to drop a single blockbuster, filled with ballast, into a 700-foot circle on the northern edge of the

47

lake. Tibbets had told Lewis that once the bomb was dropped he was to execute a 155-degree diving turn, which would take him back in the direction from which he had just come. Tibbets had emphasised: 'Keep your nose down and get the hell out of the area as fast as you can.'

Tibbets hoped the manoeuvre would provide the answer to how an aircrew could survive the expected shock wave from an atomic bomb. He had calculated that Lewis should be some seven miles away when the test blockbuster hit the ground. He did not explain to Lewis the reason for this action, 'because that would have meant telling him too much too soon'.

Shortly before boarding the B-29 Lewis had received another surprise. Beser arrived on the apron saying he was bringing along on the trip some 300 pounds of special equipment.

'Can't tell you why,' said Beser cheerfully. 'It's a matter of security.'

That didn't endear Beser to Lewis. Waiting for take-off the radar officer was squatting on the floor of the B-29, aft of the toilet in the rear section of the plane, with his spectrum analysers, direction finder, search receivers and antennae.

Beser was about to make the first flight in which he would practise how to cope with any enemy attempt to interfere electronically with an atomic bomb. Some of his instruments had been specially modified at Los Alamos. During the flight they would receive signals from the ground, simulating enemy radar beams. It would be Beser's task to recognise, anticipate and deflect the beams.

'Ready to start engines?'

Duzenbury studied the engineer's panel before answering Lewis. He was, at thirty-one, the oldest man in the crew. Duzenbury hadn't questioned why Tibbets had brought him to Wendover. It was enough for him 'to work for the finest gentleman in the Air Corps'. He also liked Lewis; next to 'the Colonel', Lewis was the best pilot Duzenbury knew.

'Start engines, Captain.'

One by one each of the four Wright Cyclone turbine engines roared into life.

The tower cleared Lewis for take-off. At the end of the runway he boosted all engines consecutively to 2300 rpm while Duzenbury checked the magnetos and generators. Then Lewis advanced the throttles to their full power position and slowly released the brakes. At 95 mph, just as the manual said, Lewis lifted the largest bomber in the world into the air.

Exactly on time he reached the I.P. Minutes later Ferebee announced he had the A.P. in his Norden bombsight.

'Bombs away. Correction. Bomb away.'

Lewis banked the bomber violently to the left, dropping its nose during the turn to give him more speed. A surprised Caron far back in the tail shouted into the intercom.

'Cap'n, it's like a roller coaster back here!'

Lewis shouted back. 'I'll charge you for the ride when we get home.'

Beser was too involved to notice the manoeuvre; two of his instruments had lost power and he simply had no idea how effective his electronic counter-measures had been against the invisible beams. Disgusted, he gave up monitoring.

The blockbuster fell within the circle. Camera-men from the Manhattan Project reported that they had managed to record its fall. Their films were flown to Los Alamos. There they were studied to see what information they offered the scientists still trying to determine the best final shape for the atomic bomb.

Measuring instruments around the A.P. calculated that Lewis was over seven miles away when the bomb impacted.

Tibbets was relieved. The manoeuvre meant that an aircraft should be able to avoid the atomic bomb's shock wave. He expressed his relief to one of the scientists who was with him on the bombing range. The man gave Tibbets a chilling response.

'Seven miles, twenty miles, fifty miles. There is no way of telling what the safe distance is until we drop a real atomic bomb. You'll just have to trust in God.'

'But, supposing,' thought Tibbets, 'God is on the other side that day.'

It was evening when Tibbets returned to Wendover. In his office he continued to review the tactical requirements for delivering an atomic bomb.

He knew a great deal more than he had a month before, but he was far from reassured. The uncertain nature of the explosion—nobody could be positive how big it would be—and the predicted shock wave, another imponderable, had helped to rule out the use of a fighter escort. To be sure of surviving the shock wave, fighters would have to be so far away from the explosion, just when the bomber was at its most vulnerable, that it was unlikely they could provide proper protection. Furthermore, a fighter escort might only succeed in drawing attention to the bomber. Tibbets made up his mind.

The bomber would have to go in alone.

That, too, raised problems: flak, and enemy fighters. It was likely that the final approach would be made over enemy-held territory, at least part of which would undoubtedly have fighter protection. The more Tibbets thought about it, the less secure the chance of success seemed. The atomic-bomb-carrying bomber could be destroyed long before it reached its objective.

Then Tibbets recalled his experience in New Mexico.

Months before, he had been there, carrying out tests to assess a B-29's susceptibility to fighter attack. He had been irritated to find that his usual B-29, the one he used for all his tests, was out of commission. He was offered another one—stripped of its guns.

He decided to fly it, to give the fighter pilots a chance to practice. Tibbets quickly discovered the stripped B-29 could operate some 4,000 feet higher than his usual bomber. It was faster and more manoeuvrable. He was able to outpace the P-47 fighters making mock attacks on him. Finally, at 34,000 feet, the fighters had to give up; the strain on their engines was too great.

As he recalled the experience, Tibbets began to feel excited. He knew that flak was largely ineffective at over 32,000 feet, and he remembered now that a P-47 fighter was similar in performance to a Japanese Zero.

With Japan 'likely to provide a target city', Tibbets reasoned that his best possible chance of survival would be to use a stripped-down B-29 for the mission. He would take out all the armour-plating and all the guns, apart from the two in the tail.

He telephoned the flight line and told the ground crews to begin work at once on stripping down the two bombers already at Wendover.

'Tonight?' asked an incredulous line chief.

'Now,' said Tibbets firmly.

The mechanics thought the idea 'plumb crazy'. Later they would christen the emasculated bombers: *Sitting Target One* and *Sitting Target Two*.

October 25, 1944
Over the Pacific

In tight formation five aircraft flew east over the Pacific. All their pilots hoped soon to die, to fulfil a sacred obligation and deal the enemy a devastating blow.

The fliers wore white scarfs, loosly knotted around their necks. Under their leather flying helmets, concealed by their goggles, each man also wore a *hachimaki*, a replica of the headband that Samurai warriors had traditionally worn in battle in ancient Japan.

This morning the band was the symbol of the Special Attack Corps, the suicide pilots, the *shimpu* or Divine Wind. Later, these pilots, and many others like them, would be called *Kamikaze*, a western translation of the characters that in Sino-Japanese are pronounced *shimpu*. The first *shimpu* were the momentous typhoons of 1241 and 1281 which, according to legend, rescued Japan from the fury of the Mongols.

The men chosen to launch this new *shimpu* had been told just before taking off a few hours earlier that they were 'gods without earthly desires'. Their Zeros contained 250-kilogram bombs. The pilots planned to crash-dive on to the ships of the American fleet now just beyond the horizon.

This plan was devised only six days before by Vice-Admiral Takijiro Onishi. To all the adjectives applied to the moon-faced commander—arrogant, brilliant, condescending and uncompromising—another could be added in these last days of October: desperate.

Onishi was no longer the confident leader who had helped devise the attack on Pearl Harbor; who had launched the crippling assault on Clark Field, Manila, which had wiped out America's air force in the Far East; who had sent his pilots marauding through the Pacific.

Those days were over. Retaliation was on the way. A huge American fleet had been spotted heading towards the Philippines. If those islands fell, Japan's supply lines would be fatally ruptured. Onishi was given command of the first Air Fleet, operating from Manila. This once-impressive force consisted now of less than one hundred aircraft. But they were enough for Onishi. On October 19, he had presented his plan for *shimpu*.

There had been an enthusiastic response from his pilots. The men now over the Pacific were about to deliver the first savage blow.

They had written their final letters and farewell poems. Some had left brief wills. Each, in accordance with the ancient tradition of Samurai leaving for their final battle, had enclosed with their words, locks of hair and nail-parings, all that was to remain of their bodies.

Before take-off, Onishi himself had poured every man a ceremonial cup of cold sake and offered him a dish of dried cuttle-fish. As each pilot took his cup he had bowed and then lifted the sake in both hands to his lips. What he had received was something close to a religious libation, like the last Communion. Onishi had then handed every pilot a small lunch box, *bento*, to provide them with the psychological comfort of a last-minute snack.

At 10.45 a.m. the suicide squadron sighted their enemy, an American carrier force with destroyer escorts.

The pilots bored in, scattering tin-foil to jam the American radar. Each pilot pulled a toggle which prepared the bomb in his plane for detonation.

At 10.53 a.m. the first Zero crash-dived on to the flight deck of the aircraft carrier *St. Lo*. Plane and pilot disintegrated in a huge explosion. This was the 'splendid death', *rippa na saigo*, which Onishi had promised.

The *St. Lo* began to sink.

By 10.59 a.m. all five planes had hit their targets.

The mission had been a total success. More would follow.

America was staggered by Onishi's barbarous tactics. Revulsion gave way to anger, and a determination that eventually Japan must be taught a terrible lesson.

November 24, 1944
USAAF Base
Wendover

The 393rd received its fifteenth stripped-down B-29 that day. The squadron was now at full strength. The removal of armour plating and all guns, except those in the tail turrets, no longer caused comment. Pilots found it gave them extra height and speed, although they were not totally convinced by Tibbets' statement that, when later they flew in combat, they would be out of range of flak and enemy fighters.

'Today,' Lewis wrote to his parents, 'was typical for its routine. Morning briefing followed by bombing practice; back for lunch (good), then more practice. I don't ask why. Nobody does.'

The letter would be read by Manhattan Project agents attached to the base post office. They would decide it did not contravene security and allow it to be mailed. Many letters failed to pass them. They ended up on Uanna's desk. The watchful major made sure the writers were sufficiently scared by the time they left his office to be more careful in future about what they wrote.

Three hundred blockbuster casings were available for the crews to use on their solitary practice missions to the Salton Sea. Camera-men continued to film the bombs dropping and the aircraft making their jolting 155-degree turns. Tibbets still believed the manoeuvre was the only protection possible against the bomb's suspected shock waves.

The action was the subject of much speculation. Pilots soon discovered that failing to execute a proper turn meant being temporarily grounded. Such punishments were an integral part of Tibbets' style. He also encouraged excellence by example. He himself had flown several runs, with Lewis as his co-pilot, and performed the manoeuvre perfectly.

The bombing circle was being steadily reduced. Now, it was no more than 400 feet in diameter. Ferebee had demonstrated that it was possible to drop a casing into the circle from 30,000 feet. Van Kirk proved that on long training flights, and over water, it was possible to navigate the distance with no more than an error of half a mile. The workshops remained open twenty four hours a day. The flight line worked around the clock keeping the bombers aloft.

Mess Officer Charles Perry was told by Tibbets to 'just use the word *Silverplate*' if he had any problems. Perry was sceptical. But one day, tired of arguing with a food supply depot, he used the code-word. His goods arrived within hours. Every Army Air Force depot in America had special orders to give priority to *Silverplate*.

The 393rd became the best-fed unit in the services. Tibbets had been known to send a transport plane 1,000 miles to collect a cargo of tropical fruit. Fresh fish from New Orleans, Miami and San Francisco were regular items on Perry's menus. On one memorable occasion, Tibbets himself flew an 1,800-mile round-trip to Portland, Oregon to pick up a load of coffee cups.

He took care of his men in other ways. When they tangled with police in Salt Lake City over traffic violation or rowdy behaviour, or 'got involved with the local married women', he intervened—if a man's work record justified it.

Exec. Officer John King struggled to maintain the standards of discipline he thought essential. But Tibbets made it clear he was not over-concerned with smart salutes, knife-edged creases in khaki trousers or gleaming toecaps. All that concerned him was a man's capacity to work. Gradually the 393rd became one of the most casually attired units in the Air Force.

A few days before, Tibbets had introduced a new pilot with the most unusual appearance of all: bobbed hair, rouged cheeks and bright red lipstick. Baggy flying coveralls could not disguise a shapely figure.

'Sure she's a lady,' grinned Tibbets as he presented the newcomer. 'And they don't fly any finer than Dora Dougherty.'

Dora was a veteran pilot who had worked for Tibbets on the B-29 testing programme. She had handled the bomber with great skill and assurance at a time when many men pilots were doubtful of its capability. Duzenbury remembered how Dora had once landed a B-29 with an engine on fire. Caron recalled how she had deliberately cut an engine on take-off and yet became airborne. At Wendover Dora flew a transport. Sometimes Tibbets wished he could have sent her up with a B-29. But Dora never complained about any assignment.

And the complaints had started.

They concerned the training schedules, the long hours, the

53

continual security checks. And above all: why doesn't somebody explain what this is for?

In the words of John King, the feeling was growing: 'That there were "them" and "us".'

Or: Tibbets, Ferebee and van Kirk; and the rest of the 393rd.

The trio worked and relaxed together. Occasionally Lewis joined the group. But the once-close relationship between Tibbets and the pilot was cooling. Tibbets felt Lewis was increasingly 'trying to take advantage of the past association we had'.

He was no longer amused by the pilot's determined forays after women, his wild partying, the aggressive way he approached everything: cards, volleyball, even conversation.

But in the air Lewis continued to excel. In the end that was all Tibbets cared about.

Beser did not like flying with Lewis 'because we had nothing in common'. The pilot had still not discovered why the radar officer 'brought along a bunch of boxes and tried to look important'.

Beser enjoyed the mystery surrounding his function. He was regularly, and unsuccessfully, pumped about his visits to the restricted Tech Area and the flights he and Tibbets made together. No flight plans were filed for these journeys. They were to Albuquerque, the gateway to Los Alamos.

There, Beser received further instruction in the intricacies of electronic counter-measures. He would return to Wendover with Los Alamos technicians. They would spend days in the Tech Area watching Beser practise analysing the intensity variations of successive return waves, or identifying the location, speed and course of a reflecting object.

After Beser had become familiar with some of the bomb's secret radar system, a security agent was assigned to guard him day and night whenever he left the base. The man took his job so seriously that he had even stood guard outside a public lavatory in a Salt Lake City restaurant while Beser relieved himself. The radar officer reacted, characteristically.

'Listen, mac. People will think there's something funny about me, with you standing there.'

'You listen, Lieutenant. I'm supposed to be in the john with you—not outside!'

Beser gave up. From now on he must share every social occasion—a date, a drink with friends, a visit home to his family. In time he would come to accept his shadow.

But only at Wendover did he feel really free. His bodyguard's duties ended when Beser set foot on the base.

Winter came early that year, making Wendover even grimmer.

54

The November wind whistled across the salt flats, numbing everything in its path.

Perry and his cooks tried hard to make Thanksgiving dinner memorable, offering pumpkin pie and an exotic fruit punch to accompany the roast turkey. The mess officer then produced an abundant supply of Cuban cigars to complete the meal.

Cuba was in fact very much on everyone's mind. The latest rumour had it that crews would soon fly south to sunny Havana to continue 'special training'.

Tibbets, as usual, remained tight-lipped. Groves was in regular telephone contact with him, wanting to be briefed on progress, chivvying and demanding. Tibbets would mention some of the difficulties he faced, bringing all the bomber crews to readiness so that any one of them was capable of performing an atomic strike. Groves would listen, grunt and only reply: 'Work them hard. That's what you are there for.'

The scientists were flying in and out of Wendover daily, making new demands which involved frequent changes. They asked for the bomb bays to be modified. Conventional bombs were held in place by shackles, but it was decided that for a plane carrying just one large, long atomic bomb, what was required was a single, safe, reliable hook from which the 10,000-pound bomb could be suspended. No such hook could be found. Bombardier Kermit Beahan was sent to Britain and brought back the specifications for the one used by the RAF in their Lancaster bombers for the British blockbusters. It was adapted and fitted to the 393rd's B-29's for carrying the atomic bomb.

There were constant changes, too, in the bomb's shape and weight. After each change, the scientists flew back to Los Alamos, telling Tibbets before they left that they were satisfied, that no more changes were contemplated and that he could plan his training programme with confidence. A few days later they would return, asking for new modifications because they had discovered further aerodynamic flow or other problems which necessitated yet another alteration in the shape of the uranium or plutonium bomb.

Tibbets often found himself in sympathy with the exasperation felt in the base machine shops where the changes had to be made by service personnel. At times they became almost openly hostile to these unknown civilians who descended on them in the company of Tibbets and scrapped a long night's work with the briefest of apologies. Matters were not helped by security insisting that the scientists should pass themselves off as sanitary engineers—a piece of flummery which led to some very ribald comments. Prohibited from answering some of the questions his own engineering officers and men asked, Tibbets knew that to many of them he seemed cold, aloof and hard-nosed. The loneliness of leadership about which his mother had once warned him was becoming increasingly clear.

His command had assumed impressive proportions. As well as the 393rd, he now had the 320th Troop Carrier Squadron, the 390th Air Service Group, the 603rd Air Engineering Squadron and the 1027th Air Materiel Squadron.

Between them they fetched, carried for and served the 393rd. To police them there was the 1395th Military Police Company; supporting them were now some fifty agents from the Manhattan Project. Under Uanna's instructions, they continued to try to get the airmen to talk about their work, although nowadays they rarely succeeded. The word was out: if Wendover was bad, Alaska was worse.

But that did not solve the problems associated with the daily management of some 1,200 servicemen. There was an outbreak of venereal disease. The security men were concerned that a number of men had shacked up with local married women whose husbands were abroad in the services. There was a renewed spate of fist fights and drunken brawls involving base personnel in Salt Lake City.

On one memorable night in the city's Chi Chi Club, a tipsy Captain Eatherly knocked out an infantry major who had ordered him to leave. Eatherly escaped through the club's back door as MP's arrived at the front.

This time Eatherly avoided arrest. But he was being regularly summoned to Tibbets' office to explain his misdemeanours. There was a wad of speeding tickets he had collected and refused to pay. Tibbets forced him to do so. Another incident concerned liquor permits. In Utah a state permit was needed to buy liquor. The permits were good for a bottle a week. Police found Eatherly with fifteen permits. Tibbets blasted the pilot and squared the law.

Eatherly continued to spend many of his nights shooting dice at $100 a throw at the State Line Hotel in Wendover. Sometimes he lost, and won back, his month's salary in a few hours. Security agents reported his gambling to Uanna.

He complained to Tibbets: 'The guy's a psycho.'

Tibbets doggedly clung to his maxim. 'Maybe. But he's a hell of a pilot. That is all that matters.'

In mid-November Eatherly had demonstrated his flying skill. Making a final approach to the field, one of the activating switches in his B-29 went into reverse, a serious mechanical failure. The B-29 began to roll 'until it was standing straight up on a wing tip'. Eatherly calmly righted the plane and made a perfect landing.

That night he lost a sizeable sum in a poker game. Eatherly shrugged aside such losses, hinting of a huge ranch back in Texas whose income could meet any of his debts. He claimed he had left the ranch at seventeen to become a pilot and later fought the Japanese in the Pacific. He told the stories well.

Nobody suspected they were pipe-dreams, the first signs of the instability which would eventually have Claude Eatherly committed to a mental hospital. His fellow fliers only recognised that he seemed to have a yearning to be famous. Eventually, though, his fantasies would make him notorious.

And none would suffer more from those fantasies than Paul Tibbets—who, ironically, would soon make them possible.

December 6, 1944
Hiroshima

Second-Lieutenant Tatsuo Yokoyama had allowed a full hour for the walk from his gun battery on Mount Futaba to Hiroshima Castle. There, he was due to attend the monthly review of the city's defences. He would not be expected to speak, merely to listen as the local commanders discussed the position. He doubted if any of them even knew his name. That did not upset him; it would be enough if, as in the previous month, the minutes of the meeting were to note again 'the alertness of the Mount Futaba battery during practice'.

The days were over when he would arrive at the meeting in a motor-pool car shared with other junior officers. Only the most senior officers were now entitled to use precious petrol, and then strictly on military business.

Yokoyama did not mind the walk. It was his way of keeping in touch with the changing situation in the city.

The tangle of black-lettered signs directing military traffic to the port were now faded. It was almost three years to the day since the commander-in-chief of the Japanese Fleet, Admiral Isoroku Yamamoto, had boarded his flagship, anchored in Hiroshima Bay along with other Japanese battleships, to hear the first radioed reports from his forces attacking Pearl Harbor and British Malaya, A few days later he was given the news of the sinking off Singapore of the two great warships *Prince of Wales* and *Repulse*. But now the revered Yamamoto was dead, killed in 1943 when the plane in which he was travelling was shot down by American fighters, and Hiroshima Harbour contained not one battleship.

Nor were there truckloads of troops winding their way through the streets of Hiroshima to the Hall of Triumphant Return, the

Gaisenkan. Almost every soldier who was fighting in the Pacific had embarked through Hiroshima's *Gaisenkan*; now it was empty, waiting in vain for the 'triumphant return' of the troops.

Three years before, the jetties were lined with thousands of civilians chanting exhortations to those departing troops; now the only civilians in the area who were not directly employed by the port authority were those tending the vegetable patches which sprouted amidst the cranes and sheds.

Everywhere in the city there were slogans urging people to grow more vegetables, and even to cultivate weeds. Also posted were warnings of severe penalties for black-marketeering, profiteering and spreading 'irresponsible rumours'.

Hiroshima's narrow streets had undergone changes in this past year. There were fewer trucks and no taxis; apart from trams, bicycling or walking was the only way to get around.

Cafés offered a tasteless green tea. Often it was served luke-warm because of the increasing fuel shortages. Coke balls for the *hibachi* stoves were regularly dampened by water to make them burn longer. Some restaurateurs had devised a method of balling up pages of the city's newspaper, the *Chugoku Shimbun*, dipping the wads in water and burning them with the coke. Four pages were sufficient to boil a pint of water in ten minutes.

As well as the vegetable allotments down in the port, there were thousands of other improvised 'victory' gardens. Flat roofs were coated with layers of soil to raise beans, carrots, marrows, spinach and Chinese cabbages. Wooden barrels, drums, even worn-out pots and pans were used for growing leeks and radishes.

Local associations had been formed to handle bulk rations, issued only to ticket holders; there were also tickets for free medicine and dental treatment. For this first week of December, the associations would distribute to each family in its care: a cake of bean curd; one sardine or small horse-mackerel; two Chinese cabbages; five carrots; four aubergines and half a pumpkin. The stalk end of a pumpkin was highly prized. Usually an inch or two long, it would be thinly sliced and stewed as an extra vegetable.

Bramble shoots were peeled and sucked as an hors d'oeuvre; sorrel was soaked in brine and used with a rice substitute for a main course. Reeds from the River Ota were cut and parboiled. Grubs found in fruit bushes and fig trees were boiled and served with imitation soya sauce. Beetles and worms of all kinds were roasted on slivers of wood.

The women of Hiroshima had never looked so drab. Most of them dressed like the men: both sexes favoured a badly-cut high buttoning jacket and trousers. The Government encouraged this apparel.

Only the girls in the red-light district continued to wear kimonos.

There were thousands of prostitutes in the rat-infested Houses of Joy. But the nights were over when 10,000 soldiers en route to the Pacific would swarm through the area.

Kindergarten and junior schools were now being closed, their pupils and teachers evacuated to the countryside to avoid air raids and to ease the city's rationing problems.

For those who remained in Hiroshima even the task of washing was an unpleasant business. The only soap available was made from rice-bran and caustic soda. It created a rash. Tooth-powder was now a black-market commodity; the accepted substitute was a vile-tasting salty paste.

Cinemas and theatres were popular. The films and plays were often inferior, but the collective heat generated from several hundred people squashed together was a pleasant experience.

Keeping warm was a problem. Many people solved it by baking flat stones or tiles in their stoves, wrapping them in layers of old newspapers and placing the bundles next to their skin. As the stones cooled, the newspapers were removed layer by layer. Then, when the heat finally evaporated, the stones were re-heated.

Yokoyama had no doubt: the city was coping. And to anybody who challenged him, he had a ready answer. Hiroshima was intact. Yokoyama thought that it was logical that the Army would soon transfer him and his battalion to a city more likely to be attacked.

From ahead came a loud concerted shout. He broke into a run. Rounding a corner, he saw a house collapse into the street. Instinctively he looked skywards. There were no aircraft.

Through the dust he saw a group of youths belonging to the Patriotic Volunteer Corps, boys and girls brought in from the country to work as labourers.

The group was gathered around the house adjoining the collapsed building. Some of them began to saw through the pillars supporting the house; others attached a stout rope to its ridge pole. One of the boys told Yokoyama they were creating a fire-break in case of air attack.

In many parts of Hiroshima, this demolition work had begun to cut swathes through the city. There had not been such an upheaval since the catastrophic floods of August 6, 1653. On that day in the seventeenth century hundreds of houses had been ripped from their foundations by nature. Now enthusiastic youths were achieving what subsequent typhoons had been unable to accomplish.

For Senkichi Awaya, the Mayor of Hiroshima, the orders to create fire-breaks was the hardest he had implemented since taking office. If it had been issued by the Army, the fifty-one-year-old civil servant would have vigorously challenged the command.

But it had come from the Department of the Interior in Tokyo, the same department which had appointed Awaya mayor in July 1943.

A few days before, Awaya had telephoned Hiroshima Castle and informed the duty officer of the order. Almost immediately, the Regional Army Headquarters there had issued instructions on which sections of the city were to be demolished; soldiers would be available to supervise and help with the work.

The Army had been ready and waiting, confident that the civil authorities must confirm the plans for the fire-lanes which the Army itself had drawn up weeks earlier. The Department of the Interior, like all branches of government, was subservient to military demands.

Throughout the morning, Mayor Awaya's frequent meetings were punctuated by the crash of falling buildings. Finally, hardly able to hear himself speak, he stood at his first-floor office window and gazed down the street to where clouds of dust were rising near the Aioi Bridge. He wondered whether the bridge itself, the most striking in Hiroshima, might also eventually be demolished on the Army's orders. Its unique T-shape linked three islands in the city centre.

He was reassured by his chief assistant, the diminutive, immaculately-dressed Kazumasa Maruyama. Maruyama had checked: all the city's bridges were safe. Without the bridges, the Army's movements within the city would be drastically curtailed; in an emergency it was necessary to be able to move troops quickly.

Together the two men watched the destruction. Outside the Town Hall, a queue was already forming composed of householders seeking compensation and new accommodation. Maruyama reminded the mayor how limited was the help the city could offer.

'We can only give them a few yen.'

'Just three years—now this. And all because of the Army.'

For Mayor Awaya to have uttered such words in public would have invited imprisonment, even execution. But in the comfortably-furnished mayor's parlour, he and Maruyama now talked openly about such matters. In the sixteen months they had worked together, each man had revealed himself to the other as a devout pacifist and fierce anti-militarist.

Vastly different in their backgrounds—Awaya was from upper middle-class stock while Maruyama was proudly working-class—the men were bound by strong personal ties.

Awaya had acted as go-between for Maruyama during his assistant's delicate negotiations with his future wife's parents. As a devout Christian, one of many in Hiroshima, Mayor Awaya found it difficult to feel his way through the complicated by-play of such discussions, an integral part of Japanese marriage. But the mayor finalised the marriage contract to everyone's satisfaction.

In the late summer of 1944, the Christian Church in Hiroshima

60

where Awaya worshipped was closed down; even those religious orders run by Germans and Italians had come to be looked upon with suspicion; it was part of the xenophobia which the militarists fostered throughout the country.

Awaya now worshipped at home, singing to himself the hymns missionaries had introduced to Japan. He wished his wife and four children, still at home in Tokyo, could be with him; when he had moved to Hiroshima they remained behind so that the children's education was not disturbed.

Awaya's Christianity had made him an enemy of the militarists. They sought every way they could to attack him. But he was one of the most popular mayors the city had known; free of any taint of corruption, easily accessible and energetic in handling cases of civil injustice. Secure in his position, he ignored the Army's sniping. He knew he was being watched, that attempts had been made to subvert his staff. Only here, in his office, with Maruyama, could he dare to express himself freely.

This morning, a familiar topic was again raised, what Awaya called the 'terrible decline in our city which can be traced to the folly of the militarists in Showa fifteen', a reference to the events of 1941.

In just twenty days' time, on December 28, the Hirohito reign of Showa would enter its nineteenth year. Both men agreed that Showa was now an ironically inept name. The word means Enlightened Peace.

Awaya raised a theme he increasingly brooded over.

'We may have to pay dearly for the mistakes that have been made.'

Both men knew how inadequately prepared was the city for an air raid. There were insufficient shelters; the water pressure to the fire hydrants was low; the few evacuation routes out of the city could easily become clogged. Nor did Awaya feel the fire-lanes would provide adequate protection.

'Whole areas within the lanes could simply burn themselves out. The lanes can only hope to stop the city being destroyed all at once.'

There was one aspect, however, for which Awaya believed they should be grateful.

'The rivers dividing our city provide excellent, natural fire-breaks. And, if necessary, the citizens could take refuge in those rivers from the heat generated by fires.'

His words were an intuitive glimpse into the future.

Four hundred years old, built on a mound surrounded by a moat, Hiroshima Castle was the centre-piece of a vast military complex. Within its keep were the divisional and regional Army Headquarters along with some 40,000 men. The area also contained an infantry training school, hospital, ammunition and supply depots. Under the Castle was the civil defence headquarters, the unit responsible for alerting the city to air attack, and the central fire control for the anti-aircraft gun batteries.

The perimeter of this multi-purpose installation was adjoined by dozens of small factories producing armaments of all kinds. The larger factories were located on the banks of the rivers.

Yokoyama relished his visits to the Castle. They provided him with visible reaffirmation of the power of the Army; there were always rows of field pieces and armoured vehicles of all kinds on display. Within the grounds which the Army had garrisoned for nearly one hundred years, the mood was permanently optimistic. Officers and men talked only of great victories to come. Nobody drew attention to shell casings made from substitute metals or the near-empty fuel tanks of half-trucks and armoured cars.

The mood of senior officers at the defence review meeting was buoyant. One after another they expounded a similar theme. Hiroshima, like all other Japanese cities, was ready to meet the enemy. There was loud agreement for the elderly officer who spoke last.

'Let the American bombers come—and soon. They will fall from the skies under our guns!'

His eyes swept the room, alighting on the coterie of young anti-aircraft officers which included Yokoyama.

'The honour will fall to you to strike the first blows. The enemy is arrogant. He believes he can enter our skies with safety, to bomb our women and children. He will be shown otherwise. Do not fail. We will repeat the success of Pearl Harbor.'

December 7, 1944
Washington, D.C.

Seated at a writing desk in his suite in the Carlton Hotel, a few convenient blocks away from the White House, Alexander Sachs, the financier who had been instrumental in alerting President Roosevelt to the possibility of atomic weapons, had little time to study the newspapers or listen to the radio programmes marking the third anniversary of Pearl Harbor.

Yet, for Sachs and millions of Americans, December 7 was a day when the media were particularly compelling. Commentators continued to return to a single theme in recalling Pearl Harbour:

the country could neither forgive nor forget Japan's treachery; the 'day of infamy' would have to be avenged.

Meanwhile, the Press and newscasters reported that the war was going well in Europe. Patton's Army was entrenched in Strasbourg. The British and French Armies under Eisenhower were helping American forces to liberate other parts of Hitler's Europe yard by yard. The Russians were 'advancing on all fronts', a phrase reporters used when they did not know where the Red Army was.

But it was the Pacific which captured America's emotions. Pearl Harbor, in the words of one editorial writer, 'has made this our war'.

Vastly better equipped on land, sea and in the air, American forces were about to pull a drawstring around the enemy. The Japanese Air Force was proving a spent force; if the kamikaze planes still struck terror in those who were facing them in increasing numbers, the newspapers in Washington and other cities played down the suicide planes as a passing phenomenon, a last reckless throw by a desperate enemy.

Tokyo was now within reach of the B-29 bombers based in the Marianas. Large formations of the Superforts were beginning to hit the Japanese mainland; each B-29 carried seven tons of bombs.

Tokyo Rose's taunt of 'Come and get us' was now receiving a confident rejoinder on Stateside radio stations.

'We're coming, Rose, we're coming!'

Nobody doubted that America's youth was paying a high price for the long journey to Rose's Tokyo lair. An average of 5,000 Americans were dying each week in the relentless push across the Pacific. But as the newspapers pointed out, the abacus was even grimmer for the enemy. The decisive aircraft carrier engagement off Guam had become known as the Great Marianas Turkey Shoot, while the loss of the islands had cost the Japanese 50,000 dead.

The mood that morning throughout America was uncompromising. The enemy, in the words of one commentator, 'must be hit with everything we've got'.

Alexander Sachs knew that 'what we've got' was likely soon to include an atomic bomb. And five years after first calling on Roosevelt to authorise its construction, Sachs now wanted the President to put a curb on when and how the bomb would be used.

The financier had been successfully lobbied by the growing band of scientists beginning to have second thoughts about the weapon. Among them were Albert Einstein and Leo Szilard, who had been so vocal in 1939 about the need for America to equip itself with an atomic arsenal. They now argued that the world situation had changed. The Nazi capability to produce atomic bombs could be discounted. They believed Japan could be beaten by conventional

63

weapons. Any brief military advantage that nuclear bombs would bring America could be outweighed by political and psychological losses. The damage to American prestige, argued Szilard, could be immense if the United States was the first to drop the bomb. If America did so, then Einstein foresaw a world-wide atomic armaments race.

Roosevelt rejected such arguments. Perhaps Niels Bohr's August visit had turned him against scientists who changed their minds at crucial moments; perhaps he felt they under-estimated the enemy's ability to keep fighting under almost any circumstances.

Those opposed to using the bomb unconditionally now had a more persuasive flag-bearer than the talkative Bohr. Sachs was a friend of the President. The scientists had persuaded the financier that just as much as they, he, too, must bear a responsibility for the development of the atomic bomb. Accepting this, Sachs prepared his draft for a startling proposal. He agonised over the words for many days. Then, in his neat handwriting, he outlined the conditions he believed Roosevelt should insist upon before dropping the bomb:

Following a successful test there should be arranged:
(a) A rehearsal demonstration before a body including internationally recognised scientists from all Allied countries and, in addition, neutral countries, supplemented by representatives of the major faiths;
(b) That a report on the nature and the portent of the atomic weapon be prepared by the scientists and other representative figures;
(c) That thereafter a warning be issued by the United States and its allies in the Project to our major enemies in the war, Germany and Japan, that atomic bombing would be applied to a selected area within a designated time limit for the evacuation of human and animal life;
(d) In the wake of such realisation of the efficacy of atomic bombing an ultimatum demand for immediate surrender by the enemies be issued, in the certainty that failure to comply would subject their countries and people to atomic annihilation.

The financier delivered his memorandum to Roosevelt in person. They discussed it alone, and no record was made of their conversation.

A few months later, with Roosevelt dead, Sachs would claim that the President had accepted his proposals. His implication was clear: those in favour of using the bomb had later persuaded the President to change his mind. There would be no acceptable way of testing the truth of this—or the claim that Roosevelt had accepted Sachs' terms.

The most likely explanation is that Roosevelt, a skilled exponent of the tactic, had led Sachs to believe he had heard what he wanted to hear.

But, with his passion for secrecy, his policy of never having witnesses to such private conversations, Roosevelt left history with one of the last riddles of the pre-atomic age.

Certainly, when Groves heard of the proposals, he thought them derisory. Sachs' suggestion that Hitler and the Japanese militarists could be swayed by a memo about an explosion in some distant place seemed to him, and many others, as naïve in the extreme. Furthermore, the financier's proposal totally removed the surprise element which Groves believed so essential. The project chief had always maintained that, forewarned, the enemy would mount an effective counter-attack, either destroying the atomic-bomb-carrying bomber in aerial combat, or by ground fire.

But one thing was sure. Scientists working on the Manhattan Project were now satisfied that the Japanese were not far enough advanced in theoretical physics or technology to manufacture an atomic bomb. Therefore, some argued, it would be 'unthinkable' to use the weapon against Japan.

The battle lines had been drawn. Even now, the more radical among the scientists were planning fresh strategies to halt the project.

December 12, 1944
Imperial Army GHQ
Tokyo

Major-General Seizo Arisue was showing increasing signs of strain; his face was a shade greyer, the pouches under his eyes darker. He was suffering from lack of sleep, proper meals and fresh air. These past two months had made severe inroads into even his considerable stamina.

His efforts to get a spy into America had been fruitless. His Lisbon contact was unable to provide further details about the mysterious American war project. And, without hard information, Arisue could not brief his agent in Brazil, who was packed and ready to slip into the United States. Experience told the head of Army Intelligence that the operation was going sour.

Increasingly, his department was under pressure from the High Command. Data was urgently requested on the B-29's which had started to raid Tokyo and other cities. The arrival of the huge bombers had astonished the Japanese. They had never seen an aircraft so big, so fast, so well-armed, so able to drop more bombs than any other aircraft. Information was requested about their bases.

Arisue had pin-pointed the Marianas, and cursed again the lack of spies he had on the islands. He was unable to answer specific questions on the number of American bomber squadrons based there, the supply back-up they possessed, the sort of intelligence which would help produce an accurate profile of the American strength.

Potential sources of useful information were proving disappointing. His special listening posts were monitoring nothing of importance in the brief air-to-air conversations between enemy pilots over Japan; ground defences had been largely unsuccessful in shooting down B-29's. Arisue's tough interrogator, Lt-Colonel Oya, was finding it difficult to get even the few American airmen who had been captured to talk.

The latest, Colonel Brian Brugge, Oya had seen soon after he was shot down nine days before, on December 3. Brugge was an important catch; he was deputy chief of staff of the 73rd Bomb Wing, based on Saipan. According to Oya the stubborn West Pointer refused to co-operate.

'We interrogated him thoroughly. He kept a tight lip. He wouldn't crack. Later he began to suffer from malnutrition. He disliked Japanese food. He died.'

Arisue was unhappy because his enthusiastic interrogator had not been able to extract any useful information from this senior American officer. Then, at his lowest ebb, knowing his reputation was being seriously challenged in certain quarters, Arisue received a further piece of unsettling news.

For some days he had been sure that Naval Intelligence, his arch rival, was in contact with a Swedish banker, Per Jacobsson, in Berne, Switzerland.

Arisue knew that even the most generous interpretation of intelligence responsibilities did not give the Navy access to Europe; that territory was strictly for Army Intelligence operations.

Thoroughly alert and suspicious, he had discovered that Jacobsson was economic adviser to the Bank of International Settlements, a bank with which Japan had had close ties before the war. The Army Intelligence registry had unearthed a file on Jacobsson. Its contents had electrified Arisue.

Jacobsson was a known contact for American Intelligence in Switzerland. He was also a friend of Dr. Frederick Hack.

Arisue knew Hack. He was a German national with a circle of friends in Japan. Among the group were admirals and several officers working in Naval Intelligence. Members of the circle had saved Hack when he fell from favour in Germany in 1938 for criticising Nazi policies. He was sent to a concentration camp. Hearing of his fate, his friends in Japan had called for Hack's release. The Nazis, anxious then to promote good relations with Japan, had complied. The Imperial Navy set up Hack as its European purchasing agent, operating from Berne. Now, Naval Intelligence was apparently using Hack to sound out Jacobsson on how best to approach Allen W. Dulles.

Dulles was European Director of Strategic Services, the American Intelligence agency. He ran his clandestine operations from Herren Street in Berne. The huge OSS organisation had direct access to President Roosevelt, who had become captivated by its derring-do.

All this Arisue had discovered some days before. Then, this morning, he had received a copy of a letter Hack had written from Switzerland to a friend, Commander Yoshio Fujimura, Naval Attaché at the Japanese Embassy in Berlin. Fujimura had forwarded the latter to the Naval Ministry in Tokyo.

Arisue could imagine the sensation it had caused in the higher echelons of the Ministry. Hack's letter calmly spelt out the economic facts of war as they pertained to Japan. Her Axis partners were beaten; her supply lines were being throttled; her credit was running out. There was only one solution: 'You must persuade your country to get out of the struggle as soon as possible and arrange a negotiated peace now before America's industrial power crushes your nation.'

Japan's sea lords, like the Army leaders, knew the dire situation Japan was facing. But there was no talk of surrender.

Now it was clear to Arisue why Naval Intelligence had responded to Hack's warning by asking him to make overtures to Jacobsson, and, he hoped, to Dulles. From there it could be but a short step to President Roosevelt—and a negotiated peace.

In Japanese eyes, there was a fundamental difference between a negotiated peace and surrender. Even so, Arisue's first reaction was to expose the plotters. Caution stayed him. They undoubtedly included some of the highest-ranking naval officers in the land. If he failed to prove a case against them he would be in serious trouble.

The desire for a peace settlement had been raised before by the Navy. Late in 1943, Arisue had obtained a copy of a top-secret survey by an admiral which had concluded that Japan faced eventual defeat and should sue for peace. The report had been presented to the *Jushin*, the powerful group of ex-premiers who had direct access to the Emperor. The *Jushin* had rejected the admiral's conclusions. In those days, Arisue had done no more than monitor these naval machinations. Now, serious questions had been raised in his mind.

What if Hack was right? Supposing Japan could not win the war? Supposing a negotiated peace was the only answer?

Even two months before such thoughts would have been unthinkable for Arisue. But throughout the day they gnawed at him. He sent for situation reports; he questioned staff officers; he studied

67

projections of enemy intentions. Whichever way he turned, the one inescapable truth faced him: the war was going badly. Japan, in his subsequent words, 'was short of everything except courage'.

By evening he had come to the conclusion that there was no way Japan could achieve victory. Equally, he knew that so long as the country kept fighting, it was not defeated.

With those thoughts in mind, without consulting anyone, Seizo Arisue decided that he would prepare the Army's ground-work for a negotiated peace.

He knew that if he was discovered he would be branded a traitor and executed. But by nightfall he was making his first moves to establish a link with Dulles in Berne.

December 14, 1944
Osaka

Penned in a steel frame, the pig grunted anxiously. At one end of a laboratory in Osaka University, Professor Tsunesaburo Asada and a group of technicians busied themselves with final preparations for a further experiment. Their attention was focussed on a large squat box. It was covered with dials and switches and had a snub gun-like barrel.

This was a prototype Death Ray.

A final adjustment was made to bring the barrel to bear on the animal.

The technicians stepped back, watching the pig.

Asada flicked a switch. A faint hum came from the machine.

The pig squealed in sudden terror as the invisible rays penetrated its body. The animal staggered and fell to its knees.

A hiss of anticipation came from the watching men.

The pig rolled over on its side, legs twitching. The technicians began to applaud.

Then the pig gave an angry squeal; its moment of shock had passed. It rose shakily to its feet and stared balefully at the crestfallen men at the opposite end of the room.

Asada pronounced the verdict of all inventors faced with a setback: it was back to the drawing-board. And for his staff it meant an end to their plan to take home portions of pork to their hungry families.

December 17, 1944
USAAF Base
Wendover

That day, the five squadrons at Wendover became formally unified under Tibbets as the 509th Composite Group, attached to the 315th Bombardment Wing of the Second Air Force. The Group's strength was 225 officers and 1,542 enlisted men.

Ferebee and van Kirk joined the 509th's headquarters' staff as Group Bombardier and Group Navigator. They rarely flew nowadays, spending their time preparing and analysing training programmes. When they did fly, they usually went with Lewis, taking the place of his regular bombardier and navigator.

Lewis' protests to Tibbets had fallen on stony ground. Their earlier friendship was outgrowing itself; while Lewis longed for the 'old days', Tibbets now had no time for reminiscing.

But Lewis' crew continued to return one of the best flying records of any. The main competition came from Eatherly's crew and Crew No. 15, commanded by the effervescent Major Charles Sweeney.

Beser liked to fly with Sweeney, 'because of the way he jollied everyone along'.

The radar officer was forming lasting judgements on many of the fliers, for 'the day was coming when I'd have to trust my life to them'.

He had warmed towards Tibbets; he saw, correctly, a shy man behind the aloof commander. Beser became aware of Tibbets' marriage problem, and decided that Tibbets was 'only truly happy in the air, but there he was magnificent'.

He did not feel the same about Lewis. On the ground he sometimes acted 'like Peck's bad boy; in the air he occasionally got over-excited'.

Van Kirk and Ferebee were tagged by Beser as 'professionals who never have any problems'.

That morning, at 30,000 feet over the Salton Sea bombing range, Tibbets and Ferebee were trying to solve a problem which had worried them for a week.

The bombardier had failed to drop dummy practice bombs with consistency into the aiming circle, now reduced to three hundred feet. There seemed no reason why some bombs fell into the circle, while others landed outside it.

Tibbets was concerned and he reminded Ferebee why precision was so important.

'Tom, when the time comes we have to be as near on target as we can get. Radar is out because it's still too uncertain. So it's got to be visual. You've got to be able to see the target and then hit it on the nose. And that means we've got to drop within that circle every time.'

Tibbets had come on the practice flight to see why this was not happening. The weather was perfect: clear skies, easily computed wind drift. With Lewis holding the B-29 steady on the run-up to the Aiming Point, Tibbets watched Ferebee crouching over the Norden bombsight.

The sight had been totally stripped and reassembled to give a mechanically perfect instrument.

Ferebee called out that he had the AP in his cross-hairs. He lifted himself a few inches off his seat to bring his face closer over the viewfinder. Below, through the optical sight, he could clearly see the bombing circle. Satisfied, he eased himself back on his seat, his head still glued to the viewfinder.

'Bomb away.'

Lewis put the aircraft into the mandatory 155 degree turn. By the time ground control reported on the drop, the B-29 was nearly eight miles away.

The bomb had fallen outside the circle.

Tibbets ordered Lewis to fly back towards the AP. He told Ferebee to repeat his actions. He watched intently as the bombardier began to line up the circle in his sights. At the last moment he rose off his buttocks.

Tibbets shouted.

'That's it!'

He had solved the problem. At the crucial moment, Ferebee, like any other bombardier, lifted himself off his seat to bring his eyes to the sight. The movement was no more than an inch or two. But it was enough. Each time he lowered his eyes to the sight, his head was at a slightly different angle to the viewfinder. If he had been bombing from a few thousand feet this small movement would have had little effect. But from 30,000 feet, nearly six miles up, with his head at a slightly different angle each time, it meant the error could ultimately work out to be several hundred feet by the time the bomb hit the ground.

Within hours Tibbets had ground crews construct and fit a padded headrest to the bombsight. Using it, Ferebee's head was forced into exactly the same position each time. From then on he bombed with consistent accuracy.

That night Tibbets received another telephone call from Groves in Washington. The General spoke in the code language of the Manhattan Project. Tibbets had recently been given a copy of the quadratic lettercode which Groves had devised.

After he had transcribed the numerals, Tibbets knew that the target city for the first atomic bomb would almost certainly be in Japan.

December 25, 1944
USAAF Base
Wendover

In the cold dawn light, mess officer Charles Perry surveyed his resources: rows of plump farm turkeys and cured hams, mounds of vegetables, trays of mince-pies and, dominating the kitchen tables, scores of huge Christmas puddings. *Silverplate* had ensured that this first Christmas of the fledgling 509th would be a memorable one.

The elements had also contributed to the festive mood. Overnight, heavy snow had fallen, covering the ground with a thick layer. At the main gate, shivering MP's fashioned a couple of snowmen, complete with hats and tree branches for carbines.

Beyond the gate, in their home, the Tibbets family were unwrapping their Christmas presents. Tibbets had given his wife, Lucie, a gift he had purchased at the last moment in the base commissary. He was always at a loss about what to buy his vivacious wife; it was another small reason why their marriage was foundering. Lucie felt that her husband was unromantic; a warm-hearted southern belle from Georgia she found the practical and pragmatic Tibbets often cool and distant. She knew there was no other woman in his life, but she could not understand how he sometimes seemed to place his work before her and the children. Once she had complained to Beser, who often used to baby-sit for the Tibbets, that 'Paul never seems to have time to sit down and talk or play with the children. And when he does talk, it's only about work'.

Tibbets had tried to explain that he was by nature 'a loner'; he had not added what many of his officers knew: that he was really only happy when he was flying.

His preoccupation with work carried over to his choice of Christmas presents for his small sons. Paul Jnr. and baby Gene both received models of B-17's.

There had been a run on the toy bombers at the PX. This morning the children found several B-17's in their stockings; presents from Lewis, van Kirk, Ferebee and Beser.

Breakfast over, the Tibbets family went to morning service in the base church.

71

Chaplain William Downey greeted his commander warmly. He could not remember when Tibbets had last attended church. Once, shortly after he had arrived on the base, Tibbets had told him in a rare unguarded moment that 'when I pray I go directly to God without a middle man'.

Downey had not been offended; he knew many men like that. He respected their views. And, in doing so, the chaplain had earned respect for himself. Articulate and refreshingly earthy, Downey was the ideal spiritual adviser for the high-living 509th. He wasn't shocked by their escapades. Though he was not much older than many of the men he cared for, he somehow gave the impression of being a tolerant, worldly-wise man, ready to have a drink, crack a joke, be a 'regular guy', without ever losing his dignity.

Even Beser, normally critical of all 'organised religion', thought Downey was a 'helluva sky-pilot; if he hadn't been a Lutheran, he would have made a fine rabbi'.

Beser was not at the service; he was spending his morning going through the newspapers in the Officers Club. He was sickened by the way Madison Avenue was using the war in its advertising. Gillette announced that its razor blade steel was being used in bayonets; Castor claimed that its oil was in the medicine chests of GI's everywhere. One newspaper announced that a New York cemetery was timing its commercials to be broadcast immediately after news bulletins describing heavy fighting overseas.

What really angered Beser was Wrigley's claim that war production would be increased if everyone chewed a few more sticks of their gum every day. He hated the product.

By midday, the Officers Club was full of officers and their wives.

Paul and Lucie Tibbets held gracious court; for the moment their private tensions and troubles were put aside. Tibbets reminisced with Ferebee and van Kirk about Europe, and wondered how London was shaping up to the 'Bob Hopes', the nickname of the flying bombs raining down on the British capital: Bob Hopes 'because you bob out of the way and hope they miss you'.

Before long a number of the officers were happily crocked and gathered around the Club radio, bellowing out carols being introduced over the air by Bing Crosby in Hollywood.

The singing was followed by a newscast which brought them sharply back to reality. American troops were fighting hard in Europe to repel a surprise German counter-attack that was to become the overture to the Battle of the Bulge. The Germans were dressing their troops in GI uniforms and creating confusion in the American lines. The news from the Pacific was encouraging: the Japanese homeland was beginning to feel the weight of American bombs.

Lucie Tibbets whispered the hope of any wife.

'Honey, maybe you won't have to go after all.'
Tibbets looked at her and smiled reassuringly.

December 29, 1944
Base P
Hiroshima Bay

A sailor carefully erased the legend 'I.58' from the conning tower of the submarine and painted on the flag of the Kikusui immediately above the Rising Sun emblem. The Kikusui was the battle standard of the ancient warrior Masashige, who had fought against overwhelming odds, knowing he had no chance of survival.

With the Kikusui flag gleaming wetly in the pale winter sunlight, Commander Hashimoto completed the transformation of his submarine by ordering a rating to raise the boat's new war banner, Masashige's war banner, the *Hiriho Kenten,* which meant 'God's will'.

Banner and flag signified that the submarine was now a human torpedo carrier, the latest weapon devised by the Imperial Navy. The human torpedoes, or *Kaitens,* were the underwater counterpart of the kamikaze.

Since January 1943 at the top-secret Base P, an island in Hiroshima Bay just south of Kure, the Navy had been experimenting with the use of human torpedoes, projectiles which could be launched from a mother-craft and steered by volunteers against an enemy ship. The Imperial Navy hoped these weapons would offset the increasing losses they were experiencing and help halt the American advance towards Japan.

Hashimoto's submarine had been chosen to be one of the flag carriers for *Operation Kaiten.* To accommodate the weapons, workmen had removed the housing for the reconnaissance plane the submarine sometimes carried, its catapault and its deck gun. That made room on the boat's deck for six *kaitens.*

The torpedoes, shaped like miniature submarines and weighing eight tons each, had explosive warheads. They had a range of thirty miles, and a top speed of twenty knots. They were not recoverable. Once a *kaiten* pilot squirmed through a narrow trunk from the parent submarine into his torpedo, and was cast-off, there was no returning. Either he exploded against his target or was blown up by the enemy before reaching it.

It took several hours to winch the *kaitens* on to the submarine's deck where they were shackled securely.

73

Late in the morning, the pilots for these craft came aboard and were greeted by Hashimoto. He was struck by the youthfulness of the *kaiten* crewmen; there was also an air of fanaticism about them that chilled him. He, too, believed in the Emperor and the traditional concept of dying. But these youths were intoxicated with their patriotism; they told him, proudly, how they literally fought for the privilege of making this *kaiten* mission, and how they longed for death. *Kaiten*, in Japanese, means 'the turn towards Heaven'.

As the moment of departure approached, the pilots sat astride their craft, white towels wrapped around their heads and brandishing their ceremonial swords.

To Hashimoto, it seemed they were 'trying hard to be strong men'.

Fenders and berthing wires were detached from the submarine's long, narrow casing. Water on the starboard quarter began to boil. Foam surged around the boat as the ballast tanks were blown to full buoyancy. The freeboard began to increase.

Farewell shouts came from the groups of dockyard workers on the wharf. The pilots raised their swords higher.

Hashimoto watched approvingly as the last ropes were released by the shore crew and hauled in by the ratings on the deck. Weeks of hard practice had paid off; the seamen moved today with dexterity and skill.

The electric motors silently drew the submarine from the shore, her bow now pointing away from Hiroshima, towards the sea. A flotilla of motor-boats accompanied the submarine, their occupants chanting in unison the names of the pilots. The submarine increased speed, the escorts fell away, the chanting faded. The boat began to tremble as the diesel motors started their rhythmic pounding. The submarine had finally shaken off her dockyard inertia.

In his log Hashimoto noted: 'Passed through Bungo Channel and turned south, proceeding on surface. Through evening haze took farewell look at the homeland.'

December 30, 1944
Washington, D.C.

The end of the year was hectic for Groves. His days stretched well beyond their regular fifteen hours; the box of candy he kept in his office safe with the atom secrets needed frequent replenishing. Steadily munching his way through chocolate bon-bons, Groves issued orders which would eventually change warfare.

He had sent for Tibbets on December 28. From an initial wariness on both sides, their relationship had passed through several phases to the present state of acceptance by Groves of Tibbets. The project chief found the flier could be as flinty as he was; he learned not to tamper with Tibbets' judgements on flying matters.

The top-secret notes of their last conversation show how far he now trusted the 509th's commander.

Tibbets had given June 15, 1945 as the date he would be ready to deliver an atomic strike.

Groves had accepted this without demur; the question was then raised 'as to what the weather conditions would be over Tokyo between June 15 and July 15'.

It was the first time the Japanese capital had been openly spoken of as a target for atomic attack.

But there might be a weather problem. The notes recorded that 'rain could be expected rather frequently [over Tokyo] up to August 15 [1945]. It is not desirable that missions be made in rain'.

Apart from weather considerations, Groves had set out the governing factors in target selection:

The targets chosen should be places the bombing of which would most adversely affect the will of the Japanese people to continue the war. Beyond that, they should be military in nature, consisting either of important headquarters or troop concentrations, or centres of production of military equipment and supplies. To enable us to assess accurately the effects of the bomb, the targets should not have been previously damaged by air attacks. It is also desirable that the first target be of such size that the damage would be confined within it, so that we could more definitely determine the power of the bomb.

Groves doubted if Tokyo would meet all these requirements. The likelihood was that the city would be heavily bombed in the coming months with conventional weapons.

Personally, he favoured Kyoto as a target. Kyoto was the ancient capital of Japan, a 'historical city and one that is of great religious significance to the Japanese'. With an estimated population of a million, Groves reasoned that Kyoto, 'like any city of that size in Japan must be involved in a tremendous amount of war work'.

It was a legitimate target.

Furthermore, he found Kyoto was 'large enough to ensure that the damage from the bomb would run out within the city, which would give us a firm understanding of its destructive power'.

At a meeting in Oppenheimer's office at Los Alamos on December 19, Groves had decided that the gun-type firing mechanism of the uranium bomb was so reliable it need not be tested before it was used on the enemy. However, the more complicated mechanism in the plutonium bomb would need proving. That was to be done at the Alamogordo firing range in the New Mexico desert, on a date still to be decided.

Now, alone in his office, Groves decided to take a momentous step. He wrote a memo to General George C. Marshall, the Chief of Staff.

> It is now reasonably certain that our operations plans should be based on the gun-type bomb, which, it is estimated, will produce the equivalent of a ten thousand ton TNT explosion. The first bomb, without previous full scale test, which we do not believe will be necessary, should be ready about 1 August, 1945.

Groves had committed the Manhattan Project to a date.

But that date was still many months away, and the war against Japan was about to enter a new phase. A tough new air commander was on his way to the Pacific with specific orders to bomb the Japanese into submission by whatever means he chose.

January 6, 1945
USAAF Base
Wendover

Tibbets knew he was facing a clear choice. He could either have Lewis court-martialled—or hope the pilot had already learned a lasting lesson.

Even now, days after it had ended, the details of Lewis' madcap adventure made Tibbets shudder.

On December 17, the day Tibbets had solved Ferebee's problem with the bomb-sight, Lewis had 'illegally borrowed' a C-45 twin-engine transport plane. With no co-pilot or proper maps, and a faulty radio, he had set off on a 2,500-mile flight to New York because he 'wanted to be home for Christmas'. His travelling companion was the 509th's senior flight engineer, hitching a ride to his wedding. Over Columbus, Ohio, the plane's radio, altimeter and compass all failed within minutes of each other. Lewis had nosed the transport groundwards 'trying to navigate by street lights'. A blizzard blocked out that hope. For two hours in zero visibility, Lewis had searched for Newark Field, New Jersey. He had eventually landed there with less than a gallon of fuel left in his tank.

Christmas over, Lewis had met the new bride and groom at

Newark. He loaned the girl his flying jacket and cap as a disguise and ignored the regulations forbidding civilians to fly in military aircraft. Over Buffalo, another snow storm forced Lewis to seek shelter. Finally, on December 29, he and the newly-married couple had landed at Wendover.

Tibbets was staggered that Lewis did not seem to appreciate he 'had broken every rule in the book'. The nearest Lewis came to contrition was a sheepish, 'Gee, I wouldn't want to do that flight again!'

Now, eight days later, Tibbets knew the time had come to make a decision about Lewis. He had taken soundings from a number of sources: the consensus was that Lewis was 'a goddam fool, but also a goddam fine pilot'.

Tibbets admitted to himself that only an exceptional flier could have flown the trip Lewis had: it had taken icy nerves and courage to handle the crippled transport in such atrocious conditions.

He decided not to court-martial Lewis, but 'any past favours I owed him were repaid. He had used my name to get that plane. From now on I was going to treat him like a flunkie; he would do exactly what I wanted, when I wanted—or God help him'.

It meant that Lewis would draw many of the disagreeable assignments: early morning flights, night duties and weekend work.

Lewis did not mind. He thought it 'a tribute. Paul was giving me all the stuff that nobody else would tackle'.

Having made his decision about Lewis, Tibbets now resolved another matter which could not be further delayed: whom he would choose to send to Cuba for 'special training'.

For days rumours about the long-awaited trip had prevailed. In sub-zero Wendover, the vision of the Caribbean was almost unbearable.

Aircraft commanders spent hours hanging around headquarters trying to pick up a whisper; gamblers like Eatherly had offered to run a book on the departure date, but there were no takers; even overseas veterans like Classen began to reminisce about tropical life. Amidst all the speculation, they did discover one fact: in two days' time Tibbets would be promoted to full Colonel. But that did not make their commander more forthcoming. Rumours reached fever-pitch when the fliers learned that Tibbets was spending this morning studying the flying reports on all fifteen bomber crews.

Then, inexplicably to the airmen, Tibbets summoned the Group's catering officer Lt. Charles Perry. In Lewis' view 'it was like sending for the dietician when you're starving'.

Perry was going to Cuba. His orders from Tibbets were clear: arrange a round-the-clock chow line serving the best food.

Beser was told he was going. He saw only one drawback to the

77

trip: his bodyguard would be travelling with him. He began to lay plans to shake off the man in Havana.

Finally ten aircraft commanders were informed they would be flying out later in the day. The Cuba-bound echelon was assembled for a pep-talk from Tibbets.

'The same rules apply in Havana as here. Don't ask questions. Don't answer questions. Do your job. The final selection for a historic mission could be made from you men.'

Everybody was too excited about going to Cuba to consider again what that mission would be.

In Cuba, they would carry out long-distance navigational training exercises over water at night, and continue their high-level bombing practice.

Before leaving, Eatherly was consulted on the legends about hot-blooded Latin ladies. He said they were all true. The flight surgeon was reported to have packed extra cartons of condoms; the studs in the group boasted they would use them up on their very first night in Havana.

At noon, Eatherly took off. Nine other B-29's followed him into the air on the long journey south. Late in the afternoon they landed at Batista Field, twelve miles from Havana.

Tibbets flew down in a transport, bringing Ferebee, van Kirk and a small headquarters staff. Another transport brought a detachment of MP's, Uanna and his agents.

All outsiders were barred from the 509th compound, but many got close enough to peer inquisitively at the planes.

The crews revelled in the curiosity they attracted. Eatherly solemnly told a bystander that the 509th was there to protect the island against an expected coup by 'unfriendly powers' planning to seize the lucrative gambling concessions. Eatherly was in high spirits. For most of the flight he had played cards with some of his crew, and had won several hundred dollars.

The three hundred fliers and ground staff all tried hard to impress the other American servicemen on the base that they were no ordinary outfit. They were coming to think of themselves as 'special', a feeling that Tibbets had encouraged; the foundation was being laid of the spirit which was to sustain them in the trying time ahead.

Rigorous security had conditioned them to do as they were told and to ask few questions. They knew their mail and telephone conversations out of Wendover were censored, their get togethers in the officers' and enlisted men's clubs reported upon. The mysterious civilians who flew in and out of the base with strange requests added to their feeling of being an élite. So did the lack of outside interference; no generals had swooped down on Wendover to cause panic with a surprise inspection. Inside the base they could do as they liked—so long as they did their jobs. For young men, many of them just out of their teens, this was heady freedom. In public they were anxious to show their worth. Here, in Cuba, from the moment of their arrival, they dazzled the local hands in everything they did.

Tibbets astonished everybody by refusing even a cup of coffee until every man had been assigned quarters and been fed by Perry's cooks. (*Silverplate* had worked its usual magic. Using the code-word, Perry raided local American military supply depots to provide a sumptuous five-course dinner.) Only then did Tibbets accept a meal tray.

He had little appetite. He had learned that evening that General Curtis LeMay was on his way to Guam.

A year ago Tibbets, Lewis and Sweeney had taken turns to teach LeMay how to pilot a B-29. LeMay was a difficult pupil, a flying general who found it hard to accept that because an aircraft was 99 feet long, 29 feet 9 inches high, with a wing span of 101 feet, it was different from any other bomber he had flown. But he finally learned to listen, respect and obey his instructors. At the end of the course, LeMay had predicted, 'We can win the war with this plane.'

Now he was going to Guam intending to do just that. If he succeeded, Tibbets knew he would not be needed to drop an atomic bomb.

January 16, 1945
N-NW of Guam
The Pacific Ocean

'Smoke on the port beam!'

The look-out's shout brought the men on the conning tower bridge scrambling down the ladder into the control room.

'Dive! Dive! Dive!'

Moments after Commander Hashimoto's order, the submarine was sealed, the main vents open, and the needle of the depth-gauge turning steadily as the boat's bow tilted towards the sea-bed.

Regularly, ever since reaching the area of the Marianas two weeks earlier, Hashimoto had been dodging anti-submarine aircraft patrols flying from Guam. Now, two hundred feet below the waves, undisturbed by the Pacific swell, he and his crew listened for the throb of ships' propellers.

Somewhere above them, approaching, were two enemy ships, probably destroyers.

Hashimoto wondered whether their presence was connected with the daring attack he had launched three days before. Then, under cover of darkness, he had surfaced eleven miles off Guam and fired four of his human torpedoes against the mass of shipping in Apra Harbour.

It was I.58's first strike and Hashimoto's first use of *kaitens*. Just before entering his suicide craft, one of the *kaiten* pilots had pressed into the captain's hands a farewell note Hashimoto would treasure all his life.

Great Japan is the land of the Gods. The Land of the Gods is eternal and cannot be destroyed. Hereafter, no matter, there will be thousands and tens of thousands of boys, and we now offer ourselves as a sacrifice for our country. Let us get away from the petty affairs of this earthly and mundane life to the land where righteousness reigns supreme and eternal.

With the four human torpedoes launched, Hashimoto had submerged to periscope depth. As daylight came he saw great clouds of smoke rising from the harbour. He stole away to safer waters. Later he had led the crew in prayer for the souls of the four warriors.

Now, the presence of the sub-chasers above them reminded the crew that they, too, could be swiftly despatched to join their dead companions.

Hashimoto ordered the submarine to be rigged for silent running so that nothing could give away their presence. Orders were relayed in sign language or in whispers; nobody moved unnecessarily. All equipment not essential to survival under water was switched off.

The crew strained their ears for the sound of propellers. It came closer: constant, on course, the high-pitched note of steel blades turning steadily through water. The ships were moving slowly, and it sounded as if each blade was striking the water separately. The screws passed overhead and began to fade.

A look of relief crossed the faces of the men around Hashimoto. He shook his head, warning.

The sound began to increase again. Hashimoto drew a circle with his finger in the air: the ships were circling. He guessed that the hunters were hoping their echo-sounders could get a fix and give cross-bearings. It would be easy then to calculate the settings for their depth charges.

The propeller noise grew fainter, almost disappeared, then returned as a new circle began.

Somebody scuffed the deck plates with his boot.

Hashimoto glared fiercely.

The propellers passed overhead, faded—and this time did not return.

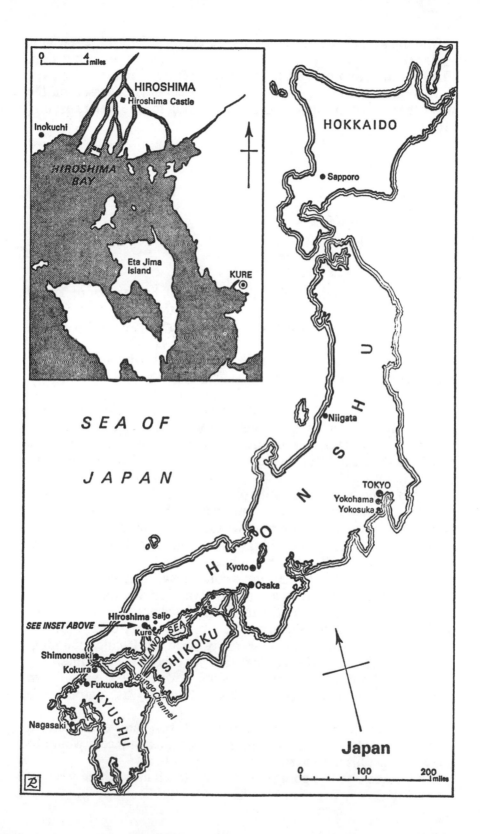

HIROSHIMA

0   4 miles

Hiroshima Castle

Inokuchi

HIROSHIMA
BAY

Eta Jima
Island

KURE

SEA OF

JAPAN

HOKKAIDO

Sapporo

H O N S H U

Niigata

TOKYO
Yokohama
Yokosuka

Kyoto

Osaka

SEE INSET ABOVE → Hiroshima Saijo
Kure   INLAND SEA
SHIKOKU
Shimonoseki
Kokura
Fukuoka
Bungo Channel
KYUSHU
Nagasaki

Japan

0   100   200 miles

The ships had either given up the search, or extended it elsewhere.

For two more hours the submarine remained silent in its position. Then Hashimoto ordered it to resume course for Kure.

There it would arrive safely on January 20, having passed on the way other *kaiten*-carrying submarines heading for the waters around Guam.

January 17, 1945
US Navy HQ
Seattle

Addressed to the Commander, Seattle Port of Embarkation, Troop Movement Order (Shipment) No. 6105 (A thru G) was a routine warning—except that it came from Headquarters, Army Air Force, Washington.

It told the Seattle port commander to have a suitable ship ready from March 1, 1945 to transport the ground echelon of a unit he had been unable to trace—the 509th Composite Group.

The order gave him no indication as to their destination in the Pacific. His request to Washington for further information was denied. A busy, overworked man, the port commander decided he should alert Pacific Fleet Headquarters (CINCPAC) on Guam about the mysterious order.

Within hours the Commander-in-Chief, Pacific, Admiral Chester W. Nimitz, was aware that a unit neither he nor his staff knew anything about was coming into his theatre of operations.

It had been a long war for Nimitz, beginning that moment at 3 p.m. on December 7, 1941 when his enjoyment of the CBS broadcast of the New York Philharmonic concert was interrupted by news of Pearl Harbor. Nimitz was up and away—and going ever since. The efforts of Japanese submarines like Hashimoto's were but pinpricks to Nimitz. His submarines had by now sunk over a million tons of Japanese shipping: his warships plied the Pacific, pounding enemy beaches before his landing craft put ashore the Marines.

Nimitz did not take kindly to receiving news of the strange group about to arrive so unexpectedly—and saltily let Washington know his feelings.

Groves was contacted. He recognised that an 'embarrassing situation' was developing. Without the Navy's assistance it would be difficult to get his atomic strike force into position.

But Groves was not going cap-in-hand to Nimitz. Three years of running the Manhattan Project had taught him how to handle such situations. He would not deal with Nimitz directly. He would ask Admiral of the Fleet Ernest J. King to inform Nimitz of the position.

More important to Groves was the implication behind the impending arrival of General LeMay on Guam. He knew LeMay was one of the finest bombing strategists in the world, able and willing to bomb Japan to its knees. And for Groves that meant that not only would he now have to be wary of the odd recalcitrant scientist, from this day on he must also concern himself with whether LeMay would leave him a suitable city to destroy.

January 20, 1945
HQ, USAAF XXI Bomber Command
Guam

General Curtis LeMay had spent his first three days on Guam listening. He was trying to find the answer to a paradox in his new charge, the 21st Bomber Command of the 20th Air Force.

Why was the B-29, the world's most superior bomber, available for the first time in sufficient numbers to strike terror into the enemy, not realising its potential?

Here in the Marianas everybody had a different answer. The training manuals said the B-29's could operate at 38,000 feet and cruise at 350 miles an hour for 3,500 miles.

The manuals were wrong.

In the Pacific, the bombers showed signs of severe strain in prolonged flights at over 30,000 feet. Long hauls caused engine breakdowns. The tremendous stress in climbing with seven tons of bombs to high altitudes showed in the daily operations reports, as bombers frequently failed to complete missions because of mechanical difficulties.

Then there was the weather.

It was impossible for the harassed Air Force meteorologists to provide accurate forecasts for the 1,300 miles of sky between the Marianas and Japan. Fierce jet-streams criss-crossed the void, buffeting the bombers and using up their precious fuel.

Over Japan the targets might be visible one minute, then obscured the next as fierce winds drove in heavy clouds. Bombs dropped from 30,000 feet were blown far from their Aiming Points by these sub-strata gales. And results using even the latest radar equipment were proving unsatisfactory.

83

Eleven targets selected for bombing that month remained almost undamaged. Intelligence monitoring of Japan Radio showed that morale was high and warwork so far virtually unimpaired by the air attacks.

The B-29's were failing.

LeMay thought he knew why. He accepted the complaints about the weather, engine strain and other malfunctions. But solving them would not answer the basic problem in the opinion of this tough, thirty-eight-year-old specialist in mass-bombing techniques. He recognised the tactics being used: they were the ones he had developed in Europe to pierce the German defences. Later, his high-flying methods were used by B-29's operating out of China, raiding Japan from airfields around Chengtu. LeMay had ordered the bombs, fuel and replacement parts to be flown into Chengtu over the Himalayas from India.

China had been a costly and hazardous venture. But LeMay had made contact with a fanatical guerrilla leader. In return for medical supplies and materials, LeMay had persuaded him to radio regular weather forecasts from that area of northern China where the partisans were fighting the Japanese. The reports were invaluable for LeMay's pilots. They often drank a toast to this Chinaman.

His name was Mao Tse-Tung.

LeMay had already contacted Mao from the Marianas and arranged for him to radio weather reports to Guam. And the man, who would soon become the leader of one of the most powerful nations on earth, was on this late January day proud and willing to act as a barometer for the American general he persisted in calling Cull-Tse Lee May.

But Mao's weather reports were only a partial answer to LeMay's problem with the B-29's.

The tactics were wrong.

The methods he had used in Europe and China were proving useless over Japan.

The solution he proposed was revolutionary. If it succeeded he believed he could break Japan. If it failed his career would be in ruins.

First LeMay intended to strip his B-29's of their arsenal of machine-guns and cannons. Then he proposed to strike in darkness—with his bombers over their targets between midnight and 4 a.m.

If necessary, they would bomb by radar, in preparation for which LeMay decided to initiate a series of intensive re-training courses. These would ensure that even 'the stupidest radar operator' was brought up to the standard he required. Most important of all, the bombers would only go in at between 5,000 and 9,000 feet.

LeMay was going to gamble that Intelligence was right, that the Japanese had not developed a night fighter, or converted their anti-

84

aircraft guns to radar control. He hoped that, manually-operated, the weapons would react too slowly to his low-level assault.

Removing the guns because of the hoped-for absence of night fighters would also increase each bomber's payload.

That, too, was crucial.

For LeMay intended the B-29's to carry only incendiaries, and thus put the torch to Japan's vulnerable wooden buildings.

While formulating his plans about the new tactics he meant to employ, LeMay went on listening, something he was very good at. Long ago, when he joined the fledgling flying service in 1928, he had learned to listen before making decisions. By now he had mastered the knack of following a number of conversations simultaneously.

This very lunch hour, while listening to a Weather Officer explaining his problems, LeMay had overheard a Naval Officer from CINCPAC saying that Nimitz was raising hell over some flying unit in the States which was trying to get itself shipped to the Marianas.

It sounded an unlikely story to LeMay. The unit was something called a Composite Group. And LeMay knew there was no such designation in the Air Force.

January 27, 1945
Washington, D.C.

Groves approved of the letter Fleet Admiral King had prepared for Admiral Nimitz. It was short and to the point, and should end the irritating queries emanating from CINCPAC. Written on King's official stationery, the letter read:

My dear Nimitz:—

It is expected that a new weapon will be ready in August of this year for use against Japan by the 20th Air Force.

The Officer, Commander Frederic L. Ashworth, USN, bearing this letter will give you enough details so that you can make the necessary plans for the proper support of the operations. By the personal direction of the President, everything pertaining to this development is covered by the highest order of secrecy, and there should be no disclosure by you beyond one other officer, who must be suitably cautioned.

I desire that you make available to Commander Ashworth such intelligence data as applies to the utilization of the new weapon.

Sincerely yours,

E. J. King,
Fleet Admiral, U.S. Navy.

Ashworth was an Annapolis graduate whom Parsons had personally engaged for the Manhattan Project. Unlike Parsons, Ashworth was a combat veteran. Groves respected both naval officers for their professionalism. They spent much of their time shuttling between Wendover and Los Alamos, helping to solve the final problems associated with fusing and detonating the atomic bomb.

Groves doubted whether Ashworth would welcome the trip to the Pacific which would take him away from his test-work. But the project chief planned to use Ashworth as more than just a courier. He wanted Ashworth to choose the overseas base for the 509th.

Groves favoured Guam. It had sophisticated military workshops for any last-minute modifications to the weapon, and a deep-sea harbour. Tibbets preferred Tinian. It was said to have the best runways in the Pacific.

Ashworth would look at both islands.

Groves made another decision. It was not yet necessary to inform General Douglas MacArthur, the abrasive American Army commander in the Pacific, about the atomic bomb. Groves saw no reason for telling the senior Allied soldier in the Far East that in some six weeks there should be delivered to his area of operations a new weapon which would alter the very concept of war.

January 28, 1945
USAAF Base
Wendover

Tibbets had surprised the rest of the 509th at Wendover by flying back from Havana to supervise personally the training of the 393rd's crews he had not sent to the Caribbean.

He was determined that when the day came every one of his fliers would be capable of carrying out an atomic strike.

He worked the five crews still at Wendover hard, sending them back and forth to the Salton Sea bombing range. Without actually saying so, he conveyed to the fliers the impression that, although they had not been sent to Cuba, they might still be chosen for the first atomic mission.

He was 'unashamedly dangling a carrot', something he had seen his father do in business. And he also remembered the advice his mother had given him on the day he became an officer. She had told him: 'Son, you can lead a man a lot better than you can drive him.'

Tibbets tried to apply that rule to his bomber crews.

That morning a transport had flown in from Havana carrying the latest flying reports: the ten crews in Cuba were making good progress with their training programme.

Tibbets was particularly pleased to see that his engineering staff were already showing their mettle; the 393rd's planes were losing less than half the number of engines through malfunction than were other Air Force squadrons based on the island. It was what Tibbets had come to expect from his men.

But he was still not prepared to do what the 393rd's Exec. Officer, John King, wanted: 'Turn the squadron into a spit-and-polish outfit.'

Tibbets knew that King meant well. But he also realised that the officer did not understand his methods: the easy familiarity he had with the enlisted men, the way he invariably called all his officers by their first names, his total disregard for 'bull'. Tibbets knew that King was 'regular Army, who had never experienced the unique camaraderie of flying as a team, where lives depend on each other, and not whether you know when to salute'.

And Tibbets would never allow anyone to stifle what he believed was a requisite for any fighting air squadron: 'plenty of spirit'.

To maintain that spirit, Tibbets was spending more time than ever with his men. His wife and small sons rarely saw him. When he did see the children, he was usually too tired or preoccupied to play with them. The shiny new model bombers the boys had received at Christmas were broken and he never seemed to find time to fix them. His wife looked accusingly at him; their marriage was continuing its slow downhill progress.

Tibbets could see what was happening—and hated himself for making no move to stem the destruction of his family life. The truth was, as he would later admit, that he did not know what to say to mend matters.

He was also not prepared to give up watching over his fliers to be with his family. When he had first married Lucie, he had warned her that 'I was a different kind of cat from the ordinary man', and that nothing would stand between him and his work.

In the first flush of marriage, she had accepted that. But now, isolated, reduced to listening to little more than long technical conversations her husband had with the officers he occasionally brought home, Lucie Tibbets knew there could be no future for them together.

Tragically, even though he was aware of her feelings, Paul Tibbets was 'only able to cry inside myself. She never knew, nobody knew, what I was feeling'.

February 1, 1945
Hiroshima

Second Lieutenant Tatsuo Yokoyama had never seen a more impressive sight. The entire East Training Field, a vast open expanse behind Hiroshima Station, was filled with soldiers. In columns, each one several hundred men long, the troops were marching past the rostrum which held the military commanders of the city. The platform was festooned with exultant slogans promising victory.

The Hiroshima garrison was staging one of its regular parades, partly for itself, partly to remind the civilian population that a sizeable segment of the Imperial Army was on hand to offer protection.

But on this cold, grey, late winter morning, disappointingly few civilians had shown up to see the review. The parade ground's perimeter was lined mostly with soldiers who had not been assigned to the march, their wives and girlfriends.

The onlookers cheered as the Army Band played stirring military music and the troops completed their march around the huge field.

The band formed up beneath the platform and the Army and Navy representatives rose to their feet.

A robed Shinto priest stepped forward to perform a traditional ritual. Rhythmically clapping his hands, he called forth the spirit of the founder of the Japanese nation in 660 BC. Then he evoked all the Shinto deities in their sanctuary of the gods. The Shinto religion, based on the simple act of worshipping natural phenomena, was now an instrument of Japanese militarism and nationalism. Having called forth these spirits, the priest then offered prayers for the dead heroes of the armed forces. Another robed figure offered a prayer for Japanese victory.

The band played a march. Then the commander of the Regional Army based at Hiroshima Castle, Lieutenant General Fujii, stepped to the front of the platform.

Fujii promised the troops that soon they could face a glorious task—defending their Emperor and country against a barbaric enemy. He warned that great hardship and sacrifice would be required. They must all accept the possibility that the war could last 'a further ten years'.

His next words seemed at variance with such a prospect as he talked of the 'magnificent' record of the Imperial Army. While the general concentrated on past victories, his speech smoothed over the present critical situation with phrases about 'strategic withdrawals', 'inflicting heavy casualties on the enemy' and the promise of the chance to deal the enemy 'a mortal blow'.

His concluding rhetoric brought a flush of pride to Yokoyama's face. He would long afterwards remember the general's words.

'The Imperial Army has proved to the world its superiority—it will continue to do so.'

Loud applause greeted this prediction. The warning about a ten-year war seemed forgotten; the mood was ebullient; victory was certain. *Banzai!*

After other speakers had reinforced the theme of an invincible Army, the band struck up a brisk marching tune and the columns of soldiers strode out of the parade ground. The crowd swarmed after them. Together, troops and spectators went to the Shinto shrine at the foot of Mount Futaba.

When the last soldier was in position, the entire parade clapped their hands three times. This was to call forth the deified souls of all those warriors who had fallen in previous wars and thereby earned the highest honour—eternal residence with the gods.

Close to tears, overcome by the emotionalism of the occasion, Tatsuo Yokoyama hoped that if he was to die, then the manner of his dying would ensure that the gods grant him a place in their company.

February 2, 1945
USAAF Base
Batista Field
Havana

Beser thought he had taken care of everything. He had planned the entire operation with the same care he had used when he once wrecked a Communist meeting back home in Baltimore; timing had been the key to his success then—as it was to this venture.

First he had spent an hour getting his bodyguard drunk. Until this evening, the man had clung to Beser: when the radar officer went on a flying mission, the agent walked with him to the aircraft; when it

89

landed, he was there waiting. They shared the same table in the mess, the same room at night.

But, tonight, the bodyguard, urged on by Beser to relax and enjoy their last few hours in Cuba, was sitting glassy-eyed in the base's Officers' Mess, staring stupidly into a fresh daquiri—the eighth he had consumed in an hour. He was too drunk to notice that Beser had gone.

Beser went to the base motor pool to collect a truck. A *Silverplate* authorisation had overcome the initial reluctance of the base transport officer to part with the vehicle.

Then Beser had driven into the old quarter of Havana and supervised a gang of Cubans in loading crates into the truck.

But now the whole secret operation which so far had gone 'like a dream' was being threatened by an MP at the gate to Batista Field.

'Lieutenant, I want to see inside this truck.'

Beser eyed the policeman: he couldn't be bribed; he would have to be threatened.

Crooking his finger—he had borrowed the gesture from his university tutor—Baser told the MP to come closer.

'What's your security rating, son?'

Beser was barely twenty-three; he sounded like a middle-aged general.

'I don't know, sir.'

'Then you had better find out—quick! Move, soldier!'

The MP backed off.

Beser slammed the truck into gear and it bounded forward into the airbase. He drove several times around the administrative blocks to make sure he was not being followed. Satisfied, he then drove to where the 509th's B-29's were parked.

A group of fliers were waiting for him. Beser jumped down from the driver's cabin and whispered to the men around him.

'Okay. Remember this stuff cost a lot. Stow it carefully. And let's not take all night. We've got a lot of living to do!'

A human chain formed between truck and bombers. The unmarked boxes were stacked in the cavernous bomb-bays of the B-29's.

It took almost an hour to transfer the cargo. Each box contained twelve bottles of best-quality whisky.

An astute Beser had discovered a Havana wholesaler offering the liquor at a quarter of the cost in the United States. The 509th had needed no persuasion to lay out the money for this bonanza.

The escapade was typical. In the past three weeks the 509th had established a reputation as hell-raisers. Havana, used to the carousing of servicemen, was astonished by the Group. They lived and loved at a frenetic pace, fought those who challenged them, and led charmed lives when authority intervened.

An MP patrol picked up some drunken 509th mechanics in a street brawl and took them to the military lock-up. Their arrest was reported to the 509th's duty officer. He checked his rosters; the men were scheduled to service a bomber in the morning. He demanded their release. When the MP's still refused, the officer used *Silverplate* to rouse the local commander. He checked his records, found the code rated the highest priority, and ordered the mechanics to be set free. The legend grew that the 509th were The Untouchables.

In the air they appeared to scorn every rule for high-altitude bombing, flying singly, unarmed, with just one huge metal ovoid which they dropped in the ocean. Their results were phenomenal; they hit the AP with relentless accuracy.

Their reputation spread. The 509th basked in their notoriety.

Now, for this, their last night in Cuba, they were given furlough; in the morning they would fly back to Wendover. They knew Tibbets was there, no doubt studying not only their flying reports, but also the complaints about the way they had conducted themselves in his absence.

The thought was enough to make many of them decide to spend their last evening on the base. There was also the need to guard the bombers stacked with Beser's booze.

March 2, 1945
Washington, D.C.

The Deficiency Sub-committee of the House Committee on Appropriations—Congress's watchdog on how public money is spent—was not placated by the prepared statement Under Secretary of War Robert Patterson had given them.

In secret hearing, the sub-committee tried to discover how almost two billion dollars had been spent on a project they could learn nothing about.

Patterson had doggedly refused to say. He pleaded that security considerations prevented him from giving further details about the undertaking.

The committee chairman, Clarence Cannon of Missouri, warned that 'as soon as the war is over Congress will conduct a most thorough inquiry into the project'.

Patterson was himself unaware of most of the Manhattan Project's ramifications. But his political instincts sensed trouble. He knew that an essential rule for survival in Washington was to write a memo.

He returned to his office and dictated one to an aide, General W. D. Styer. It was remarkable for its political expediency:

At the beginning of the project I told General Groves that the greatest care should be taken in keeping thorough records, with detailed entries of decisions made, of conferences with persons concerned in the project, of all progress made and of all financial transactions and expenditures. From time to time I have repeated these instructions and have been assured by General Groves that he and his assistants were keeping complete records. I have told him that the most exacting accounting would be demanded by Congress at some time in the future.

The size of the project, its secrecy, and the large sums of money being expended make it necessary that the utmost pains be taken in keeping records, to the end that a complete and detailed history of the project will at all times be available. This should cover fiscal, scientific and industrial phases of the work.

While I have no reason to doubt that General Groves is giving thorough attention to this matter, the importance of keeping full, accurate and intelligible records is so great that I want you personally to examine into the matter and let me have your conclusions. I want you to take any corrective measures, to make sure that a complete current history of the project is being set down on paper by competent personnel.

Patterson had covered himself. Fearful of being implicated in a future political scandal he was setting a guard dog on Groves. He was behaving as if the word's costliest weapon was a dime-store operation, with every purchase being rung up on a cash register.

Others reacted more oddly.

Fleet Admiral William D. Leahy, Chief of Staff to Roosevelt, was not impressed with what he had heard of the project. It was all far-fetched to him, this idea of a single bomb destroying a large city—and ending the war. Speaking as 'an expert on explosives' he planned to inform the President that the project was a dud, that the bomb would never explode.

Roosevelt had no lack of people prepared to offer him the benefit of their advice. Leo Szilard was one of those asking for an appointment. Szilard now believed it was no longer the Germans who threatened the world: 'Our worry [is] about what the Government of the United States might do to other countries.'

Secretary of War Stimson advised Roosevelt not to see the Hungarian scientist.

Others were not so easy to avoid. Harry Truman, the new Vice-President, was again wondering what was going on. Over a year before, Truman, then an obscure senator from Missouri, had begun asking awkward questions. Stimson had silenced him then. Now he had to be more tactful. Any day, Truman could be President. For Stimson knew that the ailing Roosevelt was hanging on to life by sheer willpower.

Stimson had told Truman no more than what Patterson had read to the Deficiency Sub-committee. There had been no mention of an atomic bomb. The Secretary of War knew that Truman was not satisfied, just as he knew that the sub-committee would return to the attack with more hearings.

Stimson was buying time for the project.

Recently, Roosevelt had asked him to conduct a review of the current situation.

Late that afternoon the two men met in Roosevelt's office. Stimson saw that the President, only days back from the taxing Yalta conference with Churchill and Stalin, looked more gaunt and senescent than ever. He was one of the few men who knew about the small box of green tablets Roosevelt kept in a desk drawer. They were digitalis. The pills were for the President's hypertension and failing cardiovascular system.

Anxious not to tire Roosevelt with a detailed summary, Stimson put the situation simply. Production of the weapon was on schedule. The bomb would be ready by August as Groves had promised. The weapon could save the million American lives Stimson believed would be lost before Japan surrendered.

Roosevelt seemed pleased. For a moment his eyes lost their lack-lustre sheen; that once-familiar set to his face returned.

But Stimson wondered whether the President would live to see those million soldiers return home safely.

March 3, 1945
Hiroshima

From the upper story of his small private hospital, Dr. Kaoru Shima had a good view of the city. It was one which was beginning to depress him. A slash of wasteland stretched away on each side of the Aioi Bridge, marking one of the fire-lanes crossing Hiroshima.

Dozens of houses, shops, tea-rooms and bars had been demolished in the vicinity of the Shima Surgical Hospital, leaving its medical director and nursing staff with the feeling that they worked 'on the brink of destruction'.

93

The morning news broadcast had reinforced this feeling. For the first time Japan Radio had given a hint that the fighting on Iwo Jima was going badly.

Iwo's eight square miles were just 700 miles from Tokyo, close enough for the Americans to covet the Japanese island as a fighter and bomber base.

For days the radio and newspapers in Japan had dwelled on the impregnability of the island's defences. They had pointed out that the enemy's seventy-four days of pre-invasion bombardment had done little to destroy those defences; the Imperial Army was sheltering in caves and deep tunnels, often protected by as much as thirty-five feet of concrete. And when the Americans had landed on Iwo, they had been led into a trap. Lured ashore by light opposition, the invading forces had gained a foot-hold on the island—only to have that hold nearly crushed by murderous cross-fire from the entrenched Army. Japan Radio had talked of slaughter on an unparalleled scale. But now the mood was changing. The latest bulletins were speaking of a 'strategic withdrawal'.

Dr. Shima, an old hand at assessing the truth of such claims, knew that Iwo was doomed.

The prospect of an invasion of the homeland came that much closer.

Hiroshima's fire-lanes were a constant reminder to him that as a prelude to invasion air raids must be expected, and that he would then have to deal with casualties. Only he knew how meagre were his resources; in practical terms he would be able to offer little more than comfort to victims of a major attack. His dispensary was in need of replenishment. He suspected that many of the city's other twenty-two hospitals and clinics, and also its thirty-two first-aid centres were in a similar position.

The materials now pouring into Hiroshima contained few medical supplies, and most of those would go to the large Ujina Army Hospital, the Red Cross Hospital and the Mitsubishi Shipyard Hospital. Dr. Shima's private clinic was low down on the Army's list of priorities.

The clinic survived solely because of the driving force of its owner. Nowadays, he was also frequently called upon to perform operations in country hospitals. The sight of the doctor peddling his bicycle, with his bag of instruments strapped to his back, was a familiar one in the area.

The construction of the fire-lanes often added to his journeys as demolished buildings blocked streets and he was forced to make lengthy detours. But Dr. Shima never complained. To those who did he had an unfailing answer.

'Be glad you are alive.'

March 4, 1945
Los Alamos

Some 9,000 miles away from the philosophical Dr. Shima, in a world that for all his scientific qualifications he never suspected existed, Tibbets and Beser thought their lives had assumed an endless treadmill pattern of travel to and from Los Alamos.

This morning they felt that 'the pressure had been notched up another few points' as soon as they arrived at the heavily-guarded gate to the compound. The sentries were more nervous than they had been when the two fliers were last there a few days before; they checked both men's ID cards more thoroughly than usual, even though Tibbets and Beser were now familiar faces.

When they eventually entered the site and were greeted by Ramsey, they found the usually unruffled scientist, in Beser's opinion, 'hot and bothered'.

It was Oppenheimer who told Tibbets the reason for the increased tension.

Groves had just ordered that the first plutonium bomb must be ready for testing at Alamogordo by the middle of July, and that the first uranium bomb must be available for 'war purposes' by early August.

The deadline had placed an additional burden on men and women who had been working under great strain for two years. They found the 'last-minute' rush hard to accept. One would complain bitterly of 'pressures to meet a mysterious deadline which we, who are working daily on the job of finishing the bomb(s), have to observe at all costs'.

Tempers had flared. They were angry exchanges between the scientists and security men.

The weather did not help. The spring rains were late coming, and an arid wind blew from the desert over the settlement, withering the grass and drying up the pond in the centre of the compound.

Shortage of water had always been a problem. Now it was rationed for personal use. Workers and their families were told to brush their teeth with Coca-Cola.

Nowadays, on his visits to Los Alamos, Beser tended to avoid any scientist who raised a doubt about the validity of their work. In Beser's opinion such men were 'misguided'. He preferred the views of Dr. Louis Slotin, a young researcher who had worked on the dangerous 'crit' experiments designed to establish how much fissionable material could be brought together before the resultant mass went 'critical' and caused a nuclear explosion. Slotin once expressed his convictions to Beser.

'Whether you die by a bullet—or a bomb, you are still dead.'

95

The words impressed the radar officer. They exactly matched his own views at a time when thousands of Americans were dying of Japanese bullets on Iwo Jima.

Beser was at Los Alamos that day to learn more about the fusing mechanism of the bomb, and how the Japanese might electronically interfere with it, causing a premature explosion.

Tibbets had come to see Oppenheimer to finalise details for the arrival at Wendover of a special new unit—the 1st Ordnance Squadron—which would be responsible technically for the atomic bomb when the 509th were overseas.

After settling on March 6 as the date when the squadron would come to Wendover, Tibbets and Oppenheimer were joined by Ashworth. The Navy commander had recently returned to Los Alamos after a thirteen-day visit to the Marianas where he had delivered Fleet Admiral King's letter to Admiral Nimitz, and explained to the Pacific commander the role of the 509th. Nimitz had made one comment: he wished the bomb was available now to be used on Okinawa, the last major island to be invaded before mainland Japan.

Ashworth told Tibbets that Guam had proven unsuitable as a base for the 509th. Instead he had agreed that the Group would use North Field, Tinian; the field had four 8,500-foot-long runways.

'I'll only need one,' responded Tibbets.

Washington, D.C.

The question of when and where Tibbets would fly from that one runway was something Groves thought a great deal about nowadays. But he would never have dreamed of raising the matter in the conversation he was having with General George C. Marshall on the scrambler telephone. Groves reported on progress once a week to Marshall. The Chief of Staff asked few questions and generally accepted without comment the information Groves chose to impart. This somewhat unusual consideration for a subordinate was a measure of Marshall's respect for the head of the Manhattan Project.

Groves had long outgrown his status as a military manager specialising in erecting atomic plants. He now considered himself capable of making scientific decisions.

He also felt he had a role as a diplomatic policy maker. Recently, he had taken steps to work against his government's policy of

96

collaborating with the British on all mattters to do with atomic research. Churchill had raised the matter privately with Roosevelt at Yalta, and the President had agreed that Britain should be kept more informed on the project. That did not please Groves: he did not trust the British to keep the atomic secrets away from the Russians. He had decided that America's allies should get as little information as possible. So deep-rooted was his anti-British feeling that earlier he had even opposed the suggestion that, if a B-29 proved unsuitable to carry the atomic bomb, then the R.A.F. could provide a Lancaster bomber.

Increasingly, Groves saw himself as a strategist, and because the use of the atomic bomb raised important political questions, also as a statesman. He knew more about the weapon than almost anyone. He was a giant among pygmies. And, to be fair, his performance had been herculean. Factories he controlled were among the largest in the United States; some were so long that works inspectors used bicycles to patrol them. He had authorised the patenting of many thousands of new inventions which accrued from the atomic research.

Yet the entire project was being threatened by some of the very scientists whose pioneering work had been invaluable. Groves could not understand them.

Now, another voice had joined the dissidents. On his desk, as he talked to Marshall, was a memo written the day before to Roosevelt by James F. Byrnes, Director of the Office of War Mobilization. Byrnes had an office in the White House and virtually ran the nation's economic affairs while Roosevelt and Stimson concentrated on foreign and military policy. Byrnes was known as 'the Assistant President'.

A copy of Byrnes' memo had been sent over from the White House to Groves for comment. That alone should have reassured him of the strength of his position. Nor was the memo totally unfriendly. It was a sensible reminder to the President that there would be a momentous political row if the project failed. Groves saw it only as the price *he* would have to pay for failure.

For a man used totally to having his own way, the memorandum's words were chilling.

... expenditures approaching 2 billion dollars with no definite assurance yet of production ... if the project proves to be a failure it will then be subjected to relentless investigation and criticism ... even eminent scientists may continue a project rather than concede its failure. Also it may be feasible to continue the experiment on a reduced scale. In any event, no harm could come from an impartial investigation and review by a small group of scientists not already identified with the project. Such a review

97

might hurt the feelings of those now engaged in the project. Still, 2 billion dollars is enough money to risk such hurt . . .

Byrnes was not asking that the project be scrapped; far from it. He merely wanted to make sure that all the money being spent could be justified.

But, in Groves' mind, the suggestion of an outside review placed Byrnes firmly in the opposition camp. Groves did not believe there was anybody competent enough to carry out such an investigation. It looked like another attempt to stop the project.

To some of those in close contact with him, Groves had begun to give the impression of coming close to obsession with his fear that the weapon which he increasingly regarded as his own might never be used. Now, he had an influential opponent in the White House, laying siege to his patron, the President, who had allowed him to spend more money than any soldier ever had before.

Groves finished briefing Marshall. He was about to break the connection when the Chief of Staff asked if he had given any thought to how the bomb could be used to best advantage.

Groves had. But he kept his ideas to himself. He merely told the Chief of Staff he thought it was time for the planners to prepare preliminary studies of suitable targets.

There was a moment's silence. Then Marshall spoke.

'I don't like to bring too many people into this matter. Is there any reason why you can't take over this and do it yourself?'

Groves eagerly accepted the offer. In his most optimistic moment he had never expected he would have the opportunity to chose atomic objectives.

He could consult, he could heed advice, but in the end he would have the responsibility for recommending which Japanese city would be the first to serve as a test-bed for the atomic bomb.

March 7, 1945
USAAF Base
Wendover

Tibbets remained impassive as Major William Uanna summed up. The security officer had spoken without interruption for many minutes, reading from one file after another. His summary was brutal and to the point.

'Colonel, you've got one convicted murderer, three men who are

98

convicted manslaughter cases and several felons. They are all on the run from the pen. Now what are you going to do?'

Tibbets restated the question.

'I know what *I* want to do. The question is, what are *you* going to recommend I do?'

Uanna was prepared.

'I'll do whatever you want.'

'Even break the law?'

'Even that.'

Tibbets began to explore other areas.

'How did these guys get into such a secret outfit as the 1st Ordnance?'

Uanna suggested that sheer chance had brought the criminals into the ordnance squadron which had just joined the 509th at Wendover. After escaping from various prisons, the convicts had presumably decided the safest place for them to remain undetected was in the Army. They would have had little difficulty enlisting under false names.

'This is wartime, Colonel. The Army doesn't ask too many questions. It's just glad for the manpower.'

Uanna's enquiries showed that the special technical talents of the criminals had been spotted by men 'scouting' for the Manhattan Project. The seven technicians—mainly tool- and die-makers—had been transferred to the 1st Ordnance.

The squadron would 'baby mind' the atomic bomb when the Group went to Tinian. Each of its members was a specialist. Together, they were capable of carrying out, under scientific supervision, any last-minute modifications to the bomb that might be required. The men were selected after a world-wide search of the American armed services. It had taken months to find the right personnel. The majority were skilled in metallurgy and allied disciplines. Twenty-seven of them held science degrees. They had been warned that from the moment they joined the squadron they might not see their family or friends until the war was over. Each was allowed to write a daily letter; the mail was posted through a special postbox in San Francisco.

The squadron had arrived at Wendover on a heavily guarded train. Its men were directed to a special fenced-off compound on the field, watched over by a detachment of Uanna's agents.

Uanna explained to Tibbets how he had spotted the criminals in the squadron. 'They were happy about all this security. Only years in prison makes men like that. We started digging.'

Tibbets looked thoughtful.

'We have them locked up here just as securely as if they were back in a State pen?'

Uanna agreed this was the case.

'I want to see them.'

Uanna raised no objection.

The escaped murderer was sent for. Tibbets studied him.

'Do you know why you are here?'

'No, Colonel, I don't.'

Tibbets picked up a file.

'Listen, fella. I know your real name, your Federal penitentiary number, the number of years you were serving, the day you broke out. I know it all.'

Tibbets tapped the file.

'It's all here. Who you murdered, the police statements, your trial, your sentence, how you came to us. Everything.'

The convict was too stunned to speak.

Tibbets thrust the file towards him.

'Here. See for yourself.'

The man began to tremble.

Tibbets withdrew the file and closed it. He looked carefully at the technician.

'This is the only record which exists of your past. The major and I are the only people who know that you are an escaped murderer. Now, it seems to me that you are real good at your present job. And we need good men. So lookit here. We're going to give you a chance. Go back to your job. Do your work exactly as you have been doing it. If we have no trouble with you, you will have no trouble from us. When the war is over, we will give you this dossier and a match to burn it.'

The dazed convict left the office, too overwhelmed to speak.

One by one the other criminals were marched in, confronted with their crimes and made to give similar undertakings.

When the last man left, Tibbets turned to Uanna.

'Major, I'm not a police department. I'm not interested in bringing people to justice. I'm interested in ending this war. All I want to do is get the proper work out of these men.'

The arrival of the 1st Ordnance caused considerable excitement. Lewis put it succinctly.

'If we think we're something special—these guys are something else!'

Even the slap-happy 509th had never seen such an untidy-looking outfit. Some of its members were middle-aged; one or two spoke with a distinct foreign accent. They were Jewish technicians who, until a few years before, had worked in workshops in Berlin and Munich, had fled Nazism, and been admitted to America.

The squadron seemed capable of anything, and were totally self-contained. They brought and erected their own workshops, connected their own electric power, installed their own special tools. The line crew of the 509th, themselves dab hands at most things, recognised their superiors had arrived.

The squadron's members only emerged from their compound at mealtimes. Then they were accompanied by several burly agents. They all sat in a corner of the mess-hall, and when strangers approached they fell silent. The curious were firmly rebuffed.

Bemused, the 509th sat back to watch this strange new outfit which had joined their Group.

This evening some of the men from the 1st Ordnance Squadron went down to the flight line to meet the regular shuttle service from Albuquerque which Dora Dougherty was now running. If they noticed a woman was flying the transport, they made no comment.

There was only one passenger. He led the 1st Ordnance men over to a B-29.

The regular flight crew had been told to answer any questions the man put to them. He seemed to be interested in the technical performances of the bomber, and spent some time examining the bomb-bay doors.

At the end of his inspection, the man turned to the Ordnance men.

'These ships are not good enough for the job. They will have to be replaced.'

With that, he walked past the gaping flight crew, boarded Dora's transport, and was on his way back to Los Alamos.

By Lights Out the whisper had spread. Beser would remember a fellow officer telling the story.

'Hear about this nut who flew in, said scrap our aircraft and flew out again? Just like he was a five-star general, not a guy in a naval captain's uniform. Doesn't he know there's a war on—nobody can scrap aircraft just like that!'

Beser asked for the man's description. He recognised it. He made a prediction to his scoffing companion.

'We'll get those planes.'

Beser knew how much power Captain William Parsons wielded.

Parsons had initially been considered as an alternate to Groves to head the Manhattan Project. He had come to Wendover to check out the planes which would fly the atomic strike. Constant test-flying and training had almost worn out the bombers. They must be exchanged for the very latest models.

These planes would have fuel-injection engines, electronically controlled reversible propellers and generally be much better than their predecessors.

Tibbets would soon have the best fleet of bombers that America could provide.

March 8, 1945
Washington, D.C.

Secretary Stimson's advice to Groves was clear. Groves should advise Roosevelt to reject Byrnes' proposal for an independent inquiry. Maintaining secrecy was all-important. Congress and the Senate should be given the minimum information needed to secure appropriations. In the past two days members of both houses had begun asking further questions about the Manhattan Project, following leakages about Under Secretary of War Patterson's appearance before the Deficiency Sub-committee.

Once again Stimson revealed himself as a man who, at the age of seventy-seven, was still able to take a commanding grasp of a situation.

Groves was delighted with Stimson's support; it enabled him to dismiss, almost defiantly, Byrnes' mild suggestion of a review.

Next, Groves dealt with Congress and the Senate. He set about the task in cavalier fashion. He was prepared, he told Stimson in a memo, to allow two Senators and two Representatives to take a peep at the project.

> I would propose to show them those things outside the secret processing areas which have been under constant observation by the construction contractors and their personnel. They would see the size and scope of the installations and have an opportunity to assure themselves of the reasonableness of the various living accommodations which have been provided. I would also like to show them some portions of the processing areas to demonstrate the scope and complexities of the project.

He was proposing to offer the sort of tour a quantity surveyor offers a client querying budget excesses. But to qualify even for this strictly limited inspection—in reality a reluctant spot of public relations to raise more money—Groves laid down conditions more appropriate for an inspection of the bomb itself than a mere glimpse of dormitories and cookhouses.

There was no possibility of anybody being allowed near Los Alamos. The visits would be to some of the less secret atomic sites whose usefulness to the project was already diminishing. And even then:

> No notes should be taken by any of the visitors. Joint conversations regarding their visits should be held only while on the project and then in secure rooms. Information ascertained would not be usable for future formal or informal conversations or addresses,

until the rules of security are changed by the Secretary of War. Some questions the members might ask would necessarily have to be unanswered and the refusal to answer must be unquestioned.

For Groves, dealing with curious Congressmen and Senators was an irritating interlude to the far more important task of selecting a target. He still favoured Kyoto, the ancient citadel of Japan.

Soon, this stubborn determination to stick to this choice would bring him into conflict with the one man whose support he could not afford to lose, the white-haired, articulate lawyer, Henry Stimson.

March 9, 1945
Guam

In the early evening, with the sun glinting on its silvered wings, the first B-29 took off. It was a pathfinder, a torch-bearer for LeMay's gamble.

Eleven other bombers followed it into the air. Between them they would pin-point the north-eastern sector of Tokyo. LeMay code-named the operation *Meetinghouse*. He had remembered that in China a meetinghouse was a place where important decisions were made.

The pathfinders were to sow their incendiaries carefully in a giant X. Its arms would embrace several square miles of one of the most congested cities in the world.

The chunky LeMay watched the main bomber force take off. In a few hours' time his bold plan would either be vindicated, or he would be in disgrace.

None of the 325 bombers climbing into the dusk were armed. Their bomb-bays were filled with a total of 2,000 tons of incendiary bombs.

LeMay had earlier ended his briefing of the crews with:

'You're going to deliver the biggest fire-cracker the Japanese have ever seen!'

Few fliers had reacted. Doubtless many of them recalled the first American air attack on Tokyo back in 1942; three of Doolittle's fliers whose planes had been forced down by the Japanese were tried for murder, found guilty and executed.

LeMay's crews were also concerned about their orders to attack at such low level without armaments. Intelligence was not comforting. Around Tokyo the Japanese were reported to have 331 heavy-calibre guns, 307 automatic-firing weapons, 322 single-engine fighters and 105 twin-engined interceptors.

LeMay had confidently predicted that this defensive arsenal would be outwitted by his surprise tactics.

Now he must wait for confirmation from General Tom Power, his chief of staff, flying in a lead bomber with orders to radio back news of the attack.

The pathfinders arrived over Tokyo at midnight. The city was in darkness. The weather forecast was correct: skies were clear; a chill, twenty-eight-mile-an-hour wind had sent most people early to bed.

Flying down-wind, the pathfinders marked the target area with magnesium, napalm and phosphorus, sowing their canisters in straight lines across wooden buildings and narrow streets.

At 0030 the main task force arrived over *Meetinghouse*. No fighters scrambled to meet them; ground fire was minimal. As LeMay had predicted, Tokyo's defences were caught totally unawares by his low-level assault.

The B-29's began systematically to bomb along the spreading arms created by the pathfinders. They dropped loads of pipe-like canisters to fuel the growing inferno.

Fifteen thousand feet above the flames, Power's plane circled the target. The chief of staff radioed a commentary back to Guam.

'It's spreading like a prairie fire . . . the blaze must be out of control . . . ground fire sporadic . . . no fighter opposition . . .'

The conflagration spread and intensified, sending great whirls of super-heated air high into the sky. The bomber pilots felt they were flying, one reported, 'In Dante's Inferno'. Turbulence from the fire-storm tossed the huge bombers hundreds of feet higher into the air, then sucked them down again. Fliers were sick from the helter-skeltering across the sky. Then a new sensation made them vomit afresh: it was the sickly-sweet stench of thousands of bodies burning.

Finally, as planned, at 0330 the last B-29 dropped its seven tons into the furnace and fled southwards.

Power radioed his final report.

'Target completely alight. Flames spreading well beyond meeting-house. All Tokyo visible in the glare. Total success.'

The fires were a funeral pyre for some hundred thousand souls. Almost half a million more were injured. Two hundred and fifty thousand buildings were destroyed in an area of about sixteen square miles.

Only fourteen of the 325 bombers which created this holocaust in under three hours were lost.

LeMay was satisfied. His gamble had worked. He had again

adapted his tactics exactly to fit local conditions. He immediately ordered further low-level sorties against Nagoya, Osaka, Kobe and Okoyama.

During the previous two months, all LeMay's efforts had been devoted to developing these tactics. There had been no time for anything else—certainly not to listen to the recurring rumour that some crack new outfit was coming to the Marianas.

But now, in his moment of triumph, the rumours took on substance. LeMay was told that part of North Field, Tinian, was being annexed on direct orders from Washington to house a 'special bombing Group'.

Echoing Groves' earlier premonition, LeMay reckoned that unless it arrived soon, there might be little left for this new outfit to bomb except ruins and paddy fields.

March 10, 1945
Above Southern California

The Group bombardier of that outfit, Tom Ferebee, laconically announced, as he always did at the Initial Point, that straight ahead and 32,000 feet below he could see the small desert town of Calipatria in Southern California.

Beyond the town lay Salton Sea and the 509th's bombing range.

Lewis knew there were now three minutes to go before the spanking new bomber reached the Aiming Point. It was the first of the replacement aircraft that Parsons had deemed necessary. It had only arrived at Wendover the previous night, and had been closely examined by Tibbets, van Kirk and Ferebee.

The new bomber *was* different. Though a lot of the armour-plating as well as the guns had been left out, it was more ruggedly built. Tibbets admired the reversible propellers. Ferebee liked the quick-action bomb doors; they were designed to close in two seconds after a bomb was released. This would allow the plane to carry out even quicker its 155-degree turn. Van Kirk appreciated his navigator's seat; it was more comfortable than the one he was used to.

A team of mechanics and engineers had flown in with the aircraft. At Tibbets' request they made a number of minor adjustments. But one of the engineers was not satisfied with the way the bomb-sight gears were working. Ferebee said he could adjust matters after a test drop or two. The engineer fussily explained that was not the way he did things. He put in a monitoring set and was given special clearance to make this one flight to observe the operation of the Norden sight.

Tibbets assigned Lewis to try out the new bomber on what was by now a regular milk run from Wendover to Salton Sea. Ferebee was on board partly because this time they were to drop one of the precious 'fused units'. These were dummy blockbusters the exact shape of the atomic bomb and containing the proximity fuse-firing mechanism. Each of these mechanisms cost the equivalent of a Cadillac.

As well as the engineer, there was another new face on board, 2nd Lieutenant Morris R. Jeppson of the 1st Ordnance Squadron. Jeppson had rigged up a control panel in the roomy cabin he shared with the navigator and radio-man. The panel was to monitor the bomb's complex internal electronics before it was dropped from the plane.

A religious and reserved young man, Jeppson quietly went about his work, oblivious of all the banter around him. He knew the fliers were curious about his presence; he sensed they were anxious to pump him about the 1st Ordnance. But he admired the way they restrained themselves. He liked that sort of discipline.

Jeppson was a physics graduate who, while in the service, had studied at Yale and Harvard Universities, and at the Massachusetts Institute of Technology. His talents were noticed and he was assigned to the 1st Ordnance. He took an immediate liking to Lewis. The pilot was friendly, suggesting where he could store his equipment and telling him what he should expect on the flight.

So far it had been uneventful. The feedback from the cables running from his control panel to the bomb revealed that the weapon was 'acting normally'.

'Two minutes to AP.'

Lewis acknowledged Ferebee's words. He prepared to slam shut the bomb-bay doors the moment the bombardier announced the block-buster was on its way down.

The engineer had a duplicate bomb-sight to the one Ferebee crouched over. If the bombardier's instrument malfunctioned, the bomb could still be dropped by Ferebee ordering the engineer to pull a lever. For his own purposes, the engineer synchronised his movements with every adjustment Ferebee was making.

'One and a half minutes to AP.'

Suddenly the B-29 leapt higher into the air.

'Je——sus!'

Ferebee's strangled cry was closely followed by another from Lewis.

'You've dropped the bomb too soon!'

Ferebee corrected him.

'I didn't. That engineer must have done it.'

Lewis yelled at the engineer over the intercom.

'Did you touch anything?'

'I thought we were at the drop point!'

Ferebee's next words stopped Lewis's flow of invective.

'It's falling straight into the town!'

He watched, transfixed, as the bomb plummeted earthwards. Though it contained only a small amount of explosive, with its ballast and electronic equipment the blockbuster weighed over nine thousand pounds; it could do considerable damage.

'Bob, hold her steady.'

Lewis held his original heading.

Jeppson calculated that the bomb needed about a minute to reach the ground.

Thirty seconds passed.

Then Ferebee spoke.

'It's going to miss.'

The bomb fell half a mile beyond Calipatria.

Within hours, Manhattan Project agents had sealed off the area, and were searching for the unit. It had buried itself ten feet underground. It was recovered and bulldozers filled in the hole. No one in Calipatria knew how close the town had been to being hit by a dummy atomic bomb.

The flight back to Wendover was a tense one. The wretched engineer's attempts to apologise met with icy silence.

At Wendover he was bundled into a car and driven to Salt Lake City. There he was put on a train by Project agents and told he would never again be allowed near the air base.

March 11, 1945
Imperial Army GHQ
Tokyo

In Tokyo, GHQ was in turmoil. Following the incendiary raid, the Army High Command was being evacuated to the more protected tree-shaded grounds of the military academy at Ichigaya Heights in west-central Tokyo.

The journey across the city was unusually difficult, for LeMay's raiders had created universal panic.

In the immediate aftermath of the attack, with air temperatures in the blitzed area reaching 2,000 degrees, the frenzy to escape had turned ordinary citizens into savages.

Thousands jumped into the Sumida River, to die either from

drowning or when the fires sucked out the oxygen from their lungs. Police and firemen were trampled in the panic.

Reports reaching Major-General Seizo Arisue that morning showed the position was still grave. Great mounds of dead were piled in the streets of north-east Tokyo.

Even here, in his Army GHQ office, Arisue's nostrils were filled with the unforgettable, stomach-wrenching stench of burned human flesh.

He decided he would delay moving his Intelligence organisation to Ichigaya Heights until the panic in the city abated.

He knew the attack had demoralised the civilian population. In the past twenty-four hours thousands had trudged out of Tokyo with nothing but the clothes they wore. Behind them they left charred families and friends.

Arisue realised this exodus posed a serious problem. The refugees could spread panic, cause confusion and lower morale. He was glad it was not his concern to deal with such matters. His immediate interest focussed on the reaction of Naval Intelligence to the raid.

For these past three months Arisue had discreetly monitored the Navy's attempts to make contact with Allen Dulles, head of the American OSS in Europe. At the same time he had been exploring the possibility of establishing his own covert link with Dulles. But the American spy-master proved more difficult to reach than Arisue had anticipated. The only consolation for the Chief of Army Intelligence was that his naval counterparts were also making little headway.

And now they had withdrawn.

It did not take Arisue long to discover why. Far from being demoralised by the attack, LeMay's bombers had strengthened the admiral's will to resist.

Naval Chief of Staff Admiral Toyoda announced that the only way Japan could survive 'with dignity' in the face of such terror was to fight on, to launch determined counter-attacks, to make America realize the Japanese nation would never surrender. The Navy, he let it be known, was considering means of carrying the war to the American shores.

The talk in Army GHQ was even fiercer. Staff officers, thirsting for revenge, put up a plan to saturate the Marianas with *shimpu* attacks, but the problems of getting the kamikazes to within striking distance proved insurmountable.

Gauging the strength of this bellicose mood, Arisue decided this was not the time to talk peace with the enemy. He decided to suspend his efforts to reach Dulles.

March 12, 1945
Hiroshima

Word of the destruction in Tokyo had not officially reached Hiroshima. The censor's office had so far refused to clear reports on the raid for the nations Press and radio.

The news reached Hiroshima unofficially by one of the few trains civilians could still use; the rail network was now monopolised by the Army to move troops and materials around the country.

Within an hour of the refugees from Tokyo arriving in Hiroshima, Major Senkichi Awaya knew what had happened in the capital.

Shamelessly using his official position, Awaya managed after several hours of anxious waiting to reach his wife by telephone. She and the children were unharmed.

He told his wife to bring the children with her and join him as soon as possible in Hiroshima.

Sachiyo Awaya hesitated. They had all survived the raid; the refugees were probably exaggerating; anyway the Army in Tokyo were saying it was unlikely the bombers would return, and if they did, next time they would receive a hot reception.

Awaya was aware that any moment an operator could interrupt the connection; nowadays telephonists had the authority to terminate any call which was not of a military nature. The mayor spoke urgently.

'The enemy will return. That is the nature of war. You and the children must come here.'

Still his wife expressed her reluctance to leave. Her husband then advanced an argument that he knew she would find difficult to reject.

'It is possible that we will all die in the battles to come. If that is to happen, I wish us to die together as one family.'

His wife promised that as a start she would bring their eldest son. The fourteen-year-old boy could continue his education at a school in Hiroshima.

March 22, 1945
USAAF Base
Wendover

Tibbets glanced in angry disbelief at one of his most trusted officers, a short, trimly-built lieutenant-colonel. Uanna, seated beside Tibbets, continued to question the officer.

'You admit you took a B-29 without authority to fly home on a weekend pass?'

The officer maintained his aggressive pose.

'I have the authority to take a plane.'

Uanna's reproof was mild.

'Nobody in the entire Air Corps has the authority to take our most top-secret bomber for pleasure purposes.'

Tibbets took over.

'You took the plane and left it unguarded for two whole days on a civilian airfield?'

'Yes. But the plane was locked.'

'And then you gave your father a conducted tour of an airplane that few servicemen on this base are allowed to go near?'

'My father's interested in flying. I didn't think there was any harm.'

Tibbets exploded.

'I don't want to hear about your father's interests! And it seems to me that you have never been able to think!'

'Colonel, I'm prepared to apologise . . .'

'Apologise! You think that settles matters! You've broken every goddam security rule. And you call yourself an officer! I'm going to make an example of you!'

The officer waited uneasily.

His decision made, Tibbets wasted no time in delivering sentence.

'You've got just sixty minutes to pack. A plane will be waiting for you. Its destination is Alaska. You're going to spend the rest of your war talking to penguins!'

'Colonel . . .'

'Another word and I'll have you court-martialled. Now get out!'

The disgraced officer left.

This was the third case that week when security regulations had been breached. Two days before, a couple of lieutenants, on duty at the telemetering station at the Salton Sea bombing range, had left their highly secret ballistic-measuring equipment and driven across the border into Mexico 'for a spot of fun'. They, too, had been swiftly sent to Alaska.

Privately, Tibbets sympathised with the three officers: they were all victims of pressures they could no longer cope with. Even if he had wanted to, he could not show them compassion; that might have opened a flood-gate and the carefully constructed security edifice he and Uanna had built up might have been swept away. Instead, Tibbets reacted toughly, ordering Uanna to close every possible security loophole. Tibbets knew his actions did not make him popular. But, as he had once told van Kirk, he wasn't 'trying to win a goddam beauty contest'.

Transferring a senior and two junior officers to the icy wilds of

Alaska would be a deterrent. But Tibbets knew it would not alleviate the tensions. For six months he had driven his men at a relentless pace.

And, until a few days ago, Tibbets himself had not been that familiar with 'the object of all this slave-driving', the top-secret nuclear mechanism inside the bomb. Then, Parsons had flown to Wendover with schematic drawings of the uranium bomb in order to discuss with Tibbets a new series of fusing tests. Tibbets already knew the bomb would be about ten feet long, twenty-eight inches in diameter and weigh something over 9,000 pounds, but what he learned from Parsons caused him to be 'amazed by the sweet simplicity of the thing'.

The bomb's uranium core would weigh only about twenty-two pounds, split into two unequal segments kept six feet apart inside the barrel of the cannon which was itself inside the bomb's casing. Between the two pieces of U-235 was a 'tamper', a neutron-resistant shield made from a high-density alloy. The tamper was to stop the two pieces of uranium from reacting with each other—to help prevent premature 'crit'—which would cause an unscheduled nuclear explosion.

The smaller piece of U-235 would weigh five pounds. This was the atomic 'bullet' which, when the gun was activated by the proximity fusing system, would be fired down the gun-barrel at the 'target', the larger piece of U-235 fixed to the muzzle of the cannon just a few feet away. The 'target' would weigh about seventeen pounds.

When fired, the force of the uranium 'bullet' would make it sever the pins previously holding it in place, break through the tamper, and ram it into the 'target'—causing the nuclear explosion.

After the description, Tibbets had been jolted by Parsons telling him that, despite all the planning and testing, the scientists at Los Alamos still did not know if the uranium bomb would actually work. Tibbets remembered how 'Parsons just sat there and said there was no way of being certain the weapon would go off—until it was used. He didn't think the risk of failure was high. But it was there'.

Parsons had refused to be drawn further and, after agreeing to a revised testing schedule for the 393rd, he had returned to Los Alamos.

Ever since, Tibbets had been mulling over what Parsons had told him. That, coupled with the security breaches by the three officers, made him edgy. Then, in the evening, he was involved in yet another security problem. He was called from dinner to interview a man who had checked into Wendover's State Line Hotel. Security agents had discovered he was using a false name. For thirty minutes the man resisted Tibbets' questions. Then one of the agents spoke.

'We're going to turn you in as a spy. Spies in this country go to the electric chair.'

The man talked. He admitted he was using an alias, in the hope of selling phoney magazine subscriptions on the base. He was escorted to Salt Lake City and warned to stay out of Utah.

But the episode further worried Tibbets. Inside the base it was now an open secret that the group was going to drop 'a big bomb' on Japan. Tibbets thought it was only a matter of time before there was a serious security leak. He expressed his fears to Uanna, then came to a decision.

'I think the moment's come for drastic action!'

Only Tibbets knew that what he had in mind might get him posted to Alaska along with the others he had already sent there.

April 1, 1945
Hiroshima

The shock of that moment, now two weeks old, was still fresh in Kazumasa Maruyama's mind. Then, on a similar balmy morning to this one, Hiroshima had finally experienced its first air attack.

Between 7.30 and 8 a.m. on March 19, four carrier-based fighter-bombers had flown across the city. Only two bombs were dropped; one fell harmlessly in a river, the other killed two people and destroyed their homes.

The planes had escaped before anti-aircraft fire could be brought to bear on them. As well as shocking Maruyama, the incident had caused widespread excitement and speculation in the city. Fierce arguments had broken out between sceptics and the proponents of the view that Roosevelt had agreed to spare Hiroshima. In the end the supporters of this theory had triumphantly pointed to the fact that the bombers had not made a second pass over the city. The two bombs they had released were dropped in error—that was why they had sheered away. And, to clinch their case, the proponents pointed to an inescapable truth: while there had been a number of air raid warnings in the past two weeks, no bombers had come anywhere near the city.

These recent warnings had delayed Muruyama's regular weekly trip into the countryside to barter for food for his wife and the man he loved almost as dearly, his employer, the Mayor of Hiroshima, Senkichi Awaya.

Though it was not usual for men to make these foraging trips, the mayor's chief assistant gladly did so because it was another small way for him to show the esteem he had for Awaya.

This morning, Maruyama had risen at five and left his wife still

112

sleeping in their tiny bedroom. The whole apartment resembled a doll's house, with its lacquered furniture, lamps and family portraits. Only the radio in the kitchen intruded upon the careful blend of traditional furnishings. The radio was important. Air raid warnings were broadcast over it. And while the newspapers were rigorously controlled, sometimes the radio announcers, by a change of inflection, the tiniest of pauses, would allow an astute listener to glean another meaning behind the strident claims of victories. It was the radio, with its first hint of a 'strategic withdrawal', which had prepared listeners for the loss of Iwo Jima.

The newscaster this morning was as confident as ever. Units of the Special Attack Force, the kamikazes, had yesterday struck another mortal blow against the enemy off the shores of Okinawa. Among their many targets was 'the pride of the enemy fleet, the warship *Indianapolis*'. The name of the ship did not register with Maruyama—nor could he know how closely it eventually would be linked with his city—but he deduced that, behind the blaring words, the radio was starting to prepare its audience for an unpalatable fact: the enemy had reached the shores of Okinawa, the last Japanese stronghold before the mainland. The newscaster reminded his listeners that if the United States dared to set foot on Okinawa, its soldiers would be decimated. To the perceptive Maruyama the unspoken message was clear: Okinawa was about to be invaded.

And if Okinawa should fall, Maruyama had no doubt the enemy would then invade Japan itself.

The thought of what that would mean was too horrible to contemplate. The newspapers and radio spoke of American soldiers as 'bloodthirsty devils'; perhaps, after all, he had been wrong to support the mayor's idea of bringing his family to Hiroshima. Perhaps they would be better off near Tokyo where the largest concentration of defending troops was stationed.

And yet Maruyama knew that he would find it almost unbearable to be separated from his own wife. Still dwelling on the dilemma the broadcast had created in his mind, the mayor's assistant headed out of the city on foot. Ahead lay an hour's walk to the farmhouse where he hoped to exchange the bundle of old clothes his wife had spared from her wardrobe.

Nowadays, commodities were more useful than money for obtaining a few vegetables and fruit to augment the legal rations.

From today, those rations were to be cut further, the rice portion reduced to three bowls a day for twenty days in any month. No food would be issued for the remaining calendar days. The quality of the rice was so poor that Maruyama would never have eaten it before the war. To give it bulk it was mixed with soya beans. Now, Maruyama ate it without demur.

113

Fish, the other staple of Japanese diet, was also becoming scarce. American bombers were systematically destroying the fishing fleet.

Yet, apart from the hunger pains in his stomach, Maruyama admitted that here in the lush green countryside, unchanged for hundreds of years, with the warm sunshine on his back, he could see or feel no signs of the war. Walking beside the paddy fields, he wondered how much of this year's crop would end up on the black market.

With a sense of guilt he realised he himself was now dabbling in that flourishing market; bartering for food was just as much of a crime as other illegal trafficking. He wondered what would happen if he was stopped by one of the dreaded Kempei Tai patrols. The Kempei Tai were the counterpart of the Nazi Gestapo. Maruyama did not know anything about the Gestapo, but he had plenty of evidence of the brutality of the Kempei Tai in Hiroshima; numerous complaints against them had been lodged with the mayor's office. Even Awaya's forceful protests were ignored by the Kempei Tai headquarters' staff in the grounds of Hiroshima Castle.

Maruyama was sure that if the Kempei Tai caught him bartering he would receive severe handling once they discovered his official position.

He reached the farm and was warmly greeted. He was the most important customer among all those who came to offer goods in exchange for food. Soon Maruyama was sitting cross-legged in his stockinged feet in the farmhouse living-room, sipping tea.

Normally the farmer plied him with questions about life in the city. This morning it was the farmer who had information to impart, and he was determined to make the most of it.

Maruyama provided the opening by mentioning that the air raid had made many people nervous in Hiroshima.

'The city will not be bombed again.'

Maruyama smiled wanly. He supposed the farmer's belief came from that tired old rumour about Roosevelt.

But Maruyama knew he must not offend the farmer; he was a touchy man and could sell his produce to whomever he liked. Maruyama said he hoped his host was right and that the city would be spared.

'It will. You see, when the war is over Americans will build their villas here. It is such a beautiful city.'

Maruyama had learned never to challenge even the wildest rumour. That only prolonged matters. He merely complimented the farmer on being privy to such interesting information.

'I cannot tell you how I learned it. But I can tell you this, Mr. Secretary, that a client almost as important as you told me.'

Nodding gravely, Maruyama stood up. It was time for business.

He opened the bundle of old clothes he had brought. Maruyama's wife had carefully packed the garments so that the most attractive ones were at the bottom of the pile. Her husband took his time with each piece, holding it up, turning it slowly before the farmer. As each item was displayed, the farmer reached into his own sacks and laid out his purchasing price in produce. The bartering continued at this leisurely pace until all the clothing had been shown.

Maruyama estimated that, with the clothes, he had purchased enough food for the Mayor, his wife and himself for three days, perhaps five if his wife was extra-careful.

He exchanged deep bows with the farmer, carefully bundled up the produce, bowed a last time and retraced his steps to Hiroshima.

He had travelled less than a mile when a peasant rushed out of his cottage and shouted that the radio had just announced another air raid alert.

Unable to resist the temptation, Maruyama did his own bit of rumour mongering.

'Don't worry. Hiroshima won't be bombed again. Haven't you heard? The Americans want to build their villas here! Maybe even Roosevelt will come!'

He walked briskly on towards the city.

April 12, 1945
Warm Springs, Georgia
Early Afternoon

Even here in Georgia, Roosevelt could not shake off the cares of war. At noon, a messenger appeared in his study with a leather pouch. The mail from Washington had arrived to intrude upon the rest that his doctors had ordered for the President.

Roosevelt began to scrawl his signature on a batch of postmaster appointments, routine correspondence and Legion of Merit awards to leading Allied statesmen. He used a fountain pen; he regarded ball-point pens as a passing fad and had forbidden their use in the White House.

He worked slowly, checking the contents of each paper carefully. It had been a troubling week, and the main problem, that of Russian duplicity, was still with him. This morning he had cabled Churchill that firmness was essential in dealing with renewed Soviet demands.

At Yalta, Roosevelt and Churchill had made a number of concessions in return for Stalin's promise to declare war on Japan 'two or three months after Germany was defeated'. Now the Russian leader wanted even more concessions.

Stalin had sat at the Yalta Conference table impassively screened by the impenetrable barrier of the Slavic language. In a rare relaxed moment the Soviet leader had demonstrated his range of English. In his deep bass voice, he had recited, like a child, his vocabulary: 'so what', 'you said it', 'what the hell goes on here?' and 'the toilet is over there'!

At the conference table Stalin had got much of what he wanted.

His gains included certain guaranteed privileges in Manchuria, an occupation zone in Korea, a United Nations veto for the major powers, the re-drawing of Poland's borders, autonomy for Outer Mongolia and a promise that after the war the Kuril Islands should be 'handed over to the Soviet Union'.

In return, as well as promising to attack Japan, Stalin agreed to sign a treaty with Chiang Kai-shek, eventually recognising Chiang, not Mao Tse-Tung, as ruler of 'all China'.

And yet the signs were that the Soviets might go back on their pledge to attack Japan unless they received further concessions.

Whatever he felt about Stalin, Roosevelt took care to present an optimistic front to those of his personal staff who had come with him to Warm Springs.

In some ways he had reason to be cheerful. The Allies were winning. Germany was on the verge of collapse. In the Pacific, landings had been made on Okinawa by 183,000 soldiers and marines. After that would come mainland Japan.

But already the death toll was high. This morning, as usual, the President had the latest casualty figures—6,481 Americans had died in battle during the past week, bringing the grand total to 196,669 American lives sacrificed in the fight against the Axis.

He was still studying these sombre figures when Madame Elizabeth Shoumatoff, the portrait painter, arrived.

Roosevelt was dressed, as she had requested, in a Harvard tie and a waistcoat, neither of which he liked. He allowed her to slip his cloak over his shoulders. Its dark cloth would contrast with the curious luminosity of the President's features. His skin had become parchment-like and this morning was aglow with an intense burning brightness which seemed to come from deep within.

She began to paint as he returned to work on his papers.

He thought he had left behind in Washington the problems surrounding the Manhattan Project. Yet here they were again, present in a memo from his chief of staff, Admiral Leahy, repeating that the atomic bomb would not work.

Back on Roosevelt's White House desk was a memo from Leo Szilard urging that the project be reconsidered; the memo from

Byrnes suggesting a comprehensive independent review; Groves' rejection of that idea on grounds of security and his alternative proposal that a small group of non-experts be shown some non-secret areas.

Madam Shoumatoff interrupted his reverie.

'Mr. President, just another fifteen minutes and then we'll be through for the day.'

Roosevelt smiled and placed another cigarette in his holder.

Suddenly, he raised his left hand to his forehead and pressed hard against the skin. His hand fell back on his lap and his fingers began to twitch. He dropped his cigarette and raised his right hand to massage the back of his neck. He closed his eyes and began to moan softly. Then his head slumped forward and he slid down in his seat, limp like a puppet.

The President's doctor arrived within moments.

Roosevelt's breathing was harsh; his neck was rigid; his left eye dilated. To the physician the signs meant only one thing: a subarachnoid haemorrhage, probably massive.

The doctor took emergency action. He injected the President with doses of papaverine and amyl nitrate, to try to stem the blood from a ruptured vessel seeping into cavities around the brain.

The only sound in the room was the gasping, anguished snores as Roosevelt struggled to live.

Between them the doctor and valet manoeuvred the President on to a nearby bed. His face was covered with a cold sweat that glistened against the ash-grey pallor of his skin.

Other doctors soon arrived. There was nothing more they could do. At three thirty-five that mid-April afternoon they pronounced the President 'clinically dead'.

The free world had lost a statesman, America a leader and the Manhattan Project, at this most crucial stage, its benefactor.

Washington, D.C.
Late Afternoon

Oblivious of what had just happened in Georgia, Harry S. Truman, the thirty-fourth Vice-President of the United States, and for that afternoon also President of the Senate, appeared to the assembled senators to be taking copious notes of the debate in progress. Many thought it was typical of the way Truman did things: he was a meticulous gatherer of facts.

Hunched over his writing block, Truman conveyed the impression that he would be happier back home in Missouri, running the family haberdashery. When he occasionally spoke, his flat, sing-song, Mid-West accent contrasted oddly with the marble pilasters and gold velvets of the Senate.

But most of the afternoon he wrote. Some Senators assumed Truman was taking notes for another of those well-researched but tepidly delivered speeches he was famous for.

In reality he was writing a letter to his mother, full of chatty news. He ended with a reminder.

Turn on your radio tomorrow night at 9.30 your time and you'll hear Harry make a Jefferson Day address to the nation. I think I'll be on all the networks, so it ought not to be hard to get me. I will be followed by the President whom I'll introduce.

At 4.56 the Senate recessed and Truman dropped in to Speaker Sam Rayburn's office for a bourbon and water. He was still there when Roosevelt's Press Secretary, Steve Early, telephoned and told Truman to 'please come over and come in through the main Pennsylvania Avenue entrance'.

Truman did not ask why. He assumed Roosevelt was back from Warm Springs and wanted to raise some minor point with him. Truman doubted if it could be important. Roosevelt rarely discussed anything of consequence with him.

Truman was a realist. He knew that most of Washington regarded his appointment to the 1944 ticket as a compromise. Roosevelt and he rarely appeared in public together. In the eighty-two days Truman had been Vice-President he had paid only two official calls on Roosevelt in the White House. All told, the two men had only met on eight official occasions. They had never discussed the Manhattan Project.

This afternoon Truman was shown up to the second-floor study of Eleanor Roosevelt. She walked towards him and grasped his arm. Her voice was calm and measured.

'Harry, the President is dead.'

Dumbfounded, Truman instinctively looked at his watch, to remember the moment he heard the unbelievable news. It was 5.25 p.m.

Mrs. Roosevelt spoke again.

'Harry, is there anything *we* can do for *you*? You are the one in trouble now.'

She invited him to use the study's telephone, and left to attend to the funeral arrangements.

Truman telephoned his wife, Bess. Her reaction of incredulous shock at the news would soon be matched in millions of American homes.

By 6.30 the Trumans' modest five-room apartment was under siege by reporters, photographers and the first callers enquiring about taking over the $120-a-month rent-controlled home now that the Trumans were moving to a larger place.

At seven o'clock, Truman went to the Cabinet Room in the White House to be sworn in. The Cabinet, including Roosevelt Administration veterans like Harold Ickes, Henry Wallace and Henry Morgenthau, watched in silence as Chief Justice Harlan Stone explained the brief ceremony to Truman.

Stone consulted a piece of paper and asked Truman to confirm that the S in his name stood for Shippe.

Truman's twangy drawl cut through the doom-laden atmosphere.

'The S stands for nothing. It's just an initial.'

The confused Chief Justice scrawled out 'Shippe' from the oath. An aide whispered to Stone that they still could not begin as they did not have a Bible. They all waited in strained silence before a frantic search of the White House produced one.

At 7.09 p.m. the Bible was handed to Truman, who repeated after Stone the Presidential Oath of Office.

I, Harry S. Truman, do solemnly swear that I will faithfully execute the office of President of the United States, and will to the best of my ability, preserve, protect and defend the Constitution of the United States.

Truman impulsively kissed the Bible. Then he motioned for the Cabinet to join him at the long table. He made them a promise.

'It will be my effort to carry on as I believe the President would have done.'

For Truman, the new President, for all the men in the room, Franklin Roosevelt was still 'The President'.

Truman asked Roosevelt's Cabinet to stay on in office. But he gave a hint of things to come when he closed the meeting with another promise.

'I will assume full responsibility for such decisions as have to be made.'

The Cabinet filed out, silent with grief. At the door Stimson lingered. When he spoke to Truman his voice was unsteady.

'Mr. President, I must talk to you on a most urgent matter.'

Truman nodded.

'I wish to inform you about an immense project that is under way— a project looking to the development of a new explosive of almost unbelievable destructive power.'

Stimson paused.

Truman waited, but the Secretary of War did not elaborate.

Stimson was an old man. He was deeply shocked by the death of his great friend. Perhaps that was the reason he continued to think of Truman as the make-weight Vice-President, the man who had never been allowed inside the White House War Room, who had never been present while the Chiefs of Staff briefed the President, who had picked up much of his knowledge of the war from the *Washington Post*.

And who still, this evening, knew far less about the Manhattan Project than, for instance, a junior Air Force lieutenant like Jacob Beser.

USAAF Base, Wendover
Early Evening

Beser, like most of the 509th, heard the news of Roosevelt's death over the radio. Some of the men were listening to NBC's *Front Page Ferrell*; others were tuned to CBS's *Wilderness Road*; by far the majority were following the adventures of ABC's highly popular *Captain Midnight*.

At 5.49 the first flash interrupted all three programmes. By 6.30—around the time the first reporters were converging on the Truman apartment in Washington—local radio stations in Utah were broadcasting details of the poignant cable Eleanor Roosevelt had sent to her four sons: two of them were in the Navy, sailing off the coast of Okinawa. To each of her children went the same message.

> Darling: Pa slept away this afternoon. He did his job to the end as he would want you to do. Bless you.
> All our love. Mother.

Beser turned off the radio. His reason for doing so was understandable.

'By switching off I believed I could deny the truth. President Roosevelt had been leading us for so long that his death was impossible to accept immediately'.

The radio networks voluntarily dropped all commercials until after the funeral as a mark of respect. That evening, for the same reason, members of the Officers' and Enlisted Men's Clubs on the base made their gesture: there would be no gambling or drinking until Roosevelt was buried. Eatherly surprised many by being one of the most vociferous supporters of this pledge.

Bob Lewis touched a popular emotional chord with his words.

'I never met the guy. But I felt that I had lost a great Buddy.'

Lewis, like all those in the group, was a product of the Depression. He remembered how Roosevelt had 'led us out of the darkness with his simple faith in the basic goodness of man, his idealism, his resourcefulness, the way he always brought out the best in everybody. He made us all proud to be Americans'.

The thought of an America without F.D.R. in the White House was impossible to comprehend for many of these young men who could hardly remember when he had not been President.

Gradually though, the talk at Wendover, as elsewhere, turned to the new President.

Bob Caron's wife, herself a Midwesterner, told her husband that Truman might well surprise everybody: 'He's a little folksy, but he knows the price of everything.'

Caron was not so sure. He felt as many Americans did. Truman would sit out Roosevelt's fourth term and then stand down.

Of more immediate concern to the 509th was the attitude of the new President to the prosecution of the war.

Eatherly remembered that Truman had made some 'good speeches' after Pearl Harbor. Mess Officer Perry recalled that Truman had shown himself to be quite 'a dime saver' when it came to defence expenditure. Exec. Officer King relied on a lawyer's logic: there was no point in speculating without the facts. And Tibbets put his finger on the salient fact.

'We just don't know what this fella thinks.'

Everybody at Wendover knew where Roosevelt had stood. Many of them could quote his speeches with their recurring theme that the enemy must be pursued to its lair. Roosevelt had almost lived to see the pursuit reach Berlin.

But would Truman be so keen to conquer Tokyo?

Lewis had a possible answer.

'Every time we look at the movie newsreels, the price we have to pay is always there. Maybe we are killing a lotta Japs. But we are also losing a lot of Americans. Maybe our new President will settle the war before we get into it.'

Those who heard Lewis began to feel that perhaps, after all, they would never drop their big bomb.

Washington, D.C.
Late Evening

When Groves heard the news of Roosevelt's death his reaction was to prepare himself for an expected call to brief the new President.

Writing fast and fluently—Groves prided himself on this skill—he prepared a survey of the project.

Now four hours later, at eleven o'clock, still with no call to go to the White House, he went to bed.

April 13, 1945
Washington, D.C.

Truman awoke at his customary hour of 6.30. This Friday the 13th was going to be another hot sticky day. Then it struck him that a President of the United States did not concern himself with forecasts unless they affected important issues. Whatever the weather, he now had to run the country.

Dressed in one of his favourite pinstripe suits, he looked more than ever the out-of-town salesman up for a spree in the big city. It was a deceptive pose, for few politicians knew Washington and its ways better than Truman. Even fewer could match his sharp analytical mind, his knowledge of world history and his quick grasp of complicated issues.

And yet he still found it hard to accept he was the nation's chief executive.

His posse of Secret Servicemen left him confused. He winced at reporters waiting outside his apartment who called him 'Mr. President'. He told the newspapermen that if they believed in prayers, they should 'pray for me now'.

Down-town he had given his security detail the biggest headache it had experienced in years when he insisted on getting out of the car and walking a few blocks to his bank to cash a cheque. Within minutes the whole area was a log-jam of gaping motorists and pedestrians watching the President strolling.

Though Truman was forced to abandon his walk because of the crowds, his image was established: he was going to be an earthy and unpretentious President.

He was also a sensitive one. The Oval Office was still filled with

Roosevelt's mementoes, ship models and ship paintings. In one of the desk drawers was a spare bottle of digitalis tablets. Gingerly, Truman cleared only a space for his writing block and seated himself behind the desk. He made it clear to the late President's personal staff that the Trumans would not be moving in until Eleanor Roosevelt was ready to leave; Harry, Bess and Margaret would camp out in Blair House, across the road from the Executive Mansion.

But when Truman got down to business, he showed himself a swift decision-maker. That morning he dealt quickly and surely with certain domestic issues and briefed members of the Cabinet.

At 2.30 James Byrnes arrived. Truman had two questions he wanted Byrnes to answer.

Firstly, would Byrnes give him a written report on the Yalta Conference? Byrnes had taken copious notes there for Roosevelt, and immediately agreed to provide a memo.

The second question was more surprising. Truman began by reminding Byrnes that, because of the way he had become President, the law did not allow him to have a Vice-President. The Constitution ruled that, if Truman died or became seriously incapacitated and unable to remain President, the Secretary of State would succeed him.

Truman asked if Byrnes would like that post. It was a surprising offer in view of their previously cool relationship. As the unofficial 'Assistant President', Byrnes had been far closer to Roosevelt than Truman, and at times had used his power to snub the Vice-President. But in asking Byrnes to become, in effect, the next President-elect, Truman was displaying the political skill which made him so formidable. He wanted Byrnes on his side; he was prepared to buy him.

Byrnes accepted.

Then, speaking in a voice Truman felt was one of 'great solemnity', Byrnes made an announcement more startling and mysterious than Stimson's had been on the previous evening.

'Mr. President, we are perfecting an explosive great enough to destroy the whole world.'

Truman said nothing.

'It might well put us in a position to dictate our own terms at the end of the war.'

Bafflingly, the new President apparently did not ask one question which could have paved the way for an early briefing on the atomic bomb. Nor would he ever offer an explanation for his silence.

The first wire service flash of Roosevelt's death had reached Army Intelligence chief Seizo Arisue in his new offices on the outskirts of Tokyo before most people in Warm Springs were aware of the event.

Since then he had been busily building up a psychological profile of Truman. Most of his information came from the Japanese military attaché in Berne, Lieutenant-General Seigo Okamoto, who had been the link-man in Arisue's so-far abortive attempts to contact Allen Dulles.

Aided as well by wire service copy and transcripts of monitored broadcasts, Arisue came to an unexpected conclusion: Truman was going to be even tougher than Roosevelt.

The new President would, in Arisue's estimation, 'overwhelm the old man' who had been Prime Minister of Japan for the past ten days.

On April 5, a serious political crisis, brewing for weeks, had finally erupted in Tokyo. On that day, General Kumaki Koiso, the compromise Premier following Tojo's resignation, had meekly suggested to the military that they allow him a share in their decision-making. The generals refused. Koiso resigned.

He was replaced by Admiral Kantaro Suzuki, a hero of the Russo–Japanese war, whose frail body still bore three bullet marks—a legacy of the days when he had fallen foul of right-wing extremists in the Army.

Arisue was astounded that Suzuki had now accepted a post where the risks of death were even greater. He would have been more astonished if he had known that the Emperor himself had virtually charged Suzuki with the task of finding a means of ending the war. Those means did not, of course, include outright surrender.

Within hours of accepting office, Suzuki had received alarming news. Japan's Ambassador in Moscow had cabled that the Soviet Union did not intend to renew its Neutrality Pact. It would be allowed automatically to lapse in one year's time. To Suzuki the news was a precursor of impending disaster. Finding an acceptable means of ending the conflict became even more urgent.

The prospect of Japan negotiating a peace was also very much on Arisue's mind. On this Sunday—the day Roosevelt was being buried on the other side of the world—he had learned that Naval Intelligence was again trying to contact Allen Dulles in Switzerland.

Arisue understood the reasoning of his naval counterparts: it coincided with his own. Truman was a hard-liner; it would be better to settle with him *now*, while Japan still had some bargaining power left. The American bombing offensive, the sea blockade, the relentless ground-fire barrage which had now crept to within 350 miles of Tokyo, to Okinawa, where a fierce and bloody battle was raging for the last major island between the enemy and Japan's westernmost mainland island, Kyushu: all these would ultimately weaken Japan to the point where the unacceptable unconditional surrender would be all that was left.

A realist, Arisue could clearly see the dimensions of the military disaster confronting the country. He believed that if Okinawa fell, attacks would be launched against Japan's four main Home Islands, Kyushu, Honshu, Shikoku and Hokkaido until every foot of their 142,000 square miles would be occupied and the population of nearly seventy-three million subjugated.

But Arisue and the other moderates did not believe Japan should surrender unconditionally; even those most pessimistic about the country's chances did not advocate that. He believed that by negotiation Japan should attempt to hold some of the territory her forces had occupied in war, and even if this proved impossible, there must as an absolute minimum be a guarantee by the Allies of the Emperor's safety and continuing omnipotent rule.

Arisue did not trust the Navy to achieve even this fundamental requirement in its manoeuvring in Switzerland.

He cabled Okamoto, the military attaché in Berne, and told him to redouble his efforts to contact Dulles.

April 19, 1945
USAAF Base
Wendover

Like a well-rehearsed team, pilot Charles Sweeney and bombardier Kermit Beahan brought the B-29 towards the Aiming Point. For this test they were using the makeshift range which had been laid out on the salt flats a few miles from Wendover.

Thirty-two thousand feet below, grouped near the AP, scientists and technicians from the 1st Ordnance Squadron waited to see if the latest adjustments they had made to the bomb's proximity fusing system would work.

The day's blockbuster was filled with ballast and a pound of explosive, enough to cause a small aerial explosion, a puff of smoke so that the scientists could see whether the fusing mechanism had set off the explosion at its pre-set height of 2,000 feet.

Sweeney's crew, No. 15, had been briefed by Tibbets on the test flight. He had reminded them of the importance and value of each fused unit, particularly as the system was still proving troublesome.

Though Tibbets had not said so, he was paying Sweeney and his fliers a rare compliment. In selecting them for a flight of considerable consequence for the scientists, he was openly acknowledging what almost all the other crews now accepted; crew 15 was probably the best in the 393rd.

The only challenge to this claim came from the vociferous Lewis and his crew.

The relationship between Lewis and Sweeney had always been cool, right from those days when both men had worked on the original B-29 test programme. Lewis suspected that the Boston–Irish Sweeney had 'kissed the Blarney stone'; certainly, Sweeney had a great deal of charm, which he used to get the very best from all those he worked with. It did not work with Lewis, a failure that Sweeney philosophically accepted. Professionally he felt that Lewis was 'lucky' to be in the 393rd, and even luckier to act on occasions as co-pilot to Tibbets.

This sort of personal tension had increased the competitive spirit between the two crews.

Tibbets, aware of how far to let the rivalry go, watched the situation carefully. He never appeared to favour any crew unduly. That, he knew, would be harmful to the morale of the entire squadron. After Sweeney had been assigned the test flight, Lewis had been asked to perform a series of take-offs and landings with a 9,000-pound blockbuster filled with high explosive in his bomb-bay. This exercise was not as pointless as it sounded to the crews. Tibbets wanted Lewis, and later the others, to become 'psychologically prepared' for the possibility that one day they might be forced to land carrying an actual atomic bomb.

Tibbets was also aware of the pragmatic view prevailing within the higher echelons of the Manhattan Project: unlike conventional bombs, the atomic bomb was far more valuable than the aircraft carrying it, or the crew. He conveyed this thought to Lewis. The pilot performed his exercises with the gentle care of a veteran Red Cross transport flier.

Approaching the Aiming Point, Sweeney watched Lewis circling far below. Then Beahan called out, in a Texas accent even Eatherly agreed was 'broad', that the AP was almost in the centre of his bomb-sight's cross-hairs. Beahan, an overseas veteran like Ferebee, was a highly efficient technician, known to his fellow fliers as 'The Great Artiste'. Crew 15 held him in such reverence that they boasted he could 'hit a nickel from six miles up'.

Beahan asked for a minute course change. Co-pilot Fred Olivi, a bulky twenty-three-year-old Italian from Chicago, watched Sweeney

126

instantly respond. Olivi thought it was 'almost magic' the way Sweeney and Beahan worked together.

The crew braced themselves for the familiar upward thrust following the bomb's release.

This flight would make another entry for the strictly illegal diary Sergeant Abe Spitzer was keeping of his time with the 509th. He was the radio operator and, at the age of thirty-five, looked upon by the rest of the crew almost as an old man. They would have been surprised at the gentle-voiced Spitzer's acid observations on some of the men he worked with. But even Spitzer had to admit that, in the air, crew 15 was a closely co-ordinated unit.

'Bomb away!'

Beahan's words were followed by a leap upwards from the B-29, cut short by Sweeney going into the 155-degree turn.

Sergeant 'Pappy' Dehart, the tail gunner and another Texan, shouted, 'It's blown up!'

The bomb's fusing mechanism had detonated prematurely, less than a hundred feet below the B-29. The spent unit continued towards the ground.

Sweeney brought the aircraft under control and landed. Tibbets was waiting on the apron. He put into words the unspoken fear of them all.

'Let's hope that doesn't happen when we've got a real one on board.'

April 21, 1945
Hiroshima

The invitation to dinner with his commanding officer, Colonel Hiroshi Abe, came as a pleasant surprise to Tatsuo Yokoyama. The anti-aircraft gunnery officer's relationship with Abe had until now been distant and formal.

Then, a week before, Abe had invited Yokoyama to dine at his home near Hiroshima Castle on Saturday night. There was one condition: an air raid would cancel the invitation. In the past weeks there had been a number of alerts. And, once, a stream of bombers had passed high over the city.

But since two bombs dropped on March 19, Hiroshima had remained free of attack.

After evening gunnery practice, Yokoyama dressed in his best uniform and told his sergeant where he could be reached.

The sergeant, the gun-post's gossip, smiled broadly and said he was sure Yokoyama's evening would be undisturbed.

'Why?'

'Because Truman's mother is a prisoner in Hiroshima!'

Yokoyama was astonished. Hiroshima was filled with the wildest of rumours nowadays. But this one was too far-fetched for anybody to take seriously.

The sergeant was insistent.

'She was on a visit to the city when war started. She has been here ever since!'

'Who told you this?'

The sergeant said he knew 'somebody' on Lieutenant-General Fujii's staff. Fujii was keeping Truman's mother in Hiroshima Castle as a hostage against air attack.

His common-sense told Yokoyama to dismiss the story, but increasingly the most outlandish tales turned out to be true. There had been the yarn about fifteen-year-old boys being taught to fly as kamikaze pilots in the Special Attack Corps. He had not believed that, until he had actually seen some of them at Hiroshima Airport. There was the tale that old women were being shown how to sharpen bamboo poles and use them like spears. That, too, he had discounted until he saw women practising in the grounds of East Training Field.

He made a note to check the Truman story with Colonel Abe.

Abe's house was a small, compact dwelling near the Castle. He was a widower and lived there with his daughter. Yokoyama was surprised to see he was the only guest; he began to wonder what lay behind the invitation.

Abe was a good host with a plentiful supply of drinks. Mellowed and relaxed, Yokoyama asked about President Truman's mother.

Abe laughed uproariously. He said he wished the story was true, then she could answer some questions about her son.

Lowering his voice, Abe told his guest still another story.

'Truman's mother is from Hiroshima! That is why we have not been bombed. She has told her son to spare this one city in all Japan.'

Yokoyama's good mood faded. He asked why, then, was Hiroshima being prepared for attack. What was the purpose of the fire-lanes?

Abe told him.

'It helps to create a mood of militancy. People who lose their homes will be ready to fight even harder for their lives, Japan and the Emperor!'

Yokoyama was not placated. He asked if this meant that, after all these months of practice, he and his men would have no chance to fight? If this was so, he would respectfully request a posting to Tokyo, or one of the other cities where air attacks were now frequent.

Abe calmed his guest and invited him to eat. Dinner was served by Abe's daughter, a plumpish, moon-faced girl in her late teens. After dishing up bowls of rice and slivers of meat and fish, she left the men to eat and talk.

Warmed sake made Yokoyama bold. He again brought up the question of a transfer.

His host looked at him carefully.

'I have not invited you here to discuss such matters, but rather something which is important to me.'

Yokoyama became respectful and silent as his host explained that he had long been impressed by the younger man's qualities. Abe revealed he had even made enquiries about Yokoyama's family background.

'It is very satisfactory. You have honourable parents.'

Knowing what was coming, for such enquiries could only mean one thing, Yokoyama waited.

Abe's next words were harsh and matter-of-fact; a businessman making an offer.

'Marry my daughter and your future will be assured. I will see to that.'

Yokoyama remembered the girl who had served dinner. She had cooked a tasty meal; he had already noticed she kept a spotless house.

Bowing gravely, Yokoyama promised his host to discuss the matter with his family. Such talks were essential before the proposed marriage could be formally contracted.

It would mean a trip home to Tokyo. Yokoyama found that prospect almost as exciting as the reason for making the journey.

April 23, 1945
USAAF Base
Wendover

Over the weekend, the 509th had made their usual journey in to Salt Lake City, and already the complaints were being received in the Duty Office.

Eatherly had set the pace by racing his roadster, hub-to-hub against that of his flight engineer, driving another super-charged automobile. They were off to chase girls. Eatherly had by now a deserved reputation for knowing more willing Utah girls than any other man on the base.

To add spice to their already hair-raising driving, they had passed a whisky bottle back and forth, from one car to the other, as they travelled at close to ninety miles an hour. The bottle was empty when they reached Salt Lake City. Like the rest of Eatherly's crew, the engineer thought the pilot 'a helluva guy'.

A number of fliers took rooms in the Hotel Utah and soon noisy parties were under way. A red-head was seen running naked down a hotel corridor, pursued by several pilots in their shorts.

The police were called—the first of several visits they made over the weekend.

Lewis got into a poker game, for once won a fistful of dollars, and announced he was going to have 'a great time'.

Nobody saw him do so. But on this Monday morning he told his bleary-eyed crew that he'd had a time he would never forget.

For different reasons the club owners, bar-tenders and hotel staffs would also remember the 509th's forty-eight-hour rampage through their establishments.

That morning the Salt Lake City police department were telephoning Wendover with a mounting list of breakages, assaults and traffic violations.

Tibbets managed once more to placate the civilian authorities. But the symptoms were clear: the 509th had reached breaking point.

The time had come to leave Wendover.

In Tibbets' mind, as well as this latest behaviour and his earlier concern about security leaks, there was another good reason for their departure. Recently, he had come to the conclusion that the scientists were 'tinkering' with the atomic bomb; they seemed 'more concerned with producing a *perfect* weapon instead of being satisfied with the one they had and using it to end the war. They wanted to improve the design, run more tests, make endless changes before they would let the bomb be used in combat'.

This had troubled Tibbets: he could imagine the physicists 'still tinkering' when the war was over—'and the whole damn thing would have been a waste of time'.

He made discreet enquiries. The 509th's base was reserved on Tinian. Weeks before, orders had been given that a ship should be standing by at Seattle to carry the ground echelon to the Pacific. All Tibbets had to do was telephone Washington, use the *Silverplate* code, 'and we could be in the war'.

The thought of seeing action again was an exhilarating one. But the prospect of what would happen to him if he actually ordered the 509th to be mobilised restrained Tibbets: 'Groves might have me stripped of my command, posted to Alaska, even sign court-marial papers.'

But Groves was also showing increasing signs of impatience with the scientists. And the special Target Committee which he had set up had not yet held its first meeting, let alone given him any recommendations to go on.

Impulsively, Tibbets asked the base telephone exchange to connect him with the Air Force Command Headquarters in Washington. Once plugged through to his liaison officer, his message was brief.

'This is *Silverplate*. We are ready to move.'

The matter was soon arranged. The Group's main ground echelon force would leave Wendover for embarkation at Seattle on May 6. The bomber crews would fly out to the Pacific later.

Soon afterwards Tibbets received a priority call from Washington, ordering him to fly there at once. His caller offered a gratuitous piece of news.

'Colonel, you're in big trouble with Gee-Gee.'

Gee-Gee was one of Groves' nicknames.

Tibbets arrived in Groves' office in the early evening.

'As I came through the door he erupted. Who the hell did I think I was, ordering my outfit overseas? For ten solid minutes he raked me over the coals, up one side and down the other, never repeating himself. I never had such a flaying. I had never seen him so mad. Then suddenly he stopped and gave me a big smile, and said "goddammit, you've got us moving! Now they can't stop us!" He was tickled to death I had done it. Without my planes, there was no way the scientists could keep tinkering with their toy.'

April 24, 1945
Osaka

Professor Tsunesaburo Asada's wife gracefully bowed to her husband as she boarded the train for Nara, bound, along with the families of other important Japanese scientists, for the comparative safety of the countryside. In the past fortnight, Osaka had been attacked three times by formations of B-29's; twenty percent of the city had been destroyed.

Mrs. Asada turned and bowed again from the train. Then she was lost behind the press of people crowding the windows to wave to loved ones on the platform.

Asada did not wait for the train to leave. He had work to do. His long period of research had begun to pay off. One of Japan's latest and most advanced long-range bombers, the *Ginga*, carrying a single 1,700-pound bomb, had flown to Saipan and attacked the main

American air base on the island. The bomb was fitted with Asada's proximity fuse, similar to the one which had exploded prematurely under Sweeney's bomber.

Asada's fuse had detonated its bomb exactly as planned, thirty-five feet above the Saipan airfield. It had caused considerable destruction. Scores of neatly parked B-29's were destroyed or damaged. The pilot of the *Ginga* reported to Asada that a large part of the air-base was 'an ocean of fire'. The photo-reconnaissance pictures showing the wrecked American planes reminded the scientists of similar ones taken at Hickam Field, Pearl Harbor. But it was a short-lived moment of triumph.

The air force could not repeat the attack because its base on Iwo Jima was now in American hands, and the round trip to Saipan from Japan was outside the 1,600-mile range of the *Ginga* bomber.

Nevertheless, Asada's proximity fuse had been proved a success. The Navy ordered 20,000 of them to be manufactured. Eventually 12,000 would be produced, many of them fitted to bombs and stored secretly on Kyushu awaiting an American invasion. When that came, it was planned that the bombs would be exploded at mast-height above the warships and troop-carrying landing craft so as to cause maximum casualties.

Asada was praised by senior naval officers for his invention. He was pleased, though secretly he thought some of the approbation was a well-meaning attempt to humour him. His Death Ray remained far from ready for use. But although it had not yet passed beyond the pig-stunning stage, he was still optimistic and spending most of his time on the project.

Meanwhile, the Navy now had another new weapon, potentially almost as lethal.

It was the brainchild of Dr. Sakyo Adachi, a scientific colleague of Asada's attached to the Naval Meteorological Department. Adachi had remembered what every Japanese high school pupil knew: although the great trade winds blow from east to west, from America to Japan, there is another wind, the Japan Current, which blows in the opposite direction. The rest was simple.

Adachi filled a balloon with gas and attached to it a small canister containing high explosive. The trial balloon-bomb was launched and tracked for some distance by a Zero fighter. It climbed steadily into the Japan Current and then headed eastwards on a journey which would take it across the Pacific, passing north of Hawaii, and eventually to the coast of the United States.

Other balloon-bombs followed.

Radar was not yet advanced enough to warn of their approach.

The Japanese, of course, did not know if the balloons had reached their target. But the Navy Chief of Staff, Admiral Toyoda, mindful of his promise to carry the war to the American shore, ordered full-scale production of the balloon-bombs.

Soon, all of America's West Coast cities would be targets. Given favourable weather conditions, the balloons might even reach Salt Lake City and Chicago.

In the coming weeks, some 6,000 balloon-bombs would be launched towards the United States. Of those that arrived most would fall in the deserts of California, Nevada and the forests of Oregon. It would never be officially revealed how many victims they claimed.

And nobody will ever know how many Japanese balloon-bombs still lie unexploded in remote areas of North America.

April 25, 1945
The White House
Washington, D.C.

On Truman's desk was a letter from Stimson. It had arrived the day before.

Dear Mr. President,

I think it very important that I should have a talk with you as soon as possible on a highly secret matter. I mentioned it to you shortly after you took office, but have not urged it since on account of the pressures you have been under. It, however has such a bearing on our present foreign relations and has such an effect upon all my thinking in this field that I think you ought to know about it without much further delay.

Truman had arranged an appointment for his Secretary of War at midday. The President would be happy to have any information which might help him keep the uppity Russians in their place. He had shown his mettle three days earlier when V. M. Molotov and Andrei Gromyko, en route for the opening session of the United Nations in San Francisco, had stopped at the White House. Truman told them the Soviet Union was going back on its Yalta agreements. His language was so blunt and without diplomatic euphemisms that Molotov bridled.

'I have never been talked to like this in my life.'

Truman's reply was crisp.

'Carry out your agreements and you won't get talked to like this.'

133

If Stimson was going to produce anything to make it easier to convince the Russians to play fair, then so much the better.

Promptly at noon, the Secretary of War arrived. Stimson said he was expecting one other person. Five minutes later Groves appeared. He had slipped in through 'the back door' to avoid arousing speculation among the pressmen stationed in and around the Executive Mansion.

Stimson said the meeting was to discuss details of a bomb equal in power to all the artillery used in both world wars.

Groves winced inwardly. He had earlier told Stimson not to lay too great an emphasis on the bomb's power; he did not want the new President to become alarmed at the sheer enormity of the weapon.

But Stimson was determined to lay out all the facts. He began to read from a prepared memorandum.

Within four months we shall in all probability have completed the most terrible weapon ever known in human history, one bomb of which could destroy a whole city.

Although we have shared its development with the United Kingdom, physically the U.S. is at present in the position of controlling the resources with which to construct and use it and no other nation could reach this position for some years. Nevertheless, it is practically certain that we could not remain in this position indefinitely.

Unlike Roosevelt, Truman enjoyed being read to, and Stimson had a mellifluous voice. In his opening statement, the Secretary had raised a vital consideration: America could not expect to retain its A-bomb monopoly.

Stimson explained that the theory behind the making of an atomic bomb was widely known. He went on to conjure up a nightmare which could come to pass.

We may see a time when such a weapon may be constructed in secret and used suddenly and effectively . . . With its aid, even a very powerful unsuspecting nation might be conquered within a very few days by a very much smaller one . . . The world in its present state of moral advancement compared with its technical development would be eventually at the mercy of such a weapon. In other words, modern civilisation might be completely destroyed.

Truman posed a question: was Stimson at least as concerned with the role of the atomic bomb in the shaping of history as with its capacity to shorten the war?

'I am, Mr. President.'

Both men were aware that while they were speaking the United

Nations was about to hold its opening session in San Francisco. Stimson had anticipated Truman raising this matter. He continued to read from his memo.

To approach any world peace organisation of any pattern now likely to be considered, without an appreciation by the leaders of our country of the power of this weapon, would seem to be unrealistic. No system of control heretofore considered would be adequate to control this menace. Both inside any particular country and between the nations of the world, the control of this weapon will undoubtedly be a matter of the greatest difficulty and would involve such thorough going rights of inspection and internal controls as we have never before contemplated.

Groves had never heard Stimson speak like this. For a moment he might have wondered whether the Secretary had been contaminated by his contact with all those 'longhairs' who had tried to make Groves' life such a misery these past months. Then, with a sense of relief, Groves heard what Stimson went on to say.

The Secretary stated that in spite of all he had said, he still favoured using the bomb against Japan; that, if it worked, it would probably shorten the war.

The meeting ended with Truman agreeing to the formation of a specialist panel, to be known as the Interim Committee, to draft essential post-war legislation and to advise Truman on all aspects of atomic energy.

Stimson agreed to be its chairman.

Groves left the White House and hurried back to his own office. There he dictated a memo 'to files', which reveals how well he too had learned the basic rule of survival in Washington: put it on paper.

The answers to the remainder of the questions [from Truman] were either considerably amplified by General Groves or were answered in their entirety by him ... The President did not show any concern over the amount of funds being spent but made it very definite that he was in entire agreement with the necessity for the project ... The Secretary [Stimson] stated that the entire work was under the charge of General Groves and expressed his entire confidence in him. The President replied that he had known General Groves for a number of years and had the highest regard for him.

Groves now felt he had the backing he needed. And if anything were to go wrong, he could at least say that the President had accepted the expenditure that those nosey Senators and Congressmen were still cavilling about.

Japan's former Naval Attaché in Germany, Commander Yoshiro Fujimura, was now one more escapee from Berlin. With the sound of Soviet gunfire ranging in on the German capital he had made his way to Switzerland. There an accommodating Swiss government had accredited him to the Japanese Legation in Berne; the city was already bulging with other Japanese diplomats who had fled from their Berlin Embassy.

In the ten days he had been in Switzerland, Fujimura had waited patiently for news of a hoped-for meeting. It was finally arranged for this lunchtime. To keep the appointment Fujimura was dressed in his one suit, an ill-fitting dark serge. He hoped his guests would understand he had had to leave most of his wardrobe in Berlin.

By contrast, his companion, the German Dr. Friedrich Hack, Japan's purchasing agent in Europe, was immaculate in fashionable tweeds and trilby hat.

The pair had come to the small restaurant at the foot of the Jungfrau to meet members of Dulles' OSS.

Promptly at one o'clock two Americans joined them on the restaurant's balcony. They introduced themselves as Mr. Blum and Mr. White. For a while they all stood talking politely about the weather and the view.

Then Fujimura suggested it was time to eat; Hack said he could recommend the cheese fondue. They all went inside and sat at a corner table. The dirndled waitress regretted that the fondue was off; they settled for veal steaks and shared a bottle of wine.

Conversation was stilted. The Americans waited for the Japanese to make some revealing disclosure; Fujimura felt he was being scrutinised.

The war was not mentioned.

The meal over, Mr. Blum and Mr. White shook hands with their hosts and left without any indication of what might happen next.

Fujimura's mood slumped. Hack also was disappointed; he, too, had hoped the Americans would be more forthcoming.

The downcast couple stepped out into the afternoon sun. So engrossed were they with their thoughts that they failed to notice Lieutenant-General Seigo Okamoto, Arisue's man in Switzerland, who had witnessed the meeting. He immediately reported it to Tokyo.

April 28, 1945
Hiroshima

When Yokoyama reached Hiroshima Airport, he found the Army transport he planned to take to Tokyo had left early.

It worried Yokoyama that he had missed the flight. He knew how much trouble his commanding officer, Colonel Abe, had gone to, to get him a seat on the plane. It was his suggestion that Yokoyama should fly to Tokyo to see his parents and discuss with them the idea of marrying Abe's daughter.

Yokoyama tried to hitch a lift on the next transport to the capital. He was told to wait. He sat on the ground outside the Operations Room and waited for his name to be called. In the meantime there was much to see.

Hiroshima's busy airport was being extended. It was too small to cater for the growing demands of the military. Now it was crammed with their aircraft. Yokoyama watched a transport taxi to its parking place. From a nearby hut a group of youngsters filed out to the plane in their cut-down coveralls.

Waiting to greet them was a handsome young flying officer, 2nd Lieutenant Matsuo Yasuzawa, one of the Air Force's most experienced instructors. Nowadays every pilot Yasuzawa trained was meant to be a kamikaze. These were his latest intake. Their average age was sixteen.

Yasuzawa was flying them to an airfield about a hundred miles from Hiroshima, on Kyushu, where they would receive their final training. Afterwards, they would leave on their suicidal missions to Okinawa, where this first month since the American invasion nearly a thousand kamikaze pilots had died. They had sunk or damaged over one hundred American ships. The fight for the control of the sixty-mile-long island was fierce and unremitting.

Second Lieutenant Yasuzawa realised how important holding Okinawa was to Japan. He hated having to remain behind as an instructor. He had recently been stopped by a senior officer just as he was about to take off in a training plane with the intention of ramming a B-29 that was bombing his airfield. Yasuzawa was considered too valuable to lose: apart from instructing experienced pilots how to fly more advanced aircraft, Yasuzawa had the ability to take a raw recruit and teach him the rudiments of flying in ten days. But the kamikaze pilots were being given only ten hours' tuition. They barely knew how to fly. To make sure they did not lose their nerve at the last moment, the cockpits of their suicide craft were sometimes screwed down shortly before take-off. Once they were airborne, the young pilots had no alternative but to die.

Today, as he settled himself at the controls of his well-used transport, Yasuzawa felt he would end the war like this: preparing schoolboys for combat while never experiencing it himself. Yet, in little over three months, at this very airport, he would undergo an experience more incredible than any either he or his pupils could possibly imagine.

Soon after Yasuzawa's transport trundled into the air, Yokoyama watched a Navy fighter-bomber land and taxi towards the Communications Room. Officers ran to meet it.

Out of the cockpit climbed an immaculate figure in spotless white naval uniform. Yokoyama recognised the flier. It was Captain Mitsuo Fuchida, the pilot who had led the raid on Pearl Harbor and was now the Imperial Navy's Operations Officer.

Listening to the respectful greetings of the other officers, Yokoyama gathered that Fuchida was in Hiroshima to attend one of the regular Army–Navy liaison conferences.

Yokoyama bowed deeply as Fuchida walked briskly past him. The flying ace did not return the greeting. Yokoyama doubted whether Fuchida even noticed him.

Shortly afterwards an officer told Yokoyama there would be no seat available for him that day to Tokyo. He left the airport, his mind still filled with the image of Fuchida. It would be something to cheer him on the long journey to the capital he now faced by train.

Across the city, in their Hiroshima home, Mayor Senkichi Awaya listened sympathetically as his wife and eldest boy told of the rigours of their night-long train journey from Tokyo. Several times the blacked-out train had been forced to stop until American bombers passed.

Although Mrs. Awaya had agreed to bring their son to Hiroshima weeks before, only recently had it become convenient to transfer him from his school in Tokyo to the one attached to Hiroshima University. They had decided the other three children would remain in the capital. Their eldest daughter was married and living in Kobe.

The mayor's secretary, the devoted Maruyama, sought to reassure Mrs. Awaya.

'They will all be safe as long as they stay out of the centre of the cities. And here you will be safe. Hiroshima is not a large city. They will bomb other places first. By the time it is our turn to be attacked the war will be over.'

The train carrying Yokoyama to Tokyo left at four p.m. Six months had passed since he last made the journey. Nothing had prepared him for the changes he now saw: city after city bore the marks of incendiary bombing. As he came closer to Tokyo, even the darkness could not conceal the destruction.

The capital was in an advanced state of devastation. Whole sections of the city's centre were levelled.

Leaving the Shimbashi railway station, Yokoyama set out to walk to the southern suburbs where his parents lived. His route took him past the Imperial Hotel. Built by the brilliant American architect Frank Lloyd Wright, the Imperial had survived the great Tokyo earthquake of 1923. Now it was a gutted ruin.

Further on, the Ginza—the business and night-life heart of Tokyo —was a scorched wasteland of ashes and craters.

Yokoyama could 'taste defeat' all around him.

He realised that he had been misled: in Hiroshima the newspapers and radio had given no inkling of the scale of the destruction in Tokyo. Worse, for the first time he felt he had been betrayed by the Army. His superior officers had lied to him. He could now see clear evidence that Japan was incapable of winning the war.

As he walked southwards, past the shanty towns of refugees, the situation gradually improved. Many of the concrete shells of buildings were being used as shops and beer halls. Men queued to get a drink.

Eventually he reached his parents' home. The house was intact, but Yokoyama wondered how long it would remain so. The American bombers seemed intent on working their way outwards until all of Tokyo was destroyed. Wearily, he entered the house, convinced that Japan must make peace or face extinction.

His parents were waiting for him. After they had made him comfortable he told them the purpose of his visit, explaining about Abe's marriage proposal. Yokoyama described what little he knew of his commander and his daughter. His parents listened gravely. Finally, Yokoyama's father spoke. Normally a marriage joining two military families was a desirable thing. But these were not normal times; values were changing. Nobody could be sure what the future attitude of people would be towards members of the armed forces. To have been in the Army might be a disadvantage. To be married to the daughter of a senior officer could even be a liability.

Yokoyama's parents would promise no more than to consider the matter further after they had made the necessary enquiries about Colonel Abe's antecedents.

April 29, 1945
USAAF Base
Wendover

Painfully aware of his age and his shyness, nineteen-year-old radio-man Richard Nelson tried to remember all their names as Lewis introduced him to the rest of the crew.

Nelson had never met an officer like Lewis; the pilot was behaving as if there was no gap in rank between him and the radio-man's buck private stripe.

After his introductions Lewis addressed the crew.

'Dick's our new radio-man. He and the rest of you are gonna get along fine. Just because he looks like a high school kid, don't be fooled!'

Lewis turned to the blushing Nelson.

'Dick, you did your basic training in Texas. Right?'

Nelson nodded.

'You wanted to be a pilot. Right. Well, we can't all be pilots. So you washed out on a physical. Eyes. Right?'

'I read too much.'

'Okay. I don't mind if you read as long as you do your job. You went to radio school where?'

'At Clovis in New Mexico.'

'Right. You sure must be good at your job. Only the best come here. And you'll hear a lotta reasons why we're all here. Forget them. We're here to win the war. You've just joined the crew that's gonna do it. Right, fellas?'

The crew chanted a familiar reply.

'Right, Cap'n.'

'Okay, let's go.'

Shoving his battered flying cap further back on his head, Lewis, looking to Nelson like a diehard combat veteran, led the way to the B-29.

Another long day of practice was beginning.

The radio operator, Sergeant Joe Stiborik, pulled the peak of his ski-cap over his eyes. Caron, the tail-gunner, tilted his brim upwards.

Nelson thought to himself that his new companions behaved as if they were actors on one of the Hollywood lots near his home in Los Angeles.

It was left to Duzenbury to remind the radio-man that this was not a film set.

'Listen, son, Cap'n Lewis runs an easy ship—if you do your job. But make a mistake and he'll come down on you like a load of concrete.'

Caron added a final warning.

'Yeah, and then he'll let you set in the stuff and dump you in the nearest ocean!'

To Nelson, Lewis sounded tougher than a combination of Errol Flynn, Alan Ladd and William Bendix.

Claude Eatherly had also established his image among his crew as a tough-talking, hard-drinking, girl-chasing gambler who would wager odds on anything.

He continued to romance about his background and war record.

He was a man, in Uanna's words to Tibbets, 'with a problem'. The security officer again urged that Eatherly should be transferred.

But Tibbets stubbornly refused, for once, to listen to Uanna. He insisted Eatherly's fine flying record was all that mattered.

Uanna never again raised the matter. And Eatherly continued to weave his fantasies.

April 30, 1945
Kure

Shortly after dawn the wife of Submarine Commander Mochitsura Hashimoto tried to arouse her husband. An air raid alert had just sounded and it was time for the family to go to the shelter.

Cradling her three small sons in her arms, Hashimoto's wife called with increasing urgency for her husband to wake-up.

Hashimoto continued to sleep. Nothing short of an earthquake would awaken him after his last, traumatic voyage.

On April 2, the day after the Americans had first landed on Okinawa, Hashimoto was ordered to attack enemy shipping in the area. The outward journey had been a foretaste of what lay ahead. American bombers had mined the coastal waters of the Inland Sea, making it hazardous even before reaching the waters of the Pacific. And when Hashimoto finally arrived off Okinawa, he was promptly bombed by American planes. During the seven days he remained near the island, he was attacked no less than fifty times. The longest period he could allow on the surface was a scant four hours in the middle of the night, barely enough to ventilate the boat and recharge its batteries.

Hashimoto had just missed seeing an American cruiser limping from the scene of battle. It was the *Indianapolis*, returning to San Francisco for repairs, after having been badly mauled by a kamikaze. When she next returned to the Pacific, the *Indianapolis* would be on a mission which would forever bind the Manhattan Project and Commander Hashimoto to each other.

At Okinawa, submarine I.58, like the *Indianapolis*, took a beating. Even so, Hashimoto was furious when he was ordered back to base. Only when he reached Kure on April 29, had he learned that his boat was the sole Japanese submarine to return safely from Okinawa. He was also informed that I.58 would have to remain in dock for a major inspection.

Too tired really to care, Hashimoto had stumbled home to bed, giving firm instructions to his wife that nothing should be allowed to disturb him.

Now, all her urgent calling did not awaken him. Then she realised it was too late: the familiar drone of aircraft engines was overhead.

Kure Harbour held most of Japan's remaining warships. It was a priority target for American bombers which regularly attacked the area in spite of its well-entrenched defences.

This morning the bark of anti-aircraft fire mingled again with the noise of exploding bombs.

Clutching her children, Mrs. Hashimoto lay down beside her still-slumbering husband and listened to the sounds of war.

Hiroshima

Just six air miles away, at precisely five minutes to seven, Dr. Kaoru Shima was awakened by a five-hundred-pound bomb exploding two streets away from his clinic. It had fallen on the Nomura Life Insurance Building. By the time the doctor had leapt out of bed and rushed to the window, nine other bombs had fallen in a ragged line across the city, killing ten people, injuring another thirty and damaging twenty-four buildings.

So swift and unexpected was the attack that no warning had been broadcast over the local radio, and no anti-aircraft fire directed against the lone B-29 which had dropped the bombs.

Dr. Shima rushed to reassure his patients and staff. Next, he made several telephone calls to Hiroshima Castle. He then waited until the usual morning staff meeting before speaking further about the matter. Dr. Shima knew it was important not to disturb the normal routine of the clinic.

Sitting cross-legged on the floor, sipping tea, discussing case histories and further treatment, his calmness soothed his staff. It was only at the end of the meeting that he mentioned the bombing.

Though the Army had imposed a news black-out about the attack, Dr. Shima had discovered that the city's military leaders believed the raid was a fluke.

He explained their view to the staff: the enemy would not have sent a solitary bomber half-way across the Pacific simply to drop a few bombs on Hiroshima. The B-29 had doubtless become separated from a larger force, missed its original target, probably Kure, and simply scattered its bombs on the nearest available city, which unhappily for them happened to be Hiroshima.

The staff were not altogether reassured by this explanation. One raised the perpetual fear that the bombers would return in force.

Dr. Shima knew that the city's good fortune in so far escaping mass air attack had increased the expectation of such a calamity occurring, among many of its people. Some actually experienced 'premonitions', which he recognised were partly psychic in origin; Dr. Shima knew that, by 'imagining the worst', people felt they could actually ward off disaster.

He himself was a fatalist, believing that, whatever lay ahead, nothing he could do would alter matters.

He now offered his staff a simple reaffirmation of his beliefs.

'If we are attacked tonight, or some time in the future, we can do nothing to prevent it. What we can do is to remain calm and cheerful and set an example to our patients.'

The staff were moved by his words. Some of the nurses were close to tears as they returned to work.

Alone in his office that night Dr. Shima did something that an increasing number of Japanese were doing. He tuned his radio to receive the short-wave transmission relayed directly from Guam, bringing, in impeccable Japanese, news of the war that Japan Radio could never broadcast.

The penalty for listening to such enemy broadcasts was death. But for men like Dr. Shima, who had come increasingly to distrust the claims of continuing victories made by Japan Radio, the risks were worthwhile.

Radio Guam had been first with the news that Iwo Jima had fallen; this morning, the modulated voice of the unknown Japanese–American speaking from 1,500 miles away, told of the terrible losses the Japanese were experiencing on Okinawa. Then the broadcaster dealt with the latest raids on Tokyo and other cities. He warned that Japan would be razed to the ground unless it surrendered.

The broadcast left Dr. Shima with a feeling of acute despair. He re-tuned the radio dial to the local station, switched off and left his office to go home to bed.

May 8, 1945
The White House
Washington, D.C.

Precisely at 9 a.m. this Tuesday morning, President Truman broadcast live to the American nation. In London, and Moscow, Churchill and Stalin gave their people the news at the same time.

The President's opening words were almost the only ones anybody would remember.

'The Allied armies, through sacrifice and devotion and with God's help . . .'

Victory in Europe was a fact.

Truman's words, delivered on this, his sixty-first birthday, confirmed what every American wanted to hear: Germany had surrendered unconditionally. For the first time in modern history, the entire armed forces of a nation became prisoners of war.

In the national rejoicing for VE Day, most ordinary Americans for the moment forgot Japan.

Truman could not. In the twenty-four days he had been President, he had thoroughly briefed himself on his predecessor's position vis à vis a Japanese surrender. Truman had come to the same conclusion: just as with Germany, only unconditional surrender was acceptable for Japan. Pearl Harbor and Japanese atrocities, particularly against American prisoners of war, made such an uncompromising attitude virtually inevitable.

However, inside the State Department, some officials were arguing that the American Government should modify this position, and that a way should be found to make peace with Japan before the Russians intervened and established a Soviet influence in the Pacific. Opposing this pragmatic view were those who felt that any leniency was unwarranted and would allow the Japanese militarists to survive, an unthinkable proposition.

While this internal debate continued, U.S. monitors listening to Japan Radio had picked up a report of a recent statement by Suzuki, the new Prime Minister of Japan. Having been secretly charged by the Emperor to bring an end to the war, astonishingly, Suzuki had then delivered a militant speech to the Diet, telling them that unconditional surrender was totally unacceptable: peace under such terms would spell the end of Japan and her Imperial system; Japan must fight to the very end.

Suzuki had also made a passionate appeal to the people:

Should my services be rewarded by death, I expect the hundred million people of this glorious Empire to swell forward over my prostrate body and form themselves into a shield to protect the Emperor and this Imperial land from the invader.

This morning Truman was ready to answer Suzuki's histrionic rhetoric. It would be his first public pronouncement on Japan since becoming President. Truman's mood was grim as he read to the assembled news and radio reporters in his White House office his prepared statement.

The Japanese people have felt the weight of our land, air and naval attacks. So long as their leaders and the armed forces continue the war, the striking power and intensity of our blows will steadily increase, and will bring utter destruction to Japan's industrial war production, to its shipping and to everything that supports its military activity.

The longer the war lasts, the greater will be the suffering and hardships which the people of Japan will undergo—all in vain. Our blows will not cease until the Japanese military and naval forces lay down their arms in unconditional surrender.

Just what does the unconditional surrender of the armed forces of Japan mean for the Japanese people? It means the end of the war. It means the termination of the influence of the military leaders who brought Japan to the present brink of disaster. It means provision for the return of soldiers and sailors to their families, their farms and their jobs. And it means not prolonging the present agony and suffering of the Japanese in the vain hope of victory. Unconditional surrender does not mean the extermination or enslavement of the Japanese people.

It was a clear statement of the American Government's position: surrender unconditionally or face Armageddon. Short-wave broadcasts beamed it to Japan.

The response was swift. Truman's warning was dismissed as propaganda. Radio Japan repeated the nation's determination to fight on.

Truman could only reflect: they have been warned.

May 9, 1945
Omaha, Nebraska

Outside Omaha, covering hundreds of acres of magnificent Nebraska countryside, the Martin aircraft plant was patrolled almost as securely as Wendover air base.

Flying low over the plant, Tibbets glimpsed the guards at the main gate and the men patrolling the high fence which surrounded the area.

He landed and taxied his transport to the aircraft reception area, passing several B-29's being towed out of the assembly sheds.

He was glad to see that here at least it was just another working day and that, unlike most of America, the aircraft workers had not taken time off to recover from their victory-in-Europe celebrations.

The night before, at Wendover, Tibbets had sipped a few soft drinks in the Officers' Mess and retired early. He had moved into the club after his wife and children vacated their house just outside the base gates; all the 509th's families had now departed in preparation for the Group moving to Tinian. Lucie Tibbets and the boys had gone home to her parents. Tibbets, caught up in an ever-increasing merry-go-round of flying between Wendover, Washington and Albuquerque, the nearest landing point to Los Alamos, felt it was 'best' that his family was away. He was being driven hard; his mind was a whirl of conferences and high-level telephone conversations, often conducted in code with Groves. He was having to cope with the strain of running a complex organisation in which he was the only one who knew 'the precise details of the end product'. Every problem ultimately ended up on his desk; every hour he had to make decisions, whether they involved flying-fitness reports, engine reports, bombing reports, security reports or sickness reports. His life, he felt, was 'just one damn report after another'.

Lucie had written to say that she and the children had settled in 'just fine' with her mother. Tibbets was pleased, but had been too busy to reply. He hoped his wife would understand. Anyway she, better than anybody, knew how much he disliked writing.

Without his wife to provide a few home comforts, life at Wendover was even emptier for Tibbets. The departure of the 800-strong main ground echelon for Tinian two weeks before had left the base 'like a ghost town'.

Tibbets was glad of an excuse to get away and come to Omaha 'to do a little shopping'.

At the aircraft reception area he presented his ID card to a waiting manager and was taken to a long cavernous building. There his credentials were checked again. Nobody without proper authority was admitted.

Silverplate ensured that Tibbets was going to be able to do something few other fliers in the American Air Force could: he was going to choose his own personal B-29, the one he intended to use on the first atomic mission.

The senior assembly line foreman escorted Tibbets down the production line. Regularly, they paused to clamber up the scaffolding

146

to look at a bomber. Once, Tibbets turned to the foreman and said the B-29 they were inspecting looked fine.

The foreman shook his head.

'First shift.'

'First shift' signified a bomber whose assembly had been started by a shift which had just returned to work after its days off, by men who were still recovering from two days' drinking and parties or just plain relaxing. They were not quite at their best; they sometimes produced a bomber 'where all the nuts and bolts haven't always been double-checked'.

Tibbets moved on.

The foreman stopped at another B-29. Gangs of riveters and fitters swarmed over the fuselage. They gave Tibbets a brief curious stare then continued their work.

Tibbets and the foreman climbed up to the cockpit. It was already fitted with its leather seats.

Tibbets sat down and looked out through the domed nose at the bustling factory floor.

The foreman's shout was reassuring.

'This is the one for you.'

The plane's assembly had been started by men who were working at their peak, where 'even the screws on the toilet seat were given an extra turn'.

The foreman told Tibbets this was the best plane in the factory.

His words sealed the transaction. Tibbets was now the future owner of a hand-picked B-29.

A delivery date was agreed upon. Tibbets told the foreman that he would send Lewis and his crew to collect the plane.

May 27, 1945
Berne
Switzerland

It was late morning when Hack's car reached the corner of Herren Street. The German stopped outside a fine old sandstone house. This was the OSS headquarters.

The last time Hack had come here, he had walked; now there was no time for such leisure. Events had reached crisis point since his previous visit on May 3 when he had delivered a message from the Japanese Naval Attaché, Fujimura, to their OSS contact Mr. Blum. The note had enquired what would be 'American opinions' on 'direct negotiations' with Japan. Although the note contained no suggestion of surrender, Blum nevertheless thought the matter was worth pursuing. He had told Hack he was prepared to continue the dialogue, provided it was based on 'official instructions' from Japan.

That had worried Hack. He knew the Naval Attaché had until then acted without the authority of the Navy Ministry in Tokyo. Hack was even more concerned when he learned that Fujimura had subsequently sent a coded cable to the Chief of Staff, Toyoda, in which the Naval Attaché had clearly hinted that it was the OSS, not he, who had made the first approach.

Hack realised that Fujimura could hardly have admitted to his superiors that he had acted without their knowledge. But he also recognised there was a danger in lying about who had made the first contact. Hack's fears had been realised. Toyoda's coded reply warned Fujimura that while 'the principal points of your negotiations with the OSS are fully understood, there are certain parts which are indicative of an enemy plot. Therefore we advise you to be very cautious'.

The warning horrified Fujimura and Hack. They suspected, correctly, that the Americans in Herren Street would have obtained a copy and decoded the cable—and would now know the prevailing view in Tokyo.

For six days the two men had pondered their next move. Fujimura contemplated travelling to Japan to urge his superiors to stop being suspicious. Hack talked him out of a pointless journey. Instead, he suggested that he call on the OSS again and tell them frankly that the delicate link with Tokyo was in danger of being broken. Fujimura agreed.

After parking his car, Hack rang the doorbell of the OSS house, was admitted, and shown into a small waiting-room.

Blum arrived and listened politely as Hack explained Tokyo's fears of a plot. He assured his visitor there was no such scheme afoot.

Blum was a student of history. He anticipated that, with the surrender of Germany, the Russians would be anxious to establish their influence in the Pacific. The Soviet promise to declare war on Japan in early August at the latest, agreed upon at Yalta, was in Blum's view little more than a Communist attempt to penetrate the Far East.

Consequently, he was prepared to offer more than coffee and sympathy to Hack. Acting on coded instructions received from Washington, Blum made a remarkable proposal.

'My Government is fully aware of the situation in Tokyo. The United States believes that the only way satisfactorily to take matters further is for Japan to send a ranking statesman, general or admiral to Berne for discussions. I am authorised to say that the United

States will guarantee the air transportation from Japan to this country.'

Hack was delighted. He drove back to the Japanese Legation to tell Fujimura the news. The Attaché immediately cabled the proposal to Tokyo. He ended his message with a realistic assessment.

'In the light of our present plight, can the Navy Minister see any other course than peace with the United States?'

May 28, 1945
The Pentagon
Washington, D.C.

There was one vacant seat at the long conference table. It was next to where Tibbets sat. Senior Naval and Army officials, and scientists from the Manhattan Project, looked pointedly at the empty space. Tibbets stared back impassively. Inwardly, he was seething. Inexplicably, Beser had failed to show up for this important Target Committee meeting.

The previous meeting, on May 12, had clarified many operational details: the proximity fuses on the atomic bomb would probably be set to detonate about 2,000 feet above ground; if the weather over the target made it impossible to bomb visually, the weapon should be brought back, 'this operation inevitably involving some risks to the base and other aircraft'; if for any reason it was found necessary to jettison the bomb, care must be taken that this was not done in water near American-held territory, since 'water leaking into the gun-type bomb will set off a nuclear reaction'.

The May 12 meeting also discussed specific targets. The Emperor's Palace in Tokyo had been considered, but was not recommended. However, the committee members 'agreed we should obtain information from which we could determine the effectiveness of our weapon against this target'.

Finally, the meeting had earmarked four cities for possible atomic attack. They were, in order of preference, Kyoto, Hiroshima, Yokohama and Kokura. All four cities had been 'reserved'; bombing of them by conventional weapons was henceforth prohibited. Now, at this third meeting of the Target Committee, these and other targets were to be further considered.

Promptly at nine o'clock, Groves took his place at the far end of the room. The meeting opened with an aide handing out target description files. Each contained large-scale maps, reconnaissance photographs and related data; as the meeting was also to review air-sea rescue procedures and navigational aids, maps of the Pacific and Japanese coastal waters were distributed.

Tibbets had wanted Beser to be present specifically to answer any questions about radar. He had allowed him to fly to Washington in advance so that the radar officer could visit his parents in Baltimore over the weekend. Beser had promised to meet Tibbets outside the conference room before the meeting began, but there was no sign of him.

Beser arrived after an MP had closed the doors to Conference Room 4E200 and posted himself outside.

The WAC officer at the reception desk near the MP eyed Beser suspiciously.

'Are you lost, lieutenant?'

'Not if this is the Pentagon, ma'am.'

She ignored his cheerful flippancy.

'This is a restricted area, lieutenant.'

'I know. And I'm late!'

Beser turned towards the guarded door. The MP stiffened. The WAC raised her voice.

'You can't go in there!'

Beser turned.

'Ma'am, if this is the Target Committee meeting, they're expecting me!'

'You want me to believe a *lieutenant* is expected in *there*, with all *that* top brass!'

'Yes, ma'am.'

'Lieutenant, why don't you go and get a coffee and forget you even walked in here.'

'Ma'am, you're making a heck of a mistake . . .'

'Lieutenant. Go!'

'Yes, ma'am!'

Beser left and waited outside the reception area. Thirty minutes later he was still there when he heard a whispered conversation going on behind him. He turned to see an angry major towering over the WAC. The door of the conference room was ajar. The major spotted Beser.

'Are you Beser?'

'Yes, sir.'

'Goddam, you should have been inside!'

'I know. Somebody should have told this lady that.'

'They're waiting for you to answer a question! Get in there!'

Beser strolled as nonchalantly as he could into the conference room.

150

A Navy captain was addressing the gathering. He stopped in mid-sentence and glared at Beser.

Tibbets motioned for Beser to sit beside him. Beser began to whisper an explanation to Tibbets.

'First the train from Baltimore was late. Then I couldn't get a cab at Union Station, and finally this Wac . . .'

The captain interrupted Beser's soliloquy.

'If the lieutenant is quite ready to answer the question?'

Beser looked around helplessly.

Tibbets saved him from further embarrassment by re-stating the question.

'The matter is this. The Navy wants to place a submarine three miles off the Japanese coast and put out a Loran Beam for us to navigate by on our approach to the target. In the event of trouble the beam could also be used to guide us to the submarine for a possible sea rescue.'

Loran was a sophisticated radar development that both the Navy and Air Force had started using.

The captain spoke again to Beser.

'The question is, lieutenant, what are your views on this proposal?'

'It's bullshit!'

The captain gaped. Tibbets groaned. The rest of the room remained deathly quiet. From the top of the table Groves' voice filled the void.

'Why do you say that?'

'Sir, I don't believe you can hold a submarine that steady. The tides are going to pull it off track. The boat's going to be fighting the motion of the sea. The submarine must be on the surface for Loran to work. And in no way can it remain surfaced three miles off the Japanese coast without coming under attack.'

Groves' next words closed the matter.

'Those seem good enough reasons. Let's move to the next item on the agenda, the positioning of rescue aircraft . . .'

Beser turned to Tibbets and whispered anxiously.

'Was that all right?'

Tibbets mouthed a one-word reply.

'Bullseye!'

May 30, 1945
Hiroshima

Shortly before dawn, Major Awaya and his family, as well as many other households in the district, were awakened by the sound of trucks, loud knocking, and cries of fear. Then the lorries drove off.

The Kempei Tai, the dreaded Military Police, was continuing the round-up it had begun in early May of people suspected simply of voicing in private the opinion that the government should make peace.

Already, almost 400 prominent public figures had been arrested in Hiroshima in the past fortnight. They included a high-court judge and a former ambassador, Shigeru Yoshida, who would one day become Prime Minister. But this morning Yoshida was detained in the city jail, accused of being a dangerous pacifist.

The Kempei Tai in Hiroshima, as elsewhere in Japan, had begun arresting all suspected radicals following the short-wave broadcast from Washington to Japan on May 8, in which Truman had bluntly spelled out there could be no conditions attached to any Japanese peace proposal. Only unconditional surrender was acceptable.

Since then, the American broadcasts had been a constant reminder to those in Japan who dared risk their lives listening, that the truth lay other than as broadcast by Japan Radio.

Many of the American broadcasts were made by Captain Ellis Zacharias, USN, speaking in fluent Japanese. His voice was becoming as familiar to some Japanese as was that of Tokyo Rose's to American servicemen in the Pacific.

Few of his listeners suspected that Zacharias' words were being carefully studied by government officials in Tokyo for a sign that the United States might, after all, change its mind about unconditional surrender.

To the bulk of his listeners Zacharias was simply an astonishingly well-informed foreigner with a rare understanding of how the Japanese thought and expressed themselves. He did not threaten or bluster; he simply presented the inescapable facts.

In Hiroshima, the Kempei Tai had carried out their customary pre-dawn arrest of those even remotely suspected of sympathising with Zacharias' reasoned argument that, unless Japan surrendered, it was only a matter of time before its cities were totally destroyed.

Operating from its headquarters in the grounds of Hiroshima Castle, the 800-strong Kempei Tai unit had full powers of arrest over every civilian and soldier in the city.

The interrogators were provided with an official manual, entitled *Notes For the Interrogation of Prisoners of War*, which contained specific instructions on how to apply a variety of tortures to the body and mind.

The Kempei Tai in Hiroshima were able to perfect their techniques on local civilians whom they had arrested. But what the interrogators hoped for were American prisoners. All units in the area had been told that if any enemy fliers were shot down they must immediately be delivered to Kempei Tai headquarters.

152

For two days, in the closest secrecy, some of the best civilian, scientific and military brains in the United States had met to consider the future of the atomic bomb.

The Interim Committee, under the watchful eye of Secretary of War Stimson, was holding the fourth and, as it was turning out, its most crucial meeting in a month.

For this meeting, the Committee's distinguished scientific panel was also present. Not only did this panel advise the Committee, it also acted as a conduit for the ideas of other scientists: this was a move to reassure the laboratories that the views of none of the physicists and chemists were being overlooked. It was hoped by this means to put an end to attempts by scientists like Niels Bohr and Leo Szilard to make independent representations to the President. In Groves' words, 'it kept things in their proper channels'.

The scientific panel consisted of Robert Oppenheimer, Enrico Fermi, Ernest O. Lawrence and Arthur Compton. Apart from Oppenheimer, all were Nobel Prize winners; apart from Fermi, all had a highly-attuned interest in the ethical and political questions surrounding the use of the bomb.

The Committee's discussions had continued well into this first day of June. Like Stimson, its members were men used to getting quickly to the kernel, and their questions were sharp and penetrating.

Oppenheimer and his colleagues answered fully and frankly.

The Committee listened intently as the Manhattan Project's scientific director revealed details of both types of bomb, the uranium gun-type weapon and the plutonium bomb, which would undergo testing at Alamogordo in seven weeks' time. Since each bomb was virtually hand-made, supplies were strictly limited, and it had been decided not to test the uranium bomb, as 'it is expected that it will work'.

The uranium bomb, like its sister, would achieve its principal effect by blast; that effect might be felt up to a mile or more away from the explosion.

In answer to another question, Oppenheimer stated that the bomb would be ideal for use against a concentration of troops or war plants, and that it might kill 'about 20,000 people'.

Shortly afterwards, the meeting adjourned for lunch. The eight members of the Interim Committee, together with the four-man scientific panel and General George C. Marshall and Groves, sat at various tables.

The physicist Arthur Compton found himself seated next to

Stimson. In the two days they had known each other, the scientist had become deeply impressed by the Secretary's vigour and vitality, and the masterful way in which Stimson had taken a long view of history, pointing out that 'atomic energy could not be considered simply in terms of military weapons, but must also be considered in terms of a new relationship of man to the universe'.

It was an argument that appealed to Compton. But what followed would forever remain a matter of dispute. No notes were taken of the lunch-time conversations; people were seated some feet apart; memories, at the best times not very reliable, would contradict each other on even small and unimportant details.

According to Compton, he asked Stimson 'whether it might be possible' to arrange a non-military demonstration of the atomic bomb, in such a manner that the Japanese would see the futility of continuing the war.

Others at the luncheon thought Stimson asked Compton whether such a demonstration 'might serve our purpose'.

Still others believe it was James F. Byrnes, present on the Interim Committee as President Truman's personal representative, who asked Lawrence for his opinion. Both Lawrence and Oppenheimer are credited with being sceptical about the suggestion.

Oppenheimer was said to have doubted 'whether any sufficiently startling demonstration could be devised that would convince the Japanese that they ought to throw in the sponge'. Byrnes, it was claimed, mentioned that 'the Japanese might bring American prisoners of war into the demonstration area'.

Nobody would later be able to swear who had said precisely what to whom or exactly what was said.

After lunch, and back in the conference room where notes were taken, the discussion continued. Stimson reportedly argued that 'nothing would have been more damaging to our effort to obtain surrender than a warning or a demonstration followed by a dud—and this was a real possibility. Furthermore, we had no bombs to waste. It was vital that a sufficient effect be quickly obtained with the few we had'.

Stimson was acutely aware that the ultimate responsibility rested with him for recommending to Truman whether and how the bomb should be used.

Privately, he had already made up his mind. He felt that 'to expect a genuine surrender from the Emperor and his military advisers, they must be administered a tremendous shock which would carry convincing proof of our power to destroy the Empire. Such an effective shock would save many times the number of lives, both American and Japanese, that it would cost'.

The Interim Committee came to the same conclusion. At the end of its deliberations, it offered three recommendations for the President about the first use of the atomic bomb:

It should be used as soon as possible;
It should be used on a military installation surrounded by houses or other buildings most susceptible to damage;
It should be used without explicit prior warning of the nature of the bomb.

June 12, 1945
Washington, D.C.

Around mid-morning Groves received a summons to see Stimson at the War Department. The Secretary's office adjoined the Chief of Staff General Marshall's, though it was larger and lined with shelves of books from Stimson's sizeable private library.

Simson's first question to Groves was casual enough. He politely asked for the names of the Japanese cities which had been reserved for possible atomic attack.

Groves hesitated. Only this very morning he had completed drafting a memo to Marshall. It was headed 'Atomic Fission Bombs', stamped Top Secret, and contained concise summaries of four targets: Kokura, Hiroshima, Niigata and Kyoto.

These were the latest revised recommendations of the Target Committee. In making that selection, the Committee had taken into account the 'psychological factors'; it was deemed desirable to make the first use of the bomb 'sufficiently spectacular for the importance of the weapon to be internationally recognised when publicity on it is released'.

Psychologically, Kyoto was seen as the best target: it had the 'advantage of the people being more highly intelligent and hence better able to appreciate the significance of the weapon'.

On the other hand, Hiroshima 'has the advantage of being such a size and with possible focussing from nearby mountains that a large fraction of the city may be destroyed'.

Groves still favoured Kyoto. Its intelligentsia would spread the word of the bomb's awesome power. Faced with such evidence, the Japanese Government would have to surrender.

Groves had always believed that bringing about that surrender was a military matter. He therefore told Stimson that he planned to submit the suggested target list to General Marshall the next day for approval.

155

'I wish to see it.'

Groves tried to conceal his alarm.

'I would rather not show you the report without having first discussed it with General Marshall, as this is a military operational matter.'

Stimson had spent thirty-five years in public service, most of it close to Presidents. He was not used to being opposed, though old age had taught him tolerance. He continued to extend it towards Groves.

'This is a question I am settling myself. Marshall is not making that decision. I would like to see the report.'

Groves continued to hedge.

'It's back in my office.'

'Then have it brought over.'

'It will take some time.'

Stimson's patience ran out. Fixing his eyes on Groves he made his point acidly clear.

'I have all morning. Use my telephone to get it over here right away.'

An unhappy Groves sent for the report. He could not imagine why the Secretary of War was being so awkward over a short-list of possible targets.

Stimson asked Groves to name them.

'The primary is Kyoto . . .'

'I will not approve that city.'

Groves was flabbergasted. What on earth could Stimson mean?

'Mr. Secretary, I suggest you will change your mind after you read the description of Kyoto and our reasons for considering it to be a desirable target.'

'I doubt it.'

Stimson explained something Groves had never seriously considered.

'Kyoto is an historical city, and one that is of great religious significance to the Japanese. I visited it when I was Governor-General of the Philippines and was very much impressed by its ancient culture.'

A messenger arrived with the target report. Groves launched into the arguments in favour of Kyoto: the city was filled with booming war plants; it was an ideal choice.

Stimson cut him short, called in Marshall and repeated his strong objections to Groves' proposal.

A discomfited Groves later produced the only detailed account of what followed.

Marshal did not express too positive an opinion, though he did not disagree with Mr. Stimson. It was my impression that he believed it did not make too much difference either way . . . Personally, I was very ill at ease about it and quite annoyed at the possibility that he might think I was short-cutting him on what was definitely a subject for his consideration. After some discussion, during which it was impossible for me discreetly to let General Marshall know how I had been trapped into by-passing him, the Secretary said that he stuck by his decision. In the course of our conversation, he gradually developed the view that the decision should be governed by the historical position that the United States would occupy after the war. He felt strongly that anything that would tend in any way to damage this position would be unfortunate. On the other hand, I particularly wanted Kyoto as a target because it was large enough in area for us to gain complete knowledge of the effects of an atomic bomb. Hiroshima was not nearly so satisfactory in this respect.

Still 'ill at ease and annoyed', Groves retreated to his office in Foggy Bottom. Despite Stimson's strictures, during the time ahead Groves would continue to press for Kyoto to be considered. Finally, Stimson would be forced to take the matter to Truman himself; Groves was told firmly that the President also opposed atombombing Kyoto.

Even so, Groves ensured that the city remained on the reserved list. Later he would claim, by a somewhat dubious twist of logic, that it was he who was responsible for actually saving the city: 'If we had not recommended Kyoto as an atomic target, it would not of course have been reserved and would most likely have been seriously damaged, if not destroyed before the war ended.'

June 14, 1945
Omaha, Nebraska

Cap tilted on the back of his head, hands on hips, Lewis looked at his crew and shook his head.

'You guys look like you haven't been outta the sack for a week!'

They all grinned knowingly. For the past seven days they had been waiting in Omaha to collect the new bomber. Ever since Tibbets had chosen the plane, it had been receiving 'special handling', and consequently there was a delay in turning it over to Lewis.

While waiting, some of the crew had picked up girls and held a succession of increasingly wild parties at a local hotel. One of the

157

men had shacked up with a married woman and they were caught in bed together by her husband. In the ensuing fight the police were called, and it had needed Lewis' considerable diplomacy to square matters. He had also placated irate motorists after another of the fliers 'bombed' passing cars with beer bottles from his bedroom window. When the hotel management complained, Lewis managed to persuade them to drop the matter.

Over the past months the pilot had become increasingly protective towards the crew. Within the group, the barriers of rank largely disappeared; there was an easy, first-name relationship between officers and enlisted men. Socially, Lewis spent a considerable time in the Enlisted Men's Club, removing his officer's jacket and often wearing one of Sergeant Joe Stiborik's instead. Stiborik was the crew's radar operator.

Nelson continued to find surprising the way Lewis treated him as an equal. Caron believed the pilot was trying to develop a close-knit inter-dependent unit 'who could rely on each other in combat'.

When flying, Lewis still did everything 'by the book'; he punished mistakes with a few choice words. But no outsider was allowed to criticise 'my crew'.

He told the men: 'You gotta problem, I'll sort it out.'

Before flying to Omaha, Sergeant Shumard, the tall soft-spoken assistant engineer, came to Lewis, visibly upset because one of the MP's at Wendover had shot and killed his red setter dog. Lewis' anger was awesome; he verbally flayed the MP. His reaction only increased the respect and affection the crew had for their unorthodox captain.

Equally, some of them resented the 'intrusion' of Ferebee and van Kirk, even Beser and Jeppson, and, on those rare days when he flew with them, Tibbets. On those occasions, Lewis was 'demoted' to co-pilot. Even then he tried to make it clear that it was 'his crew' which was flying the plane.

Caron, a wise and intuitive man, felt that Lewis and his 'over-possessiveness' could create a problem 'when the Colonel comes to fly the mission'. The tail-gunner had no doubt that it would be Tibbets who would command the first strike. He liked the days when Tibbets flew with them: 'He was just a gentleman, quiet and studious. Now Bob, he was a fine pilot, but he behaved like a cowboy.'

This morning at the Martin factory in Omaha, Lewis had only his 'regular crew' with him. It was a red-letter day for them all. With a good deal of joking and story-telling, they inspected their shiny new B-29. After pre-flight checking the plane thoroughly, Flight Engineer Duzenbury said he was satisfied. Lewis ordered the crew aboard, started engines and took off. He circled Omaha once, and then set course for Wendover. Over the intercom, he gave the crew a reminder.

'We gotta take good care of this ship. She's gonna drop the big one —and win the war!'

June 15, 1945
Berne
Switzerland

Fujimura and Hack's last chance to play a role in ending the war was crushed by a short cable sent from the Navy Minister in Tokyo. It ordered them to hand over all negotiations with the Americans to the Japanese Minister to Switzerland.

The two deduced, correctly, that in Tokyo the Naval Ministry, fearful of the military extremists now determined to fight to the death, had dumped the controversial question of negotiations on the Foreign Office.

The Navy had irrevocably broken its fragile link with the OSS, one which could conceivably have led to Truman.

But the way was now clear for Arisue's man, Lieutenant General Seigo Okamoto, to pursue his peace feelers.

June 18, 1945
The White House
Washington, D.C.

At 6.30 Harry Truman bounced out of bed for his regular early-morning foray on a refrigerator he had installed near the presidential bedroom.

Refreshed with chilled orange juice, he shaved and showered and dressed in the white shirt, bow-tie and double-breasted suit that he wore like a uniform. As Truman scorned the idea of a valet, nobody was on hand to smooth away any creases, real or imagined.

At seven o'clock precisely, as he did every morning, wet or fine, he stepped out of the White House for a brisk 120-paces-a-minute pre-breakfast stroll. A posse of secret servicemen and reporters fell in with the President.

Truman was his usual breezy self as the reporters asked a routine question: was anything big likely to break during the day?

His spectacles glinting in the warm morning sunshine, Truman gave a stock answer.

'Wait and see.'

He did not tell them about the crucial meeting he had scheduled in two hours time.

By 8.30 Truman was at his desk in the White House, going through his in-tray, initialling, ticking, correcting, rejecting, approving and occasionally adding a few extra words in the broad hand which was a throwback to his schooldays.

At 9.30 the Joint Chiefs of Staff arrived. With them came Stimson, his assistant, John J. McCloy, and other senior advisers.

For two days, on June 14 and 15, the Chiefs, the military heads of the armed forces, had been perfecting their invasion plans for Japan, code-named *Olympic* and *Coronet*.

Olympic called for an initial assault against southern Kyushu on November 1, 1945, with a force of 815,548 troops; *Coronet* was the plan for the invasion five months later, of Honshu in the Tokyo area, with a commitment there of a further 1,171,646 men.

Truman listened intently as General Marshall presented the case for invasion. A 'considerable discussion' followed on the expected casualty rate. Stimson, as usual, summed up the prospects in a few well-chosen phrases.

'A landing operation would be a very long, costly and arduous struggle on our part ... the terrain, much of which I have visited several times, has left the impression on my memory of being one which would be susceptible to a last-ditch defence.'

The possibility of a political settlement, after a warning to the Japanese, was raised by Stimson's assistant. McCloy believed there were many Japanese who did not favour the war, and, given the opportunity, their opinions might be influential.

The suggestion caught the meeting unawares.

Stimson agreed that Japan was 'not a nation composed of mad fanatics of an entirely different mentality from ours'. He also agreed that some sort of 'last-chance warning' should be given before the actual invasion, which made clear to the Japanese leaders that if they did not surrender, they would be responsible for what followed. Stimson was not yet sure whether or how this warning should be linked to the atomic bomb.

The Chiefs listened, but expressed no opinion about the atomic bomb—except that if it was used it should be dropped without prior notice. The matter was not pressed, for nobody in the room could yet know what the bomb would actually do. And nobody, in McCloy's words, could even be 'certain in spite of the assurances of the scientists that "the thing would go off"'.

Without positive proof of the weapon's viability, it was impossible

160

to plan a realistic strategy other than in terms of conventional warfare.

Truman reluctantly approved the invasion plans, aware that ultimately a million American lives could be lost as a result of his decision.

President Truman's concern about casualties would doubtless have been even greater had he known that Japanese Intelligence had already anticipated the American plans, and that at the very moment he was giving the go-ahead for the invasion of Kyushu, reinforcements were being rushed to that island.

Those forces, charged with repelling the Americans, now had their headquarters in Hiroshima.

June 19, 1945
Hiroshima

Shortly after dawn, a dull rumble awoke 2nd Lieutenant Tatsuo Yokoyama. The sound came from within Mount Futaba. Construction gangs were using compressor tools to burrow-out an underground communications complex inside the base of the hill.

Yokoyama's gun-post was immediately above the bunker, and it meant that he and his men lived from dawn to dusk with a juddering sound beneath their feet which reminded Yokoyama of the earth tremors he had often experienced in Tokyo.

The destruction he had witnessed on his last visit to that city, coupled with his parents' attitude towards the proposed marriage to his commanding officer's daughter, had left Yokoyama badly shaken. To make matters worse, he had been away during the second American air attack on Hiroshima. Nor was he consoled by Colonel Abe, his commander, saying that, with each day that passed, the chance of Yokoyama seeing action increased.

Abe was continuing to be solicitous, treating Yokoyama as if he were already a member of the family. But Yokoyama was not so sure. His mother had written a guarded letter saying his father was having to delve deeper into the girl's background. Until these enquiries were complete, she urged her son to limit his social contact with his commander.

Yokoyama found himself inventing excuses to turn down invitations to dine at Abe's home or visit him at the Officers' Mess in Hiroshima Castle.

The temptation to go was strong. Yokoyama would have given anything to escape the tedium of life on the gun-post.

Instead, he would spend this day, as he did all the others, drilling his men—and surveying through his binoculars the growing signs that Hiroshima was now the lynchpin in the defence of the whole of the western half of Japan. By road, rail and sea, in defiance of American bombers and submarines, men and supplies were pouring into the city. After further training and fitting out there, they were moved to their forward positions on Kyushu. But remaining in his command centre at Hiroshima, in charge of all troops in the west, was the man who had been chosen by his Emperor and the Imperial Army High Command to save Japan from defeat.

At the foot of Mount Futaba, not far from Yokoyama's protective anti-aircraft guns, Field Marshal Shunroku Hata, commander of the 2nd General Army, had set up his headquarters.

Hata was one of the most successful, famous and respected commanders in all Japan. He knew much better than most just how grave the situation was. He also knew that the mythology of Japan was filled with examples when the *shimpu*, the Divine Wind, had intervened to rescue it from the enemy. But Hata was more realistic than to rely on the *shimpu*; with his military forces increasing daily, he hoped to be able to turn back the foe which threatened to invade the nation he loved just as much as he did his wife and three sons.

Hata's entire life had prepared him well for this moment. He was one of the few Army commanders still close to the Emperor; in 1939 for three months he had been Hirohito's chief aide-de-camp. And his military experience was almost unequalled. From the time he had been wounded as a twenty-five-year-old officer in the Russo–Japanese war, through the period when he was Military Attaché to Germany and a delegate to the Paris Peace Conference, to 1939 when he was Japan's Minister of War, Hata's career was always distinguished.

In 1941, like a modern Genghis Khan, he had ruled over much of central China with more than 500,000 troops. While proclaiming that his policy was to 'defeat Chiang but love his people', Hata would later be accused of turning a blind eye to the repeated atrocities committed by troops under his command, both against the civilian population and American fliers who had the misfortune of falling into the hands of his soldiers. Nevertheless, for 'meritorious services' in China, Hata had in 1941 been decorated with the coveted first Class Order of the Golden Kite.

On his return to Japan in June 1944, he had been created Field Marshal. Six months later he was appointed Inspector General of Military Training, one of the highest posts in the Imperial Army.

Then, when Premier Koiso resigned, Tojo had emerged from the shadows to urge that Hata become Prime Minister.

Instead, on April 7, 1945, two days after Suzuki had been chosen, Hata was given a position perhaps as important. He was named head of the 2nd General Army and told that only he could save Japan from ignominious defeat. On April 9 Hata had travelled to his new headquarters in Hiroshima.

From then on, not only the city but the military fate of the nation lay in his hands.

His arrival in Hiroshima disturbed the officers in Hiroshima Castle. No longer were they the supreme authority in the city. Quiet-mannered but stern, Hata overawed them. The sixty-five-year-old Field Marshal had more experience of war than all of them put together. They were relieved when he decided to make his head-quarters about a mile from the Castle, at the foot of Mount Futaba.

Hata began to bring in men he had worked with before—and those whose reputations he had heard about.

By the middle of June, his headquarters staff of some 400 men included many of the best military brains in the country. Between them, they were planning to wage a war of attrition the like of which the world had never before witnessed.

Gradually, under Hata's command, the island of Kyushu was being turned into an armed fortress; from the Goto Islands in the north to the Osumi Peninsula in the south, a system of inter-locked defences was being erected. They stretched back from the coast, layer upon layer, devised to cause the maximum casualties to the enemy. Linking it all was a complicated communications network, controlled from Hiroshima and which ended at Hata's headquarters.

The city itself was a beehive of war industry; hardly a home was not involved in manufacturing parts for kamikaze planes and boats, for bombs, shell-casings, rifles and hand-guns.

Recently an order had been given to plaster the walls of the city with a new slogan

FORGET SELF!
ALL OUT FOR YOUR
COUNTRY!

Hata planned that, when invasion came, every man, woman and child in western Japan would carry a weapon.

He had authorised classes to train women and the elderly in the use of bamboo pikes; when the enemy came these civilians would throw them like spears at the advancing troops. Children were shown how to construct and hurl petrol bombs: enough bottles and fuel were being conserved to make over three million.

Even the infirm were mobilised. In Hiroshima the bed-ridden and

163

wheel-chair-bound were assembling booby traps, to be planted in the beaches of Kyushu.

For the main thrust against the invaders—an engagement now commonly referred to as 'the great climactic battle'—Hata had under his command some 400,000 men, many of whom were already in place on Kyushu. Minoru Genda, the architect of Pearl Harbor, had recently arrived there as commanding officer of a large, newly-formed fighter group. In addition, there were about 5,000 aircraft standing by, ready to be used as kamikazes.

In Hiroshima, 40,000 troops had their headquarters in the castle. Down by Hiroshima Harbor, at Ujina, a further 5,000 soldiers, mostly marines, were perfecting their own novel seaborne kamikaze tactics. Hundreds of small suicide craft, most the size of rowing boats, were being fitted with motors, filled with explosives and concealed in coves around the Bay. If an invasion force arrived, the boats would be brought out of hiding and each, manned by its crew of one, would be steered into a landing craft to blow up on impact.

Hata believed that, although it was impossible for Japan to defeat America, so also it could be made impossible for America to defeat Japan. He hoped that once the Americans sampled the welcome he was preparing, they would come to the negotiating table and drop their demand that Japan surrender unconditionally.

Preoccupied with building up the defence of Kyushu, the Field Marshal did not seriously consider that it might be Hiroshima itself which would be the first to be hit.

June 23, 1945
The Pentagon
Washington, D.C.

Tibbets looked down on Hiroshima.

Its rivers, bridges, harbor, the castle and adjoining military drill-fields were all clearly visible. So were the roads, the railway, warehouses, factories, barracks and private houses. Here and there the urbanisation was broken up by parks and woods. Beyond the city lay the hills, cocooning Hiroshima on three sides. They provided an almost perfect natural barrier to contain an atomic blast.

He noted the ground defences, an irregular chain of gun-posts stretching from Mount Futaba in the north-east to the harbour in the south.

Speaking quietly and authoritatively, using all his accumulated experience of bombing, Tibbets delivered his judgement on the suitability of Hiroshima as a target.

'The various waterways give ideal conditions. They allow for no chance of mistaking the city. Hiroshima can be approached from any direction for a perfect bombing run.'

His listeners silently considered this assessment.

Tibbets continued with his careful study, now turning to reconnaissance photographs of other Japanese cities spread out on the conference table in General Henry Arnold's office in the Pentagon.

This was the latest in a series of meetings which were settling the crucial details of how best to defeat Japan.

A few days before, LeMay had flown in specially from Guam to attend some of the meetings. He had come several thousand miles for a face-to-face talk with the Joint Chiefs of Staff, and with Groves.

LeMay, the arch apostle of low-level bombing, had already been told, on a fleeting visit Tibbets made to Guam earlier in June, that it would be too dangerous for the crew to drop an atomic bomb from below 25,000 feet. In Washington, Groves had spelled out to him the probable power of the bomb and the reason the potential targets had been chosen.

LeMay had barely reacted when Groves told him that the actual operation would be entirely under 'your control, subject of course to any limitations that might be placed upon [you] by instructions'.

Only Groves knew that those instructions would be so worded that effectual control of the operation would remain in the hands of the project chief.

LeMay had announced that he would want to carry out the bombing operation using a single unescorted plane, He pointed out that the Japanese were unlikely to pay any serious attention to a solitary aircraft flying at high altitude, and would probably assume it was either on a reconnaissance or weather mission.

Groves approved the idea. He did not tell LeMay that Tibbets had already come to a similar conclusion, and that the 509th's training had been devised with that plan in mind.

LeMay had returned to Guam believing he would soon be responsible for delivering a weapon in which he did not yet entirely have faith. Nor was he convinced that Tibbets and the 509th were the best choice for the mission. LeMay thought it might be preferable for one of his own Pacific combat-hardened veterans to do the job, a crew who had already proved their worth over the Empire.

The seeds of another conflict had been sown.

Completely unaware of this, Tibbets had flown from Wendover to Washington to attend this conference in Arnold's office. Having completed his evaluation of the reconnaissance photographs, he waited for questions from Groves and Arnold, Chief of the Air Force.

They did not come. The two men stared silently at the photographs, their eyes going first to the glossy, thirty-inch-square prints of Hiroshima, then to those of Niigata and Kokura, the two other targets now on the list of Japanese cities reserved for possible atomic attack.

Groves asked Tibbets how he would approach Hiroshima.

Using his hand to indicate a route across the photograph, Tibbets explained that he would begin his bombing run east of the city and approach Hiroshima at an angle of 90 degrees to the rivers dividing it. He pointed at a spot on the photograph close to Hiroshima Castle, where the River Ota segments into tributaries.

'Suppose that's the Aiming Point. Approached crossways, any one of the river banks would provide a handy reference point against which the bombardier could check his final calculations. If we flew up one of the rivers, the bombardier would be looking mainly at water through his bomb-sight. It would be harder for him to tell when he was close to the AP.'

Groves permitted himself a rare joke.

'Colonel, I think by the time your bombardier gets over the target he'll be able to spot it blind-folded.'

The men around the table sat down and discussion continued on other aspects of launching an atomic strike.

Groves was involving himself in such detailed discussions because he had come to believe that 'some of the Air Force people ... displayed a total lack of comprehension of what was involved. They had assumed that the atomic bomb would be handled like any other new weapon: that when it was ready for combat use, it would be turned over to the commander in the field, and though he might be given a list of recommended targets, he would have complete freedom of action in every respect'.

The chief of the Manhattan Project felt the matter was 'too complicated and all-important to be treated so casually'; that decisions about its use should be vested in him, though he did concede that 'the President would also share in the control, not so much by making original decisions as by approving or disapproving the plans made by the War Department'.

From the very beginning those plans had mainly been formulated by Groves and rubber-stamped, when required, by the War Department.

Watching Groves now, on the opposite side of the table, Tibbets was struck yet again that here was a man 'who would move hell on earth to get his own way'.

166

Tibbets had also worked out Groves' tactics: he 'didn't like a face-off, preferring to attack from the flank'.

Tibbets, on the other hand, believed in a frontal assault on any problem—or on any opposition. His mother had once told him to 'go and get what you want and don't mess'.

He thought that nowadays too much of his time was being consumed in 'messing; a lot of hours were being spent discussing imponderables'.

But one imponderable Tibbets thought well worth discussing was that of prevailing weather conditions which would be likely over the target.

Ever since April, Air Force meteorologists had been preparing summary charts of the conditions which could be expected in the coming months over Japan. The data was based on information provided by the U.S. Weather Bureau and old weather maps from the Marine Observatory at Kobe for the period 1927–1936.

The prognosis was poor. From June to September there were only a maximum of six days a month when cloudiness was likely to be 3/10 or less. For this period 8/10 cloud could be expected for at least eighteen days in any month.

Bombing by radar had been considered and rejected. After considerable study an expert had concluded:

It is apparently quite possible to completely misinterpret the images on the radar screen; a section of rural Japan could be mistaken for a city. With radar bombing and a good operator, the chance of placing the bomb within a given 1,000 feet circle is about 1% to 2%. This figure takes into account the fact that the probability of entirely missing the target area is from 70% to 50%.

By bombing visually, however, 'in clear weather the probability that a good bombardier can place the bomb within a given circle of 1,000 feet radius lies between 20% and 50%'.

Tibbets knew his own bombardiers were regularly dropping their practice bombs into a 300-foot circle.

The Air Force meteorologist proceeded to tell the meeting that, between then and Christmas, August was probably the best time to drop the atomic bomb, 'with the early part of the month offering marginally better weather conditions than the latter'.

Tibbets liked the meteorologist's next suggestion.

'Suppose no weather forecast at all was made, but that the mission started out on a given day, preceded by spotter planes who would radio back weather reports to the bomber while it was in the air. The bomber could then proceed to that target showing the clearest weather.'

167

Tibbets felt this would be a simple and relatively uncomplicated procedure. The 509th could provide the weather planes, and he himself would be free to make the final decision, in the air, clear of any outside interference and pressures and with the very latest weather information, on which a Japanese city would be atom-bombed.

June 27, 1945
USAAF Base
Wendover

Lewis held back sixty-five tons of bomber, its tanks filled with 7,000 gallons of fuel, while he watched the rev. counter. The needle climbed to 2200 and remained constant.

The bomber juddered, protesting against the brakes which held it at the end of the runway.

The co-pilot, seated beside Lewis, angled the wing-flaps for take off.

Over the intercom, Shumard and Stiborik, in the waist blister turrets, confirmed the flaps were set.

Duzenbury reported all four engines were functioning smoothly.

Only then, satisfied that all the checks prior to take-off had been made, did Lewis push the throttles forward to their full power positions, and release the brakes.

At 260 feet a second, the B-29 rushed down the runway, carrying nine men, their equipment and personal belongings on the most exciting journey any of them had ever made.

They were going to war.

Beneath them, in the bomb bay, were the remainder of the whisky that Beser had purchased in Cuba and a variety of goodies from the Wendover PX.

The ever-thoughtful Lewis, 'looking out' for his crew, particularly the enlisted men, had suggested they should stock up with 'any of those things which you might miss in the Pacific'.

Nelson had picked up a pile of paperbacks, thrillers and adventure stories. He planned to read a book on every mission he made over Japan.

Caron had stowed away some good-quality stationery to write home to his wife. Shumard had purchased a box-camera to take some photographs.

Going to the Pacific also were the crew 'trophies'—a couple of pairs of panties, snitched from bar girls in Salt Lake City, a carton of condoms, for which nobody claimed ownership, and a suspender belt, clipped over the toilet seat.

As usual Lewis had explained the 'house rule' for using the toilet. The first man to use it would be responsible for emptying and cleaning the chemical bucket at the end of the journey.

Lewis had known crew members to 'bend their guts to avoid being the first to use the can'. This always amused him, as he had trained himself to manage a ten-hour flight without once having to crawl back through the plane's central tunnel to use the toilet.

He eased the bomber into the air and began to circle over the base. He switched on the intercom.

'Hold on! We're gonna drag the ramp!'

Caron, in the tail turret, braced himself. Dragging the ramp was flying jargon for making a low-as-possible pass over the airfield.

The silvered bomber climbed several hundred feet out over the salt flats.

Lewis lined it up with the airfield, and shouted into the intercom. 'Let's give them something to remember us by!'

At full power, the B-29 swooped down on the base. Shouting 'like dervishes', the crew encouraged Lewis to fly ever lower.

Lewis tipped the plane on one wing-tip. Soon his port wing was merely inches clear of the ground as the bomber made its mad-cap way across the airfield.

Caron thought they 'must have scared the pants off anybody watching, shooting the field like a fighter plane'.

The angry voice of the controller in the tower ordered Lewis to gain height at once.

The bomber continued on its low-level course, careering over the ground, its wing-tip still only inches away from toppling plane and crew to destruction.

It was, for Nelson, a 'magnificent example of flying skill'.

Lewis eased the bomber to its cruising height and headed south. Already on Tinian were over 1,200 men from the 509th and twelve of the Group's B-29's.

The excitement on board Lewis' aircraft was unabated. None of the crew had ever before been overseas to a combat area. Most of their knowledge of the war had come from the movies and the *Saturday Evening Post* articles that Caron collected.

To them, war was a 'chance to do something for your country', to 'bring peace to the world' or, as Lewis preferred it, 'to go and beat hell outta the Japs like they tried to beat hell outta us at Pearl and other places'.

Lewis was not a blood-thirsty, vengeful young man; nor indeed were any of the crew flying south with him. They were, in Caron's words, 'just average guys going to do a job'.

It was one which would ensure at least a niche for them and their aeroplane in the history books.

But now, flying to what they hoped would be a tropical paradise, Lewis marked the moment of departure from Wendover.

'Tinian, here we come!'

Acceleration

June 28, 1945 to August 2, 1945

June 28, 1945
Tinian
Mariana Islands

Exhausted by his climb up Mount Lasso in the northern part of
Tinian, Chief Warrant Officer Kizo Imai, of the Imperial Japanese
Navy, lay flat on the moist jungle carpet of rotting leaves and fungi,
face close to the earth, frayed cap pulled down over his forehead.

Hunger and a sense of duty drove the thirty-year-old officer to
crawl regularly to this vantage point; at 564 feet it was the highest hill
on the island.

From here Imai could see many of the compounds where the
20,000 Americans on Tinian were billeted. More important, he could
watch where they dumped their food slops. They constantly changed
the sites. Imai supposed it was to make it more difficult for him, and
the 500 other Japanese troops in hiding on Tinian, to scavenge for
food.

Starvation had made them desperate. Even when the Americans
threw their rubbish into the treacherous currents around the island,
the Japanese plunged into the sea at night to grub like sharks after
plankton.

Imai's home on Tinian was a cave, 'a hole in hell', where lice, rats
and other vermin added to the misery of life. Unshaven, unwashed,
unkempt, he and others like him lived a troglodyte existence, seldom
daring to light fires in their jungle bolt-holes in case they gave away
their positions. In his cave, Imai had with him eighteen soldiers—all
who survived of the forty-eight men he had originally led into hiding
when the Americans overran the island eleven months before. Since
then, disease, starvation and American patrols had claimed thirty of
his comrades.

Now, on Mount Lasso, waiting for the refuse trucks to appear,
Imai began his other task: noting down how the American forces
were deploying themselves. This he did in preparation for an event he
still expected to happen 'at any moment': an invasion by Imperial
forces come to recapture the island. When that day came, Imai hoped
to lead his men in a *banzai* charge against the Americans.

Meanwhile, through his binoculars, he could survey almost the
whole island. Tinian from north to south is about twelve miles long;
its width is never more than five miles. Gently undulating, the island
is really a plateau jutting up from the Pacific. Most of its coastline

173

consists of sheer cliffs of rusty brown lava rising from the sea. Tinian is at the southern end of the Mariana Islands which together form an arc over 425 miles of the Pacific; clumps of coral that, until World War Two, few people knew existed.

Scanning the horizon to the north, Imai could see the coast of Saipan, less than four miles away. As usual the intervening sea was busy with American ships of all sizes and kinds. Some were making their way to the American naval anchorage at Tinian Town, three miles south-west of where Imai lay.

Inland from Tinian Town, originally only a cluster of shanty shacks but now a busy military port, the Americans had completed the work the Japanese had begun: clearing away jungle to make runways, aprons, taxi-ways. Paved roads led to fuel and bomb dumps, work-shops and warehouses. There was a growing number of hospitals. Imai concluded that the Americans must be expecting high casualties in some impending battle. His belief in the imminence of a Japanese assault on the Marianas grew. He had no way of knowing that the hospitals were being made ready to receive the casualties expected from the invasion of Kyushu.

Surveying the countryside, Imai saw that the activity this morning was familiar enough: an army was going about its normal business of war. Then his attention was attracted by something unusual. Below and about half a mile to the north-west, gangs of soldiers were com-pleting the fencing-in of a compound.

Rectangular in shape, half a mile long by a quarter of a mile wide, the compound was tucked away in a low-lying area near the coast.

The new fence around the compound was high and forbidding. Behind the wire were different-sized Nissen huts connected by paths and roads. Until this morning the huts had been occupied by Ameri-can Army construction gangs whom Imai had previously watched completing work on the giant airfield beyond the compound. Now they were vacating these quarters.

In the centre of the compound, a smaller, closed-off area had been erected; thick coils of barbed wire surrounded a group of windowless huts. Armed guards stood at the only gate to this area. There were also several guards at the main entrance to the compound.

Imai felt uneasy. The compound looked like a prison camp; perhaps the inner area was a punishment block. In Imai's mind this could only mean one thing: the Americans were planning a new drive to round up the remaining Japanese on the island.

Imai touched his weapons: a long ceremonial sword and a pistol. He did not know if damp had made the bullets useless, but he was sure the sword blade, made by the same secret process which had fashioned the swords of the ancient Samurai, was as sharp as the day

174

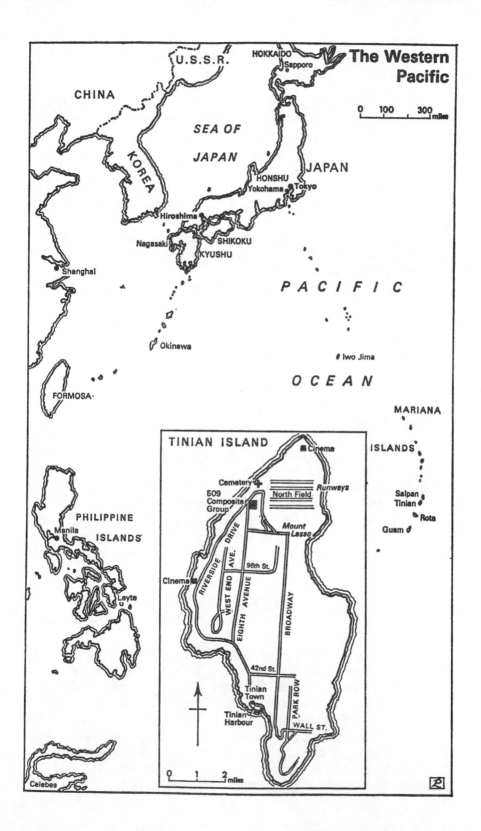

he had received it. That was shortly before he had arrived on Tinian, in March 1944.

Imai's arrival had coincided with a major change in the island's strategic role. Until then, a posting to Tinian was regarded almost as a sinecure. The Japanese garrison spent their days relaxing in the heady atmosphere of the tropics: the island's few hundred natives were mostly Japanese; there was plenty of rice and sake.

Then the atmosphere had changed swiftly and dramatically. The Americans were moving towards the Marianas, its islands were coming into the front line.

Imai had come to Tinian to help build airfields; three runways had been completed and a fourth was under construction when, in June 1944, the Americans struck.

Air attacks and naval bombardments softened up the islands for six weeks. After Saipan was overrun, heavy artillery based there systematically pounded the northern end of Tinian. In one fifteen-day period, a shell a minute fell on the island. Fighters swooped low over Tinian dropping napalm bombs, the first time they had been used in the Pacific.

In between, the Japanese garrison dug in. They believed that the Americans would attempt a landing at Tinian Town. The Japanese fortified the area; many of their guns were British six-inchers, captured at Singapore. And throughout the island, around sugar-cane fields and behind thick jungle foliage, machine-gun nests were positioned and small foxholes prepared in which a solitary soldier huddled, cuddling explosives close to his body; if an American tank passed over his foxhole, he was ready to blow himself up along with the tank.

On the fortieth day of the siege, July 24, Imai had peered through the half-light of dawn to see the American Battle Fleet slowly circling the island, pumping thousands more shells on to the ravaged landscape.

Opposite Tinian Town, the armada had halted and lowered its landing crafts. The Japanese began firing their heavy guns. The Americans quickly retreated and re-embarked. The Japanese were delighted.

Too late, they realised the attack on Tinian Town was a ruse. The bulk of the American forces had landed in the north of the island—a rugged rocky area which the Japanese had thought unassailable.

With a foot-hold established, the U.S. Marines had stormed inland. It took them eight days to reach Tinian Town and capture the island. Four hundred Americans were killed; over 8,000 Japanese died.

Chief Warrant Officer Imai had fled to the jungle, along with some 700 other Japanese survivors. In the months since then, that number had been whittled away to less than 500 hunted men.

Now, peering down on the strange, new compound, Imai was determined about one thing: he would rather die than surrender and end up imprisoned in that compound.

Tibbets continued to inspect the compound to ensure it would be a suitable final home for the 509th.

He had flown half-way round the world, from Wendover, to do so. He would have been here sooner, but had delayed his departure from the United States so that his senior navigator, van Kirk, who had come with him, could have news before leaving of his new baby son. It was a gesture in keeping with Tibbets' aim to treat his men with consideration at all times—until they tried to take advantage. Then he could treat them 'rougher than any MP Master Sergeant in a military prison'.

Tibbets took his time over the inspection: he wanted the 509th to have 'the best going', and not even Groves' personal representative on the island, Colonel E. E. Kirkpatrick, who was accompanying him on the inspection, was going to hurry Tibbets into a decision.

Impassive as usual, restricting his words to a few questions, Tibbets led Kirkpatrick and the commanders of the 509th's squadrons from one hut to another.

Kirkpatrick had hoped Tibbets would not be 'too finicky about housing'. The rule on crowded Tinian was twelve officers or twenty enlisted men in a Nissen hut twenty-nine feet wide by fifty feet long. As group commander, Tibbets would share his accommodation with three or four senior staff officers.

Tibbets responded typically.

'Before you settle my living space, I want to make sure the men are comfortable. This will be the fourth move they've had to make since arriving out here. I want it to be the last.'

Kirkpatrick considered Tibbets a 'bit cocky'—a view he would express to Groves in a secret memo—'inclined to rub his special situation in a bit, but smart enough to know how far he can go. He plays his cards well'.

Tibbets thought it essential to 'establish the ground rules' for how the 509th were to live and work.

In the past month he had made two flying visits to the Marianas to make it clear what those rules were. He was not, he would later insist, 'looking for special treatment', but simply seeking to ensure that the Group was properly settled within the framework of an existing and complicated Air Force operation.

On this second visit he detected that behind the 'glad-handing', there was opposition, muted, but discernible.

At times it had surfaced as resentment. Only this morning a CB officer, learning that he and his men were being ousted from the most comfortable quarters on the island to make room for the Group, had angrily demanded to know what was so special about the 509th. His fury deepened when he was ordered to get his construction workers to erect a high-wire fence around their old quarters.

Tibbets privately sympathised with the CB's. They were all Pacific veterans, many of whom suspected that soon they would be called upon to shed more sweat and blood in the invasion of Japan.

And from what Tibbets had gleaned, the invasion was going to be costly. The long and bitter campaign to secure Okinawa had just ended. It had taken over half a million troops three months to subdue the Japanese garrison of 110,000 who had fought fanatically and died almost to a man. If the American casualty figures for Okinawa were any guide—49,151 dead plus 34 warships sunk and 368 badly damaged —the resistance to be expected on the mainland would be formidable.

The latest American Intelligence reports indicated that some of the two million battle-hardened troops in China were being brought home to help defend the precious ground of Dai Nippon. Already in Japan were another two million soldiers, untried in battle but eager to fight. The vast mass of the Imperial Forces had not been beaten.

Tibbets had expressed to LeMay the hope that the atomic bomb would make them 'see sense', and avert unnecessary bloodshed.

LeMay had concurred. The meeting between the two men at LeMay's Guam headquarters the day before had been cordial enough, though LeMay still had reservations about being able to pin-point a target from 30,000 feet. He told Tibbets that the 509th fliers had 'better get some experience', suggesting that, initially, they could drop their practice bombs on the nearby island of Rota, which was still in Japanese hands.

In the headlong rush through the Marianas, the American forces had 'island-hopped' over Rota, isolating it, leaving its small garrison totally cut off. The Japanese on Rota, only fifty miles south of Tinian, were now a convenient target for newcomers to train on.

As their meeting was ending LeMay had made an unexpected remark.

'Paul, I want you to understand one thing. No flying for you over the Empire.'

Tibbets was stunned.

Puffing steadily on his ever-present cigar, a habit which made him look like a younger, not quite so bulldoggish Churchill, LeMay explained his reasons.

'We don't want to risk losing you. I understand you know more about this bomb than any flier in the Air Force. You're too valuable. You'd better stay on the ground'.

Tibbets had said nothing. LeMay's order made sense; if he fell into Japanese hands, the entire project could be jeopardised.

When the Japanese learned who he was, Tibbets had no doubt they would use torture to make him talk.

He also knew this was not the time and place to argue the matter. LeMay was, nominally, his field commander. To fall out with LeMay 'would be making a rod for my own back'.

But Tibbets was determined on one thing: he would fly the first atomic strike, 'come hell or high water'.

As he left LeMay's headquarters on Guam to come to Tinian, Tibbets had no inkling that there was a move afoot in the 21st Bomber Command to make sure neither he nor the 509th would make the historic flight. The internal politics which had bedevilled the Manhattan Project for the past six months had taken wing and travelled to the Marianas.

On Tinian, having completed his inspection of the new compound's living quarters, kitchens and mess hall, Tibbets examined the 'inner sanctum', the Tech. Area workshops. There, if all went well, the bomb would be finally assembled.

Two of the workshops would be ready in a few days; the other pair would not be complete until August 1.

Tibbets thought schedules were 'running tight'; he wished he could remain on Tinian 'to see things along'. But his presence was required back in America, as an observer during the critical test-firing of the plutonium bomb at Alamogordo in the New Mexico desert.

His tour of the compound complete, Tibbets expressed himself satisfied. The 509th would move into its new quarters on July 8.

For the moment there was no more he could do on Tinian. Having briefed the Group's senior officers on daily routine matters, Tibbets began the long weary journey back across the Pacific, a passenger aboard a slow transport.

He fell asleep wondering what the world's first atomic explosion would be like at Alamogordo.

'If Imai had seen Tibbets, there was no way in which he could have known who he was. In any case he was fascinated by the activity around the main entrance to the compound; a continuous procession of lorries was now driving up to the gates. There the guards stopped and checked every vehicle.

As one of the trucks pulled up, two men got out and removed a large board from the back.

Imai focussed his binoculars on the scene. Two white-helmeted MP's, carbines cradled in their arms, came into sharp focus. They looked tanned, healthy and bored. He moved his glasses slightly to bring the notice into view. Imai could read and speak a little English. Although he could not make out all the lettering, he was able to distinguished the numbers and some of the words. They were:

A feeling of relief filled Imai. It was not, after all, a prison camp.

But the compound was clearly different from all the others he had observed; it seemed to Imai that this one 'must be very important'.

Then another and more pressing thought filled the warrant officer's mind. So intent had he been on watching all the activity that he had completely neglected to note where the American garbage trucks had emptied their loads. Now, he and the men waiting back in his cave would have to forage in the darkness among the dustbins—a risky business in view of the patrols which guarded each compound.

Nevertheless, Imai's time on Mount Lasso had been worthwhile. Careful not to leave any trail, he hurried back to the cave to report to the others. They were relieved to see him; it was always an anxious time whenever any of them were out in the daylight.

Imai had chosen the cave well. He thought it was the largest on the island, yet nobody could have suspected its existence until they were upon it.

Inside, it was filthy, the ground littered with old food tins and other bits of flotsam scavenged during night forays throughout the island.

Stacked in a corner were rifles and a few cases of ammunition. Beside them was a radio transmitter/receiver.

The last message it had received was on the night Tinian fell, when the Supreme Commander of the Imperial Army in Tokyo had sent word that help would be coming. Since then there had been silence. Imai wished somebody knew how to mend the transmitter. Then he could send a message to GHQ in Tokyo about the strange new compound on the island.

Maybe they could even arrange to have it bombed.

Squatting around an up-turned crate, Beser and the other players tried to concentrate on their game. It was not easy. Even now, in the sudden tropical darkness, the cloying, enervating heat was stifling. The only garment each man wore—shorts, khaki trousers cut off about six inches below the crotch—was soaked in sweat.

As the evening wore on, the men around the makeshift card table had to raise their voices to make their bids heard. Not far away a stream of B-29's were taking off on another fire-bomb raid.

Tonight, as usual, the officers in the hut counted the number of aircraft, keeping score by the distinctive sound of engines being boosted to maximum power prior to take-off. So far, the tally was 249 bombers airborne.

Silence returned to the island. But Beser offered a side-stake that another bomber would take off within the next half-hour to make a round total of 250. Nickels and quarters were tossed on to the crate.

Soon afterwards the unmistakable roar of four 2200 horse-power Wright Cyclone engines starting up shattered the silence.

Beser collected his winnings.

Bored now with their game, he and the others listened to the bomber going through its pre-flight engine tests.

Navigator Russell Gackenbach—the young lieutenant who had survived the security snares on that first day at Wendover—went out of the hut to watch the take-off.

It was a pitch-black Tinian night, moonless, with a hot breeze blowing in off the sea.

Gackenbach sensed, rather than saw, the B-29. His ears followed the bomber as it taxied to the runway. He glimpsed short stabs of flame from the engine exhausts. The motors were boosted to full power, the stabs grew brighter, then disappeared as the bomber roared down the runway.

Gackenbach cocked his head instinctively: one of the engines was out of pitch. He shouted into the hut. The others had also heard the sound. They joined Gackenbach. The group listened as the aircraft continued to roar down the runway.

'He's airborne!'

Gackenbach's shout of relief was followed by Beser's warning.

'He's not going to make it!'

The words were followed by a bright orange-red flash, low in the sky, over the runway. It enveloped the bomber.

A split-second later the roar of high-octane fuel exploding over incendiary bombs reached the horrified watchers. The flash spilled across the night sky, briefly lighting up an area of several hundred square yards.

The flames and noise faded as the wail of crash trucks took over.

The 509th officers turned and went back into the hut. They all knew that the most the crash trucks could do was sweep up a few charred remains.

July 1, 1945
Imperial Army GHQ
Tokyo

After two weeks of study, the situation was becoming clear. While there were still some gaps, the Imperial Army's Intelligence Chief,

Major-General Seizo Arisue, had been able to make an authoritative assessment of Japan's internal political situation.

It was desperate.

The struggle had become deadly, positions more intransigent, between the militarists and the moderates. Their battles, so far confined to words, threatened to engulf the Imperial Throne. What concerned Arisue was the prospect of bloodshed after the talking between the two sides finally stopped. In his heart he believed the most extreme elements would even kill the Emperor if he opposed their stated intention of leading Japan either to victory, or else until not a single person was left alive in the country.

Opposing these fanatical die-hards were the moderates whose saving skill was reasoned argument. They were led by the Marquis Koichi Kido, Lord Keeper of the Privy Seal, the man the Emperor trusted almost above all others.

It was Marquis Kido who had kept the peace when the two factions had confronted each other at the Imperial Conference of June 8. But he had been unable to save the conference from deciding to continue the war to the bitter end. In the Emperor's presence, and without his saying a word, they had decided there must be no surrender.

Then, four days later, a moderate, an admiral, his path to the throne cleared for him by Kido, presented the Emperor with clear confirmation of what Kido had already told him.

The admiral's report detailed serious shortages of raw materials. In the war industries the workers—many of them schoolchildren—were beset by lack of experience; output was constantly falling short of expectation. Industrially, Japan was becoming moribund. Except for morale, the over-all position was dire.

On June 18, Prime Minister Suzuki called a meeting of Japan's 'Inner Cabinet'. In theory, its six members—four cabinet ministers including Suzuki and the two military chiefs of staff—formulated the policies, subject to full cabinet approval, which settled the destiny of every man, woman and child in the Japanese Empire. But their decisions had to be acceptable to the Army, or else they were unenforceable. The aged Premier could be little more than a mouthpiece for his military masters. Arisue dismissed Suzuki as having only 'the courage of the Army's convictions'.

While he had been unable to obtain precise details of the June 18 meeting—held on the same day that President Truman approved the invasion plans—Arisue did establish that the War Minister and the representatives of the Army and Navy had maintained their stated position: all forward planning must be linked to the demands an enemy D-Day would create.

However, these three hard-liners had agreed one important concession. While they still opposed direct negotiation to end the war, they now had no objection to talks starting *after* Field Marshal Hata's Army had dealt the enemy a crushing blow on the invasion beaches.

To Arisue, the fact that the three had been moved that far from their previously entrenched position, was a 'major victory for reality'.

Outwardly maintaining his careful position between the militarists and the moderates, deep down inside, Arisue had come to favour peace at any price—apart from unconditional surrender. His overriding objection to such a surrender was that it would likely mean the removal of the Emperor, and that was unthinkable.

On June 22, ten days after the admiral had delivered his report on raw materials and morale, Emperor Hirohito had requested the Inner Cabinet to initiate peace negotiations, using if possible the 'good offices' of Russia.

On June 24, a former prime minister, Koki Hirota, called upon the Soviet Ambassador in Tokyo, Jacob Malik, and declared that Japan wanted a 'strong agreement' to replace the Neutrality Pact which the Russians had recently announced they would not be renewing.

Malik, correctly, saw the move as an attempt to keep the Russians out of the war. He reminded Hirota that the Neutrality Pact was still in force, and that the Soviet Union was abiding by its terms. Any discussion about a new arrangement could be left until nearer its expiration, in April 1946.

In an attempt to obtain some concession from the implacable Russian, Hirota tried another tack. He offered some of Japan's precious rubber, tin, lead and tungsten in return for Soviet oil.

Malik bluntly refused to trade.

Hirota made a final proposal.

'If the Soviet Army and the Japanese Navy were to join forces, Japan and the Soviet Union together would become the strongest powers in the world.'

It was the incoherent hope of a drowning man.

Malik bade Hirota an icy good-bye.

Five days later, Hirota was back again. This time Malik put off the unwelcome caller by using the excuse that he would have to consult Moscow.

And there, for the moment, the diplomatic manoeuvres rested. But Arisue had growing evidence that, far from wishing to enter into a non-aggression treaty with Japan, Russia was bent on war. His staff were monitoring Soviet troop movements near the Chinese border: a formidable force was being assembled there, probably preparing to attack the Japanese troops facing them in Manchuria.

Worse, Arisue believed that a Russian attack would not be so much concerned with helping the Allies win the war, but to establish Soviet influence in the Pacific. The thought of a Soviet-dominated Japan chilled him; he found the prospect of Communism unpalatable, especially as it could mean the removal of the Emperor and the end of traditional Japan.

Arisue felt it was more urgent than ever to come to terms with the United States.

He wished his American specialist, Lieutenant-Colonel Kakuzo Oya, was still in Tokyo. But Oya had just been seconded to Field Marshal Hata's staff in Hiroshima as chief intelligence officer. Hata needed Oya at his headquarters to prepare for the anticipated invasion of Kyushu.

Arisue decided he would have to formulate, without Oya, a new approach to America through the one pipe-line he had: the OSS in Berne.

Arisue's agent there Lieutenant-General Seigo Okamoto, had been standing by for weeks to carry a message to the OSS which could then relay it to Washington.

Arisue had previously hesitated to send such a message. The risks for him were great: he would be acting without government authority; and unlike the fruitless overtures of the Navy which had been supported by some admirals, Arisue knew he could expect no backing from his Army superiors. On the contrary, if they discovered he had been approaching the enemy they would doubtless seek his dismissal, if not his death. The prospect of being branded a traitor had always checked Arisue.

But now, apart from his belief that any negotiations with Russia were doomed to failure, Arisue had another, and more compelling, reason to risk his career and life.

He had just learned that, in two weeks' time, America, Britain and Russia would be holding a conference at Potsdam.

With Germany defeated, it would not be difficult for the Big Three to agree upon a common policy towards the pursuit of the war in the Pacific. Arisue had no doubt that, at the end of their deliberations, they would issue some new threat to Japan. Then, the chances of anything but an unconditional settlement might be even slimmer.

Arisue cabled Okamoto requesting him to find out the minimum conditions that America would accept for a Japanese surrender.

July 2, 1945
Tinian

Lewis switched on the intercom and told the crew to prepare for landing.

At 200 miles an hour, the bomber—indistinguishable from other

B-29's except for its squadron identification number, 82—began its descent. Until now it had been an eventless journey. Staging down through the Pacific, through Sacramento to Honolulu and the tiny landing strip on Kwajalein, neither the plane nor its crew had received any kind of preferential treatment. The bomber that was to become the most famous in the world was not yet considered in any way special.

Some fifteen miles ahead, Tinian appeared as an indistinct mass, hidden by a morning-sun haze.

At his station, a small, windowless cubby-hole just forward of the front bomb bay, radio-man Dick Nelson tuned the radio compass to Tinian's signal. It was something to do after the hours of inactivity he had endured on the flight; three days in the air, interspersed with brief stop-overs where the food and accommodation was poor, had dampened Nelson's enthusiasm. He felt tired, in need of a bath, and, though he would never admit it to any of the men around him, a little apprehensive about the future.

He checked the IFF; the device continued to give out the silent signal which identified the B-29 as an American military aircraft.

The bored voice of a ground controller on Tinian gave Lewis the wind's speed and direction at North Field.

Lewis couldn't wait to get there and into action.

Flight Engineer Duzenbury checked the oil pressure gauges and generators. They all gave normal readings. He adjusted the fuel mixture until the needle hovered in its dial at the words 'Auto Rich'.

Stiborik, the radar scanner, checked the clearly-defined shape of Tinian on his radar; he had watched it grow from a pin-point almost to fill the screen.

Of more immediate concern to him was how soon his bandaged finger would heal. The night before, on Kwajalein, a rat had gnawed it to the bone while Stiborik slept. When he awoke he told the crew he had dreamt his finger was in a pencil-sharpener.

Caron kept quiet about his dream. In it a huge rat was straddling his chest. He had woken up in a sweat only to find a real rat squatting at his throat.

The tail-gunner thought that anywhere, after Kwajalein, must be an improvement. He switched on his intercom and asked Lewis what Tinian was like. All Caron could see from his rear turret was endless miles of Pacific.

Lewis gave the crew an enthusiastic view of the island.

"It's wonderful! The jungle looks just like in the movies! Those beaches are made for Esther Williams! And the water's the bluest I've ever seen! Guys, we're gonna have a great time!'

Some six thousand miles and three days of flying had not dampened Lewis' enthusiasm. He called out the landing orders.

'Gear down.'

When the wheels had been lowered, Stiborik and Assistant Engineer Shumard, in the waist blister turrets, confirmed the landing gear was locked in position.

'Flap check. Five degrees.'

Again, Stiborik and Shumard reported when the flaps were down.

'Flap check. Twenty-five degrees.'

The men in the blister turrets confirmed the change.

Moments later Lewis touched down on North Field and taxied to the 509th's special dispersal area.

Caron's immediate, and abiding, impression when he crawled out of the tail turret was that 'we had landed on the world's biggest latrine'.

The bomber had parked down-wind of one of the giant cess-pools dug by the CB's.

Lewis guessed he would soon get used to the stench. And if that was the only drawback to Tinian, then it really was paradise, with its Nissen huts beneath palm-fronds and paths made of crushed coral kept tidy by smiling natives.

To further a feeling of home-from-home, and because Tinian was roughly the same shape as Manhattan, the principal roads had been named and sign-posted as New York streets.

Broadway was the longest thoroughfare, running from North Field past the foot of Mount Lasso down towards Tinian Town; a splendid highway, over six miles in length, lined with living and working quarters.

Parallel to Broadway, on the western side of the island, was 8th Avenue, running from the beach-head the Marines had established when they had invaded Tinian, down past the island's second large landing strip, West Field, and eventually ending at Tinian harbour.

Hugging the west coast was Riverside Drive, a gently curving road off which were several small beaches and coves.

Forty-second street was at a busy crossroads in the southern section of Tinian, close to Wall Street, Grand Avenue, Park Row and Canal Street, which led to 2nd Avenue, and another group of familiar-sounding roads, 59th Street, 64th Street, 72nd Street and 86th Street.

The 509th were in temporary quarters just east of Broadway near 86th Street. When Lewis and his crew reached their huts they found them empty. Nine of the 393rd's crews were away on a practice mission, dropping high-explosive bombs on Rota.

It seemed to Lewis that he had arrived on Tinian not a moment too soon.

186

Sitting bolt upright on his gold and chintz chair, Harry S. Truman gave all the signs of a President enjoying a relaxed evening, listening to the Army Air Force band in concert on the south lawn of the White House.

Seated around him were members of his Cabinet, the government, diplomatic corps, and friends of Bess and Margaret Truman. Only Bess saw the signs of tension inside her husband: while the band played through a potpourri of his favourite light classics, from time to time Truman fidgeted on his seat.

Bess Truman knew what was troubling Harry, and she wished she was going with him.

Ordinarily, the concert would have marked the end of a tiring day. Since early morning a long list of callers had been to Truman's office, bringing problems, suggestions, aspirations and requests to a man whose philosophy about decision-making was encompassed in the small printed sign he had on his desk: THE BUCK STOPS HERE.

Before coming to the concert, Truman had packed the sign in his suitcase, along with his white shirts, suits, bow-ties, and a pair of combinations.

Bess had said it might be cold in Potsdam.

Clad now in a natty pin-stripe suit, Truman watched as the band's conductor brought the concert with a final crash of cymbals to a spirited conclusion.

The President jumped to his feet, clapped loudly, took Bess and Margaret by the arm and walked into the White House.

The audience drifted home, doubtless thinking the First Family would have a nightcap and then retire to bed.

Inside, safe from prying eyes, Truman kissed Bess and Margaret farewell and went out of a side-exit.

A large black limousine waited. Its chauffeur and two other men already inside were members of the White House Secret Service detail: six of them were travelling to Potsdam with the President.

Truman slipped into the back seat, and the car pulled away on its short journey to Union Station. There, it drove to track number 2, where a locomotive and four carriages were standing.

Fifty-three hand-picked passengers were already aboard, sworn to secrecy about their eventual destination: the Brandenburg city, seventeen miles south-west of Berlin. They were the assistants and advisers who would guide Truman as he made his début on the international stage.

Secretly, Truman was nervous of facing his two formidable allies,

Stalin and Churchill. But he was determined to do or say nothing which would let down America, Missouri, his family—or himself. He had taken pains to memorise everything he could about the two leaders. To mark the historic occasion when they would-all meet for the first time, Truman was taking along a pool of newsmen, and photographers—another first for an American President.

The journey was being made in utmost secrecy. The Secret Service feared a fanatic might attempt to assassinate the President. The Joint Chiefs were worried about the possibility of a Japanese submarine sneaking into the Atlantic and sinking Truman's heavy cruiser, the *Augusta*, as it carried him and his entourage to Europe.

Once Truman was settled in, the train began its seven-hour journey to Newport News, Virginia where the *Augusta* was anchored.

Truman knew that, to the sleeping America outside his compartment, the world situation looked better than it had in years.

Japan seemed on the verge of collapse, and there was no reason to doubt that the ties which had bound together the Allies in war would continue into the peace. Indeed the bonds between Moscow and Washington had been recently demonstrated when General Eisenhower was fêted at the Kremlin.

But Truman—for all the jokes the press made about his clothes and folksy sayings—was a hard-headed realist. He knew Potsdam would not be a replay of the Big Three's previous meetings at Teheran and Yalta. Then, Roosevelt, Stalin and Churchill could concentrate on defeating Germany and postpone decisions which might have estranged them. Truman believed that at Potsdam this might not be possible.

His briefing on Stalin had been skimpy; nobody in the State Department was able to offer an assessment of the Soviet leader that went much beyond 'he's a hard nut to crack'.

Truman had received plenty of advice about Churchill, much of it cautionary. He had been warned to beware of the Englishman's motives and judgements—and Churchill's winning ways.

Truman planned to handle both his allies in the same manner: he would listen to their arguments, ask questions, and then make up his mind—and stick to his decision.

That rule had stood him well throughout his long political life. He saw no reason why it should fail now.

And, in spite of his lack of experience on the international scene, Truman was travelling to Potsdam with a momentous secret: the atomic weapon was almost ready for use.

Secretary of War Stimson, who would bear much of the responsibility for the decisions which must still be made if the Alamogordo test was successful, had outlined his thoughts in a memo to Truman, dated July 2.

The atomic bomb was never mentioned in the document. But its presence loomed over Stimson's concise and far-reaching exposition.

Truman had reduced the long memo to a sentence: Stimson wanted to give the Japanese one further and final warning, an opportunity to surrender before the full might of America was brought to bear.

Stimson had couched his caveat in the measured and precise words of a diplomat. And, within it, he had included a controversial suggestion: the Japanese might be told that 'we do not exclude a constitutional monarchy under her present dynasty', so long as totalitarianism was replaced by democracy in Japan.

Truman was taking Stimson's memo with him to Potsdam, to discuss the proposals with Churchill and Stalin.

But he knew that if Japan refused to accept the conditions in the final offer—whatever it was agreed at Potsdam those conditions should be—the country faced an atomic attack. And the decision to initiate that attack would rest with him.

Another thought Truman was taking with him to Potsdam was a recent statement by General MacArthur. The general believed it possible that, once the American invasion forces had established a beach-head on Kyushu and were driving inland, they might find that formal Japanese defence was replaced by guerilla warfare. In that case MacArthur predicted it could take up to ten years to conquer Japan—and there was virtually no ceiling on what the Allied losses might be.

It was an appalling prospect for the President to consider.

July 9, 1945
Hiroshima

Even with a dozen radio sets tuned to different stations, the room was almost totally silent except for the gentle whirring of the fans suspended from the ceiling. Each radio had been adjusted so that it could be heard only through the head-set of the man seated before it. Each of the men was doing something that for others in Japan would have been an offence punishable by death. They were listening to American broadcasts.

The men were radio monitors, the morning shift of a round-the-clock watch being kept on the air-waves of the Pacific, and beyond. They were a part of the Communications Bureau of Field Marshal Hata's 2nd General Army Headquarters.

The Bureau was the nerve-centre of Hata's headquarters. It was housed in a former school, a long two-storey building at the foot of

Mount Futaba, near the East Training Field. Special land-lines linked the Bureau to General Army Headquarters in Tokyo; other lines ran to military centres on Kyushu—Fukuoka, Sasebo, Nagasaki and Kagoshima; nearer to hand, the Bureau was linked to the Naval base at Kure, Marine headquarters at Ujina and to the regional defence command in Hiroshima Castle.

The monitoring room was the Bureau's show-piece; only the large transmitting and monitoring centre just outside Tokyo rivalled the listening post at Hiroshima. And never had it been so busy as in these past few weeks, following the arrival in Hiroshima of Lieutenant-Colonel Kakuzo Oya, Arisue's tough-minded specialist in American affairs, seconded to Hata's staff as chief intelligence officer.

Hata and Oya knew that the monitoring room could provide the first indication that an actual landing on Kyushu was about to take place. Prior to that, they expected the Americans would spend weeks bombarding the invasion area by sea and by air. But Hata hoped he would have sufficient warning of an impending landing for Kyushu's kamikaze planes and suicide motor-boats to attack the invasion armada.

Much of the success of this plan depended on the personnel manning the monitoring room. All of them were either too old or otherwise unfit for combat service. Each had an excellent command of English.

In eight-hour shifts, they sat in dull, enervating stillness, staring at their radios, pads at the ready, listening to an endless stream of words and music relayed from as far away as Washington D.C. Recently a short-wave transmission from the American capital had mentioned that President Truman was so confident of victory that he had been able to take an evening away from his duties to attend a White House open-air concert. The fact had been noted and passed on.

The busiest time was from midday to midnight. During these hours, half the sets in the room were tuned to transmissions from Okinawa, Iwo Jima and the Marianas.

The monitors strained to hear orders being broadcast by the Americans from as far south as Guam. Many of them were in code, but a sufficient number were made in clear so as to provide the monitors with information which could be acted upon speedily. These intercepts included not only military radio traffic, but also brief radio tests made by B-29 radio-men just before take-off.

There was an hour's time difference between Japan and the Marianas—Hiroshima was one hour behind Tinian—and if the radio tests were made around three to four p.m. Hiroshima time, then the monitors knew that a raid could be expected that night. They used the number of tests they picked up as a rough-and-ready guide to the number of aircraft to be expected.

Bob Caron

1 Colonel Paul W. Tibbets, commander of the 509th Composite Group and aircraft commander of the *Enola Gay*, on Tinian, August 6, 1945; pinned to his coveralls is the Distinguished Service Cross which he had received the same day

Dick Nels[...]

2 Major Thomas Ferebee, Group bombardier, August 6, 1945

3 Captain Robert Lewis in the pilot's seat of the *Enola Gay*, August 1945

Ted van Kirk

4a Captain Theodore 'Dutch' van Kirk,
Group navigator, August 1945

Dick Nelson

4b S/Sgt George 'Bob' Caron,
tail-gunner, August 1945

Dick Nelson

4c S/Sgt Wyatt Duzenbury, flight
engineer, August 1945

5a 2nd Lt Morris Jeppson, electronics officer, August 1945

Jacob Beser

5b Chaplain William Downey, who composed a special prayer for the atomic mission

William Downey

6a The crew of the *Enola Gay*. Left to right, rear: Ferebee, van Kirk, Tibbets, Lewis; front: Caron, Stiborik, Duzenbury, Nelson, Shumard

6b On the tarmac, just before take-off from Tinian in the early hours of August 6 1945: Tibbets (centre) talking to radar operator Stiborik (back to camera, wearing knife and water bottle) and radar counter-measures officer Beser (wearing pistol). Navigator van Kirk is on right of picture and bombardier Ferebee third from left

7a Bob Caron in his tail-gunner's position on the *Enola Gay*

Bob Caron

7b Flight engineer Duzenbury in the tunnel connecting the rear and forward sections of the *Enola Gay*. Beneath the tunnel is the hatch leading to the bomb bay

John King

Kakuzo Oya

8 Senior officers of the 2nd General Army Headquarters, Hiroshima, July 15, 1945. Field Marshal Shunroku Hata, commander, is in the front row, third from right; third from left is Korean prince Lt Col RiGu. Middle row: third from left, Colonel Katayama; fourth from left, Colonel Imoto; far right, Lt Col Oya

9a 2nd Lt Matsuo Yasuzawa and the plane in which he was to have such an incredible flight

Matsuo Yasuzawa

9b Chief Warrant Officer Kizo Imai on Tinian before he went into hiding on the island following the American invasion in mid-1944

Kizo Imai

10a Mayor of Hiroshima,
Senkichi Awaya

Authors' collection

10b Corporal Kanai Hiroto
who helped capture and
interrogate American
prisoners of war in
Hiroshima

Kanai Hiroto

11a August 6, 1945: Colonel Paul Tibbets about to take off on the world's
first atomic strike

11b The return of the *Enola Gay*

12a Hiroshima—before

12b After

13a Tinian Island in the Marianas; the four long parallel runways
of North Field comprised in 1945 the world's largest operational
airfield. It was from one of these runways that the *Enola Gay* took
off on its historic flight. Note the lone B-29 top left of picture

13b Hiroshima—after

14a General Spaatz (left), just after decorating Colone Tibbets on Tinian, August 6, 1945

Bob Caron

14b The debriefing following the atomic mission. General Spaatz (head of table, centr listens as van Kirk (lower left) reads from his navigator's log. Caron is lower right in dark Brooklyn Dodgers baseball cap; on his immediate right is Ferebee; Lewis leans forward on table, with cigarette; Captain William 'Deak' Parsons, balding, is upper right. Group Captain Leonard Cheshire can be seen centre-left seated behind man with cigar

Bob Lewis

15a Hiroshima, August 1945: the ruins of the city's Industry Promotion Hall

15b Hiroshima today: the same building, now known as the A-bomb dome and left as a reminder of August 6, 1945, seen through the arch of the Memorial Cenotaph in the city's Peace Park

Photo copyright Keystone Press

16 The atomic cloud above Hiroshima, August 6, 1945

The monitors passed their notes to supervisors who in turn sent the information to the central communication room. From there the entire air raid alert system of western Japan was informed. The whole operation took only minutes.

As the bombers entered Japanese air space, the monitors picked up snatches of conversations between air crews, enabling the supervisors to estimate which areas of Japan the planes meant to attack. The information, along with the intercepts of radio messages to and from ships at sea, were typed up for subsequent analysis. It all helped Hata and Oya to gauge the enemy's strength and intentions with remarkable accuracy.

Since coming to Hiroshima, Oya had regularly visited the monitors, hoping his presence was an indication to them of the importance he placed on their work.

But his real speciality was interrogation. From the days when he had first come to work with Arisue, he had shown an aptitude for questioning. It was Arisue's proud boast that if Oya couldn't make a man talk, then nobody could.

Oya still regretted that he had arrived in Hiroshima too late to be the first to interrogate the ten American fliers who had been shot down over Okinawa and brought to the city before the island fell.

So far, they were the only American POW's in Hiroshima. They were kept at Kempei Tai headquarters in the grounds of Hiroshima Castle.

Although the American's were either non-combatants or junior officers, men whom Oya would not normally have bothered to question, he was now anxious to interrogate prisoners of almost any rank. But these had already been thoroughly grilled, and the short time Oya had spent with them had produced nothing additional of value.

Oya knew he had got to them too late; the most successful interrogations generally come soon after capture, when prisoners are confused or disorientated. The ten Americans had had too much time to prepare themselves. It was doubtful if even torturing them would now produce anything further—not that Oya used torture; piercing a man's mind by sharp questioning was one thing; piercing his body another.

Oya always tried to give the impression to a prisoner that he was merely seeking confirmation of facts he already knew. Those who refused to succumb to his wiles were told they might be questioned by the Kempei Tai, who had 'other methods'. Oya knew that fear of the unknown was a powerful persuader.

To make the best use of his talents, Oya was in need of 'a few new prisoners', preferably senior aircrew from the Marianas. The intelligence officer knew that was where the Americans had their largest bomber bases.

191

July 12, 1945
Tinian

The sun was still a glowing ball rimming the horizon when Charles Perry, the 509th's catering officer, rose from his bunk. He stepped gingerly on to the floor. The night before one of the other officers in the hut had set traps to catch the rats which roamed the Group's compound. The 509th had moved into their new quarters on Tinian four days earlier, and, in spite of the rodents, the consensus was that this time 'the Old Man has done us proud'. The men accepted Tibbets' absence without question: back at Wendover they had become accustomed to their commander disappearing.

Perry hoped that, when Tibbets returned from the States, he would bring a few 'presents'—liquor and cigarettes. In the deft hands of Perry these items were valuable commodities to barter. The usually urbane, sophisticated Mess Officer was nowadays behaving 'like an Arab trader'.

Because of his efforts, the Group enjoyed a selection of dishes not available to the 20,000 other Americans on Tinian. It was Perry's proud boast that 'in the 509th a PFC eats better than a five-star general'.

Today's breakfast menu gave substance to the claim: chilled grapefruit juice, hot cereals, pineapple fritters, eggs and plenty of fresh coffee. For lunch and dinner there would be choice steaks, rib roasts, chickens, ducks, new potatoes, fresh salads and cold milk.

Many of these items were acquired by Perry in exchange for the liquor which he traded with the Navy and CB quartermasters, the acknowledged 'food barons' on Tinian.

This morning, as usual, before doing anything else, Perry climbed a coral outcrop near North Field to witness a sight that made him 'just tingle with pride': bombers from other squadrons on Tinian returning after their all-night forays to Japan.

To Perry, the B-29's were 'like beads on a string. As soon as one landed, another made its approach. There was always the same number of planes in sight. It was thrilling to watch'.

It was broad daylight when the last returning bomber landed. The weary crews, who had been almost thirteen hours in the air, would spend most of the day 'in the sack'. As they went to bed, some of the 509th's crews were preparing, yet again, to practice-bomb the Japanese on nearby Rota. None of them had yet been allowed to fly over Japan.

Their B-29's were parked on segregated aprons on North Field and guarded round the clock. The sentries had orders to shoot any unauthorised person who attempted to approach the aircraft after being challenged.

192

This stringent security had already attracted the curiosity of other squadrons. Their questions remained unanswered. Now, as planes from the 509th took off for Rota, cat-calls and jeers from a group of combat veterans drifted across North Field.

The muted resentment, which Tibbets had detected, was out in the open; the 509th had become an object of derision.

Soon the taunts about the humiliated fliers would be turned into verse, penned by a clerk in the island's base headquarters:

NOBODY KNOWS

Into the air the secret rose,
Where they're going, nobody knows.
Tomorrow they'll return again,
But we'll never know where they've been.
Don't ask us about results or such,
Unless you want to get in Dutch.
But take it from one who is sure of the score,
The 509th is winning the war.

When the other Groups are ready to go,
We have a program of the whole damned show.
And when Halsey's 5th shells Nippon's shore,
Why, shucks, we hear about it the day before.
And MacArthur and Doolittle give out in advance,
But with this new bunch we haven't a chance.
We should have been home a month or more,
For the 509th is winning the war.

Thousands of copies of this doggerel were mimeographed and distributed throughout the Pacific command. From Hawaii to the Philippines, men read about this strange outfit on Tinian who stirred themselves to make occasional sorties against a tame target, the Japanese on Rota.

In public, the 509th laughed off the poem, but it touched a raw nerve among many in the Group. Six weeks had now passed since the ground echelon arrived on Tinian. For them in particular the weary waiting, having to parry relentless sniping questions, dividing their time between the beach, mess-hall and movie theatres—all had combined to help dent their pride. Some of the 509th even wondered if their compound, with its tough-talking guards, was not just fenced in as a security precaution, but because the Group needed 'baby-minding'.

Men began to react in all sorts of ways to the strains and pressures.

Beser awoke late, having been until the early hours of the morning in the Tech. Area workshop where the atomic bomb would be finally

193

assembled. There, Jeppson and members of the 1st Ordnance Squadron were preparing for the arrival of the bomb's component parts. Jeppson and the five other specialists on the proximity fuse mechanism had been among the first to reach the island. In their spare time they had made for themselves a porch out of bomb crates which formed the entrance to the tent they chose to live in; carefully sited on a high bluff where it received any possible breeze, the accommodation was the envy of almost all in the 509th.

Beser was in a hut close to the cemetery where the Americans who had died taking Tinian were buried. It was also where the remains of the crew he had seen crash were interred; Beser had come to learn that such crashes by B-29's loaded to the maximum with incendiary bombs, were a frequent and disturbing fact of life on Tinian.

Now, as he dressed, Beser saw that his Nissen hut was empty. He guessed his fellow officers had gone to the beach.

He turned on the hut's radio. The strains of *Sentimental Journey* came through the static. It was followed by a dulcet voice that Beser was both fascinated by, and hated.

Tokyo Rose was making one of her regular propaganda broadcasts to the American forces in the Pacific.

Twice already she had startled the 509th by making specific references to the Group. The first was shortly after the ground echelon landed on Tinian on May 30, Memorial Day.

Tokyo Rose noted their arrival and urged them to return home before they fell victims to the victorious Japanese forces.

Some of the 509th had jeered. Others showed concern. They wondered how she could possibly know about the most secret unit in the entire American Air Force. Two weeks later Tokyo Rose had mentioned them again. She warned that the Group's bombers would be easily recognisable to Japanese anti-aircraft gunners because of the distinctive 'R' symbols on the B-29 tails. This time nobody scoffed. The insignia had only just been painted on.

But even if Beser found disturbing the omnipresent sources of Tokyo Rose, he still listened to the beguiling voice from Japan.

This morning, as usual, she had all the latest baseball scores from the States; news of the dramas and comedies playing on and off Broadway; details of the fiction and non-fiction best-sellers, all interspersed with current selections from the Hit Parade.

There was no mention of the 509th. Beser switched off the radio, leaving Tokyo Rose to entertain other lonely men thinking of home.

And, Beser knew, there were plenty of them on Tinian. In the time he had been on the island, he had received 'a crash course in the basics of life'. The young man who had blushed at the sight of a naked Katherine Oppenheimer at Los Alamos, turned almost scarlet when, as Duty Censor Officer, he read the contents of some of the enlisted men's letters home.

Beser was shocked 'so much sexual intercourse was conducted by mail'.

He was even more horrified to learn that several of the island's native women were running a brothel in one of the laundries. He was tempted to report the matter, but had persuaded himself it 'was probably better for the men to have some real sex than to write all that primitive stuff'.

They did not write only about their sexual fantasies; several of them described combat missions they had never flown, targets they had never bombed, attacks they had never repulsed.

Men whom Beser had judged to be 'sane ordinary guys were daredevils on paper'. He guessed they had spent too many nights at the island's movie theatres. There they sat on hard wooden benches, under their ponchos, feeling the rain, which regularly fell every night during the main feature, dripping down their necks as they watched Spencer Tracy and Errol Flynn mopping up all the Japanese-looking extras Hollywood could muster.

Beser felt the 'real thing' would be different. He wondered how he would face being shot at. A buddy in another squadron had confessed that, flying to Japan, he 'always filled his pants on the way up in fear and on the way back in relief'.

The fastidious Beser resolved that when his time came, he would somehow ensure the same did not happen to him.

July 13, 1945
Washington, D.C.

Over a month before, when the bomb's opponents had geared themselves for a further effort to inhibit the Manhattan Project, Groves decided on a new strategy. He would do or say nothing. Safe in the knowledge that Stimson and the Interim Committee had so far supported the use of the weapon, Groves sat back and watched what he regarded as still only a small group of outspoken dissidents launch their attacks.

By early June, the rumble of their arguments had been heard in all the atomic plants. Strong feelings about many aspects of nuclear energy were put on paper. But none of this seriously interrupted work; and indeed, at the key laboratory of Los Alamos, there was little discussion and virtually no dissent.

While the internal jockeying was going on, Leo Szilard and two other scientists had made yet another attempt to impress their views on the government. They had travelled to Spartanburg, South Carolina, to talk to James Byrnes, Truman's new Secretary of State. The scientists had not thoroughly prepared their arguments, their thoughts about giving Japan 'a warning' were blurred by ideas of 'a public demonstration'. The confused and unsympathetic exchange ended with Byrnes refusing to pledge any help.

Then, on June 12, seven scientists from the Chicago laboratory submitted a petition to the Secretary of War urging a demonstration before international observers in an uninhabited area. It was the Franck Report, destined to become arguably the most famous document concerned with the use of the atomic bomb.

The report was delivered to George Harrison, Stimson's assistant. He passed it to the Interim Committee's Scientific Panel.

On June 16, the Panel met in Oppenheimer's office in Los Alamos to consider the report. They acknowledged it was a fair-minded and serious attempt to present all sides of a complicated issue.

But, in the end, the Panel reported 'with heavy heart' to the Interim Committee that 'we can propose no technical demonstration likely to bring an end to the war; we see no acceptable alternative to direct military use'.

The Committee agreed with the conclusion of its advisory Panel.

In four momentous days the Franck Report had been delivered, discussed and discounted.

Then, a surprising new opponent emerged to threaten the project. He was a member of the Interim Committee, Under-Secretary of the Navy, James Bard. On June 27 he wrote to Harrison, dissenting from the Interim Committee's recommendation that the bomb be used without warning. Bard suggested that Japan be given several days' notice, including 'some information' about the weapon. But he did not ask for a demonstration. His idea died a natural death.

The unrest continued. And, as Groves had always expected, opposition was centred on the Metallurgical Laboratory in Chicago. For years he had regarded some of those working there as difficult die-hards: '. . . a small group of scientists, mostly, though not entirely, European-born, who felt they should be given complete control of the entire project . . . They seemed to feel that no one who was over forty years old, no matter how distinguished a scientist he might be, could possibly understand the intricacies of atomic energy. This was quite absurd, for it was not and is not extraordinarily difficult for anyone who will apply himself to learning them to understand the basic principles of atomic physics.'

On July 12, a poll had been taken among the Chicago scientists. 150 were asked to choose between five alternative proposals: the

196

choices offered ranged from not using the bomb under any circumstances, to using it in the 'most effective' manner. The results seemed to suggest that scientists favoured some kind of demonstration.

But now, a day later, complaints were already being made by those polled that insufficient time had been allowed for answering, that the questions were imprecise, that the choice of a 'military demonstration' was interpreted by some as meaning that the bomb should first be used on a Japanese city.

The poll was inconclusive. Like other efforts in the past—and those yet to be made—its only effect was to cause further argument.

It seemed to Groves that nothing could now stop the atomic age dawning on schedule in just three days' time at Alamogordo. There, if all went well, he would preside over an act of creation unique in mankind's history.

And even as he anxiously awaited the result of that momentous curtain-raiser, preparations were in train at Los Alamos for the main event that would follow.

July 14, 1945
Los Alamos

From Oppenheimer's office, a telephone call was made to the guard house further down on the mesa. The call ordered the sentries to let the approaching convoy pass unhampered.

Sandwiched between seven cars was a closed black truck. Four men sat in each car. Beneath their coats were pistols in shoulder holsters; on the floor were shot-guns, rifles and boxes of ammunition. The men had orders to shoot to kill anybody who attempted to stop the convoy.

In the car immediately behind the truck rode two Army officers. Their field artillery collar insignia were upside down—an indication of the hurry with which Major Robert Furman and Captain James Nolan had assumed their disguises.

In reality Furman was a Princeton engineering graduate, attached to the Manhattan Project. His normal role was to procure strategic materials and help recruit scientific personnel. Nolan was a radiologist at the Los Alamos hospital.

Today, the two men were beginning a journey scheduled to end on Tinian. Until they reached that destination, they had strict orders not to let out of their sight a fifteen-foot-long crate—it contained the atomic bomb's inner cannon—and a lead-lined cylinder two feet high and eighteen inches in diameter in which was the uranium projectile. Crate and cylinder were now being carried in the truck.

Oppenheimer had impressed upon both men the virtual irreplaceability of the material they were accompanying.

Only a mile down the mountain road from Los Alamos, near-disaster struck. The car in which Furman and Nolan were travelling blew a tyre, and slewed out of control, threatening to plunge with its occupants into a nearby ravine.

The truck screeched to a halt. Security agents cocked their guns.

The car was brought under control; its wheel was changed and the journey resumed. In a cloud of dust the convoy passed through Santa Fe and reached Albuquerque's airfield.

Three DC-3's were waiting. Furman and Nolan were given parachutes and boarded the centre plane.

The crate and bucket-shaped cylinder were put on the same plane; they too had their own parachutes.

The crew had been given one instruction: in the event of an emergency, the crate and cylinder were to be jettisoned before the passengers.

The planes reached Hamilton Field, San Francisco, without incident. A new team of agents then escorted the crate, cylinder, Furman and Nolan to their next means of transport—a heavy cruiser whose recent battle-scars, earned at Okinawa, were hidden under a fresh coat of paint. It was the *Indianapolis*.

July 15, 1945
Wiesbaden

As he sat silently at the breakfast table, the only sound Swedish banker Per Jacobsson heard was that of his host, Allen Welsh Dulles, sucking noisily on his briar pipe.

There was no more Jacobsson could say to his old friend. During much of the previous night, often in heated argument, he and Dulles had moved from one room to another in the large house the OSS had requisitioned for Dulles in the southern German city of Wiesbaden. Dulles liked to conduct important talks in this manner. And, in the month Dulles had been in Germany, ostensibly to seek out Nazis, nothing was as important as the discussions he was having with Jacobsson. They were new proposals for an early Japanese surrender.

Both men knew that the crunch had finally come in the delicate negotiations which had begun in December 1944, when first a high

Japanese naval officer, and then Arisue, had sought to use Jacobsson as a channel to Dulles, and he hoped to the American government.

Twelve days ago, Arisue's man in Berne, Lt. General Seigo Okamoto, had been told to establish the minimum surrender terms the Allies would accept from Japan—other than unconditional surrender.

Okamoto, mindful of how the naval peace initiatives had collapsed, discussed the matter with the Japanese Ambassador to Switzerland. They had called in two senior officials of the Bank for International Settlements—to which Jacobsson was financial adviser.

For several days this consortium debated what surrender terms they believed would be acceptable to Japan. They had received no guidance or encouragement from Tokyo, but the group had devised a ploy so daring that even the conservative Jacobsson thought it had a good chance of success.

They proposed that if the American Government would accept the terms of surrender that they, the consortium, had devised and believed the Japanese Government would accept—then America should publicly advance those terms as emanating from Washington. In this way, Japan would be offered a face-saving opportunity to surrender.

Jacobsson recognised this could be one of the greatest coups in diplomatic history: a handful of men, working alone, without encouragement, actually bringing to an end the world's costliest war.

He had contacted Dulles. The OSS director, sensing the barely-concealed excitement behind Jacobsson's cryptic words on the telephone, had sent an OSS car to bring the banker from Switzerland to Wiesbaden.

Jacobsson arrived the previous night. He had immediately outlined the suggested terms to Dulles.

Unconditional surrender should be modified so as to include: a guarantee of the continuing sovereignty of the Emperor; no changes in the Japanese constitution; internationalism of Manchuria; continuation of Japanese control over Formosa and Korea.

Acutely aware of the Allies' insistence on unconditional surrender, Dulles had reacted to the terms coolly, arguing against them in the slow, measured tones which infuriated so many of his subordinates.

Jacobsson had grown steadily more angry in the face of such opposition. Finally, temper and arguments exhausted, well past midnight, he had gone to bed.

Five hours later, in a more conciliatory mood, over breakfast he explained that all the terms were negotiable—except the clause relating to the Emperor. Now he awaited Dulles' response.

For a long time, the head of the OSS sat silently puffing his pipe, the morning sun catching his rimless spectacles. His deep eye-pouches and snow-white moustache made him look far older than his fifty-two years; dressed in *lederhosen*, he could have passed for one of the wood-carvers in the nearby Black Forest. Only his eyes told of his concentration.

Dulles was tired. In the thirty-two months he had been in Europe, he had achieved some brilliant espionage coups, including helping to arrange the surrender of General Wolff's forces in Italy shortly before V-E Day. To those who expressed surprise at his methods, Dulles replied he would trade with the Devil if it was for the benefit of the United States and the Free World.

But he knew the weakness of his present position. Roosevelt had given him a free hand; Truman had shown himself unwilling to grant such latitude. Dulles was not authorised to speak for the new President or the American Government. Furthermore, he was aware of the possible repercussions in America which could result from any sign of appeasement towards the Japanese. The first reports were being published about Nazi concentration camps; the fear was that the Japanese had committed even greater atrocities. America would continue to insist on unconditional surrender as part of the punishment to be meted out to Japan.

And yet Jacobsson's view, that if the Japanese could keep their Emperor they would probably surrender, interested Dulles.

Like Stimson, he took a long view of history. The Russians were crouched, committed to leap at Japan's northern flank in August—less than a month away. But Dulles believed the Soviet Union would not stop there. Once she was in the Far East Russia would stay there —permeating the whole area with her influence.

Dulles, the man who would one day become head of the CIA, already saw it as his life's mission to protect the American way of life from Communism.

He made up his mind.

Dulles gave Jacobsson a counter-proposal. Carefully couched in lawyer's language, it drew a clear distinction between a firm promise and an 'understanding'. But what Dulles was saying, between all the qualifications, was clear: there was a good chance that America would let the Emperor stay, *providing* that Hirohito took a public stand *now* to help end the war.

Jacobsson was relieved. Dulles' proposal, if not what the banker wanted, was at least something.

He hurried back to Berne.

Dulles told an aide to find out about flights from the nearby Frankfurt air base to Berlin. He wanted to report to Stimson, who was due in Berlin shortly to take part in the Big Three Conference.

USAAF Base
Wendover

A few hours after Dulles was making his plans to travel to Potsdam, in Wendover Paul Tibbets watched a transport plane make its final approach. It descended over the salt flats, banked to avoid the town and then touched down, rolling past the three B-29's still on the base.

How long the bombers would remain there depended on the news the transport had brought. The plane carried a Manhattan Project courier, who shuttled between Washington, Wendover and Los Alamos, carrying instructions too secret to be delivered by other means.

The courier brought news that part of the atomic bomb had been delivered to the *Indianapolis*. The other part—the U-235 'target', the lump of uranium which would be placed at the muzzle-end of the gun inside the bomb—was to be flown to Tinian in pieces by the crews still at Wendover.

The operation was code-named: Bronx Shipments. Tibbets often wondered who invented the endless cover-names which were given to everybody and everything associated with the project. He was still surprised each time Groves came on the telephone with the words 'This is Relief', or when Ashworth announced himself as 'Scathe', sometimes bringing news from 'the Co-Ordinator of Rapid Rupture', the pseudonym given to one of the scientists working on the plutonium bomb.

Today's memo confirmed a recent one from 'Judge' (Captain Parsons) giving details of how the 'target' for the 'Little Boy' (the uranium bomb) should travel to 'Destination' (Tinian). Little Boy was just one of a variety of names for the bomb. It was also known as 'the gadget', the 'device', 'the gimmick' (an expression Tibbets favoured), 'the beast' (often used by scientists now critical of the project), 'S-1' (preferred by Stimson) and 'it' (used by the 509th, still mystified about what the weapon exactly was).

Groves had originally called the uranium bomb the 'Thin Man', after Roosevelt. When it was found necessary to shorten the bomb's gun-barrel, Groves re-named it 'Little Boy'. The plutonium bomb, from its conception, was known as 'Fat Man' after Churchill.

Work in Britain on the bomb was hidden under the guise of 'The Directorate of Tube Alloys'.

To keep track of who was who and what was what in the codified world of the Manhattan Project was hard even for the retentive memory Tibbets possessed.

But these instructions were clear enough. One of the B-29's at

Wendover was to carry certain of the remaining bomb parts to Tinian; others would travel on board 509th C-54 transport planes.

Tibbets assigned crews for the flights, and then prepared to travel to Alamogordo for the test-firing of the 'Fat Man'.

With the 509th's presence at Wendover now reduced to a handful of officers and men, Tibbets was more anxious than ever to leave the bleak desert base.

Packed and just about to leave for New Mexico, he received an unexpected and urgent message from Tinian. It was signed by Ferebee, the one man above all others in the 509th whose judgement in all matters Tibbets totally trusted. The easy-going bombardier, who had just arrived on Tinian, was not a man to 'press the panic button'. Yet there was no mistaking the gravity of Ferebee's words urging Tibbets to fly at once to Tinian to deal with a major crisis. It looked as if the 509th were going to be dumped from the 'atomic bomb ticket'.

Pausing only to send a coded message to Groves that he would not be at Alamogordo—and thus would miss the world's first atomic explosion—Tibbets set off at top speed on the 5,500-mile flight to Tinian. He was coldly angry that the internal bickering and manoeuvring which he was aware of, and had carefully avoided, had now finally embroiled the 509th. In all his career Tibbets had never spoiled for a fight. But this time, if somebody wanted 'an eye-ball to eye-ball confrontation', he would provide it. He had not spent the past ten months working himself 'to the bone', sacrificing his family life, his leisure and his friendships only to have some 'wheeler-dealer' snatch the atomic mission from him at the last moment.

July 16, 1945
Alamogordo, New Mexico
Pre-Dawn

Using for illumination the jagged shafts of lightning which intermittently broke through the pitch blackness before dawn on this chilly Monday morning, many of the 425 scientists and technicians gathered at the test site carefully rubbed sun lotion on their faces and hands. Though some of them were twenty miles away from its source, they feared the flash, when it came, might cause instant sunburn. But that could be the least harmful of its side-effects. They all knew the radioactive fall-out accompanying the flash could kill. If it reached them, no lotion or potion could prevent them being contaminated.

And, since nobody knew for certain what were the outer limits of an uncontrolled nuclear chain reaction, it was conceivable the destruction could spread beyond this semi-desert area of land which Groves and the scientists called Site S, and the natives *Jornada del Muerto*, the Tract of Death. Even those scientists who, along with Groves, believed that the world's first atomic explosion would not spread too far, shared a feeling of taking a huge leap into the unknown.

Nine miles from the Base Camp where Groves and Oppenheimer spent most of these early morning hours, the atomic bomb with its plutonium core stood on a hundred-foot-high structural steel scaffold. This point in the desert was code-named Ground Zero.

Two months earlier, when the tower was still under construction, the Air Force had bombed the site, mistakenly believing the area to be part of a practice target range. Two buildings had been hit and fires started, but miraculously there were no casualties. Then, a few days ago, during a rehearsal using a conventional bomb, a bolt of forked lightning had struck the tower and detonated the explosive. Again no one was hurt.

Now, with the test scheduled for 2 a.m., everyone hoped there would be no further mishaps. But the weather began to get worse. Lightning was accompanied by showers. Sporadic rain could be a serious danger, causing shorts in the electrical circuits leading to the bomb; heavy rain could prevent the test firing altogether.

It was one more worry for Groves, already concerned that Tibbets was not at Alamogordo. And, because of the weather, the B-29 Tibbets had ordered to be in the air at the time of the explosion was grounded. Now there was no way of knowing what effect the bomb would have on the aeroplane which would drop it over Japan.

Apart from Tibbets' absence, Groves was 'distressed' by the way some of the scientists were trying to pressurise Oppenheimer to postpone the test. The brilliant physicist was now wound-up 'like the spring in a very expensive watch'.

Groves decided to cast himself in the unusual role of the man who would dispel the tension. Clutching his scientific director firmly by the arm, the project chief marched him up and down around the Base Camp area, assuring him that the weather would improve. In Groves' opinion:

All the personnel had been brought up to such a peak of tension and excitement that a postponement would be bound to result in a let-down which would affect their efficiency . . . We simply could not adequately protect either our own people or the surrounding community or our security if a delayed firing did occur . . . [another] point of concern was the effect of a test delay on our schedule of bombing Japan. Our first combat bomb was to be a U-235 one, and

203

while a successful test of the plutonium bomb without the complications of an air drop would not be a guarantee, it would be most reassuring. Moreover, it would give credence to our assurance to the President as to the probable effectiveness. A misfire might well have weighed heavily on the argument by some, particularly Admiral Leahy, that we were too optimistic and that we should wait for a successful test. After all, this was the first time in history since the Trojan Horse that a new weapon was to be used without prior testing.

The test was delayed while the harassed weather men tried to predict conditions in the coming hours.

Finally, the firing was scheduled for approximately 5.30 a.m. Mountain War Time.

At 5.25 a.m. the observers who were out in the open took up their final pre-atomic positions, lying flat on the earth, faces down, feet towards the blast.

At 5.29 : 00 the last in a series of automatic timing devices took over. There were forty-five seconds to go.

Oppenheimer and his senior staff waited tensely in a concrete bunker. Groves was in a slit trench a short distance away from the scientific director, because, 'I wanted us to be separated in case of trouble'.

5.29 : 35.

From another dugout, a man spoke into a microphone linked to the four look-out posts around the Base Camp.

'Zero minus ten seconds.'

A green flare flashed from the ground and burnt against the low cloud base, briefly and eerily lighting up the darkness.

5.29 : 40.

'Zero minus five seconds.'

A second flare cascaded.

5.29 : 43.

Silence and darkness reigned once more over the desert.

5.29 : 44.

At 5.29 : 45 everything happened at once. But it was too fast for the watchers to distinguish; no human eye can separate between millionths of a second; no human brain can record such a fraction of time. No one therefore saw the actual first flash of cosmic fire. What they saw was its dazzling reflection on surrounding hills; even that was, in the words of the observer from *The New York Times*:

. . . a light not of this world, the light of many suns in one. It was a sunrise such as the world had never seen, a great green super-sun climbing in a fraction of a second to a height of more than 8,000

204

feet, rising ever higher until it touched the clouds, lighting up earth and sky all around with a dazzling luminosity. Up it went, a great ball of fire about a mile in diameter, changing colours as it kept shooting upward, from deep purple to orange, expanding, growing bigger, rising as it was expanding, an elemental force freed from its bonds after being chained for billions of years. For a fleeting instant the color was unearthly green, such as one only sees in the corona of the sun during a total eclipse. It was as though the earth had opened and the skies had split. One felt as though he had been privileged to witness the Birth of the World—to be present at the moment of Creation when the Lord said: Let There Be Light.

Many of the observers were transfixed, rooted to the ground by a mixture of fear and awe at the immensity of the spectacle. Oppenheimer remembered a line from the *Bhagavad Gita*, the sacred epic of the Hindus:

'I am become death, the destroyer of worlds.'

The sinister cloud continued to billow upwards, its internal pressures finding relief in one supramundane mushroom after another, finally disappearing into the dawning sky at well over 40,000 feet, far higher than Mount Everest.

Then, thirty seconds after the first flash of atomic fire, a wind of hurricane force buffeted the Base Camp. Behind it came a deafening roar.

Panic-stricken, one of the military officers in the Manhattan Project screamed.

'The longhairs have let it get away from them!'

A physicist shouted in excitement.

'The sun can't hold a candle to it!'

He rushed out of his bunker and began to do an impromptu war dance. Other scientists joined him, forming a crocodile, whooping over the ground, elated by an event which had produced a light brighter than a thousand suns. At Ground Zero, the temperature at that moment of explosion had been one hundred million degrees Fahrenheit, three times hotter than the interior of the sun and ten thousand times the heat on its surface.

Within a mile radius of Ground Zero all life, plant and animal, had vanished; around what had been the base of the tower, the sand had been hammered into the desert to form a white-hot saucer five hundred yards in diameter. There had never before been sand like it on earth. When it cooled, it turned into a jade-green, glazed substance, unknown to scientists.

The steel scaffold, impervious to any heat known in the pre-atomic age, had been transformed into gas and dispersed.

Groves was among the first to regain his composure. He turned to his deputy, General Farrell, and uttered a prediction for the new era.

'The war's over. One or two of these things and Japan will be finished.'

San Francisco
Morning

Furman and Nolan, the two young Manhattan Project specialists masquerading as Army gunnery officers who were escorting some of the vital components of 'one of these things' to Tinian, watched the final sailing preparations of the *Indianapolis*.

Knowing as little about ships as they did about guns, Furman and Nolan were impressed by the *Indianapolis*' towering superstructure and her eight-inch gun-batteries. They had been told she was the flagship of Admiral Spruance, Commander Fifth Fleet. They had not been told that he was now on Guam helping to plan an invasion of Japan which the priceless parts they were escorting might even yet make unnecessary. Nor did they know that the Admiral's verdict on the cruiser they so much admired had been far from comforting. In his judgement, the ship's centre of gravity was entirely too high and, as a result, he had once remarked that if she ever took a clean torpedo hit she could capsize and sink in short order.

The *Indianapolis*' problem was age. Her keel had been laid in 1932, well before the advent of radar. To remain on active service, the lookout aids had been fitted following Pearl Harbor; her superstructure, from the bridge aft, bristled with radar devices which were efficient but heavy. To those who knew her well, the venerable old warship seemed always to be in danger of toppling over.

She was a curious choice to carry the crucial components of the world's most sophisticated weapon.

For Furman and Nolan, the journey to Tinian would have all the trappings of a luxury cruise. There would be nothing for them to do except take turns to sit in their spacious cabin, watching over the lead bucket containing the uranium projectile. It had been welded to the cabin floor. The fifteen-foot-long crate carrying the cannon was lashed to the deck and guarded round the clock by Marines. With an armed man at each corner, it resembled a bier.

Gossip spread to every corner of the ship. In ward rooms and mess halls, bets were laid that the mystery cargo was anything from a secret rocket, to gold 'to bribe the Nips to quit'.

Even the rosy-cheeked Captain Charles Butler McVay, III, the ship's forty-six-year-old commander, knew little more than any rating about what his ship was carrying or why she was making this head-long dash to the Marianas.

The previous day Parsons had come from Los Alamos to brief McVay. The two men had met in Admiral Purnells' office at the Embarcadero in San Francisco. Parsons had spelled out the mission in words McVay would always remember.

'You will sail at high speed to Tinian where your cargo will be taken off by others. You will not be told what the cargo is, but it is to be guarded even after the life of your vessel. If she goes down, save the cargo at all costs, in a lifeboat if necessary. And every day you save on your voyage will cut the length of the war by just that much.'

Mystified, but having the good sense not to ask questions, McVay had returned to his ship still wondering what his cargo was and why his ship had been chosen.

Pure chance had decided on the *Indianapolis*. She was available and, from the point of speed and space, she was right.

But nobody could be sure how well the cruiser had recovered from the mauling she received at Okinawa, when a kamikaze plane had killed nine of her crew and blown two huge holes in her hull. Skilled artisans at Mare Island, the largest repair yard on the West Coast, had given her a new port quarter, radio and radar equipment, and fire-control mechanisms. She had also received a new 'team'. Captain McVay and some of his senior officers were still there, but over thirty officers, almost half the cruiser's complement, and 250 enlisted men had come aboard as replacements for the veterans of Okinawa. Most of the new officers were distinctly junior; twenty of them had come straight from midshipman's school or the Academy, and many of the enlisted men from training camp.

McVay had planned to work them up in a series of training exercises off the California coast.

Now, these plans were scrapped. With untried officers and crew, with a ship that had undergone the skimpiest of sea trials after major repairs, he was about to set off on a momentous voyage, not knowing what he was carrying—except that it could shorten the war.

He sent for Nolan, who, as Parsons had suggested, told the captain he was not a gunnery officer but 'a medical orderly', and that, as such, he could state 'the cargo contained nothing dangerous to the ship or crew'.

McVay looked at Nolan and made a guess.

"I didn't think we were going to use bacteriological weapons in this war.'

Nolan did not reply. He re-joined Furman in their cabin keeping watch over the bucket, leaving McVay as baffled as ever.

At exactly 8 a.m., the *Indianapolis* sailed with the crew still at morning colours. Thirty-six minutes later she passed under the Golden Gate bridge, outward bound. McVay rang for full speed and soon the thirteen-year-old ship's four screws were turning to produce very nearly flank speed of twenty-nine knots.

On the same day, at almost the same time, some 7,000 sea miles away, at Kure, Commander Hashimoto edged his submarine, I.58, away from her moorings, also outward bound.

July 17, 1945
Potsdam

Bess Truman's fears about a chill in the German air proved groundless. Potsdam was mild and sunny in July; her husband's combinations remained in the suite he occupied at No. 2 Kaiserstrasse, Babelsberg, midway between Berlin and Potsdam.

Babelsberg was in the Soviet Occupation Zone. The Russians had insisted on equipping the American and British residences, situated a couple of blocks from each other. The Americans noted that Churchill's residence was 'perhaps a bit better furnished than the President's'. Truman's second-floor suite was in a three-story stucco building which was immediately christened the 'Little White House'. Stalin's house, a mile away, was the most palatial of all.

Soon after his arrival, on the morning of July 16, Churchill had paid a brief call on Truman. It was the first time the two men had met. Truman took an 'instant liking' to Churchill, who entered into an 'amiable relationship' with Truman, showing a 'marked disposition to agree with him as far as possible'.

The two leaders parted after discussing the news that Stalin was unwell and would be one day late for the conference, They guessed, correctly, that the Soviet leader was recovering from a minor heart attack.

Truman took advantage of the delay to go sightseeing in the ruins of Berlin. He was much affected by what he saw, remarking that the destruction 'is a demonstration of what can happen when a man [Hitler] over-reaches himself'.

Upon his return to Babelsberg, Truman was given a message by Stimson which had just arrived from Washington. It made Truman the most powerful of the three leaders soon to meet over the negotiating table.

The message read:

TOP SECRET
WAR DEPARTMENT
Classified Message Center
Outgoing Message

Secretary, General Staff
Col. Pasco 3542
16 July 1945

TERMINAL
Number WAR 32887
To Humelsine for Colonel Kyle's EYES ONLY from Harrison for
Stimson.

OPERATED ON THIS MORNING. DIAGNOSIS NOT YET COMPLETE
BUT RESULTS SEEM SATISFACTORY AND ALREADY EXCEED
EXPECTATIONS. LOCAL PRESS RELEASE NECESSARY AS
INTEREST EXTENDS GREAT DISTANCE. DR. GROVES PLEASED.
HE RETURNS TOMORROW. I WILL KEEP YOU POSTED.

END

ORIGINATOR:SGS
CM-OUT-32887   (Jul 45) DTG 161524Z hjm

Terminal was the code-name for Potsdam. Humelsine was in charge
of the Military Communications Centre. Kyle was Stimson's military
aide in Potsdam; Harrison was his special assistant in Washington
and also chairman of the Interim Committee in Stimson's absence.
And Harrison's message let Truman know that the Alamogordo test
had been a success, so much so that a fake pre-prepared press release
had been fed to the wire-services claiming that an ammunition
magazine had exploded, 'producing a brilliant flash and blast', which
had been observed over two hundred miles away.

As Truman read the message, he realised 'that the United States
had in its possession an explosive force of unparalleled power'. He
ordered Stimson to respond to Harrison's news. From Potsdam had
gone the message:

TOP SECRET
From: TERMINAL   16, July 1945
To: WAR DEPARTMENT
To Secretary General Staff for Harrison's EYES ONLY from
Stimson.

I SEND MY WARMEST CONGRATULATIONS TO THE DOCTOR
AND HIS CONSULTANT.

SVC 384

Now, at noon on this Tuesday, as Stimson met Churchill and told
him the good news from Alamogordo, Stalin called on Truman. The

Generalissimo apologised for being late, saying his health was not as good as it used to be.

Truman had been told that Stalin had a withered arm, but he could see no signs of any deformity. And he was surprised that the Soviet leader 'was not over five feet, five or six inches tall', which later caused the President to complain that 'when we had our pictures taken, he would usually stand on the step above me. Churchill would do the same thing. They were both shorter than I'.

Nevertheless, Truman was sufficiently impressed by the Soviet leader to feel that at this first meeting he could 'talk to him straight from the shoulder. He looked me in the eye when he spoke and I felt hopeful that we could reach an agreement that would be satisfactory to the world and to ourselves'.

But the President was not sufficiently impressed by Stalin to confide in him what he had just learned about the atomic bomb. Nor did he do so later in the day when they met again at the opening session of the Potsdam Conference.

Not that it much mattered. The Russians already knew about the bomb—through the treachery of scientists in the Manhattan Project. Even now, Russian scientists were engaged in an attempt to catch up with the Americans. The nuclear arms race that Einstein had predicted would occur if America dropped the bomb was already under way.

When Truman returned to the 'Little White House' early in the evening, another message from Harrison had arrived. It read:

TOP SECRET
WAR DEPARTMENT
Classified Message Center
Outgoing Message
                    Office, Special Consultant
                    George L. Harrison, 72501
                    17 July, 1945
TERMINAL
Number: WAR 33556
Secretary of War from Harrison
DOCTOR HAS JUST RETURNED MOST ENTHUSIASTIC AND CONFIDENT THAT THE LITTLE BOY IS AS HUSKY AS HIS BIG BROTHER. THE LIGHT IN HIS EYES DISCERNIBLE FROM HERE TO HIGH HOLD AND I COULD HAVE HEARD HIS SCREAMS FROM HERE TO MY FARM.
                    END
ORIGINATOR: OSW (Mr. Harrison)
CM-OUT-33556   (Jul 45) DTG: 172017Z   bg

Translated, the message gave Stimson and Truman a better idea of the size of the explosion. 'High Hold' was Stimson's estate on Long Island, 250 miles from 'here' (Washington); that was the distance at which the atomic flash had been discernible. Harrison had a farm at Upperville, Virginia, fifty miles from Washington; that was the distance the sound had travelled. 'Doctor' Groves was confident that the still-untried uranium bomb would produce similar spectacular results.

Truman immediately discussed the matter with Stimson, Secretary of State Byrnes, and Admiral Leahy, who had stubbornly refused to believe the bomb would work. Over dinner, the Joint Chiefs of Staff—General Marshall, General Arnold and Admiral King—joined in the discourse.

Truman forebore to ask Leahy if he wished to revise his estimate. Instead, in his later words:

We reviewed our military strategy in the light of this revolutionary development . . . we did not know as yet what effect the new weapon might have, physically or psychologically, when used against the enemy. For that reason the military advised that we go ahead with the existing military plans for the invasion of the Japanese home islands.

The die was cast. The bomb was ready. There would be no further tests to indicate what it might do in war. If the Japanese did not react positively to the final appeal for surrender Truman was planning, then he knew the responsibility was his to decide whether to use the new weapon.

And Truman never was a man to flinch from taking even the most agonising of decisions.

July 18, 1945
Tinian

Paul Tibbets, who shared a similar sense of confidence, now regretted that he had not taken a stronger stand during his earlier visits to LeMay's headquarters on Guam. He was 'fairly certain' that LeMay was not personally involved in the situation that had arisen; rather it was the work of LeMay's staff officers, motivated by reasons that Tibbets could only suspect.

Ferebee, on the other hand, had no doubts.

'Jealousy, that's what it is, pure and simple jealousy. Everybody's trying to get in on the act.'

Tibbets had never known the master bombardier so angry. The

two men were alone in Tibbets' office in the 509th headquarters building, near the centre of the Group's compound on Tinian.

Ferebee had met Tibbets when his plane landed after its three-day flight from Wendover. His first words had been prophetic.

'It's bad news, Paul, really bad news.'

After listening to Ferebee, Tibbets knew he had been right to come pell-mell to Tinian. The future of the 509th, the unit he had built up from scratch, was endangered. In Ferebee's words, 'they're trying to tear your outfit apart'.

A determined effort was underway to break up the tightly-knit 509th and reassign the flying and ground crews to other groups based on the island.

A number of reasons were advanced for this astonishing move: the 509th's fliers could benefit from working alongside combat veterans; they were needed to plug gaps in squadrons who had lost men over Japan; the ground crews were needed to help already harassed line chiefs keep the endless flow of bombers moving into the air.

Tibbets suspected these were mostly excuses. Like Ferebee, he now thought the trouble was caused mainly by others envious of the 509th's special situation.

Matters were not helped by a brush Ferebee had just had with LeMay on Guam. The two men knew each other from Europe; their mutual respect was strong. It was based partly on the fact that while there was a considerable gap in rank between Major Ferebee and General LeMay, they had always spoken frankly to each other.

Ferebee had a 'slow-burning fuse'; it took a lot to rile him. But once aroused he was a formidable foe. LeMay had succeeded in angering Ferebee by casting doubt on Tibbets' ability to fly the atomic mission.

Ferebee had exploded.

'Look, General, if Colonel Tibbets is not qualified, then I'm not qualified, so neither one of us is qualified, so you don't have anybody qualified, and the Navy doesn't have anybody qualified!'

LeMay had told Ferebee to cool down.

The advice had not been heeded. Today, the bombardier was as nettled as ever, not only over LeMay's remarks, but over an 'attempt by the Navy to have their own man fly the mission'.

Tibbets knew the naval pilot—and disliked him from those days back at Wendover when, before the 393rd was fully operational, the pilot had done some early test-flights. To Tibbets, the flier was 'a prima donna, quite the wrong personality for the job'.

Tibbets promised Ferebee that he would go to LeMay 'tomorrow, and settle the whole shooting match once and for all'.

The return of their commander acted as a tonic for the 509th. The sniping and sneering by other units had intensified: at night some of the fliers lobbed stones on to the roofs of the Group's huts as they passed by on their way to North Field for another mission over Japan.

Tibbets' popular deputy, Lt. Colonel Tom Classen, had tried to ease the situation; privately, Tibbets felt that Classen was himself finding the strain of a second tour overseas barely endurable.

Nor had the Group's Intelligence Officer, the roly-poly Colonel Payette, behaved as Tibbets might have expected. Payette was a trained lawyer and had always concerned himself with facts not feelings, results not excuses. But on Tinian he had carried this to extremes; 'in trying to keep the men on their toes he trod on too many feet', was how radio operator Dick Nelson saw Payette's behaviour. Payette had also managed to ruffle Colonel Kirkpatrick, Groves' energetic engineering officer on Tinian, the man who had worked wonders to prepare the island's facilities for the 509th before and since its arrival.

Unknown to Tibbets, Groves was receiving regular reports on the 509th from Kirkpatrick; it was a classic example of the way Groves worked: in his perfect world everybody would watch everybody else.

On this very day of Tibbets' return, Kirkpatrick was preparing his latest top secret newsletter containing the sort of tittle-tattle he believed Groves appreciated.

> The attitude of a few of the people in the Group has been most unfortunate. At times they have acted as spoiled children as I sometimes think they are. There have been a few irritating petty jealousies on the part of some of the personnel, but certainly nothing that couldn't have been promptly corrected by bringing it to the attention of responsible people. Colonel Tibbets is taking action to straighten things out. It is to be regretted that he was so late in joining his command; his prolonged absence has made it difficult for everyone here.

> I don't believe that Col. Tibbets or other late arrivals of the Group will ever appreciate how fortunate they have been. They have the best camp on the island—ready-made, and the best working area. I don't believe that any other organisation has had half the deference and consideration they have, yet their tone is one of not having had enough consideration.

> But this is all petty and will not affect the final outcome. There is no doubt in any one's mind about Col. Tibbets being good or the Group being well qualified but it is unfortunate that they suspect the motives of everyone they are connected with.

To the 509th, Kirkpatrick was just one more 'outsider' who had

213

become attached to their unit. Scientists from Los Alamos, men most of the 509th had never seen before, were now flying in and bedding down in the compound.

They created unexpected paper-work for Charles Perry. The Mess Officer had received written orders from the Air Force Quartermaster's office that he must collect 35 cents for every meal the civilians ate, get receipts for the money, and send them in a special pouch by air to Washington.

Perry thought the idea 'plain stupid'. He did not suspect that behind it all was a continuing Manhattan Project concern about using civilian scientists working alongside military personnel, to make and maintain and eventually to help deliver a military weapon. At Los Alamos, some of the scientists refused to wear a uniform; here, on Tinian, they wore khaki without insignia or markings.

By charging them for their meals, a 'distance' was kept between them and the military.

Beser had no patience with such niceties. To him, it was 'simply a matter of trying to play it both ways. The fact was they were part of the American war effort like everybody else'.

In the seven weeks he had been on Tinian, Beser had made only a few short flights to check out his equipment; the nearest he had come to seeing action was when a solitary flak battery on Rota opened up as the B-29 he was in cruised high overhead.

A few days ago a friend in the 504th had invited Beser to fly with him as a passenger for a fire-raid on Japan.

Classen and Sweeney, now the commanding officer of the 393rd Squadron, refused Beser permission to go.

Beser saw Tibbets' arrival as fortuitous: the raid was scheduled for this very night. He found Tibbets in his Nissen hut and repeated the request.

'I'm sorry, Jake, you can't go.'

Beser looked miffed. Six months before, he would never have dared challenge a decision of Tibbets, but now, 'having been through so much with him, I felt more confident'.

'Colonel, it's just one raid—'

'No.'

Tibbets had himself been stopped by LeMay from flying over Japan; he could see no reason why Beser, who knew almost as much as he did about the atomic bomb, should be allowed 'to go joy-riding where there was a chance he could get shot down'.

Tibbets settled back on his bunk, indicating that the interview was over.

Beser misunderstood the gesture. He thought Tibbets was merely tired after his trip from Wendover and with a little more persuasion would let him go.

214

'Paul, all I want to do is just this one mission to see what it's like—'
Tibbets leapt from his bed.

'Godammit, Lieutenant Beser, I've said no and I mean no! Now get the hell out of here and go about your business. And the next time you come with a request, it's Colonel Tibbets. Understand?'

A chastened Beser backed out of the hut. He spread the word that 'the Old Man's on the rampage'.

Sergeant Abe Spitzer, Sweeney's lanky and articulate radio-man, was glad to hear this. He had sorely missed the guiding driving force that Tibbets provided; if only 'the Colonel' had been on Tinian all the time, Spitzer was sure he would not have had to write the sort of entries he was making in his diary. He did not like much of what he saw.

On the way to chow I passed the officers' beach. It is a stretch of sand and water and sunshine. When we first arrived on the island, it was open to everyone, officers and enlisted men. Now it's for nurses, Red Cross workers and officers. Officers' Country—a kind of never-never land for enlisted men, a place for whose inhabitants there is whiskey and whatever other luxuries can be imported by plane or ship. Officers' Country: no enlisted men or dogs allowed. What a crock. It is not a good feeling for a soldier in what is supposed to be a democratic army.

Spitzer was not the only enlisted man beginning to feel frustrated. Much of the feeling of 'belonging' which Tibbets encouraged at Wendover had evaporated during his enforced absences from Tinian.

In Spitzer's acerbic view, the 509th was becoming 'just another outfit waiting to do a job that nobody seems to think will ever happen'.

Tibbets' long absences had convinced Lewis of one thing: when it came to the mission that really mattered, his commanding officer would not be on board; it would be Lewis himself who would fly the strike.

Lewis' reasons for coming to this conclusion were based on a number of premises.

He believed that he and his crew's record fitted them for the mission. Furthermore, he assumed that Tibbets saw his own role as a 'chairborne commander, planning the operation, leaving its execution to men who regularly flew B-29's'. But Tibbets probably knew more about flying B-29's than anybody else in the Air Force; it was, after all, Tibbets who had initiated Lewis in handling the bomber.

Lewis also believed that Tibbets 'didn't have an airplane'. Technically that was true. The 509th's commander had not assigned himself the aircraft; instead, he had chosen almost always to fly with Lewis. In Tibbets' view this made it clear to everyone with 'a couple of dimesworth of sense that Lewis and his boys were actually my crew. When I went aboard, Lewis was co-pilot and I drove the plane'.

Lewis interpreted the position 'somewhat differently. First of all, Tibbets had never been inside my airplane since I collected it from the factory; secondly, he had not flown on Tinian with us; thirdly I could do the job as well as he could—as well as anybody could'.

Nobody doubted Lewis' flying ability. But the first atomic strike called for more than professional flying expertise. It called for decision-making of the highest order. And indeed it was Tibbets' *duty* to command the mission. The tragedy was that Lewis now believed he should do the job.

Only Eatherly matched Lewis in keenness to make the mission. He had even named his B-29 the *Straight Flush*, after the high-ranking poker game, partly because of his obsession with gambling and partly because he believed his crew was the best in the Group.

Whatever flying standards the officers of the *Straight Flush* had achieved, nobody could match them for the comfortable life they lived on the ground.

Through Eatherly's 'good offices', they had 'inherited' a group of five nurses on Tinian. On an island filled with men starved of female companionship, this was the most desirable gift Eatherly could bestow.

Equipped with perfumes and silks that they had brought from America, the officers, in the words of Flight Engineer Eugene Grennan, 'came, saw and conquered'.

From then on, they had lived 'in the laps of goddesses who waited on us hand and foot'. The *Straight Flush*'s officers regularly dined at the nurses' mess, eating off white linen, food almost matching that provided by Perry. And there was the further advantage that, having dined, the officers could dance and smooch with the nurses—a thrill the 509th Mess Officer could in no way match.

For other officers the Tinian evenings were long; some, like the navigator Russell Gackenbach, relieved their boredom by playing endless practical jokes. His speciality was to creep through the stygian darkness tossing rescue flares into the camp fires which at night flickered all over the compound. The flares created considerable panic —and provided much amusement for Gackenbach.

Caron devised a different way to spend his nights. When he was not at the movies, he was stealthily removing, plank by plank, parts of the Officers' Club, and using the wood to build himself a porch at the back of his hut. The job was coming along nicely; he hoped he could finish it before the mission took place. If he was selected for that, he planned to wear the new Brooklyn Dodgers baseball cap which the team had just sent him.

Flight Engineer Duzenbury had found potentially the most dangerous way of all to spend his free time. Despite having heard that the Japanese on Tinian had recently killed two GI's, at night he and a handful of friends, armed with carbines, went out in the jungle 'in search of souvenirs—Japanese guns and bayonets'. So far, during his scrambling down caves, Duzenbury had discovered three bottles of sake; he did not much like the taste.

Tokyo

Nearly 2,000 miles to the north of where Staff Sergeant Duzenbury had come across the cache, the Japanese soldiers on duty around the Imperial Army GHQ sprang to attention as Major-General Seizo Arisue left the building.

He wanted fresh air, solitude, time to think about the deteriorating situation.

Walking through the grounds surrounding the GHQ complex, he came to one inescapable conclusion: the recent unprecedented intervention by Emperor Hirohito to help terminate the war had come too late; His Majesty had urged Prime Minister Suzuki to let the Soviet Government know openly that the Japanese Government would like it to mediate; the Emperor was even ready to send a special envoy to Moscow with a personal message and full authority to explain the desires of the Japanese Government.

The Imperial wishes had been made known in Moscow five days ago. The Russians had reacted since then only with 'a deafening silence'. Worse, Arisue could sense a cold wind blowing from Potsdam.

For the first time since his appointment as Army Intelligence chief, Arisue felt totally helpless. 'Whichever way I looked there was no ray of hope. The great gamble which had begun at Pearl Harbor was finally coming to an end.'

Late in the evening, on Tinian, Tibbets received a coded message. It was from Groves. It told him that the Alamogordo test had been a total success. Tibbets went to sleep knowing the 'next atomic bang would be the real thing'.

July 19, 1945
Guam

The confrontation between Tibbets and LeMay was short and sweet. LeMay listened attentively while Tibbets explained that it was necessary for the 509th to be left 'alone and intact', that he hoped there would be no more 'meddling', and that *he* 'intended' to fly the first atomic mission.

LeMay had already 'crossed swords' with Groves a month earlier in Washington over the question of who would be in charge once the weapon was ready for combat use. LeMay believed he had won that round, that 'it was my baby once it came to my area'. Groves thought otherwise.

It was still not entirely clear to LeMay why everyone was so insistent that the delivery of the bomb should be entrusted to a unit which had not yet been fully tested in combat over Japan. But he could see that 'to turn it over now to someone else was a little more than they could swallow'.

He decided to agree to Tibbets' request, with one proviso. LeMay's Operations Officer, Colonel William 'Butch' Blanchard, still felt strongly that a 'regular' crew, a 'known quantity' from one of the more battle-experienced groups, should fly the mission. LeMay told Tibbets he wanted to 'send Butch up on a training ride with you and your crew just to satisfy the requirement that you guys know what you're doing'.

Tibbets said he would be glad of the opportunity to take Blanchard 'up for a spin'. The test was fixed for later in the day.

Far to the east, at 10 a.m., the *Indianapolis*, with its nuclear cargo, completed the first leg of its journey. The 2,091-mile trip from San Francisco to Pearl Harbor had taken just seventy-four and a half hours; the old cruiser clipped thirty minutes off the previous record.

Its crew was delighted. They were anxious to continue the run to Tinian.

Commander Hashimoto in submarine I.58 was having no success, lying in wait for American ships off Okinawa. After giving orders to head slowly south towards the Marianas, he walked to the sub's Shinto shrine, aft of the diesel engines, and prayed.

Tibbets took his time over the pre-flight checks. He was keenly aware that Blanchard was watching and listening to each instruction and every response of the crew.

Blanchard was seated on a pile of cushions, just behind Tibbets and Lewis, who was strapped in the co-pilot's seat. Van Kirk was at the navigator's table, Ferebee in the bombardier's position. Duzenbury was at the engineer's panel, Nelson at the radio, Shumard and Stiborik in the blister turrets and Caron in the rear turret.

In the bomb-bay was a single blockbuster filled with high explosive; the fuel tanks carried enough for the round trip from Tinian to Rota.

Tibbets was only able to give the crew a few hours' notice of the flight, but he warned them that Blanchard would be 'looking for the slightest excuse to trip us up'.

He taxied out to the end of the airstrip and awaited clearance for take-off. Then, Tibbets sent the B-29 thundering down the central runway on North Field. Just as the wheels were about to leave the ground, he feathered an engine. Many of the Tinian crashes on take-off happened because an engine failed at this critical moment. Tibbets fought the yawing movement, brought the bomber back on course and began deftly to coax it into the air.

Then he ordered a second engine to be cut. On the same side.

'Yes sir!' replied a confident Duzenbury. There was no doubt in the engineer's mind this was going to be some flight.

Pulled by only two engines, both on one wing, the huge plane, carrying its five-ton bomb, very slowly began to climb.

Banking the B-29, dipping the wing with the silent engines towards Tinian, Tibbets offered Blanchard an excellent view of what was now the world's largest operational airfield.

Tibbets saw that Blanchard was not interested in sight-seeing; his eyes were glued on the two propellers gently windmilling in the air.

Tibbets winked at Lewis—and increased the aircraft's bank until the bomber seemed to be standing on one wing.

Blanchard's anxious voice called Tibbets on the intercom.

'Okay, I'm satisfied with engine performance. Let's head for Rota.'

Tibbets levelled off and, at full power, the B-29 roared towards the island. They arrived over the Initial Point at exactly the time van Kirk had predicted. Tibbets called Blanchard.

'Guess we can agree navigational error was nil.'

'Agreed'.

'Now it's Ferebee's turn.'

The bombardier was in the nose, head glued to the bomb-sight head-rest.

From 30,000 feet the blockbuster plummeted down. Tibbets let Blanchard 'watch it fall and watch it hit. It came so close to the target that there was no use even talking about it'.

Then, without warning Blanchard, Tibbets put the B-29 into the usual 155-degree turn. Strapped in, the crew felt the gravity-force building up as Tibbets 'racked up the plane as tight as I could pull it. I had the tail chattering and the whole airplane juddered like it was coming to pieces'.

A strangled cry came from Blanchard.

'What . . . what's happening . . . ?'

'The damn tail is stalling on me!'

'What'ya mean?'

In all his career, Blanchard had never experienced such a sensation.

219

Pinned to the cushions by centrifugal force, it felt as if he was riding a bone-shaker at full speed down a mountain track.

Tibbets shouted to him.

'This is the only way I can make a tight turn. I've got to keep the tail stalling and then I know I'm doing it right. Now you wouldn't want me to do it any other way, would you?'

'Okay, that's enough. I'm satisfied . . .!'

Tibbets continued to chide him.

'Oh no, we're not through yet!'

Coming out of the 155-degree turn, he yanked back the control column, sending the huge bomber up into a sickening stall. It hovered momentarily on its tail, then slid back, turned and began to spin towards the ground.

Blanchard turned white with fear.

'For Chris' sake, you're going to kill us!'

The bomber continued its dive. Then, judging the moment perfectly, Tibbets brought the B-29 under control and headed back for Tinian. He touched down within fifteen seconds of van Kirk's estimate.

Still stunned and speechless, Blanchard climbed out of the bomber. Only when his feet were firmly on the ground did he speak.

'Okay. You've proved your point.'

Tibbets laughed, now certain Blanchard would pose no further challenge to his authority.

July 20, 1945
Potsdam
Morning

Secretary of War Stimson was just finishing breakfast when Allen Welsh Dulles was shown in to his quarters. His nearby desk was strewn with confidential papers and reports, including one dealing with the thorny question of when and what to tell the Russians about the atomic bomb. Churchill was at first strongly against disclosing any information about the weapon to Stalin, but now seemed to be coming to the same conclusion as Truman and Stimson; the Russians should be told something, but how much?

Official American guidelines on the question of sharing nuclear knowledge had, in fact, been laid down in April by Stimson himself. During his first serious discussion with Truman about the bomb, the Secretary had argued that the pooling of atomic research information was not possible until agreement was reached on international inspection and control. Some scientists had challenged this view, either on the grounds that the Soviet Union could build an atomic bomb whenever it wished without America's help, or in the belief that all scientific knowledge should be shared by the entire world.

Stimson was still fretting over how much the Russians should now be told when Dulles arrived.

Five days had passed since the OSS Director had seen Per Jacobsson, the banker, in Wiesbaden. In that time Dulles had critically examined with his staff the counter-proposal he had made to Jacobsson, that America might allow Emperor Hirohito to remain on the Imperial Throne *if* he took a public stand now in ending the war. Both Dulles and his aides agreed that while there were many uncertainties in the proposal—was the Emperor free to act, was just one question they could not answer—it was still worth exploring.

Stimson respected Dulles' reputation and judgement. But it did not seem that peripheral peace feelers stemming from Switzerland could possibly represent, or indeed influence, official Japanese Government thinking at home.

The Secretary of War's reaction to Dulles was complicated by the fact that Stimson himself had come to Potsdam thinking that, in the final appeal to Japan to surrender, some assurance might be given for continuance of the Imperial system. But already Stimson was aware that such a view was unpopular.

Secretary of State Byrnes, among others, was strongly against making any commitment with regard to the Japanese Throne. And Stimson knew that, for many American intellectuals, the very idea of an Imperial dynasty was repugnant and smacked of 'feudal privilege' and the perpetuation of a 'ruling caste'. To the average American citizen, the concept of Kings and Emperors was totally foreign, inexplicable and generally undesirable; for a great many, Hirohito was simply Hitler, writ large.

Furthermore, to Stimson the story that Dulles presented perfectly illustrated a prediction contained in an important report by the Combined Intelligence Committee. The Washington-based group had recently warned that Japan would:

> Put out intermittent peace feelers, in an effort to bring the war to an acceptable end, to weaken the determination of the United Nations to fight to the bitter end, or to create inter Allied dissensions . . . In general, Japan will use all political means for avoiding complete defeat or unconditional surrender.

Stimson thanked Dulles for coming, but made it clear that he could have no great faith in the Jacobsson connection achieving a breakthrough with the intransigent cabal in Tokyo. Increasingly, Stimson feared that only the pole-axe shock of an atomic bomb would succeed in doing that.

Dulles returned to Wiesbaden as inscrutable as ever, his part in the story over.

In Berne, the Japanese Ambassador and Lt. General Seigo Okamoto would begin to bombard the Foreign Office and Army General Staff in Tokyo with telegrams advocating surrender. Jacobsson would add his voice in cables to Japan's financial leaders. All to no avail. Eventually, Okamoto, in despair, would commit ritual suicide, bringing to a tragic end the strange cloak-and-dagger drama which had for a time involved the secret services of both the United States and Japan.

Now, other players, some familiar, some newcomers, were moving to centre-stage.

Moscow

Physically and mentally wearied by the events of the past few days, Japan's Ambassador in Moscow, Naotaki Sato, was trying, yet again, to make Foreign Minister Togo in Tokyo realise the extreme gravity of the situation.

As he attempted to formulate his message, Sato could not but reflect on the communiqués Togo had been sending him. They seemed to suggest that there was a total lack of reality prevailing in the upper echelons of the Japanese Government.

Having cabled Sato to ascertain how the Soviet Union 'might be used to terminate the war', Togo had added a caution which exemplified the baffling nature of the orders the Ambassador was receiving.

As you are skilled in matters such as this, I need not mention this, but in your meetings with the Soviets on this matter please bear in mind not to give them the impression that we wish to use the Soviet Union to terminate the war.

The same cable indicated to Sato what those in Tokyo thought he should tell the Russians:

We consider the maintenance of peace in Asia as one aspect of maintaining world peace. We have no intention of annexing or taking possession of the areas which we have been occupying as a result of the war; we hope to terminate the war with a view to establishing and maintaining lasting world peace.

The endless flow of words had continued, keeping Sato and his small staff in Moscow decoding day and night. There were proposals and counter-proposals, instructions and counter-instructions, all couched in the confusing courtly language of diplomacy.

Then three days ago, the harassed Ambassador had received a cable in language which was unequivocal:

Not only our High Command but also our Government firmly believes that even now our war potential is still sufficient to deal the enemy a severe blow . . . if the enemy insists on unconditional surrender to the very end, then our country and His Majesty would unanimously resolve to fight a war of resistance to the bitter end. Therefore, inviting the Soviet Union to mediate fairly does not include unconditional surrender; please understand this point in particular.

In other words, nothing much had changed. And, on July 18, Sato was told by the Soviet Government that as they did not know the purpose of the proposed visit to Tokyo by the Emperor's special envoy, they were 'unable to give any definite reply' to this suggestion.

Sato was not to know that the delaying tactic had been ordered by Stalin in Potsdam with the approval of Truman. Even so, it was now clear to him that the Russians were not interested in any Japanese overtures.

He started to write his report to Tokyo, beginning by stating that what followed was his 'unreserved opinion' on the fate facing Japan.

He could see no hope of avoiding an ultimate, total defeat. The enemy had the capacity to destroy not only Japan's industry, but also her life-sustaining rice crop, by burning up the plants when the paddies were dry. To avoid such a calamity, Japan should yield quickly to all the enemy's demands, holding out for only one absolute condition: the national polity must be preserved.

Like Arisue in Tokyo and Dulles in Potsdam, Sato in Moscow was suggesting that Japan should attach no conditions to surrender apart from insisting that the country's form of government, including the Monarchy, be maintained.

His final words indicated how far he had stepped out of line in what he had said:

I realise that it is a great crime to dare to make such statements, knowing that they are contrary to the views of the government. The reason for doing so, however, is that I believe that the only policy for national salvation must coincide with these ideas.

Once his message was received in Tokyo, Sato feared that, if Foreign Minister Togo rejected his plea, then there would be little hope left for his country.

Over Tokyo
Aboard the
Straight Flush

Completely oblivious of the fact that what he intended to do was not only against the bombing policy of the United States in its attacks on Japan, but would also affect the Potsdam Conference, the likely course of the war, and not least, and probably most important of all, the attitude of every Japanese towards fighting on, Claude Eatherly was circling at 30,000 feet just south of Tokyo while his navigator plotted a course which would allow the *Straight Flush* to drop its 10,000-pound high-explosive bomb slap-bang on the Emperor's Palace.

If Eatherly succeeded, he would not only remove Hirohito from the diplomatic chess-board—thereby destroying instantly the one link with Japan's heritage its leaders sought above all others to preserve— he would also trigger a series of events whose course nobody could predict. Bereft of their Emperor, the Japanese nation might do anything.

None of that concerned Eatherly. What did was his craving for fame: if he succeeded, he would forever have a place in the history books. He thought he might end the war.

Eatherly and his men comprised one of the ten crews which Tibbets had chosen to fly the very first 509th missions over Japan on this July 20. They flew separately, against pre-selected targets. The purpose was to accustom the fliers to combat, and the Japanese to seeing single high-flying aircraft which dropped only one bomb.

The crews had strict orders that if their given targets were weather-bound, they must 'under no circumstances' drop their blockbusters on Hiroshima, Kyoto, Kokura or Niigata. Otherwise, their choice of alternative targets was unrestricted.

The B-29's arrived over Japan in the morning, the first having taken off from Tinian at 2 a.m. On the way, one of them had engine trouble and had to jettison its bomb in the sea; five managed to drop their blockbusters in or around their target areas; four, including Eatherly, found the weather so bad that they were forced to seek alternative targets.

Eatherly chose Tokyo—and the Emperor's Palace.

He drawled into the intercom for his navigator, Francis Thornhill, to hurry up with the heading. Thornhill was having trouble. Tokyo, like the original target they had been assigned, was socked-in with cloud.

Although Eatherly had told his crew—and they believed him— that he was a combat-experienced Pacific War veteran, this was in fact, for him, as for them, the very first flight where there was a real possibility they might be shot down. If he was nervous, he concealed it from his crew, showing only mounting enthusiasm at the prospect of bombing the Palace.

And the more he thought about it, the more Eatherly liked the idea. He and his crew would be heroes; it would almost certainly end all the jeering and cat-calling that followed the 509th around Tinian.

Thornhill reported he was still having weather problems.

Bombardier Ken Wey said he could see no gaps in the clouds through which he could sight the Palace.

'Then drop it by radar!'

'Right,' replied the bombardier.

Wey lined up the *Straight Flush* for a radar drop, and released the bomb. Eatherly immediately threw the B-29 into a 155-degree turn, whooping with excitement into the intercom.

They left the Tokyo area without being able to see where the bomb had fallen.

But they knew that, if they had succeeded, there was little doubt Tokyo Rose would mention the fact in her next broadcast. Only then did they plan to reveal to the world it was all their doing.

Tinian

Kizo Imai, the Japanese naval warrant officer in hiding on Tinian, waited until the images flickered on the screen of the outdoor cinema. Then he wriggled towards the high-wire fence, moving swiftly and surely, covering the ground between jungle and fence in seconds.

He ran his fingers along the barbed strands. The gap was still there. Imai eased himself through, moving slowly now, careful not to snag his clothes and leave a clue for the guards who patrolled the 509th's compound.

Having negotiated the wire, he squirmed on his belly towards the nearest Nissen hut. Reaching it, he carefully checked himself and his surroundings. The mud he had smeared on his tunic buttons and belt-buckle was still there; so was the sacking he had wrapped round his boots to deaden his footsteps. Just before he left the safety of the jungle, Imai had dipped his arms into a mud-hole and rubbed his face and neck: he could feel the mud-pack drying on his skin. Imai doubted whether in the darkness anybody could spot him from more than a few feet away. And then, if he was lucky, he could kill them before they raised the alarm; he carried a small knife in his belt for just such a purpose.

Satisfied now that he was as protected as he could be, Imai moved away from the hut, running in a half-crouch, pausing from time to time to get his bearings. From somewhere behind him, the film soundtrack carried clearly through the darkness; the glow from the screen outlined nearby buildings.

He knew he had to travel in the opposite direction to the cinema. Like a dog's sniffing for a bone, Imai's nose directed him towards Perry's kitchens.

He reached the area undetected, found a kitchen door unlocked and slunk inside.

Standing on the table were rows of cooked chickens. He grabbed a couple, stuffed them in his tunic and was reaching for another when he heard a sound. He darted outside just as someone was entering by another door.

Imai stealthily retraced his footsteps, stopping in the shadow of the hut near the hole in the fence. There was a dustbin outside the building. He began to rummage through it. Garbage cans often provided food: partly-consumed tins of meat, potato salads, over-ripe fruit. Tonight's haul was typical: a chunk of smoked sausage, a half-full jam jar and some peanuts. Wrapping his haul carefully in old newspapers he found in the dustbin, Imai stuffed the package inside his tunic and trousers, giving his thin frame an odd, bulbous shape. Then he began to move towards the wire.

A voice stopped him.

The words were in English, but there was no mistaking the accent: it was a Japanese woman's.

Imai felt a sudden surge of excitement as from a nearby hut came the voice of Tokyo Rose, making her nightly broadcast from Japan.

He was tempted to stop and listen. If Radio Japan could penetrate this mysterious compound, then perhaps, soon, Japan's Army would also arrive to drive the Americans back into the sea and bring to an end the scavenger existence of him and his friends.

His spirits raised, Imai fled into the jungle, anxious to return to his cave where he would scan the American newspapers he had stolen for reports of a Japanese advance towards Tinian.

Grouped around their hut's radio, Eatherly and his crew listened impatiently to Tokyo Rose's diatribe. Finally she gave them the news they were all eager to hear.

The tactics of the raiding enemy planes have become so complicated that they cannot be anticipated from experience or common sense. The single B-29 which passed over the capital this morning was

226

apparently using a sneak tactic aimed at confusing the minds of the people.

Tokyo Rose could not know that it was not the minds of the people Eatherly was after, but Hirohito himself.

No further reference was made to the raid. Clearly the bomb had not hit the Palace.

Disappointed, Eatherly turned away from the radio, his hopes of world-wide fame temporarily quashed.

July 21, 1945
Hiroshima

Precisely at 6 a.m., as he did every morning, Field Marshal Hata awoke, bathed, dressed in a kimono and breakfasted with his wife.

Then, around seven o'clock, he padded in his slippers to the Shinto shrine which was an integral part of his home. There he prayed for victory in the great battle he now deemed inevitable. He was not concerned about his own fate. He had faced death too often for that prospect to worry him now.

His prayers said, he changed into his uniform and was ready to begin the next part of his daily ritual.

Hata's house was newly-built, comfortable and close to his head-quarters. But nowadays, apart from praying at the shrine, the Field Marshal's domestic involvement with his home was confined to working in the 'victory' garden he had planted at the rear of the dwelling.

By Hiroshima standards it was a large and well-stocked plot, surrounded by young trees. Every morning after his prayers, Hata tended his vegetables. They provided a significant portion of his household's food. This manual outdoor work kept him lean and fit; his appearance belied his sixty-five years.

He was still confident he could give the Americans a severe blow when they landed, but he also believed they would prove the most formidable foe he had ever faced. Long ago, in that period of early Japanese victories, Hata had dismissed the Americans as soft, with no stomach for fighting; he had even thought the United States might seek peace after Pearl Harbor. Now, he knew better: the Americans were certainly as tough as the Chinese or British, and were probably the best-equipped army in the world. When they came, Hata expected an assault of unparalleled fury.

He was ready for it.

In a few short months, behind a fantastic jungle of obstacles and minefields, Hata had prepared his inland defences. From the shores of Kyushu they stretched as far back as Hiroshima on the main island of Honshu where he now stood, almost two hundred miles behind the Kyushu beachheads. Designed to allow for an orderly falling back to prepared positions, the defence system utilised the natural terrain to the maximum: murderous arcs of cross-fire, tank traps and booby-traps awaited the Americans at every turn.

At nearly eight o'clock Hata completed his gardening and went into the house. There, an overnight situation report, prepared with the help of Oya, acting in his capacity as Hata's intelligence chief, awaited the Field Marshal. This morning's summary offered no clues which would help Hata harden up his estimate of where on Kyushu the Americans intended to invade, or when. The report stated there had been the usual air raids during the night on a number of cities. Army Intelligence was particularly puzzled by the solitary B-29's which had bombed Japan yesterday. Not only did they fly alone, but at a great height and in the daytime, precisely the opposite of the Americans' usual bombing tactics. Furthermore, each plane had dropped just one large bomb, often on targets with no apparent military significance. One of the bombs was said to have fallen in the moat around the Imperial Palace. Apart from its size, the weapon seemed conventional. Intelligence suggested it could have come from Europe, where similar large bombs had been used by the R.A.F. against the Germans.

The report noted that American and British warships had again been shelling the coast of Honshu, concentrating mainly on the areas north of Tokyo.

Hata put aside the summary and finished his tea. Then, at about 8.15 a.m., again as he did every morning, the most important soldier outside Tokyo left for his headquarters.

Hata's staff car was one of the few vehicles heading for 2nd General Army headquarters this morning. Most of his officers preferred to ride on horseback to work, and this equestrian parade was a sight which regularly earned admiration from the milling crowds on their way to, or from, Hiroshima's war factories.

The animals, like their owners, and in marked contrast to the civilians, were sleek and well-groomed.

Particular approbation was reserved for the Korean prince, Lt. Colonel RiGu, who was attached to Hata's staff. His was arguably the most superb horse in Hiroshima, a huge stallion, sixteen hands high, snow-white with black fetlocks.

Sitting bolt upright on his steed, ceremonial sword at his side, the handsome young prince in his polished boots and carefully pressed

228

uniform was a reassuring sight. RiGu was a reminder of past glories, when the Imperial Army's cavalry had swept all before them; even his haughty manner was accepted: in civilian minds such an attitude was regarded as being part of the Army's invincibility.

RiGu enjoyed his morning canter through the streets and parks of the city. He was well aware of the Japanese attitude towards his people: most Koreans were there to do the dirty jobs, to live in a segregated ghetto outside the city and usually to be treated as socially inferior. Seated on his magnificent mount, Prince RiGu could look down on a population which treated his people so badly.

Mayor Awaya and his personal assistant, Kazumaso Maruyama, chose to walk to work each morning. They found it allowed them to discuss the city's problems unhindered. Today, their conversation turned to a recurring topic: what could be done for the children who still remained in Hiroshima? Many of them worked in the factories, and were receiving only a token education. Teachers travelled from one war plant to another, holding short classes on the factory floors.

Awaya thought the situation appalling and wanted to enlarge the city's industrial college. Maruyama believed all children should be evacuated.

The problem unresolved, the two men entered the City Hall and were at once confronted by others. There were complaints about some of the local associations and the way they distributed food; about the lack of fuel; about shops overcharging; about Kempei Tai brutality; about the need for more large air raid shelters. A man wanted the mayor to support an application for travel; a woman wanted Maruyama to fill in the forms needed to obtain compensation for losing her home to a fire-lane.

The question of how best to deal with the neglected children of Hiroshima was lost in a welter of demands and decisions which overwhelmed Awaya and Maruyama.

Two miles away from where the embattled mayor and his assistant dealt with a myriad of problems, 2nd Lieutenant Tatsuo Yokoyama at his Mount Futaba gun-post struggled to cope with an issue which threatened his whole future.

For weeks now, his commander, Colonel Abe, had been pressing for a decision from Yokoyama's parents as to whether he could marry Abe's daughter.

Yokoyama had finally received their answer this morning in a letter from his father in Tokyo. Carefully couched and bearing all the signs of having had each of its words considered before it was committed to paper, the letter rejected the marriage proposal.

Yokoyama's parents had decided that Abe's daughter was unsuitable because their investigation had shown, 'she has an unhappy disposition. Her school teachers indicate she is not obedient or good at her work. In spite of his high position, we do not see from our most patient enquiries that your colonel's antecedents are always what we would desire for uniting our two families'.

The gunnery officer read the letter a number of times; its message was clear and, as a dutiful son, he must accept his parents' decision. What troubled him now was how to break the news to Colonel Abe. His commander, he knew, was an unpredictable man. Yokoyama had no idea how Abe might react to what he would surely regard as an unforgivable insult.

Yokoyama was certain that once he had told Abe of his parents' decision, the commander at the very least would banish him to some other part of the country.

He had folded the letter and placed it in his tunic pocket, still undecided on what to do, when his reverie was disturbed by excited shouts from his gunners. Yokoyama looked at his watch and then rushed out of his quarters. It was midday, and American bombers were back over Kure to bomb and machine-gun the port. Nowadays, they came regularly at noon and at midnight. From his vantage point, just seven miles away, Yokoyama could clearly see the flashes from the Kure ground batteries.

The feeling of hopelessness which he had brought back from Tokyo now lifted. Tokyo, indeed, might be in ruins. But here, in the west of Japan, the Army was fighting back as hard as ever; he desperately wanted to be part of that fight. Suddenly he knew what he must do about the letter: he would pretend he had never received it; he would tell Abe that his parents were still considering the matter, that it might be some months before they were able to give a decision as their life had been disrupted by the bombing. That would buy him time—perhaps enough time for one of the planes he could clearly see in the sky above Kure to come over Hiroshima and within range of his guns.

Some hundred miles south of Hiroshima, and 32,000 feet above the ground, Lewis was flying in an unfamiliar B-29 on what he regarded as 'a shit job'.

He had been asked to establish whether a fellow pilot was a coward.

The pilot had told Tibbets that the reason he had aborted his mission to Japan was because one of his engines had over-heated and cut-out near the Japanese coast. The pilot had dropped his bomb into the sea and returned to Tinian.

Tibbets suspected the story. He ordered a thorough ground test of the aircraft's engines. They all behaved perfectly. His suspicions increased; he told Lewis to take the bomber up and test it in the air.

Lewis was ebullient because Tibbets had entrusted such a 'delicate matter' to him; he saw it as a clear sign that any past misunderstandings were forgotten, that the 'special relationship' between them was being re-established. Most important of all, in Lewis' mind was planted the thought that, if he did a good test flight, it would further establish his right to drop 'the big bomb' on Japan. He did not like the idea of 'reporting on a fellow pilot', but equally, he had no time for cowards; in his view 'a man who got chicken had no place in our outfit'.

When Lewis returned, Tibbets was waiting for him on the apron. 'Well?'

'No problem. She flies like she's brand-new.'

Tibbets turned away. He had known the pilot who had flunked the mission a long time; he had a good record. Tibbets had even considered using him to fly one of the support planes for the atomic mission—unthinkable now in view of his behaviour. Yet to post him from the 509th would ruin the flier's career. Tibbets remembered a piece of advice his mother had given him: 'Son, if you don't have to hurt somebody who's weaker than you, then don't.'

Tibbets decided that the pilot would henceforward only be given harmless trips around the Marianas.

July 22, 1945
Potsdam

This Sunday morning saw no let-up in the pace President Truman was maintaining. He had been up since 6.30 reviewing the decisions reached so far during the Big Three sessions in the lofty, dark-panelled conference room at the Cecilienhof. The position did not please him. Both Stalin and Churchill were tough-minded negotiators, and the President was getting 'tired of sitting and listening to endless debates on matters that could not be settled . . . I was anxious to avoid any sharpening of the verbal clashes in view of the more immediate and urgent questions that needed to be settled'.

Paramount among them was Japan.

The matter had been brought to a head the day before when Groves' ecstatic report on the Alamogordo test had arrived. Stimson had read it in full to the President.

Groves had made no attempt to present a concise, formal military report, but had produced an account that bore the stamp of having been written with the test still vividly in his mind. The result was a personal narrative of great power.

Stimson's excellent voice made the most of the prose, and Truman had sat entranced, listening to details which were quite fantastic: the flash brighter than many suns, the massive cloud, the steel tower vapourised into gas, a window shattered 125 miles away.

The Manhattan Project director wrote of:

feeling that the faith of those who had been responsible for the initiation and the carrying on of this Herculean project had been justified. I personally thought of Blondin crossing Niagara Falls on his tight-rope, only to me this tight-rope had lasted for almost three years, and of my repeated confident-appearing assurances that such a thing was possible and that we would do it.

Groves noted, as an aside, that although he saw no reason to expect the loss of the bomber which would deliver the bomb, 'we cannot guarantee [its] safety'. He also added that he no longer regarded 'the Pentagon a safe shelter from such a bomb', a sobering thought for a man whose previous claim to fame was that he had helped to erect the building.

Truman said the report gave him an 'entirely new feeling of confidence'.

Now, this Sunday morning, Stimson arrived with more good news. Harrison in Washington had cabled that the uranium bomb would be ready for use 'the first favourable opportunity in August'; furthermore, if the mission was to go ahead, then its complicated preparations must be set in motion no later than July 25, three days hence.

To the Secretary of War, Truman seemed 'intensely pleased with the accelerated timetable'.

At 10.40 a.m., Stimson called on Churchill, who read Groves' report in full. He looked at the Secretary of War and, in that familiar resonant voice, fired off two questions which he himself immediately answered.

'Stimson, what was gunpowder? Trivial. What was electricity? Meaningless. The atomic bomb is the Second Coming in wrath.'

Stimson made it clear that the President intended to tell Stalin about the weapon—although he would 'withhold all details', merely 'divulging the simple fact that the United States and Britain had the bomb'.

The Prime Minister agreed; he believed the fact should be used as 'an argument in the negotiations' going on at Potsdam.

Back in his quarters, at 12.15 a.m., Stimson summoned General Arnold, chief of the Air Force, and showed him the report from Groves and the cables from Harrison.

Stimson asked for Arnold's views.

The air chief confirmed that it would 'take considerable hard work to organise the operation'.

He suggested that, in place of Kyoto, Nagasaki should be considered as one of the potential targets—the first time the city had been ear-marked for possible atomic destruction.

Arnold told Stimson that General Carl A. Spaatz, recently promoted commander of the Strategic Air Forces and about to travel to the Marianas, could make the final choice in consultation with LeMay.

While Stimson talked with Arnold, Truman met Churchill.

To the Prime Minister, the weapon was 'a miracle of deliverance'. It might make invasion unnecessary. It could end the war in 'one or two violent shocks'. Its almost supernatural power would afford the Japanese an excuse which would save their honour and release them from the Samurai obligation to fight to the death. Nor would there now be a need to beg favours of Stalin, to rely on Russian intervention to help bring Japan to her knees. And, with the war over in the Far East and the balance of power redressed, the United States and Britain could face European problems on their merits.

Churchill concluded that, 'while the final decision lay in the main' with Truman, there was no disagreement between them, for, as he later put it:

> The historic fact remains, and it must be judged in the after time, that the decision whether or not to use the atomic bomb to compel the surrender of Japan was never an issue. There was unanimous, automatic, unquestioned agreement around the table.

All that now remained in question was whether Japan would first accept the terms of surrender which were about to be offered by the Allies. When those terms were received, to paraphrase Churchill, only 'a miracle of sanity' on the part of Japan's leaders could prevent the weapon being dropped.

July 23, 1945
Tinian

Deep in the Tinian jungle at the foot of Mount Lasso, hemmed in by the pitch-black night, Jacob Beser also doubted whether he would see his idea of a Japanese miracle: 'a Nip popping out of the bush and saying "me very glad to surrender to honourable American".'

Beser was taking part in what had become a favourite Tinian pastime.

Clutching a carbine he had traded for a quart of whisky, the skinny young radar officer had persuaded a Marine patrol to take him with them into the jungle in search of Japanese.

The Marine officer had explained the hunting rules to Beser.

'First we surround the area where we think the Nip is hidden. Then we work inwards, pen him into a few square yards and illuminate the area with flashlights. Then we try to talk him into surrendering.'

'And if he doesn't?'

'Wait and see.'

At night-fall, the Marines, with Beser in their midst, had entered the jungle.

Since then they had twice encircled suspicious patches, but had drawn blanks.

Now the patrol was stalking the rising ground around Mount Lasso.

The Marines kept up a fast pace, moving in a crocodile with Beser in the middle.

Suddenly the soldiers froze.

Beser could hear nothing.

The Marine in the lead turned and tapped his nose.

Beser sniffed. Faint but unmistakable, he detected a human odour. Once before, when he had been a student, he had encountered a similar smell—on the night he had led a gang of students to bust up a Communist meeting in Baltimore. Beser had always remembered the pungent sweaty stench from some of his fellow students just before the encounter.

Now, it was here in the darkness.

The Marine officer swiftly deployed his men, ordering Beser to remain stationary while the soldiers melted into the dark.

Alone, clutching his carbine, Beser wondered what he would do if a Japanese soldier appeared before him. He had never killed a man; he prayed he would not have to do so now. He wished he had stayed in his hut playing poker.

For long minutes nothing happened.

Then Beser heard the sound of branches being moved. He cocked his gun, preparing to shoot into the impenetrable wall of jungle around him.

Suddenly, beams of light probed the darkness. An American voice called out in Japanese.

'Surrender! You are surrounded. Come out with your hands up.'

Beser started to rise to his feet. Another American voice stopped him.

'Stay down—or you'll be shot!'

Beser resumed crouching.

The talking continued.

There was a grunt from the jungle, following by a movement through the foliage.

'He's coming out!'

The torches followed the sound.

Then, from out of the undergrowth in front of Beser, a figure emerged.

The lights held the Japanese soldier, blinding him, forcing him to close his eyes.

As Beser took his first view of an enemy soldier, all he could think was that, 'he didn't look much like the Nips in *Yank* cartoons'.

Beser joined the Marines milling around their prisoner. The torches were lowered. The captured soldier opened his eyes. He spoke his first words in passable English.

'Please. Cigarette.'

He was given one. Inhaling deeply, he stood still while a Marine patted down his uniform and fished out of a pocket a silver cigarette case. In halting English, the prisoner explained he had taken the case from a dead Australian soldier in New Guinea.

The Marine officer looked at the captured man, shook his head in disgust and turned away. Two Marines fell in beside the prisoner, pinioning his arms. In silence the patrol returned to their base.

That night there was one man less in Imai's cave to pick over the garbage scavenged from the American refuse dumps.

Grouped around the desk in his office, Tibbets, Ferebee and van Kirk carefully studied the latest reconnaissance photographs of the Japanese cities so far 'reserved' for the atomic attack.

All three agreed that, given the chance, they would prefer to bomb Hiroshima.

July 27, 1945
Tokyo

In his office at Imperial Army GHQ, Major-General Arisue listened carefully as Lt. Colonel Oya described the network of defences which radiated outwards from Hiroshima.

Oya had travelled 550 miles by train to Tokyo to make a personal report to Arisue on Field Marshal Hata's plans for repelling the invaders from Kyushu's shores.

His report was the most welcome news Arisue had heard in days.

He only wished that the area around Tokyo was in the same high state of readiness. But every time he looked out of his office window, the bleak reality was visible: for miles, to the left, right and centre, the landscape was devastated. Tokyo and its environs were prostrate, its industries either obliterated by bombs or paralysed by lack of manpower and materials. The bombs had driven millions of workers from the city, reducing its population from seven to less than four million. Without factories, the army around Tokyo could not be supplied with goods—yet no way had been found to induce workers to return to their benches when there were no facilities to feed, clothe and house them.

Arisue knew that, without efficient production and supply lines, the Army could not last long against American forces. Oya still clung to the conviction that there was one element even more important than war materials—a determination to resist. He believed the Army would wage war until the end, defending His Majesty, the Emperor, and the holy soil of the homeland.

Arisue was spared from commenting by the arrival of a messenger from the radio monitoring unit he maintained as a part of Army Intelligence.

He took the batch of flimsies and laid them out on his desk. Excitedly, Arisue realised this was the long-expected communiqué from Potsdam. He began to study the sheets of paper crammed with hurriedly prepared Japanese script, the result of transcribing and translating at high speed the words of a monitored short-wave transmission from Washington.

It was the text of the Potsdam Proclamation, perhaps the most important message the Japanese received from the Allies in the entire war. It read:

July 26, 1945

(1) WE—THE PRESIDENT of the United States, the President of the National Government of the Republic of China, and the Prime Minister of Great Britain, representing the hundreds of millions of our countrymen, have conferred and agree that Japan shall be given an opportunity to end this war.

(2) The prodigious land, sea and air forces of the United States, the British Empire and of China, many times reinforced by their armies and air fleets from the west, are poised to strike the final blows upon Japan. This military power is sustained and inspired by the determination of all the Allied nations to prosecute the war against Japan until she ceases to resist.

(3) The result of the futile and senseless German resistance to the might of the aroused free peoples of the world stands forth in awful clarity as an example to the people of Japan. The might that

now converges on Japan is immeasurably greater than that which, when applied to the resisting Nazis, necessarily laid waste to the lands, industry and the method of life of the whole German people. The full application of our military power, backed by our resolve, *will* mean the inevitable and complete destruction of the Japanese armed forces and just as inevitably the utter devastation of the Japanese homeland.

(4) The time has come for Japan to decide whether she will continue to be controlled by those self-willed militaristic advisers whose unintelligent calculations have brought the Empire of Japan to the threshold of annihilation, or whether she will follow the path of reason.

(5) Following are our terms. We will not deviate from them. There are no alternatives. We shall brook no delay.

(6) There must be eliminated for all time the authority and influence of those who have deceived and misled the people of Japan into embarking on world conquest, for we insist that a new order of peace, security and justice will be impossible until irresponsible militarism is driven from the world.

(7) Until such a new order is established *and* until there is convincing proof that Japan's war-making power is destroyed, points in Japanese territory to be designated by the Allies shall be occupied to secure the achievement of the basic objectives we are here setting forth.

(8) The terms of the Cairo Declaration shall be carried out and Japanese sovereignty shall be limited to the islands of Honshu, Hokkaido, Kyushu, Shikoku and such minor islands as we determine.

(9) The Japanese military forces, after being completely disarmed, shall be permitted to return to their homes with the opportunity to lead peaceful and productive lives.

(10) We do not intend that the Japanese shall be enslaved as a race or destroyed as a nation, but stern justice shall be meted out to all war criminals, including those who have visited cruelties upon our prisoners. The Japanese Government shall remove all obstacles to the revival and strengthening of democratic tendencies among the Japanese people. Freedom of speech, of religion and of thought, as well as respect for the fundamental human rights shall be established.

(11) Japan shall be permitted to maintain such industries as will sustain her economy and permit the exaction of just reparations in kind but not those which would enable her to re-arm for war. To this end access to, as distinguished from control of, raw materials shall be permitted. Eventual Japanese participation in world trade relations shall be permitted.

(12) The occupying forces of the Allies shall be withdrawn from Japan as soon as these objectives have been accomplished and there has been established in accordance with the freely expressed will of the Japanese people a peacefully inclined and responsible government.

(13) We call upon the government of Japan to proclaim now the unconditional surrender of all Japanese armed forces, and to provide proper and adequate assurances of their good faith in such action. The alternative for Japan is prompt and utter destruction.

All Arisue's calculations on how the war could be brought to an end had been based on the Allies giving some sign, however tenuous, that the Imperial System would continue.

There was no such sign.

The Intelligence chief believed that, without a guarantee that the Emperor would rule a post-war Japan, the nation would fight on.

Arisue also anticipated that the militants would suspect 'as a trick' phrases such as 'we do not intend that the Japanese shall be enslaved as a race or destroyed as a nation'. For such men, the Samurai influence would continue to prevail.

And for Oya, the statement that 'stern justice shall be meted out to all war criminals' had an ominous ring. He thought it was entirely possible he 'might be accused of war crimes'.

Oya, for all his specialist knowledge of America, could offer no explanation of why the Proclamation excluded any reference to the Emperor.

Neither he nor Arisue had any way of knowing that Stimson had agreed to leave out mention of the Throne on the understanding from Truman that if the Japanese, in their reply, raised the question, it would be treated sympathetically, if not at first publicly.

Now, with the terms of surrender so plainly stated, Seizo Arisue, in common with other Japanese, saw the Potsdam Proclamation as a 'warning of annihilation unless we give up what we hold sacred'.

A few miles away, the person most directly concerned with the absence of any mention in the Proclamation of the Royal Family, the Emperor himself, studied the document that some thought threatened his dynasty.

Foreign Minister Togo, who had brought the copy of the communiqué to Hirohito, sat bolt upright on one of the hard sofas, watching the Emperor slowly read it.

His Majesty was in no hurry, pondering every word, weighing the implications of each sentence. The increasing paralysis gripping the Japanese nation had not penetrated to the Audience Hall of the

Imperial Palace's *Gobunko*—the Library Building, screened by trees near the North Gate.

The *Gobunko* was one of the few buildings within the Palace grounds which was unscarred by war. On May 25, the Emperor had suffered the agony of seeing many of the buildings and pavilions within the Imperial compound burn to the ground. During the previous night there had been a fire-bomb raid; LeMay's bombers had concentrated on the two districts adjoining the Palace. Though the Americans intentionally avoided dropping incendiaries within the Imperial precincts, they had converted the surrounding areas into such tornadoes of flame that the conflagration had jumped the moat around the Palace and set fire to dry brushwood on the far side. In minutes the flames had spread and engulfed the old wooden Imperial residence, built by Hirohito's grandfather, the revered Emperor Meiji.

At dawn, Hirohito and his Empress had emerged from their shelter and surveyed the destruction. As well as structural damage, twenty-eight members of the Palace staff, including twelve firemen, had died; the firemen could easily have escaped, but no one gave them direct orders, and they were burned at their posts. It took fourteen hours to extinguish the flames; it took even longer for a Palace official to grasp the significance of what the Emperor had told him:

'We have been bombed at last. Now the people will realise that I am sharing their ordeal with no special protection from the gods.'

Hirohito was astute enough to make use of the blaze to remind his people that he was mortal, and was also sharing their hardships. At the same time he took steps to ensure that the nation was not misled into believing there had been a deliberate attempt by the Americans to bomb the Palace or to kill him. He knew that, if that thought was allowed to take root, it would only weld his people even more firmly together in a solid wall of hatred against the enemy, and that was not something His Majesty desired.

Now, as the Emperor studied the Allies' Proclamation, Togo kept to himself the reservations he had about the document.

But even the manner in which it had been sent to Japan—as the main story in one of the short-wave newscasts emanating from Washington—disheartened the protocol-minded Togo. To him, steeped in the tradition of diplomatic exchanges, conveying such an important document by public broadcast 'did not seem the way for government to speak to government'.

Yet, under the Emperor's questioning, Togo conceded that the communiqué did give detailed assurances of humane treatment, freedom of speech, religion and thought. There was also the unwelcome mention of an occupation of strategic points of the Home Islands, but this would end once stability was restored. And the Japanese people were to be consulted on the form of government they wished after the surrender.

The Emperor continued to discuss the Proclamation clause by clause, asking his questions and making his points. He was probably one of the best-informed men in Japan. He knew, perhaps better than anybody else, that the war was lost. And, not for the first time, Hirohito must have wished that the short, dapper Togo, his formal dress showing traces of wear, would bluntly state his opinion.

But the Foreign Minister, like so many others who came into regular contact with the Emperor, continued to speak in polite circumlocutions, which were often so stylised and elaborate that the sense of what he was saying was completely obscured.

Togo, the man who had no difficulty in finding the right words to mislead America's Ambassador in Tokyo on the day of Pearl Harbor into believing that war was still avoidable at the very time Japanese bombers were about to attack, now found it a tortuous business to make his points clearly.

It would, of course, have been unthinkable for him to raise the one issue that troubled him most: the possibility that the Proclamation's demand for unconditional surrender meant the end of the national polity.

Finally, the Emperor asked his Foreign Minister whether he accepted that the terms 'were the most reasonable to be expected in the circumstances'.

Togo agreed this was the case.

'I, too, agree. In principle they are acceptable.'

Silence enveloped the Audience Chamber.

Then, abruptly, Shigenori Togo rose to his feet and faced the Emperor. It was the traditional gesture of the Imperial Court to signify that a visitor had no more to say.

The Emperor also stood and, controlled by another act of ritual, without speaking further he turned and left the room.

Togo bowed from the waist to the retreating Emperor. As Hirohito disappeared through the door of the Audience Hall, the Foreign Minister bowed again.

He had not revealed to the Emperor the hardening attitude of Japan's government and military leaders to the Potsdam Proclamation.

Prime Minister Suzuki and his colleagues were inclined to ignore the communiqué, partly on the grounds that officially they had not even received it. Furthermore, the Cabinet still pinned its hopes on the Soviet Union mediating for them towards a 'reasonable surrender'. There was total agreement that to 'accept Potsdam would be to insult Russia'.

That reaction was misguided enough, but the aged Suzuki would compound the folly.

He arranged a press conference with a reporter planted to ask the Cabinet's view of the Proclamation.

Hands trembling, the Prime Minister read a prepared statement. He dismissed the Proclamation as 'no more than a repetition of the Cairo Declaration'—which in fact had been much tougher—and added that the government 'does not regard it as a thing of great value. We have decided to *mokusatsu* the Proclamation.'

Translated into English, *mokusatsu* meant either to 'take no notice', 'treat with silent contempt', 'ignore' or 'kill' it 'with silence'.

The Prime Minister did not specify which interpretation should be placed on his *mokusatsu*. The reporters did not ask; they felt there was no need to. Suzuki's tone, coupled with his concluding phrase— 'we will press forward resolutely to carry the war to a successful conclusion'—could only mean that the Cabinet had rejected the Potsdam Proclamation, contemptuously brushing aside the guarantees it contained.

Within minutes Suzuki's words would be broadcast by the official Japanese news agency.

In Potsdam, Secretary of War Stimson was tersely to record the conclusion that was drawn by the Allies when they heard the news:

In the face of this rejection, we could only proceed to demonstrate that the ultimatum had meant exactly what it said when it stated that if the Japanese continued the war, 'the full application of our military power, backed by our resolve, will mean the inevitable and complete destruction of the Japanese armed forces and just as inevitably the utter devastation of the Japanese homeland'. For such a purpose the atomic bomb was an eminently suitable weapon.

Now, there was no need to countermand the preparations for dropping it.

Before attacking Pearl Harbor, Japan had intended that diplomatic relations with the United States should have been formally broken.

They were not.

Before using the atomic bomb, America had intended that the Japanese should understand what would happen if their terms were rejected.

They did not.

The road to Hiroshima was paved with good intentions.

This was the day when Beser finally discovered he was being watched by the 509th's flight surgeon, Dr. Don Young, for signs of psychological strain.

On orders from Tibbets, Young was observing all the Group's air crews for such symptoms. Tibbets 'didn't want somebody to goof-off just as we were about to drop the bomb'. Young did his work so discreetly that few fliers suspected they were under survey.

Beser was delighted to discover he was: 'It meant we must be getting close to mission time.'

Young himself still did not know exactly what the mission entailed. He had simply been told to report any flier showing the first signs of 'unusual behaviour'.

The surgeon watched every crew going off on a flight; he carefully noted the way they walked and carried their gear. He eavesdropped on their conversations, listening for complaints of lack of sleep or loss of appetite—possible indications of inner tension.

When the planes returned he was on the tarmac, smiling, a gentle unobtrusive man with a sharp clinical mind. Young observed the fliers drinking their ration of bourbon, issued at the end of each mission; he was looking for the crew-man who gulped his whisky too quickly or asked for a second shot.

He sat in on de-briefings, assessing the way the fliers made their reports: their choice of words provided him with clues to their mental states and attitudes.

And, against all regulations, he read their mail after it had cleared the Censor Office: he was looking for further signals which might indicate instability.

In between, he dropped into the fliers' huts, searching for the man who laughed too loudly, lost his temper too quickly, played too boisterously. His quest took him into the Officers' and Enlisted Men's Clubs, where he would move from one table to another, anticipating signs of homesickness, depression or hypertension.

Finally, he would prowl the sports field, watching the fliers at play, looking for signs of 'undue aggression' or bad sportsmanship.

Then, late at night, the indefatigable Dr. Young would collate his findings in confidential reports for Tibbets.

He had tabbed Beser as one of the most normal men in the 509th, 'balanced, filled with healthy aggression, calm under pressure'.

And, in the heavily-guarded Tech. Area where Beser worked, the pressures had markedly increased with the arrival from Los Alamos of Captain William 'Deak' Parsons.

At Los Alamos Beser had hardly known Parsons, whose punctuality, reserve and exacting manner intimidated many of his scientific subordinates.

But, here on Tinian, the middle-aged naval officer revealed himself to be a relaxed as well as dynamic leader; the faster the pace, the calmer he became. He made a lasting impression on Beser; in the radar officer's book of instant character assessments, Parsons was 'a dignified officer and a fine gentleman'.

Parsons had come to Tinian to supervise the final assembly and delivery of the atomic bomb.

Group Captain Leonard Cheshire, R.A.F., an authentic hero from the skies of Europe, was on the island as an observer for the British Government. He firmly believed he would be going on the mission to drop the atomic bomb.

Cheshire was one of two Englishmen on Tinian. The other was a fair-haired scientist, William Penney, whose brilliant mathematical calculations had played a part in developing the weapon. Penney had also been on the all-important Target Committee, responsible for recommending which Japanese cities should be ear-marked for bombing. He now expected to be present to witness the results of his work.

The War Cabinet in London had insisted that Britain should be represented when the bomb was dropped. President Truman had agreed 'in principle' to this at Potsdam. As a result, Cheshire and Penney believed themselves to be official representatives of the British Prime Minister, charged with watching the event and afterwards reporting their observations to London.

But already things had begun to go wrong. While everybody in the 509th was helpful 'and very jolly', others were vague and evasive when the two Englishmen mentioned going on the flight.

Tibbets did not mind, either way, whether he would have to fit in Cheshire and Penney. He was much too concerned with the well-being of his own men.

Recently there had been a mysterious outbreak of diarrhoea in the 509th. Dr. Young put it down to 'a generous quantity of soap' having been slipped into the cooking vats. Uanna, the Group's security chief, suspected that 'a mischievous Jap who had gotten into the compound was responsible'. He was right; that was exactly what had happened. Security around the cookhouse was increased. There was no further trouble.

But a continuing, even increasing, concern for Tibbets was the hostility the Group encountered outside the compound. While every other flying unit on the island was putting in the maximum number of airborne hours, the 509th, apart from practice missions around the Marianas, had so far been just three times to Japan—and even then, on each of these occasions, had used only ten bombers from its fleet of fifteen.

At night, furious fliers from other groups were still hurling showers of rocks into the compound; it was a humiliating experience for the self-confident 509th.

Tibbets tried to dispel the frustration by holding regular pep-talks.

He encouraged Perry to excel himself in the kitchens; the Mess Officer devised a series of 'gourmet nights from around the world'— offering classic dishes from Italy, Poland and Russia.

Chaplain Downey, Tibbets was also pleased to see, was acting 'like a cheer-leader, always on hand to lend support'. Downey dealt with men whose wives and sweethearts had left them or whose children were ill in the States or whose parents had died. In an ordinary outfit some of these cases would have qualified for compassionate furlough. But nobody was now allowed to leave the 509th; those with personal problems could only rely on an overworked Downey to offer solace, and sometimes a solution.

Tibbets encouraged jokes and parodies about life in the compound; he reasoned that if the men could laugh at their hardships they would not seem so unendurable. One of the most successful jests was a song, sung to the tune of *Rum and Coca-Cola*, whose words accurately counterpointed reality:

> Have you ever been to Tinian?
> It's Heaven for the enlisted man.
> There's whisky, girls and other such,
> But all are labeled: Mustn't touch.
>
> This tropic isle's a paradise,
> Of muddy roads and rainy skies.
> Outdoor latrines and fungus feet,
> And every day more goat to eat.
>
> Enlisted men are on the beam,
> Officers say 'we're one big team'.
> But do they ever share the rum and coke?
> Ha, ha, ha, that's one big joke.

When some of his officers complained that the song was in poor taste, Tibbets sharply rebuked them: it was helping raise morale among the enlisted men.

As always, he was careful to hide the increasing strain he, personally, felt. His working day often stretched from 7 a.m. until midnight. His sleep was frequently disturbed by 'eyes only' messages from

'Morose', the new code-name Groves had adopted for his head-quarters in Washington, or from 'Misplay', Groves' new name for Los Alamos. Messages from 'Morose' inevitably ended with a request for the latest readiness report for 'Centerboard', the code-name for the actual atomic strike.

Tibbets patiently answered all the queries, though there was one piece of information he could not yet provide: the names of everyone who would be flying on the mission.

Tibbets knew it would be a hard choice; in his view most of the crews deserved to go. Their flying fitness reports were only matched by the high ratings which Dr. Young had given the fliers.

Psychologically, he had told Tibbets, 'your crews are probably among the most balanced in the Air Force'.

Extraordinarily, Young did not spot that Claude Eatherly, for all his brilliance as a pilot, had shown sufficient signs of instability to warrant being grounded.

Tragically, Tibbets, well aware of Eatherly's quirks, still felt the pilot's skills outweighed all else. In making that judgement, he would give Eatherly the chance to become world-famous—at the expense of himself.

Hiroshima
Early Afternoon

At 12.50 p.m., the field telephone rang in 2nd Lieutenant Tatsuo Yokoyama's anti-aircraft gun-post on Mount Futaba. One of the controllers at central fire control in Hiroshima Castle was calling to warn of the possible approach of bombers from the south, the direction of Kure. Yokoyama already had his guns pointed that way; he and his men were anxiously watching to see whether any of the American planes bombing the port would be forced by the gun batteries there to flee towards Hiroshima.

Simultaneously with the warning he received, Radio Hiroshima interrupted its programme by announcing an alert. All over the city people began to run for shelter.

Dr. Kaoru Shima was in the operating theatre, performing an appendectomy, when a nurse gave him the news of the air-raid warning. He continued with the operation. Outside the theatre, the staff were hurrying the patients to the ground floor shelter, carrying those too sick to walk by themselves.

Mayor Senkichi Awaya and his assistant, Kazumasa Maruyama, were in the Mayor's office when they heard the alert siren. Maruyama rushed to the window and stared into the sky, but could see nothing. He and Awaya resumed their discussion.

An aide interrupted a staff meeting chaired by Field Marshal Hata to say bombers were approaching.

Hata invited his officers to join him at the windows of the conference room to watch developments.

Not far away, as he peered through his binoculars, Yokoyama could see at least two B-24's coming towards him. They were still some distance off, climbing after their bomb run over Kure Naval Dockyard. A towering pall of smoke was now rising from that area.

With growing excitement, the gunnery officer estimated that if the oncoming aircraft maintained their present course, even under full power they would still be below 20,000 feet when they crossed Hiroshima. That would bring them well within range of his guns.

He began to call out his orders, instructing his aimers to hold the nearer of the two planes in their sights. He reminded the gunners that he would treat them to beer and sake if they scored a hit.

The bombers approaching Hiroshima were from the 866th Bombardment Squadron of the 494th Bombardment Group of the VII Bomber Command, based on Okinawa.

They were part of a force of thirty B-24's which had taken off earlier in the morning to attack the *Haruna*, one of the last battleships the Imperial Navy still had afloat. Each bomber carried 2,700 gallons of fuel, three 2,000-pound bombs, and propaganda leaflets giving the Potsdam Proclamation surrender terms.

The bombers had arrived over Kure at exactly 12.40. But even from the designated attack altitude of 10,000 feet, the *Haruna* proved a difficult target to hit; she was well camouflaged and, apart from her own guns, she was protected by shore batteries.

By the time the B-24's from the 866th began their bomb run, some thirty near misses had exploded at a distance of between 200 and 600 yards from the *Haruna*. A number of other bombs had fallen on nearby dockyard buildings, and the immediate target area was shrouded in dense smoke—the pall that Yokoyama could see seven miles away on Mount Futaba.

Flying through heavy flak, the first 866th B-24, nicknamed *Taloa*, had dropped her three bombs into the smoke and broken away to the left, on a course now taking the bomber towards Hiroshima.

The crew of the *Taloa* were in an understandable state of nervousness. It was common knowledge that the Japanese often executed captured American fliers. Just over a month before, on June 20, in the Kyushu city of Fukuoka, eight airmen had been publicly put to death

246

—their bodies prodded into the ritual kneeling position and their heads chopped off by ceremonial swords.

American Intelligence had learned of the incident, which was then broadcast over the Armed Forces Radio as a solemn warning to all crews of what might happen if they were captured.

The pilot of *Taloa*, Joseph Bubinsky, co-pilot Rudolph Flanagin and navigator Lawrence Falls, all 1st Lieutenants, were doubtless too busy trying to gain height and chart a new course for home to dwell on such gruesome thoughts.

Bombardier Robert Johnston, also a 1st Lieutenant, was still in the nose of the B-24, peering through the perspex at the countryside below. His relief was considerable as the bomber cleared the concentration of gun batteries which made Kure one of the most heavily defended cities in Japan.

Miraculously, the bomber was still unscathed. Ahead of Johnston, coming up fast, were the port facilities of Hiroshima, and just beyond, the welcome sight of wooded countryside.

Johnston began to relax; in a minute they would be out of danger.

Not far behind *Taloa* came the *Lonesome Lady*, carrying a crew of nine, commanded by 2nd Lieutenant Thomas Cartwright.

The men aboard both B-24's knew of the standing orders which forbade them to bomb Hiroshima; but as far as they all knew there was no restriction on actually flying over the city.

First Bubinsky in *Taloa* and then Cartwright in *Lonesome Lady* were following a course which would take them over the centre of Hiroshima, above Mayor Awaya's office, and to the left of where Hata and his staff officers were standing in the 2nd General Army Headquarters at the foot of Mount Futaba. The flight path would also bring the bombers within range of Yokoyama's battery.

None of the fliers knew anything at all about the ground defences of Hiroshima. When the city had been 'reserved' for possible atomic attack, all information about it was restricted. To the crews of the *Taloa* and the *Lonesome Lady*, the city below them was as alien as a foreign planet.

As they approached the southern end of Hiroshima, the anti-aircraft guns situated there began sending up a concentrated stream of shells from batteries sited near the *Gaisenkan*, the Hall of Triumphant Return, and from those in Eba Park, guarding the Mitsubishi factory.

The bombers continued their headlong dash over Hiroshima, getting closer and closer to Mount Futaba.

And then, with the time nearing 1 p.m., with two-thirds of the city behind them and open countryside and safety immediately ahead, the fate of the twenty crew members in the two bombers, although never publicly reported by the American Government, was about to become inextricably linked with that of Hiroshima.

Yokoyama could not believe his good fortune. The B-24's were flying on to his guns.

As soon as they were within range, he ordered the battery to commence firing.

The first salvo bracketed the *Taloa*. Pretty puffs of smoke exploded above and below the B-24.

Yokoyama shouted an immediate correction.

The next salvo seemed to hit the *Taloa* squarely on the nose.

A frenzied cheer came from the gunners. Yokoyama shouted at them to keep firing.

The clear sky around the stricken bomber was now pock-marked with shrapnel bursts. Trailing smoke, the plane abruptly changed direction, turning left, away from Mount Futaba.

Behind, the *Lonesome Lady* seemed also to have been hit.

Standing impassively at the conference room windows, Field Marshal Hata and his staff watched the first tiny figures tumbling from the *Taloa*. Moments later, as the B-24 began to cross western Hiroshima, their parachutes opened.

The bomber plunged into a hill between the two small villages of Itsukaichi and Inokuchi. A great cloud of flame and oily smoke rose into the air.

The sound of the crash brought people from nearby farms and hamlets out into the open. Some, workers from the local market, brandished fish-knives and hatchets.

At least three men from the *Taloa* were now floating earthwards. They were: the pilot Joseph Bubinsky, the bombardier Robert Johnston and the tail-gunner Julius Molnar.

All were deeply shocked and suffering superficial wounds. But instinctively they tried to juggle their parachute cords so that they would drift away from the packs of civilians they could clearly see converging below.

After the *Taloa* had turned away, Yokoyama had brought his guns to bear on the *Lonesome Lady*, already trailing smoke and coming under accurate fire from a battery sited near Hiroshima Castle.

As it did so, the bomber banked sharply to the right, turning back in the direction of Kure. Yokoyama's gunners would forever believe it was they who delivered the *coup de grâce* to the stricken plane.

The *Lonesome Lady* began to descend, passing over the Toyo factory and heading for the dense forest area south-east of Hiroshima. Eight men managed to jump from the bomber. Only the navigator,

248

Roy Pedersen, remained inside the plane. He was still on board as *Lonesome Lady* crashed to the ground.

The scenes of excitement at the Mount Futaba gun-post knew no bounds. For Tatsuo Yokoyama, 'this was my most thrilling day in all the war'.

He promised his gunners the biggest celebration they could imagine.

Then he turned to look through his binoculars across Hiroshima, to the west, where those who had baled out of the *Taloa* were about to touch down.

Squads of Kempei Tai military policemen were fanning out from Hiroshima in pursuit of the parachutists.

One of those squads, led by Warrant Officer Hiroshi Yanagita, stopped to check its bearings with Imperial Army corporal Kanai Hiroto, who lived locally and had been furiously pedalling his bicycle in the direction of the crashed plane.

Hiroto explained to Yanagita that he spoke English and would be happy to offer his services as an interpreter.

He stepped on to the running board of the Kempei Tai car and they continued towards Inokuchi.

Hiroto had been partly educated in a Pasadena High School, near Los Angeles. He had returned to Japan in 1934 and afterwards been drafted. Following three years' fighting in Manchuria, he had experienced an uneventful war.

Yanagita was one of the senior Kempei Tai leaders in Hiroshima. He was a tough, professional soldier, and proud of it.

When they reached the foot of the hill into which the *Taloa* had crashed, the Kempei Tai officer, his men and Hiroto raced up towards the parachutes which they could see were caught in the trees.

Hiroto stopped by the still-smouldering bomber. It had split into two sections, lying some two hundred yards apart. Near the front portion was 'a leg, tossed out of the plane, severed at the ankle'. He was about to go into the wreckage when Yanagita returned, saying one of the Americans had been caught and was being held prisoner a little way down the hill.

It was the tail gunner, S/Sgt Julius Molnar.

Even before reaching him, Hiroto saw that Molnar was in grave danger. The slightly-built sergeant was surrounded by civilians who 'wanted to beat him to death. I forced my way in, took hold of him and tried to ward off their blows.'

Hiroto turned and faced the enraged mob, shouting for them to stop. He received another blow.

Yanagita stepped forward, brandishing a pistol. He threatened that his men would shoot the next civilian who moved.

Sullenly, the crowd stood back.

Then, flanked by Hiroto and Yanagita, Molnar was escorted to the relative safety of a nearby farmstead. There, Molnar was surrounded by Kempei Tai policemen.

Hiroto could see the effort the young airman was making to control his trembling. He spoke to the tail-gunner for the first time, telling him in English that he had once lived in the United States. The terrified Molnar began to calm down.

Prompted by Yanagita, Hiroto began to question Molnar. He willingly gave his name, serial number 36453945, rank, and said that he was twenty-one years old, had been trained in Texas, and that they had taken off from Okinawa to attack the port of Kure. He claimed he did not know the names of the other crew-members of the *Taloa*.

Hiroto was then called to another part of the farmyard where a second American, bombardier Robert Johnston, was being held. The crowd of villagers menacing the officer were again warned back by the Kempei Tai.

Johnston concealed his fear better than Molnar, but Hiroto 'could tell from his eyes that he was very frightened'.

Johnston also gave his name, serial number 0698565, and rank.

Hiroto guessed the bombardier's age at about thirty-five. He noticed his parachute was beside him. His pistol had been taken by one of the Kempei Tai policemen.

When Johnston refused to say more, the Kempei Tai leader told Hiroto his translation services were not needed further. Hiroto returned to the crashed bomber, where he began searching in the wreckage for food, and for radio components.

Yanagita and his men rounded up a further three crew-members from the *Taloa*, including its pilot, Joseph Bubinsky, and drove them to Kempei Tai headquarters at Hiroshima Castle where specialist interrogators could question them more thoroughly.

By now the eight crew from the *Lonesome Lady* had also been caught by Kempei Tai patrols and were on their way to the Castle.

Of the twenty original fliers in the two bombers, thirteen had survived being shot down, and the first frightening moments of capture. When they arrived in Hiroshima, there would be a total of twenty-three American prisoners of war being held in the city.

For them, the most terrible experience of all was yet to come.

Soon after midnight, eighty-one fliers assembled to be briefed for the fourth—and, as it was to turn out, the last—practice mission the 509th would make over Japan. The usual facetious patter, a useful cover for nervousness, died away as Colonel Hazen Payette, the Group Intelligence Officer, re-confirmed the targets allocated at an earlier briefing to each of the nine crews.

Lewis was going to bomb a factory complex at Koriyama; Captain Frederick Bock was to drop his 10,000-pound blockbuster on Osaka, not far from where Professor Asada was still trying to perfect his Death Ray. Eatherly was to bomb the railway sidings at Maizura; others were to attack targets at Kobe, Shimada, Ube, Nagoya, Wakayama and Hitachi.

For this mission, Lewis would be flying Sweeney's plane, nick-named the *Great Artiste*, while his usual B-29 was being given a special inspection and service by Group technicians. He also had on board van Kirk, who was taking the place of Lewis' regular navigator.

The combination of having to fly an unfamiliar plane, and taking van Kirk, made Lewis uneasy. He wondered why Ferebee was not coming along. He did not know that the Group Bombardier, like Tibbets, had been forbidden to fly over Japan until the atomic mission.

Another of the B-29's was, for this one flight, not to be commanded by its usual pilot but by Major James Hopkins, the 509th's Operations Officer. Hopkins, normally desk-bound, was keen to add to his flying experience.

The briefing was routine. It dealt with weather and rescue facilities should any plane be forced down into the sea. Anti-aircraft fire was not expected to be a problem; it would probably be 'moderate to light', and was in any case generally believed to be inaccurate.

Van Kirk spoke to the navigators about the routes to the targets, where they planned to arrive, as usual, around nine in the morning.

Trucks took the crews to their planes. The B-29's were impressively grouped together. With their long thick snouts poised above the ground, in the darkness they looked like sinister, antediluvian beasts.

Eatherly was the first to take off. The *Straight Flush* slipped into the air with its pilot bent on making a record flight to Japan and back in order to resume an unfinished poker game.

Minutes later *Bock's Car*, commanded by Captain Bock, trundled down the runway.

251

Then it was the turn of Hopkins in *Strange Cargo*. Lewis, in the *Great Artiste*, was parked about a hundred feet from him. He watched the four engines spin into life. Then *Strange Cargo* started to move from the apron.

Suddenly, there was a rasping sound of metal grinding upon metal. The bomb-bay doors of *Strange Cargo* were being slowly forced open, their reinforced steel hinges screeching under the pressure.

Hopkins brought the plane to a stop, as with a sickening thud *Strange Cargo*'s blockbuster dropped on to the asphalt.

Lewis stared boggle-eyed at the huge bomb a few feet away, which, if it exploded, would destroy everything within a radius of several hundred yards.

Quietly, trying to supress the panic in his voice, Lewis warned his crew of what had happened. Over the radio he could hear Hopkins calling the control tower for help. In moments, the sound of crash trucks, ambulances and MP's jeeps began to fill the air.

The flying control officer told Lewis and Hopkins that, for the moment, the safest course seemed for both B-29 crews to remain on board; the slightest jarring might detonate the 10,000-pound blockbuster.

Portable searchlights were brought to bear on the bomb.

Through binoculars, firemen and armourers studied the brightly-painted, orange-coloured bomb, its fins bent and twisted from the impact after its fall.

The firemen were the first to move in, advancing cautiously until they stood under the wings of *Strange Cargo*. They began to blanket the blockbuster with foam, which they hoped would help deaden any explosion.

A volunteer gang of armourers pushed a dolly and winch-crane under the gaping belly of the plane. Working in total silence, they gently placed shackles around the bomb and began to winch it up, inch by inch. Then they slid the dolly under the bomb. A small tractor was backed into position, the dolly hooked up and towed away.

A relieved voice from the control tower told both crews they could relax.

Lewis, once more full of confidence, bellowed a characteristic reply. 'Like hell! We gotta a mission to fulfil!'

Within minutes, the engines of *Great Artiste* thundered into life, and without giving *Strange Cargo* a second look, Lewis and his crew took off on their night flight to Koriyama.

Guam
Morning

General Carl Spaatz, commanding general of the newly-created Strategic Air Forces, formed for the impending invasion of Japan, looked at the group of expectant officers assembled in General Curtis LeMay's office and carefully unfolded a document.

Spaatz, a greying, lean-faced Pennsylvania Dutchman, did not tell the watchful officers of the confrontation he had staged in order to obtain the document. Six days earlier in the Pentagon, he had faced General Thomas T. Handy, acting Chief of Staff while Marshall was in Potsdam, and stubbornly insisted that 'if I'm going to kill 100,000 people I'm not going to do it on verbal orders. I want a piece of paper'.

Spaatz had just arrived in Washington D.C. from Europe on his way to command the Strategic Air Forces in the Pacific. Groves had briefed him on the atomic bomb. Spaatz, like General Dwight D. Eisenhower, the Supreme Commander of the Allied Forces in Europe, wished that the United States did not have to be the first to use the weapon. Groves, and later Handy, expressed the anxiety felt over the loss of lives expected before Japan admitted defeat. Spaatz had repeated his request and received 'the piece of paper' he wanted.

The document was drafted by Groves on July 23. It was then transmitted to the Little White House in Potsdam for approval, immediately granted. On July 25 the document had been handed to Spaatz after being prepared by Handy.

Spaatz brought it with him to Guam. His new Chief of Staff, LeMay, suggested that Spaatz should hold an immediate meeting with some of the key personnel involved in the atomic mission. Spaatz agreed, and assembled now in LeMay's office were: LeMay, Tibbets, Parsons, Blanchard—fully recovered from his hair-raising flight with Tibbets—and LeMay's senior meteorologist. The exact date of the first mission would depend on his forecast of 'a good bombing day', when there would be a maximum of 3/10's cloud cover and favourable winds over Japan. To make such a forecast the officer was relying heavily on the weather reports radioed from northern China by Mao Tse-Tung.

The document Spaatz now read to these officers bore the unmistakable imprint of Groves:

To: General Carl Spaatz, CG, USASAF:

1. The 509 Composite Group, 20th Air Force will deliver its first special bomb as soon as weather will permit visual bombing after about 3 August 1945 on one of the targets: Hiroshima, Kokura, Niigata and Nagasaki. To carry military and civilian scientific

personnel from the War Department to observe and record the effects of the explosion of the bomb, additional aircraft will accompany the airplane carrying the bomb. The observing planes will stay several miles distant from the point of impact of the bomb.

2. Additional bombs will be delivered on the above targets as soon as made ready by the project staff. Further instructions will be issued concerning targets other than those listed above.

3. Dissemination of any and all information concerning the use of the weapon against Japan is reserved to the Secretary of War and the President of the United States. No communiques on the subject or releases of information will be issued by commanders in the field without specific prior authority. Any news stories will be sent to the War Department for special clearance.

4. The foregoing directive is issued to you by direction and with the approval of the Secretary of War and of the Chief of Staff, USA. It is desired that you personally deliver one copy of this directive to General MacArthur and one copy to Admiral Nimitz for their information.

Signed: Thos. T. Handy,
General, G.S.C.
Acting Chief of Staff.

At last, America's senior soldier in the Pacific, MacArthur, was to be told about the revolutionary weapon.

Spaatz refolded the document and placed it back in his briefcase. He had one question.

'Gentlemen, are your preparations on schedule?'

The men around the table nodded. Parsons then read a memorandum he had just received from Oppenheimer in Los Alamos.

Following the Alamogordo test, Oppenheimer had calculated that the energy release from the bomb to be dropped on Japan would be in the region of 12,000 to 20,000 tons, and the blast should be equivalent to that from 8,000 to 15,000 tons of TNT.

Tibbets knew that it would need nearly 2,000 B-29's, carrying full loads of conventional high explosive bombs, to match one atomic bomb. Even now, after almost a year with the Manhattan Project, he found such a thought 'just awesome'.

Perhaps Oppenheimer felt the same when he wrote his memo to Parsons. In it, after mentioning that the bomb would probably be fused to go off 1,850 feet above the target city, he stated:

It is not expected that radioactive contamination will reach the ground. The Ball of Fire should have a brilliance which should persist longer than at Trinity [Alamogordo] since no dust should be mixed with it. In general, the visible light emitted by the unit should be even more spectacular. Lethal radiation will, of course, reach the ground from the bomb itself.

Oppenheimer ended his memo: 'Good luck.'

The meeting in LeMay's office concluded with the introduction of two further code-names. LeMay was to be known as 'Cannon'; General Farrell, on route to Guam to function as the senior representative of the Manhattan Project in the Marianas, would be 'Scale'.

As he flew back to Tinian with Parsons, whose code-name was 'Judge', Tibbets mused that, if he had a choice of pseudonym, he would like to be known as 'Justice'.

Tinian
Afternoon

Soon after landing on the island, in mid-afternoon the commander of the 509th was again out on the tarmac, waiting to greet the crews as they returned from their solo missions to Japan.

None had been hit by flak. The weather over the targets was reasonable, and each aircraft had been able to bomb visually.

When Lewis landed, Tibbets congratulated him and his men for not being unnerved by the experience with the errant bomb just before take-off. Lewis took the opportunity to remind his commander, not for the first time, that 'my crew is the best you've got'.

There then occurred a short conversation whose meaning Tibbets and Lewis would later dispute, agreeing only that they were alone when it happened.

Although Lewis had once expected to fly the first atomic flight with 'his crew' in 'his plane', Tibbets had already told him that van Kirk and Ferebee would be going along. Lewis did not like the idea, but had come to accept it, viewing van Kirk's flight with him today as confirmation of the fact.

Now, according to Lewis, Tibbets told him that he 'would be flying the mission'. Wishful thinking or not, Lewis took that to mean that he would be the aircraft commander.

Tibbets would not deny that he made the remark, but he would differ radically from Lewis in how it should have been interpreted: 'Lewis would fly as co-pilot, van Kirk and Ferebee would replace his usual navigator and bombardier. It was clear to anybody that on such a mission I had to be in the driver's seat.'

The misunderstanding would not end here. The confused conversation was merely a curtain-raiser for the real clash between the two men which was to follow.

S.W. of Tinian
Close to Midnight

Some 650 miles to the south-west of where Tibbets and Lewis had held their disputed talk, Commander Mochitsura Hashimoto told his officer of the watch something about which there could never later be any doubt. As the officer awakened him from his cat-nap shortly before midnight and reported that all was well aboard submarine I.58, Hashimoto told him he thought 'it was going to be a good night for hunting'.

The Captain dressed and went to the boat's shrine to pray.

After previous prayers, I.58 had finally produced one 'probable' victim. The day before at 2 p.m., Hashimoto had sighted a tanker escorted by a destroyer. Judging it unwise to approach close enough to use conventional torpedoes, he had decided instead to launch two of his six *kaitens*. After quickly saying goodbye to Hashimoto, each suicide pilot had climbed through a hatch from I.58 into his human torpedo, lashed to the mother submarine's deck. When Hashimoto heard the young officers shout over the intercom 'three cheers for the Emperor', he knew it was the signal they were ready to be launched. In poor visibility, the *kaitens* had steered towards the tanker. Hashimoto tracked them through his periscope until the rain squalls blotted them out. He waited. Then, faint, but unmistakable, came the sound of explosions. Hashimoto guessed the tanker had been hit, but not being absolutely sure, he had logged it as a 'probable'.

After leading the crew in prayers for the departed *kaiten* pilots, Hashimoto had then set course for 'the crossroads', the intersection of American shipping lanes connecting Guam with Leyte in the Philippine Islands, and Okinawa with Peleliu in the Palau Islands.

The crossroads was exactly 600 miles from Guam. The I.58 arrived there earlier that Sunday; the sea was calm and the submarine remained surfaced for most of the day. Towards evening visibility dropped rapidly as mist drifted over the area. Hashimoto had ordered the submarine to submerge until moonrise at about 11 p.m. The boat had edged westward at two knots, ninety feet below the surface, with most of the crew, like their captain, dozing completely naked in spite of the loud scampering of rats.

But now, having been awakened by the watch officer and his visit

256

to the shrine over, Hashimoto ordered 'Night action stations'. As the chief engineer increased speed to three knots, the crew moved to a state of alert.

Hashimoto ordered the submarine to sixty feet, and then sent the night periscope hissing upwards to break the Pacific's surface. After adjusting the eye-piece, he began slowly sweeping the quarters of the compass.

The moon was some twenty degrees high in the east, and there were a few scattered clouds. There was nothing else to be seen.

He ordered the submarine brought to within ten feet of the surface. 'Stand by type thirteen radar.'

The mechanism for detecting aircraft rose from its mounting to just above the swell. Its operator reported no sign of planes.

'Stand by type twenty-two radar.'

The surface radar, the receiver which indicated the presence of other ships within a three-mile radius of I.58, rose out of the water. From past experience Hashimoto knew that the device was erratic, capable of mistaking driftwood, shoals of fish and outcrops of rock for ships.

Only when the operator was thoroughly satisfied that the vicinity was empty did the Captain give his next order.

'Stand by to surface.'

Hashimoto lowered the periscope handles.

'Blow main ballast.'

High-pressure air entered the main tanks, expelling the last of the water, and sending the boat swiftly to the surface.

As soon as the deck was awash, Hashimoto ordered the conning-tower hatch opened. The signalman and navigator climbed up to the bridge with the watch officer, and each began looking through high-powered night binoculars.

Below, in the control room, Hashimoto continued to watch through the night periscope; the operator of the surface radar continued monitoring.

The normal routine was broken by the navigator shouting from the bridge.

'Bearing red-nine-zero degrees. Possible enemy ship.'

Hashimoto lowered the periscope.

'Action stations!'

The alarm bells rang and the crews closed up to battle stations as Hashimoto bounded up the ladder to the bridge. Peering through his binoculars, he could see in the moonlight a black spot clearly visible on the horizon. He leapt for the ladder shouting one word.

'Dive!'

The bridge watch shinned down behind him; the hatch was slammed shut; the main vents were opened and I.58 crash-dived, with Hashimoto glued to the night periscope so as not to lose sight of the target.

It was the *Indianapolis*.

The aged cruiser had sailed from Tinian on Thursday, July 26, having safely delivered her mysterious cargo. After stopping at Guam, the *Indianapolis* had headed for Leyte in the Philippines; from there, it was likely she would be ordered back to San Francisco to collect yet more nuclear material.

This Sunday at sea had followed a familiar pattern: morning church service on the fantail, no smoking about the ship until after the service was over and no work before the noonday meal was served.

By evening the small chop of the sea had increased to a rough swell, but not enough to affect the standard zig-zag course the ship was following. Its engines were phased to produce 'staggered turns' on her four screws, ensuring an uneven pattern of sounds to hamper further any enemy submarines listening to hydrophones.

At dusk, Captain McVay told the watch officer that the ship could be secured from zig-zagging after twilight.

It was a fateful order.

At 10.30 p.m., with visibility still poor, McVay signed the night orders; they contained no request to resume zig-zagging if the weather improved. He retired to sleep in his cabin close to the bridge.

At sixteen knots, the *Indianapolis* steamed in a direct line towards submarine I.58.

Now, close to midnight, less than ten miles of sea separated them.

Thirty feet below the surface, trimmed level, I.58 swung slowly to port to face the approaching ship. Hashimoto remained bent to the periscope, pressing so hard on the rubber eye-piece that his eyes began to water. He quickly blinked the tears away and resumed watching. As the target came closer, the black spot changed into a distinct triangular shape. Hashimoto felt a sense of growing excitement: this was no mere merchantman, but a large warship. He began to call out final orders.

'All tubes to the ready—*kaitens*, stand by!'

Suddenly, panic seized Hashimoto: was it perhaps a destroyer about to make a depth-charge attack? Surely that could be the only explanation for the straight-as-a-line course the enemy ship was maintaining. He kept the fear out of his voice as he issued his next command.

'All torpedoes to be fired in one salvo. *Kaiten* Six, embark. *Kaiten* Five, stand by.'

The gap between the submarine and the *Indianapolis* was now five miles.

His eyes still firmly pressed to the periscope, Hashimoto assessed the ship's masthead height as ninety feet. She was too big to be a

258

destroyer; he guessed she was either a battleship or a large cruiser—a plum target indeed.

The range fell steadily. The hydrophone operators reported they could pick up engine noises. At three miles' separation, Hashimoto fixed a set of earphones over his head. The target, clearly outlined in the moonlight, was approaching on a near-collision course with his submarine.

Hashimoto could not believe his eyes. He suspected a trap: was the approaching ship acting as a decoy, drawing his fire while destroyers waited to pounce? Nervously, he scanned the rest of the field of view. There was nothing else in sight.

He continued to focus on the approaching ship. She was showing no change of direction or speed. She was behaving, in Hashimoto's opinion, 'like a ship passing in review'. She presented a target so perfect and simple that he still could not believe his luck.

At two miles, he realised that his luck would hold. Turning to the men grouped around him, Hashimoto allowed himself a prediction.

'We've got her!'

Silence fell over the boat. Entirely dependent on the eyes of their captain, the crew waited tensely for the order to fire.

Suddenly, the *kaiten* pilots began clamouring to go.

Hashimoto curtly told them they would be used only if the ordinary torpedo attack failed.

The suicide pilots subsided into sullen silence.

The range was 3,000 yards as Hashimoto began his final calculations before firing.

One and a half miles away from the I.58, aboard the *Indianapolis*, the 12.00 to 4.00 a.m. watch arrived on the bridge. There were now thirteen officers and men there, monitoring course and speed. At various points of the ship other watch-standers were on duty. One by one they made their rounds and found everything in order. No lights were showing, no gear was adrift, all ports, doorways and hatches were secure. The sea continued coursing by the hull as midnight came and passed and another day began.

It was to be the shortest and last day in the life of the *Indianapolis*.

July 30, 1945
S.W. of Tinian
Past Midnight

Aboard the I.58, Hashimoto made a critical decision. He revised his original estimate that the *Indianapolis* was travelling at twenty knots.

259

Based on what he could see through the periscope, and hear through the hydrophones, he now estimated that her true speed was twelve knots. He decided to delay firing until the range had closed to under a mile. The torpedoes were set to travel through the water at a depth of twelve feet and a speed of forty-eight knots. Wakeless, they would be invisible to the most vigilant watch-keeper on the *Indianapolis*.

Around him, Hashimoto could sense the men straining for him to give the order. With less than 1,500 yards separating the cruiser and submarine, Hashimoto finally shouted the words.

'Stand by. Fire!'

At two-second intervals, the torpedo-release switch tripped. After twelve seconds the torpedo officer reported.

'All tubes fired and correct.'

Six torpedoes, launched to give them a spread of three degrees, were speeding fanwise towards the *Indianapolis*.

It was two minutes past midnight.

Less than an hour had elapsed since the cruiser was sighted.

Hashimoto began to count off the seconds, his eyes still fixed to the periscope.

Aboard the *Indianapolis*, one of the officers on the bridge commented that the visibility was improving as the moon rose higher in front of the ship.

Below the bridge, on the open deck, several hundred men slept on mattresses and blankets, preferring to do so rather than endure the broiling heat below decks.

A party, far forward in a starboard cabin, was coming to an end. And in his emergency cabin, behind the bridge, just as Hashimoto had been ninety minutes before, Captain McVay was in his berth, asleep, stark naked.

In I.58, Hashimoto's count-down continued as the submarine turned on a course parallel with the cruiser.

'Fifty-one, fifty-two, fifty-three—'

A huge column of water rose into the air, blocking out the forward turret of the *Indianapolis*. Another column spouted near the aft turret. Then bright red flashes of flame leapt from various parts of the ship's superstructure. As each of the torpedoes struck home, Hashimoto signalled the strike with an exultant cry.

'A hit! A hit!'

The crew of I.58 began to dance with joy, shouting and stamping their feet until the submarine resembled some underwater madhouse.

There was no panic aboard the *Indianapolis*, only stunned disbelief that the ship had been hit. And this swiftly passed as the crew moved to deal with the emergency.

There was nothing they could do. The cruiser was straining and groaning and settling at the bows.

Captain McVay ordered the radio room to transmit a distress message. Moments later, with smoke and flames enveloping the foredeck, without lights or power—certain indication of mortal damage—McVay gave the order to abandon ship.

The *Indianapolis* rolled on to her starboard side. Then, as the cruiser began to fill rapidly with water, her stern rose higher and higher into the air, until a hundred feet, and more, of hull reared straight up out of the Pacific, towering over hundreds of men living and dying and already dead, floating in the sea.

For a few awesome moments the glistening hull remained poised to crush the bodies strewn over the water and to suck them down as it sank to the sea-bed. Screams of blind panic filled the air. Then, swiftly and cleanly, barely disturbing the Pacific swell, the *Indianapolis* plunged out of sight—the last major vessel to be lost in World War Two, and destined to become the greatest disaster at sea in the history of the United States Navy.

It was 12.14 a.m., July 30, 1945.

After re-loading his six torpedo tubes, prepared, if necessary, to fire a second salvo or to use his *kaitens* to finish off the enemy ship, Hashimoto brought I.58 to the surface. There was nothing to be seen in the darkness. It was over an hour since the action began. He now knew he had sunk the vessel, but wanted proof—a piece of flotsam, a survivor. Finding nothing, he ordered course set for the north-east. Hashimoto feared reprisals from other ships or aircraft he felt sure must have been accompanying his victim.

A full ninety-six hours would pass before the first rescue ship began to drag from the water the few remaining survivors from the *Indianapolis*. When the news of the loss of four-fifths of its crew reached Tinian, it would cause shock and horror, and, in the case of Jake Beser, a sense of personal grief; before the *Indianapolis* had left Tinian, he had dined with an old classmate aboard the ship. Now his friend was dead, one of the nearly 900 victims of Hashimoto's torpedoes.

In Washington, when Groves heard of the loss, he reacted predictably: he was relieved the ship had delivered her precious cargo of uranium before sinking. On the very day that the *Indianapolis* was sunk, Groves signed a memo to the Chief of Staff in which he presented his projected production schedule for atomic bombs after August: 'In September, we should have three or four bombs . . . four or three in October . . . In November at least five and the rate will raise to seven in December and increase decidedly in early 1946.'

Clearly, the Manhattan Project chief would have to think carefully whether delivery by ship, as with the *Indianapolis*, was the most sensible course.

That was for the future. And so, too, was the next encounter between Commander Hashimoto and Captain McVay. They were destined to meet again—in a Washington D.C. court-room—when Hashimoto would be called as star witness against McVay in the only court-martial in U.S. Naval history of a commanding officer for the loss of his vessel in wartime.

But now, heading away from the scene of the action that would eventually lead to that court-room clash, Hashimoto could only think of the captain of the American ship in coldly impersonal terms.

'I was the predator. He was the prey. And he was the victim.'

Most of all, Hashimoto thought of his wife and children. He wanted badly to get back to them, for now he had quite a story to tell his three young sons, waiting for him at his home in Kure.

Hiroshima

Fifteen hundred miles away from where the survivors of the *Indianapolis* struggled to stay alive in shark-infested waters, in Hiroshima, the city whose fate they had helped to settle by delivering their atomic cargo, a handful of other Americans, shot down after bombing Hashimoto's home port, also wondered how long they would live.

The thirteen surviving crew from the two B-24's were all being held prisoner within Hiroshima Castle's grounds. Soon after their arrival, just two days before, they had been split up and put in individual cells at three different locations: some were still being held captive at Kempei Tai headquarters, others were incarcerated in the dungeon of the Castle itself, and two of the crew were at the 2nd Infantry Divisional Headquarters in cells normally reserved for insubordinate Japanese soldiers.

The newly-arrived airmen had no knowledge of the ten other prisoners of war who had already spent weeks in solitary confinement within the Castle confines.

For all twenty-three Americans now in Hiroshima, life was a mixture of despair and fear. Their cells were uniformly bereft of all furniture except for a washbasin and one blanket on which they slept. They had no clothes other than those they had been wearing when captured. Long hours of solitude were interspersed with bouts of hard questioning. The bowls of corn-meal mush or rice which they received three times a day in their cells were barely enough to sustain them.

Regularly, squads of curious Japanese soldiers came to stare into the cells at the enemy they had been taught to hate. Peering through the grilles, they heaped insults on the prisoners as they attempted to squat, Japanese-fashion, over the stinking toilet-holes set into the floor of the cells.

The prisoners tried to ignore the jeering, just as they also struggled to disregard the threats when they were taken to the special interrogation room used by the Kempei Tai. Some of the Americans began to invent stories, hoping to stay alive by telling their captors what they imagined they wanted to hear.

Those held at the Infantry Headquarters were guarded by Private Second Class Masuru Matsuoka. They were perhaps the most fortunate of the twenty-three prisoners in Hiroshima. Matsuoka was not a member of the Kempei Tai, but a regular soldier. He stood guard, rifle and fixed bayonet at the ready, just outside adjoining cells whose occupants could look past the bamboo poles which formed one wall to the open courtyard beyond.

During his shift of three hours on, three hours off, Matsuoka never spoke to the airmen, but he noticed their dress. He and his fellow guards thought their uniform looked so worn out and faded that 'America must be in bad shape—we can win the war yet'.

Matsuoka pitied his prisoners. He could not understand why they had not killed themselves to avoid capture, as 'we would have done'. To him, the disgrace of being shot down would have been sufficient reason to die.

The belts and shoelaces of the prisoners had been taken away, and, when they asked for a razor to shave, the request was refused. The Japanese feared the Americans might yet commit suicide.

Matsuoka believed his solemn, and main duty, as he stood guard outside the prisoners' cages in the grounds of the Castle, was to protect the Americans from themselves.

July 31, 1945
Washington, D.C.

Seven thousand miles—and metaphorical light years—away from those twenty-three prisoners, Groves studied a copy of an urgent cable from Spaatz on Guam, raising questions about other American POW'S in Japan. The cable read:

Reference CENTERBOARD operation scheduled after August 3rd against Nagasaki. Reports, prisoner of war sources, not verified by photos, give locations of Allied prisoner of war camp one mile north of center of city of Nagasaki. Does this influence the choice of this target for initial CENTERBOARD operation? Request immediate reply.

Groves was 'bothered' by the message, not so much because the lives of several hundred Allied POW's could be at risk, but:

by the fact that the intelligence estimate that both Spaatz and we were using was apparently incorrect in its details. If it was correct, the camp was on the west side of Nagasaki Bay; yet it seemed much more likely that it would be on the other side, which was much closer to the docks where it was believed that the prisoners were being worked. No matter which location was right, however, it did seem likely that at the probable time of an explosion POW's would be working in the dock area and would be fully exposed to the expected hazards.

Even Groves had to admit that 'Spaatz query was not an easy one to answer'.

For in his report of the previous day to the Chief of Staff, General Marshall, in which he described his production schedule for bombs, Groves had drawn a graphic portrait of what could be the fate of all those in the vicinity of an atomic explosion:

Exploded about 1800 feet in the air [and] measured from the point on the ground directly below the explosion the blast should be lethal to at least 1000 feet. Between 2500 and 3500 feet, blast effects should be extremely serious to personnel. Heat and flames should be fatal to about 1500 to 2000 feet. At 10 miles for a few thousandths of a second the light will be as bright as a thousand suns; at the end of a second, as bright as one or possibly two suns. The effect on anyone about half a mile away who looks directly at the explosion would probably be permanent sight impairment; at one mile, temporary blindness; and up to and even beyond ten miles, temporary sight impairment. To persons who are completely un-shielded, gamma rays may be lethal to 3500 feet and neutrons to about 2000 feet.

Groves knew that the prisoners in Nagasaki could, at the very minimum, be blinded. More likely, they would die.

Unwilling for once to assume total responsibility for everything involving the Manhattan Project, he discussed the matter with General Handy, the officer who had given Spaatz the 'piece of paper' authorising the atomic strike. Handy thought the query should be brought to the attention of Stimson who had just returned from the Big Three Conference.

Groves agreed, noting this would give the Secretary of War 'an opportunity, if he chose to take advantage of it, to overrule us before any harm was done'.

Before going to see Stimson, Groves prepared a reply to Spaatz telling him there was to be no change in the targets because of the POW situation; Spaatz could, however, adjust the aiming points 'in such a way as to decrease the possibility of hitting any POW camps'.

Mindful of his confrontation with Stimson over the proposal to bomb Kyoto, Groves presented the Secretary with the Spaatz cable and the proposed reply, on the understanding that 'I was showing them to him for his information. I added that this was our responsibility and we were not passing it on to him. I did not emphasize that he could change it if he wished, though I told him that I was sending it as soon as I left his office. His only reaction was to thank me for showing him the cable before it was sent'.

In the meantime, Spaatz had sent another Top Secret message to Handy. It read:

Hiroshima according to prisoner of war reports is the only one of four target cities for CENTERBOARD that does not have Allied prisoners of war camps. Advise.

Handy's reply was made after a brief telephone talk with Groves, who had just returned from Stimson's office relieved that the Secretary had not interfered over the POW issue. The cable to Spaatz stated:

If you consider your information reliable Hiroshima should be given first priority.

Spaatz had no reason to doubt his information was reliable. Hiroshima was put at the top of the target list.

Tinian

All morning the island had buzzed with a rumour that the biggest-ever task-force from the Marianas was off to bomb Japan. For once rumour did not exaggerate: almost 1,000 bombers were scheduled to begin taking off at midday to attack a dozen selected Japanese cities.

By noon, scores of ground staff had forsworn lunch to go to North Field, Tinian and watch part of the armada take off. Beser was one of the few from the 509th who thought it worthwhile to miss Perry's chow to 'see the show'. Beser's craving for action had still not been satisfied in spite of his having by now made a number of trips over Japan. Today, as usual, he wished he was flying.

Shortly after noon the first Wright-Cyclone engine banged into life. Then the next one started, and the next, until the sound of hundreds of engines echoed back from the jungle.

To Group Captain Leonard Cheshire, the scene was another example 'of the prodigious American art of running the Pacific war on Big Business lines'. He only wished that one of the directors of this vast enterprise could confirm that he and the scientist William Penney would one day soon be climbing into a B-29 and rolling down the runway on the first atomic mission. But the 'top brass' were being as evasive as ever.

After moving to the taxi-ways, the bombers were now taking off four at a time from the 8,500-foot parallel runways of North Field.

Beser could imagine the scene in the aircraft still waiting to take off: men would be making secret promises to God, fingering lucky objects, or finding any excuse to talk to somebody on the intercom. It had been like that on the missions he had flown; he supposed it was the same on all strikes.

It took two hours for all the bombers to become airborne; by the time the last plane rose from North Field, the lead bomber was almost 500 miles away.

Beser knew one other staggering fact: the planes carried a massive combined pay-load that, in explosive power, was still less than that expected of the first atomic bomb.

And the radar officer was one of the few men on Tinian who knew that the weapon had now been finally assembled. It was resting on a cradle in a workshop in the Tech. Area, ready for delivery. To the earthy Beser, the bomb 'looked like an elongated trash-can with fins —only this one had cost more to produce than all the cans in the free world'.

Tibbets met the bomber force streaming northwards as he was flying southwards, returning to Tinian from Iwo Jima. He had gone to the island with Ferebee and van Kirk to check plans to use Iwo Jima as an emergency 'pit stop' for the atomic mission. Months before it had been decided that if, for any reason, the atomic bomb-carrying plane developed a serious malfunction on the outward leg of its journey, it should land on Iwo; it was better to put at risk the few thousand U.S. servicemen stationed there than to endanger the over 20,000 on Tinian—not to mention Tinian's second priceless piece of ordnance, the plutonium bomb.

Tibbets, Ferebee and van Kirk had spent the morning on Iwo carefully checking out arrangements. Almost no one on the island knew who they were or what they were doing.

One of the parking places was fenced off; in its centre was a large, deep, open pit whose dimensions were precisely the same as those of another pit in a similarly fenced-off area on North Field, Tinian. The atomic bomb would first be lowered into the Tinian pit, then the B-29 wheeled into position over the hole so that the bomb could be winched up into the bomb-bay. The pit on Iwo would permit the quick transfer of the bomb to a standby plane if the original aircraft had to force-land on the island.

Ferebee and van Kirk checked the specially prepared communications centre on Iwo; it would act as a relay station between the strike aircraft and Tinian. Shortly before the mission, 509th personnel would fly to Iwo to man the centre. They would be under the command of Uanna, the Group's security chief.

Satisfied, Tibbets and his companions had left Iwo Jima as mysteriously as they arrived. Now, flying south again, they found the air space on the 600-mile journey back to Tinian 'a log jam of bombers'. Tibbets thought to himself that' soon all this will be obsolete—if the atomic bomb works'.

Paul Tibbets was a cautious man. Long ago his mother, Enola Gay Tibbets, had advised him: 'Son, until you see something work—it doesn't work.'

He decided to continue to apply that rule to the atomic mission; he would have doubts about its viability right up until the moment of explosion.

August 1, 1945
Tinian

After one of Charles Perry's magnificent breakfasts, Tibbets adjourned to his office in the 509th Headquarters, closed the door, sat at his desk and began to write rapidly. It took him only minutes to draft the top-secret order for the first atomic attack in history.

He sealed the order in an envelope and sent it by special courier to LeMay's headquarters on Guam.

The order specified that a total of seven B-29's would be used for the historic mission. One would be needed at Iwo Jima to serve as the stand-by aircraft. Three would fly well ahead of the bomb-carrying plane, one to each of three potential target cities, to appraise the local weather and to relay the information back to the bomb-carrier. This aircraft would be accompanied by two observer planes.

Tibbets now had to decide which of his crews would fly with him on the mission, and what role each would have.

He started by assigning Major Claude Eatherly to fly the weather plane to Hiroshima.

Manila

As Tibbets was drawing up his fateful battle order, General Carl Spaatz was briefing the commanding general of the Allied Pacific ground forces: at his Philippines headquarters, General Douglas MacArthur now finally heard about *Centerboard*.

If his pride was injured by his being one of the last commanders in the Pacific to learn of the weapon, MacArthur did not show it. When Spaatz had finished, MacArthur restricted his comment to a single sentence.

'This will completely change all our ideas of warfare.'

Tinian

On Tinian, at noon, Tibbets sent for his Group Intelligence officer, Lt. Colonel Hazen Payette, and the Intelligence Officer of the 393rd Squadron, Captain Joseph Buscher. It was Buscher who on that first day at Wendover, almost a year ago now, had urged the complaining fliers to 'give the place a chance', and who had ignored Eatherly's crack, 'what about broads?'

Tibbets told the two men about the impending mission and ordered them to be ready to begin briefing the selected crews on what the target cities looked like from 30,000 feet.

Guam

On Guam, Brigadier-General Thomas Farrell, Groves' deputy who had just arrived in the Marianas to act as the Project's 'eyes and ears',

received his first cable from 'Morose', Groves' Washington headquarters. It read:

Is there anything left undone either here or there which is delaying
initiation of Little Boy operations?

Farrell, a man of commendably few words, cabled:

'No.'

Tinian

After lunch on Tinian, Tibbets sent, in rapid succession, for Perry,
the Mess Officer; Sweeney, the commander of the 393rd; Classen,
deputy commander of the 509th.

Among other instructions, he ordered Perry to make sure he had 'a
goodly supply of pineapple fritters ready from August 3 onwards'.
The fritters were Tibbets' favourite meal; he liked several helpings
before he flew.

Tibbets briefed Sweeney on the forthcoming mission. He told the
Boston-Irishman that his plane, the *Great Artiste*, would be turned
into a flying laboratory, carrying sensitive instruments which would
measure the blast and other effects of the bomb. Sweeney, and a B-29
carrying photographic equipment, would accompany Tibbets' plane
to the target.

Classen received a general briefing. Tibbets sensed that his somewhat neglected deputy 'was glad to be put in the picture'.

Tibbets did not send for Lewis to tell him that he would be flying as
his co-pilot on the flight. He felt that was 'so self-evident it didn't
warrant stating'.

He was wrong. Lewis was still under the impression that he would
actually command the first atomic mission.

Washington, D.C.

In Washington D.C., Groves received a further laconic cable from
Farrell. It reported that 'as of 1000 hours Eastern War Time' the
atomic bomb was ready to drop over Japan. Truman had insisted

269

on giving Japan's leaders several more days to reconsider their original reaction to the Potsdam Proclamation, but since then everything they had reportedly said seemed to confirm their initial rejection of its terms. For Groves, this reaction 'put our operation fully into motion'.

August 2, 1945
Guam

In the early afternoon, Tibbets and Ferebee arrived at LeMay's headquarters. They were there to finalise the details which Tibbets had been unable to incorporate in the draft mission order he had sent to Guam the previous day.

LeMay had just been promoted to Chief of Staff of the Strategic Air Forces. He was in a receptive mood.

The first thing the two fliers needed to know was which target city was LeMay's personal preference. Previously, when Groves had recommended Kyoto, LeMay was totally against the idea. In his view, Kyoto 'wasn't much of a military target; only a lot of shrines and things of that sort there, and anyway, bombing people gets you nowhere—it's just not profitable'. But LeMay was happy with Hiroshima—he knew it contained a very large number of troops and war factories. He turned to Tibbets and said, almost casually, 'Paul, the primary's Hiroshima.'

Tibbets response was immediate.

'I've always preferred it as the target.'

LeMay led his visitors over to a large map table, its surface covered with the latest reconnaissance photographs of Hiroshima. As Tibbets and Ferebee studied the photographs, LeMay called in Operations Officer Blanchard, who exchanged a slightly uncomfortable look with the airmen. LeMay broke the silence.

'Bombing from the height you intend, cross-winds can be a big problem.'

Ferebee agreed, saying that his bombsight 'could handle 25–30 degrees of crosswind, but it sometimes gets to 40–50 degrees up there'.

Blanchard proposed a solution.

'You should fly directly downwind. That would have the double advantage of increasing your speed, so you wouldn't be vulnerable over the larget so long, and you wouldn't have to worry so much about crosswinds.'

Tibbets disagreed. He thought it better to head directly into the wind, which could eliminate crosswind effect and give Ferebee the best chance to bomb accurately.

LeMay pointed out that going against the wind would also reduce the aircraft speed, making the journey over the target more hazardous.

Ferebee looked at Tibbets and then spoke for them both.

'Our primary purpose is to hit the target. We're going up there to bomb, not to play safe.'

'Okay, the heading will be into the wind.'

LeMay then raised the one other question that mattered. He asked Ferebee to select his Aiming Point.

The bombardier unhesitatingly placed his index finger on the T-shaped Aioi Bridge in the centre of Hiroshima.

LeMay nodded.

Tibbets agreed: 'It's the most perfect AP I've seen in this whole damn war.'

Fission

August 3, 1945 to 8.16 a.m., August 6, 1945

August 3, 1945
Hiroshima

Less than half a mile from the Aioi Bridge, a solitary blindfolded American stood, quite motionless, in the centre of an open space, inside the keep of Hiroshima Castle. His guard, Private Matsuoka, moved to the airman and, grasping his arms, lifted them up and down. Once the prisoner began doing the movement himself, Matsuoka took hold of his knees, forcing him to bend them.

Each morning, in turn, the twenty-three POW's in Hiroshima received such exercise.

Although it was now barely eight o'clock, the August sun beat down on the prisoner, and as he continued the enforced actions, his soiled coveralls became soaked in perspiration. Afterwards, still blindfolded, he was marched for fifteen minutes around Hiroshima Castle's courtyard.

Only some fifty yards away from the American, in his City Hall office, Mayor Senkichi Awaya listened to his assistant, Kazumasa Maruyama, counting off the latest statistics. Up to this morning, about 30,000 adults and 11,000 students, aged between eleven and seventeen, had been drafted into labour battalions to work on the fire-breaks. Over 70,000 dwellings had been demolished; some 60,000 of the city's peak war-time civilian population of 340,000 had already been evacuated; a sixth forced exodus was due to begin within a few days as more and more people lost their homes in the destruction produced by the fire-breaks. This morning, Maruyama estimated there were 280,000 civilians left in the city.

Both men knew that was still too many for Hiroshima's dwindling number of suppliers to cope with. Before the war there had been nearly 2,000 food shops in the city; today there were less than 150. Many of the larger ones were only allowed to supply the military. And Awaya also knew it was the demands of the military which made it necessary for so many of the citizens to remain in the city. The Toyo factory, for instance, needed 10,000 employees to turn out its 6,000 rifles a week. The Mitsubishi company also required a huge labour force and, like Japan Steel's complex on the edge of Hiroshima, it was working seven days a week, twenty-four hours a day.

The money earned by the workers was almost worthless—even the hungry whores in the brothel quarter were refusing to accept

275

cash; for them, like many others in Hiroshima, a mouthful of food was now the only acceptable payment.

Listening to Maruyama's long catalogue of complaints, Awaya knew there was only one way 'of changing the situation and ending this madness'.

He told Maruyama he would seek an immediate interview with Field Marshal Hata.

Maruyama cautioned him. A formal interview would be a mistake; in such situations Hata was reputed to be stiffly uncompromising. Far better to catch the Field Marshal in a more relaxed and convivial surrounding. And in two days' time, on August 5, there would be just such an opportunity: the Mayor had been invited to a cocktail party in the Officers' Club, almost next door to the City Hall. That evening, between toasts, Awaya could make his points to Hata.

Awaya said he would think over the suggestion.

While the two men continued to talk, not far away and less than three hundred yards from the Aioi Bridge, in the Shima Surgical Hospital, its medical director, Dr. Kaoru Shima, permitted himself a brief smile at the earnest manner of his visitor. The man was a farmer who had walked several miles into the city to ask Dr. Shima to make a house call on his wife. From the farmer's description, Dr. Shima guessed that the woman was probably pregnant. He arranged to call at the farm the next time he was in the area.

Tinian

In a hospital twenty times as large as Dr. Shima's, on Tinian, the 509th's Group Navigator, Ted 'Dutch' van Kirk, was beginning to wonder if there was any connection between being told by Tibbets that he was going on the mission, and being suddenly struck down by a mysterious skin rash.

The day before, when Tibbets briefed van Kirk on the strike, he had stressed the importance of accurate navigation. That did not worry the experienced van Kirk. But what did concern him was the fact that Tibbets, Ferebee and he had never flown together from Tinian, and now there would be no chance for them to do so.

Furthermore, some of the men he would be flying with were virtual strangers to him. Van Kirk thought 'they probably all knew their jobs, individually, but we'd never been tested as a team, we'd had no opportunity to become a co-ordinated, tightly-knit crew'.

The pensive van Kirk did not share his worries with Tibbets.

But when he had left Tibbets' office, the matter was still 'bugging' the navigator.

Shortly afterwards, he noticed a painful rash had erupted on various parts of his body.

Alarmed, he reported to Flight Surgeon Young, who promptly despatched van Kirk to the hospital and reported the incident to Tibbets.

Tibbets was even more alarmed than van Kirk about the strange outbreak. In Tibbets' view there 'just wasn't anybody in the same class as Dutch when it came to accurate navigation'. He sent Ferebee to the hospital to find out how ill van Kirk was.

It was an inspired choice. Ferebee made light of van Kirk's complaint, 'accused me of lying in bed just to get attention from some of the prettiest nurses you ever did see'.

After Ferebee left, convinced that van Kirk would be fit for the mission, Dr. Young visited the navigator. He began to question van Kirk, seeking 'a possible emotional basis' for his illness.

'Are you worried about the mission?'

'No.'

'Do you really want to go? You've got a wife and son now.'

'I want to go.'

'Then go.'

Within a few hours, van Kirk's rash had completely cleared up.

He left the hospital as suddenly as he had entered it.

From his headquarters office, Tibbets continued to receive and dispense orders. He ordered a round-the-clock guard to be mounted at the fenced-off bomb pit on the North Field apron. He carefully considered the idea of evacuating the entire northern half of the island just before his mission plane took off; he rejected the thought when he remembered that a premature atomic explosion 'would probably turn the whole of Tinian into a spectacular Krakatoa'.

LeMay flew in with the order for Special Bombing Mission No. 13. It was essentially the same document which Tibbets had drafted on the morning of August 1, though a number of details had been added since the meeting at LeMay's headquarters. The order set the date for the strike as August 6. It listed the targets:

Primary—Hiroshima urban industrial area.

Secondary—Kokura arsenal and city.

Tertiary—Nagasaki urban area.

The order confirmed that no friendly aircraft, 'other than those listed herein, will be within a fifty-mile area of any of the targets for this strike during a period of four hours prior to and six subsequent to strike time'.

Thirty-two copies of the order were distributed to commands on Guam, Iwo Jima and Tinian. Tibbets locked his copy in the office safe, and then departed with LeMay to inspect the Little Boy, nestling on its cradle in the Tech. Area.

At the entrance to the area a security agent politely divested LeMay of his cigar and matches. It was a gesture worthy of Groves.

August 4, 1945
Tinian

Shortly after 2 p.m., the 509th's briefing hut was sealed off by carbine-carrying MP's who barred its only entrance and entirely ringed the long, narrow, purpose-built building. There was an hour to go to the briefing for the first atomic mission.

Inside, intelligence officers Hazen Payette and Joseph Buscher drew the curtains over the windows. The hut's naked lights made its interior look even starker and more cheerless.

Almost filling the room were rows of plain wooden benches facing a platform which supported two blackboards and several chairs. The walls were covered with maps of Japan, and posters reminding readers that 'careless talk costs lives'.

Payette and Buscher began to pin enlarged reconnaissance photographs of Hiroshima and the alternative targets on to the blackboards. They then draped both boards with large cloths.

At 2.15 p.m., a technician arrived with a movie projector and screen. Supervised by Payette, he set up the screen in the middle of the stage and positioned the projector at the back of the room.

At 2.30 p.m., Captain 'Deak' Parsons arrived with a group of scientists. They included Norman Ramsey and Ed Doll. With Doll was 2nd Lieutenant Morris Jeppson, who a few days before had flipped a coin with another electronics officer to decide which of them would assist Parsons on the mission. Jeppson had won. A thoughtful, reserved young man, he sat quietly among the scientists, on the left-hand side of the room.

Parsons produced a roll of film from a briefcase and the technician laced it on to the projector. The film was a copy of the photographic record made of the Alamogordo test.

At 2.45 the British contingent arrived. Both Cheshire and Penney were grim-faced, having just been told that they were to be excluded from flying on the first atomic mission. LeMay had promised they would get 'the official reports' after the flight. The offer had irritated

278

Cheshire. He reminded LeMay that he had been instructed to go on the flight by the British Government, 'and if I wasn't going on it, why on earth was I sent here?'

LeMay would not budge; he could not; he was only carrying out orders from Washington, doubtless on the instigation of Groves.

Cheshire was not to be baulked. He and Penney had sent a 'really stiff signal' to the British Joint Staff Mission in Washington describing the position they were in.

So far they had received no reply. Now, with the briefing about to begin, Cheshire and Penney felt they 'were still on a sticky wicket with time running out'. They seated themselves behind the scientists.

Caron, Duzenbury, Shumard, Stiborik and Nelson arrived in a bunch, the first of the crews to do so. They wore flying coveralls, having just returned with Tibbets after a local test flight. During this practice mission, van Kirk, fully recovered, had navigated to Rota. Tibbets had made a four-minute bomb run, then banked sharply to the right after Ferebee released the practice bomb. All the bomber's equipment had functioned perfectly.

When the plane had landed back on Tinian, Tibbets taxied it to the special area where the pit had been dug. He positioned the bomber so that the bomb doors were directly over the hole. MP's took up station around the plane. From now on, until it next took off, the B-29 along with the hole in the ground would be under constant guard.

During the entire practice flight, Lewis, in the co-pilot's seat, had said little. Prior to flying he had 'performed the painful task' of telling his regular bombardier and navigator that 'they were being superseded by rank', and would not be flying the atomic strike. And even though Tibbets had at last made it clear to Lewis that his role would be as co-pilot, with Tibbets in command, Lewis still felt it was 'basically my crew' which were about to go into the history books.

When the enlisted men on the crew learned of the change-over, they accepted it without question. For them it was enough to be going.

Inside the hut, Caron had 'never seen so many strangers at a briefing'. Apart from the scientists, there were Parsons and Ashworth, in crisp naval uniforms. The tail-gunner wondered what the Navy had to do with an Army Air Force briefing. But he was determined on one thing: even in the presence of all this brass, nothing but a direct order would make him remove his Brooklyn Dodgers cap. The night before, in a moment of drunken euphoria, Caron had succumbed to Shumard's prompting for a haircut. An equally tipsy GI barber and Duzenbury had trimmed Caron's head until he 'resembled a cross between a Blackfoot Indian and a patch of sprouting prairie'.

Lewis arrived with Eatherly's crew, who were in boisterous good spirits after a night's carousing with their nurses. They seated themselves next to Sweeney's crew, who, taking a cue from their commander, were in a more thoughtful mood. Before coming to the briefing, Sweeney had gone down the flight line with three scientists who were installing a range of radio receivers and automatic film-recording devices aboard the *Great Artiste*. The scientists had explained to Sweeney that three parachutes, carrying cylinders similar in shape and weight to fire extinguishers, would be dropped from the plane near the target. Radio transmitters in the cylinders would send back data to the plane. Sweeney realised he would have to fly in perfect synchronisation with Tibbets to make sure the instruments fell into the designated area.

Beser arrived with Tom Classen, deputy commander of the 509th; they seated themselves at the rear of the room, near the projector. For Beser, the briefing was a welcome respite 'from the murderous pace up at the Tech. Area'. Having worked on the uranium bomb, he had now been switched to assist with the final assembly of the plutonium bomb; shortly before coming to the briefing, Doll had told him to 'stand by to go on a second mission as well'. Beser had asked how many missions were planned and Doll replied, 'just as many as it takes to make them quit'.

In the briefing hut, Beser felt the atmosphere was 'supercharged. After a while even Eatherly and his boys became subdued. We all just sat there, staring at the platform and the shrouded blackboards'.

Shortly before 3 p.m., Ferebee and van Kirk entered the building, taking seats near General Farrell close to the front.

At three o'clock precisely, Tibbets arrived in freshly-pressed khakis. Flanked by Payette and Buscher, the trio walked to the platform. The two intelligence officers positioned themselves by the blackboards. Parsons joined Tibbets on the dais.

Sergeant Abe Spitzer, Sweeney's radio-man, was concentrating hard to remember his impressions for the secret diary he was keeping. He saw that Parsons was 'perspiring and kept clearing his throat and shuffling his papers'.

Spitzer had no idea of the awesome responsibility that rested on Parsons. He and Tibbets were the key men of the mission. Better than anybody, Parsons knew what could go wrong—and that long list included the very real possibility of crashing on take-off, producing a premature nuclear explosion which 'could blow Tinian to Kingdom-come'.

The fear was not new. Two months earlier, at a Los Alamos

280

conference, one of Parsons' staff had proposed 'arming' the bomb in flight. Groves and Oppenheimer had opposed the idea, believing it would be too easy for something to go wrong. Nevertheless, provision had been made for the insertion of the conventional explosive and its detonator into the rear of the bomb after the plane was airborne. Without this explosive charge, the uranium 'bullet' would not be fired at the 'target' at the muzzle-end of the gun, although if the plane crashed, the 'bullet' might still slip down the barrel and cause a nuclear explosion. But inserting the explosive later was one way of reducing the risk, and Parsons, increasingly troubled by the spate of crashes on Tinian, decided to go against Groves and arm the bomb after take-off. He had told nobody yet of his plan—fearful that even now, if Groves heard about it, he would reach out across nearly 7,000 miles and stop him.

The hushed murmuring in the room ceased as Tibbets began to speak.

'The moment has arrived. This is what we have all been working towards. Very recently the weapon we are about to deliver was successfully tested in the States. We have received orders to drop it on the enemy.'

He nodded to Payette and Buscher. They removed the cloth from the blackboards.

Tibbets announced the targets in order of priority: Hiroshima, Kokura, Nagasaki. He next assigned the three B-29's to serve as weather scouts. Eatherly's *Straight Flush* would go to Hiroshima; *Jabbit III*, commanded by Major John Wilson, would fly to Kokura; the *Full House* piloted by Major Ralph Taylor was given Nagasaki.

Assistant engineer Jack Bivans sensed Eatherly's disappointment over the fact that they had drawn only a weather-scout role. A wise-cracking, good-looking, talented 'child star' of pre-war soap operas, Bivans had a clearly-defined, albeit unofficial role within the crew: keeping Eatherly laughing. Bivans guessed he would have his work cut out for him on the Hiroshima run.

Sweeney's *Great Artiste*, and *No. 91*, commanded by Major George Marquardt and carrying photographic equipment, would accompany Tibbets to the actual target—whose final selection would still depend on the weather reports radioed back by the scouting B-29's. If all three targets were clear, Tibbets would go for the primary one; only if Hiroshima was socked-in would he fly to one of the alternates. If all three were ruled out by weather conditions he would return to Iwo Jima, after Parsons had 'disarmed' the bomb in the air—a manoeuvre that both men had agreed upon that very day.

The seventh B-29, *Top Secret*, commanded by Captain Charles McKnight, was assigned to fly to Iwo and park on the guarded apron by the specially-constructed pit.

Jeppson stared intently at the reconnaissance photographs; the young Mormon had 'mixed feelings' about the impending mission.

Although he was not against dropping the bomb on a purely military target, he 'wished it wasn't going to be dropped on a city'. With his scientific background, he knew that the after-effects of exposure to radiation could be both severe and lingering.

On the platform Tibbets introduced Parsons, who came directly to the point.

'The bomb you are going to drop is something new in the history of warfare. It is the most destructive weapon ever produced. We think it will knock out almost everything within a three-mile area.'

A stunned gasp swept the room.

Parsons sketched in the background of the Manhattan Project. In his 'numbed mind', Spitzer was trying to compose a suitable sentence to include in his diary which would convey his reaction to what he had heard. He tried, 'It is like some weird dream conceived by one with too vivid an imagination.'

Boggle-eyed, Lewis watched Parsons walk to the projector. All the pilot could think of was, 'Is this guy for real?'

Parsons signalled to the technician to switch on the projector. Nothing happened. The operator began to fiddle with the mechanism. Buscher moved to help.

Suddenly the machine started and began to rip up the film as the celluloid became entangled in the sprockets.

Boot-faced, Parsons told the operator to stop the projector. He walked back to the platform and addressed the room.

'The film you are not about to see . . .'

He paused, and a roar of laughter lifted the tension.

'. . . was made of the only test we have performed. This is what happened. The flash of the explosion was seen for more than ten miles. A soldier 10,000 feet away was knocked off his feet. Another soldier more than five miles away was temporarily blinded. A girl in a town many miles away who had been blind all her life saw a flash of light. The explosion was heard fifty miles away. For those of us who were there, it was the beginning of a new age.'

The tension returned.

Parsons turned to a blackboard. After Payette had hurriedly removed some of the target photographs, the naval captain drew a mushroom shape.

Every man in the room was transfixed. Even Tibbets, who knew what was coming, was 'overwhelmed by the presentation'.

Parsons continued.

'No one knows exactly what will happen when the bomb is dropped from the air. That has never been done before. But we do

282

expect a cloud this shape will rise to at least 30,000 feet and maybe 60,000 feet, preceded by a flash of light much brighter than the sun's.'

He paused to let his words sink in. Van Kirk thought: *what's a naval officer doing telling us about a strange cloud twelve miles high?* Unlike Ferebee, the navigator did not yet know that Parsons was going on the mission.

Parsons turned to Buscher who brought forward a cardboard box, pulled out a pair of tinted goggles similar to those worn by welders, and handed them to Parsons.

Parsons explained that these would be worn by every crew member of the planes which would be near the target at the time of the explosion. He slipped them over his eyes, adjusting a knob on the nose bridge, telling his audience that by doing so he was changing the amount of light admitted by the glass. He said that over the AP the knob must be turned to its lowest setting.

Payette and Buscher began to distribute the goggles. Beser felt 'like a kid with a new toy'; Nelson wondered what the glass was made of; Lewis thought 'this is sure going to be some mission'.

Tibbets reinforced the view with a warning.

'You're now the hottest crews in the Air Force. No talking—to anyone. No talking even among yourselves. No letters. No writing home. No mentioning of the slightest possibility of a mission.'

He then gave details of the route to be taken to Japan, the altitude along various stages of the flight, the bombing height and the likely take-off time: the early hours of Monday, August 6. Some seven hours later, if all went well, they would be over the target city. That would be about forty hours from now.

The Air/Sea Rescue Officer took over. He said that no 'mission at any time' had been so thoroughly supported. Flying off the Japanese coast would be Superdumbos—B-29's specially equipped to co-ordinate rescue operations and fight off any enemy opposition. Dumbos—Navy flying boats—would be patrolling the flight path to and from Japan, ready to swoop down and rescue any crew that ditched. Supporting the aircraft would be cruisers, destroyers and 'lifeguards'—submarines prepared to 'come almost on to the enemy beaches to pick you up'.

Before the briefing, Ed Doll had told Jeppson that if he fell into enemy hands, Jeppson 'should tell the Japs everything you know. Then we'll know what you've told them. They'd find out anyway in the end'.

Doll was a civilian expressing the reality of the situation. Buscher was a military man, and delivered the formal Air Force attitude: captured crews were to give only their name, rank and serial number. He reminded them to search through their flying kit to make sure

283

they had removed all personal belongings—items which could be useful to the enemy.

Tibbets concluded the formal briefing with a short homily. Later he would not be able to recall his exact words; it would be left to Spitzer to produce the only record.

The colonel began by saying that whatever any of us, including himself, had done before was small potatoes compared to what we were going to do now. Then he said the usual things, but he said them well, as if he meant them, about how proud he was to have been associated with us, about how high our morale had been and how difficult it was not knowing what we were doing, thinking maybe we were wasting our time and that the 'gimmick' was just somebody's wild dream. He was personally honored and he was sure all of us were, to have been chosen to take part in this raid, which, he said—and all the other big-wigs nodded when he said it —would shorten the war by at least six months. And you got the feeling that he really thought this bomb would end the war, period.

August 5, 1945
Tinian
Morning

On this last day before the mission that Tibbets had waited so long for, in the 509th Operations Room, a duplicating machine turned out the single-page Operations Order, numbered 35, which described the final preparations for the strike.

The order was primarily a timetable of the day's activities, from meal-times for the various crews to the last moment when they could rest in their huts before the specialised briefings just before take-off. Officers began to use the order to plan lectures and prepare diagrams which would constitute the late-evening meetings. Down on the flight line, the order gave the mechanics all the details they needed about which planes were going, and when, and how much fuel and ammunition each would carry. The one bomb to be taken was described only as 'special'.

The crucially-important forecast of the weather expected over western Japan in the next twenty-four hours was based partly on information radioed from northern China on the orders of Mao Tse-Tung. The future ruler of Communist China had played his part in introducing nuclear warfare to the world.

After attending morning Mass, Sweeney was to make the last pre-atomic flight of the 509th. He was ordered by Tibbets to take the *Great Artiste* to 30,000 feet and release an inert, concrete-filled bomb over the ocean while the scientists on Tinian tracked its fall through binoculars.

The fusing test was similar to the one Sweeney's crew had performed at Wendover. Then, the firing system had been triggered prematurely, providing a stark reminder of what would have been their fate if they had been dropping an atomic bomb.

At altitude, Sweeney radioed that he was ready.

Among the knot of scientists waiting to track the falling bomb was Luis Alvarez, the son of a well-known surgeon at the Mayo Clinic. While at the Massachusetts Institute of Technology, Alvarez had invented the ground-control approach system that would one day be used on almost every airfield in the world. He had later headed the Los Alamos team which built the complex release mechanism for the bomb. On Tinian he had developed a device which would be carried by Sweeney's plane and dropped over the target city to help measure the atomic bomb's shock-wave.

Now, Alvarez was waiting for the steady tone he was hearing through his earphones to be broken, signifying that Sweeney's test bomb had left the plane. He knew exactly the sequence of events which, if everything worked properly, would follow. It was precisely the same as for the real atomic bomb to be dropped on the morrow.

When the bomb fell from the plane, wires attached to it would be pulled out, not only cutting a tone signal, but also closing a switch within the bomb—the first of a number of switches which had to be closed in sequence before the electricity travelling from batteries within the bomb reached the end of the circuit, the electrical detonator. Once the electricity reached the detonator, it would ignite the explosive powder. If there were no hitches tomorrow this would send the uranium 'bullet' down the gun-barrel, causing the atomic explosion.

Alvarez heard the signal stop. He knew the test bomb was on its way. The first switch should have closed. Sweeney started his 155-degree turn. A timing device in the bomb now waited a pre-set number of seconds before closing the second switch in the electrical circuit. Once that switch was closed, the electricity continued a little further along the line, stopped by another still-open switch which was controlled by a height-detecting device that measured barometric pressure. That device was set to close its switch when the bomb was 5,000 feet above the ground. Then the final and most sensitive instrument in the chain took over. This was a miniature radar set, also enclosed within the bomb. Its transmitter sent out radio waves which hit the ground, bounced back, and were received by the bomb's radar antennae sticking out like strange feelers near the front of the weapon. If all went well, the radar was set to close the final switch in the chain when the bomb was still 1,850 feet up in the air.

For this test run, at 1,850 feet, to signify that the fusing system had worked properly—that each switch had been snapped shut in the correct order—the bomb was to emit a slight puff of smoke.

Through binoculars, Alvarez and the other observers watched carefully for the smoke.

In vain.

The test bomb plunged, smokeless, past the planned height of detonation and splashed into the ocean.

Alvarez turned to his colleagues, filled with dismay.

'Great, just great. Tomorrow this time we're going to drop one of these on Japan and we still haven't got the thing right.'

Sweeney wasn't surprised by what had happened. He knew that, whereas Japanese bombs had a tendency to explode prematurely, among the conventional bombs produced by the United States were a fair number of duds. With such a new complex bomb, the chances of success must be less. Apart from that, Sweeney simply believed 'first bombs never work'.

He predicted the bomb Tibbets dropped tomorrow would be a dud.

Afternoon

In the hot glaring sun down on the flight line, a group of men led by one of the scientists, Bernard Waldman, a physics professor on loan from Notre Dame University, completed the fitting-out of *No. 91* for its photographic role; a fast-acting camera was to replace the plane's Norden bomb-sight. Waldman himself would be acting as camera man.

At 2.15 p.m., the telecon machine in the 509th Operations Room clattered out confirmation from LeMay on Guam that the take-off time for the atomic bomb-carrying plane was to be in just over twelve hours, making the time-over-target between eight and nine o'clock the following morning.

At 2.30 p.m., Ed Doll sent an encoded telegram to Los Alamos. It was based on an interview he had conducted with Beser, who reported that a rigorous search 'had so far detected no Japanese using the frequency on which the bomb's radar set will be operating'.

286

By 3 p.m., Morris Jeppson and three officers from the 1st Ordnance Squadron had completed installing a control panel just forward of the bomb-bay and just aft of the engineer and pilot compartments of the bomber Tibbets would be flying. The console was thirty inches high and about twenty inches wide. It contained switches, meters and small, coloured, indicator lights. Attached to its back were four thick cables, each containing twenty-four individual wires. These cables stretched like umbilical cords back to the bomb-bay where, once the bomb was in place, they would be plugged in to the weapon. They would automatically disconnect from the bomb when it was dropped.

The console was designed to monitor the bomb's batteries, to check for any electrical shorts along its firing circuit, to look out for a premature closing of any switch, to spot a malfunction in the barometric pressure device, the timing mechanism or the radar set.

While Jeppson and his team toiled inside the bomber, a sign-painter placed a ladder against the nose of the B-29 and grumpily climbed to the top, carrying a can of paint and a brush.

He had been dragged away from a softball game on the specific orders of Tibbets. The 509th's commander had handed the painter a piece of paper and told him 'to paint that on the strike ship, nice and big'.

The paper contained two words.

Enola Gay.

The choice of name indicated not only the esteem Paul Tibbets had for his mother, it also suggested that the commander of the 509th was not as confident about the safety of the mission as he had led his men to believe. Tibbets chose his mother's name because she had once promised him that whatever happened in his life, 'you will be all right'.

Tibbets felt the need to take that assurance with him to Japan.

At 3.30 p.m. a group assembled around the atomic bomb, now resting on a trolley. They included scientists, MP's and a number of Manhattan Project security agents.

On a signal from Major Uanna, after he had carefully draped the bomb with a tarpaulin, the trolley was trundled to a tractor and connected up. It began to be pulled slowly out of the hut, flanked by seven MP's on one side and an equal number of project agents on the other. Outside, jeep-loads of MP's fell in fore and aft of the bomb.

Looking to some observers for all the world like a military funeral cortège, complete with draped gun-carriage, the strange procession moved from the Tech. Area.

Half a mile away, on the apron, another detachment of MP's

reinforced the trio of guards already around the *Enola Gay*. A ground crew was led through the cordon to roll back the bomber from its position straddling the pit.

At 3.45 p.m. the trailer and escort arrived. A mobile winch was manoeuvred alongside the trolley and gently swung the weapon down into the pit. The *Enola Gay* was pushed back into position and, for a moment, the B-29, its bomb below, roosted like a great mother bird over her nest. Then the weapon was winched up into the *Enola Gay*'s front bomb-bay where it was clamped to its special hook. The fifteen-foot-long doors banged shut.

At 4 p.m. MP's posted warning signs around the bomber:

NO SMOKING WITHIN 100 FEET

There were just over ten hours to take-off.

At 4.15 Tibbets, Ferebee and van Kirk joined Lewis and the regular crew of the *Enola Gay* to pose for an official Air Force group photograph outside 509th Headquarters. The mood was relaxed; there was some joshing of Caron over his refusal to remove his baseball cap; Lewis made a joke about being famous.

Tibbets returned to his office to go over the final details of the mission; Ferebee and van Kirk went to the Operations Room to study route maps and target photos.

Lewis and the rest of the crew, with little to do before final briefing, decided to drive down to inspect the bomber.

Near the *Enola Gay*, their progress was barred by the MP's, one of whom explained that nobody was allowed near the bomber before take-off. Disappointed, but still mellow, Lewis began to walk around the plane. The rest of the crew started to drift back towards their truck.

Suddenly, Lewis bellowed, as Caron would recall: 'What the Hell is *that* doing on *my* plane?'

The crew joined the pilot who was staring up at the words *Enola Gay*.

Lewis, on his own later admission, was 'very angry, so I called the officer in charge of maintenance and said, "Who put this name on here?" He refused to tell me. He could see I was boiling. So then I said to him, "All right, I want it taken off. Get your men and remove the name from the plane." So then he said, "I can't do that." I says, "What the Hell you talking about, you can't? Who authorised you to put it on?" He says, "Colonel Tibbets." I said, "Colonel Tibbets? Okay."'

An enraged Lewis drove the truck to Group Headquarters and stormed into Tibbets' office.

What followed is a matter of dispute. In Lewis' version, 'Tibbets knew what in the Hell I was coming in there for. I says, "Colonel,

288

you authorised men to put a name on my airplane?" He says, "I didn't think you'd mind, Bob." I guess he was embarrassed.'

Tibbets would maintain he was anything but embarrassed. He had in fact consulted Ferebee, van Kirk and Duzenbury before naming the bomber *Enola Gay*; none of the three had raised any objection. Tibbets had not consulted Lewis, 'because I wasn't concerned whether Bob cared or didn't care'.

Tibbets firmly told Lewis that the name stayed. It was a decision which would lead to a lasting conflict between the two men.

Evening

During the morning in the Tech. area, and later, into the early evening in the stifling heat of the *Enola Gay* bomb-bay, Parsons practised inserting the explosive charge and detonator into the weapon, a delicate manoeuvre made more difficult by the cramped conditions and poor light.

When he finally emerged from the *Enola Gay*, General Farrell was waiting for him on the tarmac.

Concerned, Groves' deputy pointed at Parsons' lacerated hands and offered to loan him a pair of thin pigskin gloves.

Parsons shook his head.

'I wouldn't dare. I've got to feel the touch.'

At 7.17 p.m., Farrell sent a message to Groves letting him know that Parsons intended to arm the bomb after take-off. By the time Groves received the message, it was too late for him to do anything about it.

At 7.30 p.m., Classen, the 509th's deputy commander, following instructions from Tibbets, briefed a dozen ground officers on their various duties between then and take-off.

They were to escort scientists and key military personnel to 'safe' areas well away from North Field; there was to be no chance of losing irreplaceable atomic experts in an unscheduled nuclear explosion. When the time came, many of the scientists refused to budge, pointing out that almost nowhere on Tinian would be safe if an accident occurred.

Fire-trucks were to be stationed every fifty feet down the sides of runway A, the North Field airstrip selected for take-off.

Flight Surgeon Young was told that, in the event of a crash, his rescue teams must not touch anything until a specially detailed squad from the 1st Ordnance Squadron had monitored the crash area for radioactive contamination. It was the first, and only, inkling Young would receive that the weapon was an atomic bomb.

By eight o'clock, Mess Officer Charles Perry's cooks had begun to prepare the meals he would be offering the combat crews just after midnight: they could select a full-scale breakfast, dinner or supper from a choice of thirty dishes. Afterwards the crews could collect packed sandwiches to be eaten over Japan in the morning. Satisfied that the fliers were catered for, Perry began personally to prepare the pineapple fritters which Tibbets had requested.

All Perry had been told about the mission was that it 'was the most important in the war'. That was enough for him. He started to lay plans for 'a full-scale culinary celebration', to take place after the airmen returned.

Hiroshima

In Hiroshima another celebration was already in full swing. Since six o'clock guests had been arriving at the Imperial Army Officers' Club to attend a reception in honour of Field Marshal Hata's new Chief of Staff. The civilian guests included the local governor, senior civil servants and Mayor Senkichi Awaya. They, together with some fifty senior staff officers, were grouped in one room with Hata and the new Chief; the remainder of the guests had drinks in an adjoining reception area. Hata and his Chief had briefly visited this room, paid their respects, and then returned to the inner salon, moving from group to group, sipping sake and making polite conversation.

Periodically, Awaya drifted to the door of the salon where his assistant, Kazumasa Maruyama, would be patiently waiting with a sake container, filled with cold tea. Awaya was a teetotaller and it was Maruyama's duty to replenish the mayor's cup so that Awaya would be spared the embarrassment of having to refuse sake.

So far, the party was not proving a success for Mayor Awaya. His attempts to have a 'serious discussion' with Hata about the deteriorating situation in Hiroshima had failed. The Field Marshal had fobbed him off.

Now, fortified with another cup of tea, the mayor turned back into the room, determined to try again to make his views clear to his host.

Lt. Colonel Oya, Hata's intelligence chief, had, by contrast, no problem communicating with the Field Marshal. As soon as he arrived at the reception, Hata had sought him out, anxious for a first-hand report on the situation in Tokyo, from where Oya had just returned. While not making light of the massive destruction the capital had endured, Oya reported that morale in the city, as in the rest of Japan, was still high. The two men had discussed briefly the latest up-to-date report of the military situation which Oya had spent the day preparing; it was to form the basis for discussion at a full-scale communications conference called by Hata for tomorrow morning.

In less than twelve hours, gathered together in Hiroshima would be many of the senior commanders crucial to the defence of western Japan. They were to assemble in this very room at 9 a.m.

Oya wondered how many from the party tonight would turn up with hangovers. Some of them were already drinking too much. But the most senior officers from 2nd General Army Headquarters, the two divisional chiefs, Colonel Imoto and Colonel Katayama, and the Korean Prince RiGu were drinking only moderately. Katayama explained he had to be at the dentist's at eight in the morning, and did not want to be suffering from drink.

When Mayor Awaya again cornered Hata, the Field Marshal gave a vague promise to discuss matters in a few days. The disconsolate mayor decided it was time to go home. His wife had just returned to Hiroshima with their three-year-old grandchild, the latest member of the family to be taken into their care.

Maruyama drove the mayor home and said he would see him in the morning, as usual, soon after eight o'clock. They were the last words the two men would ever exchange.

Shortly after they parted, at 9.22 p.m. Radio Hiroshima broadcast an air raid stand-by alert. Eight minutes later came the all-clear.

For Dr. Shima, travelling towards the outskirts of Hiroshima, the warning presaged another nervous night for the patients in his clinic. He always worried about them when he was away. But it would have been unthinkable for him to have refused to carry out the house-calls he was off to make around the countryside. He had a busy night's work ahead of him, moving from one farmstead to another. He did not expect to be back in Hiroshima much before eight o'clock the following morning.

Dr. Shima had no way of knowing that if he stuck to his time-table his arrival in Hiroshima would coincide with that of the *Enola Gay*.

Scattered around the precincts of Hiroshima Castle, each man isolated in a cell, the twenty-three American prisoners of war prepared for another night of deprivation. Threatened and abused, in fear of their lives, they knew that at any moment they might have to face death.

Tinian
Night

Kneeling, head bowed, Joe Stiborik, the *Enola Gay*'s radar scanner, calmly prepared himself for that eventuality. With four hours to take-off, he had gone to the Catholic Church on Tinian to make a sacramental confession because, 'if something happened to me, I wanted to be sure to go to Heaven'.

In the confessional, Stiborik asked the priest on the other side of the grating to absolve him from all mortal sins. Satisfied that he had 'obtained a bit of insurance', Stiborik went back to his hut to await the call to the final briefing.

Within the 509th compound, many of the men scheduled to fly the atomic mission were also thinking of their spiritual well-being.

Tibbets believed in 'talking directly to God, asking for His help one more time, to make things come out the way I wanted them to and to get us back home after it's all over'.

Lewis prayed that 'we'd do our mission properly and that we would be safe and help end the war, that's all'.

Some of the crew-men went to the mess hall, to sample the line of chafing dishes Perry's cooks had prepared. Tibbets, Ferebee and van Kirk ate several plates of pineapple fritters. But for many the thought of food was unpalatable. They lay in their bunks and thought of their loved ones, became a little maudlin and drowned their homesickness and fears with surreptitious shots of whisky. A few slept.

At 11.30 p.m., the crews of the three weather planes went to their final briefing. By then Ferebee was heavily involved in a poker game, one of many being held that night. Between bids, he told a favourite Tinian story about the day when one of the 509th officers had gone swimming with a nurse in the nude; the clothes they had left on the beach were stolen, and the two were forced to walk, naked, back to their huts almost two miles away.

The tale helped to relieve the mounting tension everyone felt.

Van Kirk occupied his time checking his flight bag, making sure all his navigational instruments were there and his pencils sharpened; Caron sat quietly and thought of his wife; Nelson read the latest copy of the *Reader's Digest*; Shumard and Stiborik tried to sleep; Parsons and Jeppson ran over a check-list of what they would do once they were airborne; Lewis prowled around outside the combat crew lounge where the final briefing would be held at midnight.

In the lounge, Tibbets was talking to William Downey, the 509th's chaplain. Downey had no doubt that what Tibbets and his men were about to do was right. Although as a Christian he despised killing, in war, 'killing is the name of the game; those who don't accept that have to be prepared to accept the alternative—defeat'.

Beser was busy with a task ideally suited to his temperament. Tibbets had assigned him the job of briefing Bill Laurence, the *New York Times* reporter attached to the Manhattan Project. Beser's vivid descriptions helped Laurence later to collect a Pulitzer Prize for his work.

Beser was still talking when, shortly before midnight, he was called to the briefing.

Outside the crew lounge, the scientist Ed Doll waited for him. He handed Beser a piece of rice paper with numbers on it, specifying the radio frequency the bomb's radar would use to measure the distance from the ground as it fell. The numbers were written on rice paper, explained Doll, so that Beser could swallow the paper if he was in danger of being captured. It was a sobering thought for the twenty-four-year-old radar officer.

August 6, 1945
Midnight to 8.16 a.m.
Tinian

At midnight, Paul Tibbets walked to one end of the lounge and addressed the twenty-six airmen who would be flying with him to Japan.

'I'm going to keep this short, because there is not much left to say. I want you to remember this bomb we are going to drop is different from any you have ever seen or heard about. Secondly, I want you to remember that it contains a destructive power equal to about 20,000 tons of TNT.'

Not once in the year he had commanded them had Tibbets ever mentioned to anyone in the 509th the words 'atomic' or 'nuclear'. Now, in this final briefing, he continued to preserve security by merely referring to the weapon as being 'very powerful' and 'having the potential to end the war'.

He reminded the crews that at the time of the explosion they must be wearing their welders' goggles. Then, in a crisp few sentences, he spelled out the rules for a successful mission.

'Do your jobs. Obey your orders. Don't cut corners or take chances.'

The Weather Officer stepped forward and gave the forecast: the route to Japan would be almost cloud-free with only moderate winds;

clouds over the target cities were likely to clear at dawn. The Communications Officer read out the frequencies to be used on various stages of the mission and gave the positions of rescue ships and planes.

Tibbets had a few final words for each of the specialist disciplines on the mission: navigators were reminded of the rendezvous point above Iwo Jima where the three planes were to meet; tail-gunners should check that each aircraft had its 1,000 rounds of ammunition; engineers, that they were carrying 7,400 gallons of fuel, except for the strike aircraft, *Enola Gay*, which would have 400 gallons less to make its take-off easier; radio-men, the new call sign was 'Dimples'.

Tibbets had dropped the usual call sign, 'Victor', in case the Japanese had somehow learned of it.

At 12.15 a.m., the briefing over, Tibbets beckoned to Downey who bounded to his side. The chaplain invited the gathering to bow their heads. Then, in a richly resonant voice, consulting the back of an envelope he was carrying, Downey began to read the special prayer he had composed for this moment.

> Almighty Father, Who wilt hear the prayer of them that love Thee, we pray Thee to be with those who brave the heights of Thy heaven and who carry the battle to our enemies. Guard and protect them, we pray Thee, as they fly their appointed rounds. May they, as well as we, know Thy strength and power, and armed with Thy might may they bring this war to a rapid end. We pray Thee that the end of the war may come soon, and that once more we may know peace on earth. May the men who fly this night be kept safe in Thy care, and may they be returned safely to us. We shall go forward trusting in Thee, knowing that we are in Thy care now and forever. In the Name of Jesus Christ. Amen.

Beser looked at Spitzer, the only other Jew scheduled to fly the mission, and thought, 'This is a truly interdenominational strike—Jews, Catholics and Protestants all combining.' His own reaction to Downey's prayer was that 'as a Jew, the way I pray is to thank God *after* coming through a trying experience, not to ask him for a special favour beforehand'.

Hiroshima

Tibbets' concern about Japanese Intelligence was not fanciful. In the Communications Bureau of 2nd General Army Headquarters, radio monitors regularly picked up brief exchanges between aircraft and control towers in the Marianas, Okinawa and Iwo Jima.

Tonight, as usual, the monitors had indications that Japan was in for another brutalising series of raids. Thirty bombers were en route to Japan to drop mines in the Inland Sea; 65 bombers were coming to bomb Saga; 102 planes were about to launch an incendiary attack on Maebashi; 261 bombers were heading for the Nishinomiya-Mikage area; 111 bombers were bound for Ube; 66 for Imabari.

As the bombers came closer to Japan and began to change course, the monitors could make a rough prediction of their general target areas. The information helped to alert local batteries and the airfields where Japan's handful of night fighters were based.

On one of those bases, at Shimonoseki, some hundred miles to the south-west of Hiroshima, was 2nd Lieutenant Matsuo Yasuzawa, the flying instructor Yokoyama had seen at Hiroshima airport with the kamikaze student pilots.

Tonight, Yasuzawa was sleeping badly, his mind brooding over why he had once again been rejected for combat flying. The excuse his commanding officer had given him was the same as before: Yasuzawa was simply too valuable an instructor to risk in battle.

But, sensing Yasuzawa's rebellious mood, his commander had promised that soon they would each climb into a training aircraft and attempt to ram an attacking B-29. For Yasuzawa this would be the *rippa na saigo*, the 'splendid death' the kamikazes so often spoke to him about.

Now, tossing and turning in his bunk during this first hour of a new day, the eager young instructor wondered whether his commander intended to keep his promise or whether, instead, Yasuzawa was destined only to perform the sort of task he had to carry out later that morning. In just over six hours' time, at 7 a.m., he was scheduled to fly a major to Field Marshal Hata's communications meeting in Hiroshima. He expected to arrive in the city just before eight o'clock.

Edgy, unable to sleep, Yasuzawa turned on his bedside radio. He was just in time to hear the radio broadcasting a new air raid stand-by alert for western Honshu.

Moments after, at 12.25 a.m., in Hiroshima, the city's radio station advised the civilian population to evacuate to their designated 'safe areas'.

They would have to wait in their shelters for two hours before the all-clear sounded. It would do nothing to improve the temper of a weary populace called for the second time from their homes by false alarms.

295

Tinian

At 1.12 a.m., on Tinian, trucks picked up the crews of the two B-29's assigned to fly alongside the *Enola Gay:* the *Great Artiste* piloted and commanded by Sweeney; and *No. 91*, piloted and commanded by Marquardt. The *Great Artiste* was carrying scientific sensing devices; *No. 91* was carrying photographic equipment.

At 1.15 a.m. a truck picked up the crew of the *Enola Gay*. Tibbets and Parsons sat up front with the driver. Squeezed in the back were: van Kirk, Ferebee, Lewis, Beser, Jeppson, Caron, Shumard, Stiborik and Nelson. They all wore pale green combat coveralls; the only identification they carried were dog-tags around their necks. Beser's was stamped with an 'H' for 'Hebrew'.

At 1.37 a.m., the three weather-scout planes took off simultaneously from separate runways on North Field. Eatherly's *Straight Flush* was bound for Hiroshima; *Jabbit III* and *Full House* for Kokura and Nagasaki.

At 1.51 a.m., *Top Secret* took off for its stand-by role at Iwo Jima.

Ever since the final briefing, Duzenbury had been with the *Enola Gay*. He always took at least two hours for his 'pre-flight' for, whatever Tibbets and Lewis might have thought, the flight engineer '*knew* she was *my* ship'.

First, Duzenbury walked slowly around the bomber, checking it visually, 'watching out for the slightest thing that didn't look normal', checking even that every rivet was in place on all the control surfaces. Then, around one o'clock, Duzenbury went aboard *Enola Gay*, alone, check-list in hand.

At about that time, trucks and jeeps began arriving on the apron. The cordon of MP's drew back and a small army of technicians started to roll out cables and equipment.

Duzenbury went first to his own station, immediately behind Lewis' seat. There he began ticking off items on his list. It took him little enough time to inspect his instrument panel; he prided himself that it was always in perfect working order. Then he stepped into the cockpit and examined the controls, switches and dials. After he had verified that all was in order there, Duzenbury turned and made his way back into the spacious area he shared with navigator van Kirk and radio-man Nelson. Now it also contained Jeppson's console for monitoring the bomb. Duzenbury thought the panel was 'the prettiest gol'darn thing you ever saw in your life, all coloured lights and dials'.

After admiring the panel, Duzenbury opened a small, circular, airtight hatch, situated just below the entrance to the long tunnel which led to the after-end of the plane, swung himself feet first through the hatch and found himself facing the back end of the bomb, its fins almost touching the hatch door.

Using a flashlight, he crawled to the right-hand side of the weapon and on to the catwalk that ran along the length of the bay; from there he had his first overall view of the world's most expensive bomb.

The methodical Duzenbury played his torch over the weapon, suspended from its special hook and taking up almost the entire length of the bay. Duzenbury, who had worked as a tree surgeon before enlisting, thought the bomb resembled a long, heavy, tree trunk. The cables leading into it from Jeppson's monitoring panel, and its antennae, made it look like no bomb he'd ever seen before. He continued along the catwalk, checking everything as he went, past the nose of the bomb and back down along the other side. When he once again reached the fins, he noticed two unusual containers. Duzenbury thought they shouldn't be there. Almost subconsciously, he kicked them.

'Get these darn things the heck out of here.'

The flight engineer had not been told they contained the explosive powder and tools Parsons would use later to arm the bomb.

He was about to remove the containers when a bright shaft of light shone through the hatch into the bomb bay. Puzzled, Duzenbury climbed back through the hatch into van Kirk's compartment. The light filled the area. Duzenbury stumbled forward into the cockpit. He stopped open-mouthed.

The *Enola Gay* was ringed by floodlights.

Interspersed between the lights were mobile generators, photographers and film crews. Mingling among them were senior officers, scientists, project security agents and MP's. All told, there were close to a hundred people on the apron.

Dumbfounded, and not a little annoyed, Duzenbury turned back to his check-list.

The lights and camera crews had been specially ordered by Groves, over 6,000 miles away in Washington, D.C. He wanted a pictorial record made of as much as possible of the *Enola Gay*'s flight; only space had precluded a movie crew actually flying on the mission.

And, with a touch worthy of an epic production, the 'extras' on the tarmac formed an avenue for the 'stars' in their crew truck to drive down.

Tibbets stepped from the truck and found himself surrounded by a film crew. He had been warned in a message from Groves that there would be 'a little publicity, but this was full-scale Hollywood premiere treatment. I expected to see MGM's lion walk on to the apron or Warner's logo to light up the sky. It was crazy'.

297

The 509th's commander realised there was no point in objecting; resignedly, he complied with shouted requests to turn first *this* way, then *that* way, to smile, look serious, 'look busy'.

Parsons, mystified by the carnival atmosphere, turned to anybody who would listen and said, 'What's going on?' Not recognising that he was speaking to a Naval Captain, a brash photographer shoved Parsons against one of the *Enola Gay*'s wheels and said, 'You're gonna be famous—so smile!'

Parsons glared at the camera-man and said he didn't want to be famous and the hell he was going to smile.

The photographer shrugged and joined the group of camera-men swarming around Beser, who was still busily briefing Bill Laurence of the *New York Times*.

Beser was enjoying 'my first moments of fame'; everywhere he turned there was a camera clicking, a microphone ready to pick up his every word.

He himself was carrying a portable sound machine on which he planned to record the crew's reactions to the atomic explosion. That moment was a scheduled seven hours away. Here, now, nearing two o'clock in the morning, Beser was undoubtedly the star performer of the crew.

In the end the radar officer laughingly told the camera-men to 'go and plague somebody else'. They continued filming around him until Beser led them to where the enlisted members of the bemused crew were standing.

In expansive mood, Beser told the photographers to take some shots of them, adding that 'these guys are every bit as important as the rest of us'.

Shumard and Stiborik bowed in mock obsequiousness; they had always thought Beser never knew they existed.

Radio-man Dick Nelson, raised on Hollywood's doorstep, thought 'some of the people were behaving as if they were a bunch of guys in some low-budget production'.

Lewis walked over to the enlisted men. He was as flushed and excited as Beser, and perhaps with more cause. The reporter Laurence had just asked Lewis to keep a log of the *Enola Gay*'s flight, which the *New York Times* would later publish. No money was mentioned, but Lewis thought it might earn him 'a few dollars'. In the end it would make him a small fortune.

Now, on the tarmac, Lewis prepared to address the crew. Nelson watched him carefully: 'He gave us a good long stare and said, "you guys, this bomb cost more than an aircraft carrier. Don't screw it up. We've got it made; we're gonna win the war, just don't screw it up. Let's do this really great!" He made it clear that as far as he was concerned we were still his crew, and we were doing it for him.'

With the photographers clicking away, Lewis completed his pep talk.

Jeppson, like van Kirk and Ferebee—once Tibbets explained that Washington had ordered the filming 'for the historical record'—accepted it. In van Kirk's view it was 'a chore that would soon be over'.

Caron kept peering around owlishly in the bright lights, smiling enigmatically when somebody said they had never before known a tail-gunner who wore glasses. He doggedly refused to take off his baseball cap.

In common with many on the apron, Caron could not quite believe what was happening. He found the scene 'a trifle bizarre. I had to put my guns in their mount and all the time I was getting stopped to have my picture taken'.

Caron had only one regret: he had planned to take his camera on the mission; in all the excitement he had left it on his bunk.

But in the end he would take the most historic pictures of all. An army captain thrust a plate camera at Caron and told him, 'Shoot whatever you can over the target.'

At 2.20 a.m., the final group photo was taken, Tibbets turned to the crew and said, 'Okay, let's go to work.'

A photographer grabbed Beser and asked for 'one last goodbye look'.

Beser bridled.

'Goodbye, hell! We're coming back!'

The photographer was unabashed.

'Hope you're right, Lieutenant, hope you're right. In the meantime just give us a goodbye look!'

Beser turned and climbed up the ladder and through the hatch behind the *Enola Gay*'s nose wheel, suddenly tired of all the publicity.

He was followed by Ferebee and van Kirk, who, like Tibbets, were wearing baseball caps; Shumard and Nelson wore GI work caps; Stiborik a ski cap. None of the head-gear matched Caron's Brooklyn Dodgers cap with its large 'B' emblazoned on the front.

Finally only Parsons and Tibbets remained on the apron, talking to General Farrell. He suddenly turned and pointed to Parsons' coveralls.

'Where's your gun?'

Parsons, who usually thought of everything, had forgotten to draw a weapon from supply. He motioned to a nearby MP, who unstrapped his gun-belt and handed it to Parsons. He buckled it around his waist and after a quick thank-you, climbed clumsily up the nose ladder. Like all the others, Parsons wore beneath his coverall a survival vest with fish hooks, a drinking water kit, first aid packages and emergency food rations. Over this came a parachute harness with clips for a chest 'chute and a one-man life raft. On top came the armourlike flak suit for protection against shell fragments.

Unknown to the others, Paul Tibbets also carried a small sealed metal box in a pocket of his coveralls. Inside the box were twelve capsules. Each contained a lethal dose of cyanide. At the first sign of trouble over Japan, Tibbets was to distribute the cyanide capsules to the men on the plane. He would then explain to them the alternatives they faced before capture: they could either blow out their brains or commit suicide by poisoning. Tibbets knew this 'wasn't normal' Air Force procedure, but had been devised specially for the atomic mission because, 'if you were shot down, can you imagine the way and the measures the Japanese would take to find out what it was you were doing? So the alternative was, if you don't want to go through the torture that they might submit you to, the best way out is either with the gun or with the capsules'.

But that was a worry for later. Now, as he said farewell to Farrell, Tibbets had a more immediate concern—the possibility of crashing on take-off. During these past weeks on Tinian he had seen so many planes do just this that Tibbets had taken every possible step he could think of to avert a disaster. The *Enola Gay* was probably the most thoroughly-checked aircraft in the world. But no check devised could ensure there would be no last-minute failure of some crucial component.

Outwardly smiling and relaxed for the clamouring photographers, Tibbets boarded the *Enola Gay*, acutely aware that in a few minutes the camera teams could be recording the world's first nuclear disaster—if they themselves survived it.

Down on the tarmac, the camera-men continued to photograph the *Enola Gay* from all angles. One of them climbed a step-ladder and photographed Ferebee's bomb-aiming position in the nose. The bombardier was glad he had earlier ordered the ground crew to make a thorough search of the bomber and to remove 'any unauthorised items'. Among those found were six packs of condoms and three pairs of silk pants. Ferebee thought 'such things had no place on a bomber'.

When Tibbets reached his seat he automatically felt his breast pocket to make sure his battered aluminium cigarette case was still there. He regarded the case as a lucky charm, and he never made a flight without it.

Caron strapped himself in by his twin rear guns; although he need not have been there, in the event of a crash on take-off, he believed 'there was a marginally better chance of survival in the tail'. Even so, for good luck, Caron carried a photograph of his wife and baby daughter stuck in his oxygen flow chart. Shumard, squatting in one of the waist blister turrets, had with him a tiny doll; across from him, at the other turret, were Beser and Stiborik. They did not believe in talismen, though Stiborik thought his ski cap was as good as any.

At his station by the entrance hatch to the bomb-bay, Nelson fished out a half-finished paperback and placed it on the table beside him. A few feet away, van Kirk laid out his pencils and chart.

Forward of the navigator, Parsons and Jeppson sat on cushions on the floor, beside a pile of parachutes. They waited patiently, listening to the final preparation for take-off going on around them. Finally Tibbets called up Duzenbury.

'All set, Dooz?'

'All set, Colonel.'

Tibbets slid open a side window in the cockpit and leaned out.

A battery of camera-men converged to photograph his head peering over the gleaming new sign, *Enola Gay*.

'Okay, fellows, cut those lights. We've gotta be going.'

Normality returned to the apron.

Tibbets ordered Duzenbury to start no. 3 engine; when it was running smoothly, he ordered no. 4, then no. 1 and finally no. 2 engine to be fired.

Lewis added another note on the scratch pad he was keeping for the *New York Times:* 'Started engines at 2.27 a.m.'

The co-pilot looked across at Tibbets, who nodded. Lewis depressed the switch on his intercom.

'This is Dimples eight-two to North Tinian Tower. Ready for taxi out and take-off instructions.'

'Tower to Dimples eight-two. Clear to taxi. Take-off on runway A for Able.'

At 2.35 a.m., the *Enola Gay* reached her take-off position.

The jeep which had led the bomber there now drove down the runway, its headlights searching for any obstacle and briefly illuminating the fire-trucks and ambulances parked every fifty feet down each side of the airstrip.

At 2.42 a.m., the jeep flashed its lights from the far end of the runway, then drove to the side, joining the watching ranks of emergency vehicles.

Tibbets told Lewis to call the tower.

Their response was immediate.

'Tower to Dimples eight-two. Clear for take-off.'

Tibbets made a final careful check of the instrument panel. The take-off weight was 150,000 pounds; or, put another way, the 65-ton *Enola Gay*, with 7,000 gallons of fuel, a five-ton bomb and twelve men on board, would have to build up enough engine thrust to lift an overload of 15,000 pounds into the air. Tibbets made a decision: he would hold the bomber on the ground until the last possible moment.

He did not tell Lewis of his intention.

The co-pilot was feeling apprehensive; he, too, knew that the *Enola Gay* was well overweight, and he sensed that the next few seconds 'could be traumatic'.

Ferebee, on the other hand, felt completely relaxed and confident that Tibbets 'had worked everything out'.

Tibbets had—as far as was possible. But in the end it would be a 'gut reaction', experience, which would tell him what to do.

Van Kirk watched the second hand of his watch reach 2.44 a.m. Until the bomber was actually airborne, there was nothing for him to do. He momentarily wondered what would happen if Tibbets discovered a technical fault and had to return to the apron. How would the photographers react then, mused the navigator. The thought was too painful to pursue.

At precisely 2.45 a.m., Tibbets said to Lewis 'let's go', and thrust all throttles forward.

The *Enola Gay* began to roll down the runway, Tibbets keeping a careful eye on the RPM counter and the manifold pressure gauge.

With two-thirds of the runway behind them, the counter was still below the 2550 rpm Tibbets calculated he needed for take-off; the manifold pressure gauge only registered forty inches—not enough.

In the waist blister turrets, Shumard and Stiborik exchanged nervous glances. Beser smiled back at them, oblivious of any danger. Far forward, at his panel, Duzenbury stirred uneasily: he knew what Tibbets was trying to do—hold the *Enola Gay* on the ground to build up every knot of speed before lifting it into the air—but the engineer began to wonder whether he 'was *ever* going to take her up!'.

Lewis was staring anxiously at the instruments before him, a duplicate set of those in front of Tibbets. Outside, the ambulances and fire-trucks flashed by.

'She's too heavy!'

Tibbets did not reply to Lewis' shout.

'Pull her off—now!'

Tibbets continued to ignore Lewis, holding the bomber on the runway. Instinctively, Lewis' hands reached for his control column.

'No! Leave it!'

Lewis' hands froze on the wheel.

Back in the tail, Caron thought to himself: 'The Colonel's taking a hell of a long time to lift off!'

Beser suddenly sensed the fear Stiborik and Shumard felt. He shouted: 'Hey, aren't we going to run out of runway soon?'

Lewis was feeling the same way. He glanced quickly at Tibbets who was staring fixedly ahead at a break in the darkness where the runway ended at the cliff's edge.

Lewis could wait no longer. But, even as his hands tightened around the control column, Tibbets eased his wheel back. The *Enola Gay*'s nose lifted and the bomber was airborne at what seemed to Lewis the very moment that the ground disappeared beneath them and was replaced by the blackness of the sea.

Watching the take-off from his hiding place near the peak of Mount Lasso was Warrant Officer Kizo Imai. For the past ninety minutes he had peered fascinated at the lights, the flashbulbs, the cameras and the people. He could not imagine what it all meant.

And then, when the bomber which was the centre of all the attraction had taken off, it left from the very runway which Imai had originally helped to build.

Two minutes after the *Enola Gay*, the *Great Artiste* took off, followed, at 2.49 a.m. by *No. 91*.

The three weather-scout planes and now all three combat planes of Special Bombing Mission No. 13 were airborne and strung over several hundred miles of airspace, heading, on course and on time, for Japan.

At 2.55½ a.m., ten minutes after take-off, van Kirk made his first entry in the navigator's log. Position: N. Tip Saipan. Air Speed: 213. True course: 336. True head: 338. Temperature: +22C. Distance to Iwo Jima RV 622 miles. Height: 4700.

To make these calculations van Kirk had begun the close collaboration he would maintain with the radar-man Stiborik during the entire flight. Between them the two men would continually check bearings and make radar wind runs.

Nelson was also busy. Just before take-off he had switched on the IFF; now he adjusted the A and B band screws. Next he tuned the transmitter, checked the marker beacon and the compensation on the radio compass.

The *Enola Gay* was at the pre-determined height and on the north by north-west course it would maintain for the three-hour leg to Iwo Jima. And as the plane burrowed through the Pacific night, ten of the twelve men on board continued to busy themselves.

Ferebee had nothing to do and sat relaxed in his seat. There would be another six hours before the specialist skills of this self-contained professional bombardier were called into use. To tire himself now in pointless activity could have a detrimental effect on the role he would play later.

Beser had adopted a similar policy. Exhausted from over forty hours without sleep, he was slumped on the floor at the back end of the tunnel, quietly snoring. He would only be needed to man his electronic surveillance equipment after the *Enola Gay* passed over Iwo Jima.

Apart from giving routine orders, Tibbets had not yet exchanged a word with Lewis. Both men were aware that Lewis had tried to take over at the crucial moment of take-off. Lewis was anxious to explain he had acted instinctively, that he had in no way intended his action to be a reflection on Tibbets' flying ability. But he could not bring himself to say so. In turn, Tibbets recognised that his co-pilot's reaction had been perfectly understandable—'it was the response of a man used to sitting in the driver's seat'. But Tibbets, too, could find no way of expressing himself. And so they sat in uncomfortable silence, Tibbets intent on flying the plane, Lewis watching the instruments and adding a few lines to the 'log' he was keeping:

Everything went well on take-off, nothing unusual was encountered.

Caron called Tibbets on the intercom and asked, and received, permission to test his guns. He had 1,000 rounds to defend the *Enola Gay* against attack. He now expended fifty of them. The sound rattled through the fuselage. In Caron's tail turret there was a smell of cordite and burnt oil. Behind him, in the darkness, he watched tracers falling towards the sea.

Satisfied, and for the moment free of responsibility, Caron crawled forward into the rear compartment of the bomber. There, Stiborik was studying photographs of Hiroshima as the city would later appear on his radar screen. The unreal-looking pictures meant almost nothing to the tail-gunner.

Close to 3 a.m., Parsons tapped Tibbets on the shoulder.
'We're starting.'
Tibbets nodded, switched on the low-frequency radio in the cockpit and called Tinian Tower.
'Judge going to work.'
As arranged, there was no acknowledgement. But, in the control tower on North Field, a small group of scientists studied a copy of a check list that, on board the *Enola Gay*, Parsons had taken from a coverall pocket. It read:

Check List for loading charge in plane with special breech plug.
(after all 0–3 tests are complete)

  1: Check that green plugs are installed.
  2: Remove rear plate.
  3: Remove armor plate.
  4: Insert breech wrench in breech plug.
  5: Unscrew breech plug, place on rubber pad.
  6: Insert charge, 4 sections, red ends to breech.

7: Insert breech plug and tighten home.
8: Connect firing line.
9: Install armor plate.
10: Install rear plate.
11: Remove and secure catwalk and tools.

This bald recital gave no clue as to the delicate and ticklish nature of the task Parsons was going to perform.

The naval officer lowered himself down through the hatch into the bomb-bay. Jeppson followed him, carrying an inspection torch.

The two men squatted, just inside the bay, their backs almost touching the open hatch, and faced the tail-end of the bomb. Parsons began to take tools out of the box which Duzenbury had kicked during his pre-flight check.

Ferebee, wanting to be present at this critical stage of the mission, left his bombardier's seat and came back to watch.

Shielded by half a ton of ballast, at the muzzle-end of the gun inside the bomb, was a ring of uranium.

At the breech-end was a metal slug, the 'bullet'. About six inches long, it resembled a tin of soup. This contained the remainder of the fissionable material.

It was Parsons' task to insert a charge of high-quality gunpowder, along with its electrical detonator, into the breech, behind the 'bullet'. When the time came, the detonator would ignite the powder, which would propel the uranium slug down the fifty-two-inch barrel at 900 feet per second, into the centre of the uranium ring. As the 'bullet' travelled down the barrel, a small device made of Polonium 84 would begin emitting neutrons, initiating the chain reaction. The tiny mechanism was nicknamed 'Abner', after Al Capp's comic strip powerhouse, Li'l Abner.

To Ferebee, the two men crouching in the bomb-bay resembled car mechanics, with Jeppson handing tools to Parsons whenever he was asked.

As each stage on the check list was reached, Parsons used the intercom to inform Tibbets, who radioed the news to Tinian.

But by stage six—the actual insertion of the gun-powder and electrical detonator—Tinian was out of radio range of Tibbets' set. For security reasons he had decided against using Nelson's more powerful transmitter: Tibbets feared that his messages would be picked up by Japanese monitors.

At 3.10 a.m. Parsons began the task of inserting the gunpowder and detonator. He worked slowly and in total silence, his eyes and hands concentrating on the task; he, better than anybody, knew that the bomb had more built-in fail-safe devices than any other weapon. And yet there was still an element of risk which was very real: not even

Parsons knew what would happen if a stray bullet penetrated the bomb's casing and detonated the powder he was now inserting.

Gently, he placed the powder, in four sections, into position. Then he connected up the detonator. Afterwards, with sixteen measured turns, he tightened home the breech plate, then the armour and rear plates.

The weapon was now 'final' except for the last, crucial operation which Jeppson would perform when he returned to the bomb-bay and exchanged three green 'safety' plugs for red ones. Jeppson knew that, until then, the weapon could not be detonated electrically— 'unless, of course, the plane ran into an electrical storm.'

At 3.20 a.m., the two men climbed out of the bomb-bay.

Parsons went forward and informed Tibbets that they had finished. Then he sat on the floor beside Jeppson who was now checking the bomb's circuits on his monitoring console.

Five minutes after Parsons and Jeppson completed arming the bomb, in Hiroshima, where the time was 2.25 a.m., the all-clear sounded. People returned from the air raid shelters.

On Mount Futaba, Lieutenant Tatsuo Yokoyama staggered sleepily back to his quarters. This was turning out to be a bad night: three alerts and not a sign of a bomber. He ordered the gun-crews to stand down, and asked his orderly to bring him a pot of tea.

In Hiroshima Castle, the twenty-three American prisoners of war had waited nervously for the sound of planes. During the alert, they had remained in their cells. Their captors had decided the prisoners should be offered no protection if the city was attacked.

Tibbets stared into the night. The stars were out, pricking the inky blackness of the sky; below them, looking very white, were the clouds. Inside the *Enola Gay* it was comfortably warm, room temperature.

Beside him, Lewis was making an entry in his 'log'.

Tibbets had finally broken the silence between them by asking his co-pilot what he was writing. Lewis replied he 'was keeping a record'. Tibbets did not pursue the matter, and the two men continued to sit side by side, not speaking, peering into the darkness.

Nelson completed his check of the Loran equipment. Loran was a long-range navigational device designed to determine a plane's position by the time it took to receive radio signals from two or more transmitters whose positions were known. Nelson had tuned to transmitters on Iwo Jima and Okinawa.

Duzenbury and Shumard were paralleling generators, to ensure that the four motors remained smoothly synchronised.

At 4.01 Tibbets spoke first to Sweeney and then to Marquardt, both of whom were following some three miles behind. The *Great Artiste* and *No. 91* reported 'conditions normal'.

At 4.20 a.m., van Kirk called Lewis on the intercom to give the estimated time of arrival over Iwo Jima as 5.52 a.m.

Lewis noted this in his 'log', and then added 'we'll just check' to see whether the navigator's estimate turned out to be correct.

By now Lewis was expanding his 'log' from its original stark time-table to contain such observations as 'the Colonel, better known as the "old bull", shows signs of a tough day; with all he had to do to help get this mission off, he is deserving a few winks'.

Tibbets, in fact, had never felt more relaxed or less tired. The trip, so far, was 'a joy ride'.

At 4.25 a.m., he handed over the controls to Lewis, unstrapped himself and climbed out of his seat to spend a little time with each man on the plane.

Parsons and Jeppson confirmed that the final adjustments to the bomb would only be made in the last hour before the target was reached.

As he reached Duzenbury's position, Tibbets felt Lewis trim the controls so that the *Enola Gay* was flying on 'George', the automatic pilot; the elevators gave a distinct kick as 'George' engaged.

Tibbets chatted to Duzenbury for a few minutes, and then moved on to Nelson. The young radio-man hurriedly put down the paper-back he was reading and reported, 'Everything okay, Colonel.' Tibbets smiled and said, 'I know you'll do a good job, Dick.' Nelson had never felt so proud.

Tibbets next watched van Kirk make a navigational check. Ferebee joined them and the three men talked quietly about whether conditions would allow them to bomb the 'primary'. Tibbets said that whatever Eatherly reported the weather over Hiroshima was like, he would still go there first 'to judge for myself'. Van Kirk thought it would be an 'easy target to find'. Ferebee said he had memorised what the city would look like so well that he 'could see it in my sleep.'

Tibbets then crawled down the thirty-foot-long padded tunnel which ran over the two bomb-bays and connected the forward and aft compartments of the *Enola Gay*.

In the rear compartment were Caron, Stiborik, Shumard and a still-sleeping Beser, surrounded by his equipment.

Stiborik and Shumard were not well-known to Tibbets, though their flying reports stamped them as top-grade. But Tibbets knew, and trusted, Caron. He turned to the tail-gunner.

'Bob, have you figured out what we are doing this morning?'

'Colonel, I don't want to get put up against a wall and shot.'

Tibbets smiled, recalling that day last September in Wendover when Caron had fervently promised to keep his mouth shut. Since then the tail-gunner had been an example to everybody when it came to security.

'Bob, we're on our way now. You can talk.'

Caron had already guessed the *Enola Gay* was carrying 'a new super-explosive'.

'Are we carrying a chemist's nightmare?'

'No, not exactly.'

Caron tried again.

'How about a physicist's nightmare?'

'Yes.'

Tibbets turned to crawl back up the tunnel. Caron reached in and tugged at his leg.

Tibbets looked back.

'What's the problem?'

'No problem, Colonel, Just a question. Are we splitting atoms?'

Tibbets stared at the tail-gunner—then continued crawling up the tunnel.

Caron had recalled the phrase about splitting atoms from a popular science journal he had once read. The tail-gunner had no idea what it meant.

Back in the cockpit, Tibbets disengaged 'George' and began to climb the *Enola Gay* to 9,000 feet for its rendezvous at Iwo Jima.

Jeppson, who had flown less than one hundred hours, went into the navigator's astrodome; to the east he could see a waning moon, flashing in and out of the cloud banks. Ahead, apart from a high thin cirrus, the sky was cloudless and cerulean. All his life Jeppson would remember the grandeur of this night as it began to fade into dawn.

Lewis leaned forward towards Ferebee, sprawled in his chair, eyes half-closed.

'Won't be long now, Tom.'

Ferebee made no reply

Sitting back, Lewis confided to paper, 'Our bombardier has been very quiet and methinks he is mentally back in mid-west part of the old U.S.'

Ferebee, in fact, was reviewing in his mind's eye the future targets.

Outside, the night was being swiftly folded back. By the time the *Enola Gay* arrived over Iwo Jima, the whole sky was a pale incandescent pink as the first rays of the sun probed through the cockpit windows.

Exactly on time, the *Enola Gay* reached the rendezvous point.

Circling above Iwo Jima, Tibbets waited for the other two bombers.

At 4.55 a.m. Japanese time, Sweeney's *Great Artiste* and Marquardt's *No. 91* joined the orbit, swimming upwards to 9,000 feet.

At 5.05½ (6.05½ on van Kirk's chart, as the navigator was to remain on Tinian time as far as his entries went), with daybreak in full flood, the three bombers formed up into a loose V, Tibbets in the lead, and headed towards Shikoku, the large island off the south-west coast of Japan.

Crossing the pork-chop-shaped Iwo Jima for the last time, Tibbets used his cockpit radio to call Major Bud Uanna in the communications centre specially set up on the island for the mission.

'Bud, we are proceeding as planned.'

Through the early morning static came Uanna's brief response.

'Good luck.'

On Iwo Jima, McKnight and the crew of *Top Secret* relaxed, their stand-by bomber unlikely now to be needed.

At a comfortable 205 miles an hour, the *Enola Gay*, the *Great Artiste* and *No. 91* headed northwards. Aboard all three bombers there was a constant routine of checking wind velocity and calculating drift.

Lewis, with little to do except fill in his 'log', found his entries becoming more spaced out, more cryptic. Finally, when the bomber had reached 9,200 feet, he simply wrote that 'we'll stay here until we are about 1 hour away from the Empire'.

Beser's sleep was unexpectedly disturbed when an orange was slowly rolled down the tunnel from the forward compartment and dropped gently on his head.

He awoke with a start, to see Shumard and Stiborik grinning at him. Caron thrust a cup of coffee into his hands. Gulping it down, Beser began to 'wind up' his equipment. He had arranged it so that all the dials he needed to see were at eye-level when he sat on the floor; instruments which he would only listen to were higher up the special racks which reached to the bomber's roof. There were several such racks of receivers, direction finders, spectrum analysers and decoders. Between them they allowed Beser to monitor enemy fighter control frequencies and ground defences, as well as radar signals which could prematurely detonate the bomb. He wore a special headset which allowed him to listen to a different frequency in each ear.

Beser began to fiddle with the sets; tuning dials and throwing switches. Into one of his ears came the sounds of a ground controller on Okinawa, talking down a fleet of bombers returning from a mission; in his other ear were brief air-to-air exchanges between Superdumbos circling off the coast of Japan. With a sense of relief Beser realised the rescue craft were on station for the atomic strike.

Then, suddenly, Beser stiffened. His eyes glued to the monitoring equipment, he saw 'the Japanese Early Warning Signal sweep by us.

309

It made a second sweep, and then locked on to us. I could hear the constant pulse rate as they continued to track us'.

Beser now knew that the greatest protection the *Enola Gay* had—surprise—was gone. And nothing could be done to shake off a competent enemy radar scanner.

Instead of informing Tibbets that the Japanese had located them, Beser decided to keep the knowledge to himself: 'It wasn't Tibbets' worry at this stage. And it would be upsetting for the rest of the crew to have somebody say, "hey, they're watching us". So I just used my discretion.'

Sometime after 6.30 a.m. Japanese time, Jeppson climbed into the bomb-bay carrying the three red plugs. Once he had exchanged them for the 'safety' plugs, the bomb would become a 'living, viable weapon'.

Jeppson edged along the catwalk to near the middle of the bomb. The bay was unheated and the temperature about the same as outside the plane, 18 degrees Centigrade. Carefully, he unscrewed the green plugs and inserted the red ones in their place. They fitted flush with the casing. As he gave the last plug a final turn, even the ice-cool Jeppson had to reflect that 'this was a *moment*'.

The electrical circuit to the weapon's fusing chain was now open. The bomb was ready for dropping.

Jeppson climbed out of the bay, leaving the atomic bomb suspended motionless from its one powerful hook.

He reported to Parsons what he had done. Parsons went forward and informed Tibbets, who switched on the intercom and addressed the crew.

'We are carrying the world's first atomic bomb.'

An audible gasp came from several of his listeners. Lewis gave a long low whistle; *now* it all made sense.

Tibbets continued.

'When the bomb is dropped, Lieutenant Beser will record our reactions to what we see. This recording is being made for history. Watch your language and don't clutter up the intercom.'

He had a final word for Caron.

'Bob, you were right: we are splitting atoms. Now get back in your turret. We're going to start climbing.'

Still bemused, the diminutive Caron crawled back to his position in the tail, wondering what he would say on the recorder and thinking that 'if we're going to be recorded for history, then Jeez, this has to be *some* bomb!'.

At 6.40 a.m., nearing Japan, the *Enola Gay* began climbing to its bombing height of 30,000 feet.

In Hiroshima, some three hundred miles from the *Enola Gay*,

Lt. Colonel Kakuzo Oya arrived at seven o'clock at Second General Army Headquarters to read over the intelligence report he intended to submit to Hata's Communications meeting in two hours' time. While he checked the report, Colonel Imoto and other senior officers were arriving in the room. There they would wait for Lt. Colonel RiGu and Colonel Katayama, before taking transport to the Officers' Club in the grounds of the Castle where the meeting was to be held. Field Marshal Hata was still at home, praying at the family shrine. Soon he planned to be host to the most distinguished gathering of commanders assembled in Hiroshima since the outbreak of war.

There would be one noticeable absentee—Captain Mitsuo Fuchida, hero of Pearl Harbor and now the Imperial Navy's Air Operations Officer. For the past ten days, Fuchida had been in Hiroshima attending an Army-Navy liaison conference at Hata's headquarters, discussing defence plans for the expected American invasion. The previous afternoon, Fuchida had been summoned from the conference to deal with some technical snags at the Navy's new headquarters in Nara, near Kyoto. In spite of working late into the night, Fuchida had not solved the problems. At about the time that Oya was checking over his report, Fuchida was again grappling with the bugs in the communications system at Nara. Those stubborn bugs probably saved his life.

In the countryside to the west of Hiroshima, unforeseen circumstances were also deciding the fate of Dr. Kaoru Shima. On his house calls he had encountered cases which demanded more time than anticipated. He did not expect to be back in his Hiroshima clinic much before noon.

Further west, 2nd Lieutenant Matsuo Yasuzawa started the engine of his two-seater training plane, turned to check that his passenger was strapped-in behind him, taxied to the runway, received clearance to take off and commenced the forty-minute flight from Shimonoseki to Hiroshima. Yasuzawa's course was roughly at right angles to the *Enola Gay*, now approaching Japanese air space.

At over 500 feet a minute, the *Enola Gay* was climbing to her bombing height of almost six miles.

Though the sun beat warmly on the pressurised aircraft, the outside temperature was now below freezing.

At the monitoring panel directly linked to the bomb by its thick cables, Parsons and Jeppson maintained their vigil. Both men hoped there would be no reason for them to go down into the unpressurised bomb-bay where icy conditions now prevailed. But if the console showed a fault—a winking red light—then they were prepared to don oxygen masks and re-enter the bay to try and remedy it.

The lights all remained green.

At 7.09 a.m. Radio Hiroshima interrupted its programme with another air raid alert. Simultaneously, the siren wailed its warning across the city. Everybody tensed for a second and more urgent sound—a series of intermittent blasts of the siren—which would indicate that an attack was imminent.

At the very moment the Hiroshima siren sounded, Claude Eatherly's *Straight Flush* reached the designated Initial Point, just sixteen miles from the Aioi Bridge which Ferebee had chosen as his Aiming Point.

Below, all Eatherly could see was a solid undercast.

At 235 miles an hour, at a height of 30,200 feet, on a heading of 265 degrees, almost due west, the *Straight Flush* began a straight run from the Initial Point to the Aiming Point, following exactly the course Tibbets and Ferebee had selected for the *Enola Gay*. This short flight would provide the basis for all Eatherly's later extravagant claims—claims which would, as he wished, make him world famous.

He looked for a break in the clouds. At first he could find none.

Then, immediately ahead, directly over Hiroshima, he saw a large rent in the cloud. Six miles below, the city was so clear that the crew of the *Straight Flush* could see patches of greenery.

Whooping with delight, Eatherly flew across Hiroshima. Above the city's outskirts, he turned, and made another pass to make sure the break in the cloud was still there.

It was.

A huge hole ten miles across, ringed by thick cloud, hovered over Hiroshima. Shafts of light shone down through the gap, as if to spotlight the target city for the fliers.

At about the same time, the planes checking the weather over Nagasaki and Kokura found conditions there nearly as good.

All three cities were available for the *Enola Gay*, now at 26,000 feet and still climbing at a steady 194 miles an hour.

At 7.24 a.m. Nelson switched off the IFF. A minute later, on 7310 kilocycles, he received a coded message from the *Straight Flush*. When he had transcribed the code it read:

Cloud cover less than 3/10ths at all altitudes.
Advice: bomb primary.

After Tibbets had read the message, he switched on the intercom and announced: 'It's Hiroshima.'

Minutes later *Full House* and *Jabbit III* reported in. Nelson took the transcribed messages to Tibbets who shoved them into his coverall pocket. He told Nelson to send a one-word message to Uanna on Iwo Jima.

Primary.

Lewis noted in his log: 'Everyone has a big hopeful look on his face.'

He couldn't have seen Beser's face, concentrating hard on the enemy radar, silently tracking the *Enola Gay*. Its signal was growing stronger all the time.

On board Eatherly's *Straight Flush*, just about to leave Japanese air space, an extraordinary debate broke out.

Eatherly, like the other two weather-scout planes, was under strict instructions to return directly to Tinian.

Instead, according to his flight engineer, Eugene Grennan, Eatherly switched on the intercom and suggested they orbit until Tibbets passed them, 'and then follow him back to see what happens when the bomb goes off'.

Grennan suggested this 'wouldn't be smart'. Somebody else, the engineer would recall, disagreed, arguing that '"if Tibbets and the others get knocked out, we would be there to report what happens". So it started: everybody arguing, should we, shouldn't we go? Then Eatherly says "Listen fellas, if we don't get back to Tinian by two o'clock we won't be able to get into the afternoon poker game" '.

Still the argument raged.

Nobody, as Grennan would recall, was much concerned about future consequences: 'We wouldn't have stopped because of any discipline reason. When the argument was going on Eatherly asks me, "do we have enough gas to go to Hiroshima again and get back to base?" I said we could always land in Iwo Jima. He wasn't very keen on that because I guess he didn't want to play poker there. Then we all polled each other and the consensus was that going back to watch one bomb drop wouldn't be much of a thrill. "What would we see?" asked Eatherly.'

The crew of the *Straight Flush* decided to give the atomic bomb a miss.

At 7.31 a.m. the all-clear sounded in Hiroshima. People relaxed, lit kitchen stoves, prepared breakfast, read the *Chugoku Shimbun*.

Warrant Officer Hiroshi Yanagita, the Kempei Tai leader who had rounded up some of the American POW's now in their cells at Hiroshima Castle, had not heard any of the night's air raid alerts.

He was in bed, sleeping off a heavy hangover.

On Mount Futaba, 2nd Lieutenant Tatsuo Yokoyama kept his men at their anti-aircraft gun-post.

Yokoyama was suspicious. He thought it strange that the lone plane had circled and made a second run high over the city.

He ordered a breakfast of rice, soup, pickles and stewed vegetables to be served to the gunners at their posts. Yokoyama had a similar meal brought to his quarters. As a sign of respect his batman carried the breakfast tray high above his head, 'to ensure that his breath did not fall on the food'.

Within the precincts of Hiroshima Castle, bowls of mush were unceremoniously left on the cell floors of the American prisoners.

In Mayor Senkichi Awaya's home, in the more modest apartment of his assistant, Kazumasa Maruyama, in tens of thousands of other homes in Hiroshima, frugal breakfasts were being eaten against the background of Radio Hiroshima's regular programme of martial music.

Eight hundred feet from the Aioi Bridge, the Shima Hospital's staff changed shifts while the patients had breakfast. As was the custom in Japanese hospitals, the food was prepared and served by relatives. By 7.35 a.m. most of them were hurrying from the clinic to put in another long day for the war effort.

Few of them noticed 2nd Lieutenant Matsuo Yasuzawa's twin-seater aircraft descending over the city towards the airport.

At 7.40 a.m., Yasuzawa taxied to a dispersal bay, cut his motor, and climbed out of the trainer. It had been a short, undemanding flight. He now had to find out for his passenger, a major, where Hata's communications meeting was being held. Yasuzawa felt he was becoming an errand boy.

The Korean Prince, Lt. Colonel RiGu, had waited until Yasuzawa's trainer passed overhead before mounting his handsome white stallion.

The sound of aero engines made the horse nervous. RiGu was in no hurry. There were still seventy-five minutes to go before Hata was scheduled to open the communications conference. At a gentle trot his stallion took him towards the Aioi Bridge and 2nd Army GHQ.

Just over a mile from the bridge, in the first-floor office of Colonel Imoto, at GHQ, Oya finished reading his report and joined the four other officers in the room. They were discussing the war. One of them mentioned the demoralising news that the American Fifth Feet was continuing to shell the Japanese coast.

In the centre of Hiroshima, at eight o'clock, hundreds of youths began work on the fire-lane leading to the Aioi Bridge.

Close by, in the grounds of Hiroshima Castle, many of the city's 40,000 soldiers were doing their morning calisthenics. Not far from them, a solitary American was also being exercised.

Fifty miles from the Aiming Point, the Aioi Bridge, at 30,800 feet, the *Enola Gay* flew on, followed a few miles behind by the two observer planes. The only person speaking was van Kirk, calling out tiny course corrections to Tibbets.

It was 8.05 a.m. Van Kirk marked the moment.

'Ten minutes to AP.'

Isolated from the rest of the plane by an unpressurised compartment, connected to the crew only by intercom, in his cramped tail turret, Bob Caron began to put on his armoured vest. Hemmed in by his guns and holding the unwieldy camera he had been given just before take-off, he found it 'too tight a squeeze'.

Caron put his only protection from flak on the floor.

It was 8.06 a.m. Nine minutes to go.

Beser was monitoring the Japanese fighter control frequency. There was no indication of activity. Stiborik was glued to his radar screen. Shumard was peering out of a waist blister turret, also on the look-out for fighter planes.

Ferebee settled himself comfortably on his seat and leaned forward against the special bombardier's head-rest he and Tibbets had designed months before at Wendover.

Dick Nelson was watching Parsons and Jeppson, kneeling a few feet away at the bomb console. Neither man touched anything, but to Nelson they seemed to be 'willing all those lights to remain as they were'. Parsons rose to his feet and walked stiffly towards the cockpit.

It was 8.09 a.m.

Left alone, Jeppson also stood up, and buckled on his parachute. He saw Nelson and van Kirk look at him curiously. Their parachutes remained stacked in a corner.

Van Kirk called out another course change, bringing the *Enola Gay* on to a heading of 264 degrees, slightly south of due west. At 31,060 feet and an indicated airspeed of 200 miles an hour, the bomber roared on.

It was 8.11 a.m.

Stiborik took his eyes off his radar screen. Just by his left hand was a lever. Opposite the lever, attached to the outside of the B-29's fuselage, was a camera. It was totally enclosed but had two small bomb-bay-like doors beneath the lens. Stiborik turned the lever and saw the miniature doors slowly swing open. The moment the bomb fell from the plane, the camera would begin taking pictures.

Van Kirk called Tibbets on the intercom.

'IP.'

It was 8.12 a.m.

Exactly on time, at the right height and pre-determined speed, van Kirk had navigated the *Enola Gay* to the Initial Point.

There were now three minutes to go.

At that moment, at Saijo, nineteen miles east of Hiroshima, an observer spotted the *Enola Gay* and behind, the *Great Artiste* and *No. 91.* He immediately cranked the field telephone which linked him directly with the Communications Centre in Hiroshima Castle, and reported what he had seen. The centre was manned by school-girls drafted to work as telephonists. Between them they handled all such calls and passed on warnings to the duty announcer at the Hiroshima radio station. Having written down the details furnished by the Saijo look-out, one of the girls telephoned the station. At dictation speed, the announcer wrote down the message.

8.13 Chugoku Regional Army reports three large enemy planes spotted, heading west from Saijo. Top alert.

The announcer rushed to a nearby studio.
It was now 8.14 a.m.

One minute to go.
Tibbets spoke into the intercom.
'On glasses.'
Nine of the twelve men slipped the polaroid glasses over their eyes and found themselves in total darkness.
Only Tibbets, Ferebee and Beser kept their glasses up on their foreheads. It would otherwise have been impossible for them to do their work.
Before covering his eyes, Lewis had made a notation in his 'log'.
'There will be a short intermission while we bomb our target.'
Thirty seconds.
Simultaneously, several things happened. Ferebee shouted that Hiroshima was coming into his viewfinder. Beser called Parsons, saying that no Japanese radar was threatening the bomb's proximity fuse. Parsons, who was standing immediately behind Tibbets, raised his glasses and agreed with Tibbets that 'this was the target'. As Parsons lowered his glasses, Tibbets spoke quickly into the intercom.
'Stand by for the tone break—and the turn.'
They were his last words in the pre-atomic age.
Glasses still on his forehead, eyes fixed on the target, Ferebee watched the blacks and whites of the reconnaissance photographs transform themselves into greens, soft pastels and the duller shades of buildings cramming the great long fingers of land which reached into the dark blue of Hiroshima Bay. The six tributaries of the Ota River were brown; the city's principal roads a flat metallic grey. A

gossamer haze shimmered over the city, but it did not obscure Ferebee's view of the Aiming Point, the T-shaped Aioi Bridge, about to coincide with the cross-hairs of his bombsight.

'I've got it.'

Ferebee made his final adjustments and turned on the tone signal, a continuous low-pitched hum, which indicated he had started the automatic synchronization for the final fifteen seconds of the bomb run.

Now, unless the weapon stuck in the bay, there was no more Ferebee need do.

A mile behind, in the *Greate Artiste*, bombardier Kermit Beahan waited to toggle open the bomb doors and drop the blast gauges parachuting earthwards.

Two miles behind, Marquardt's *No. 91* had begun to make a 90-degree turn to be in position to take photographs.

The tone signal was picked up by the crews of the three weather planes, including Eatherly's, now about 225 miles from Hiroshima and heading back to base.

It was heard on Iwo Jima by McKnight, still sitting in the pilot's seat of *Top Secret*, the stand-by aircraft that would not now be needed. McKnight told Uanna, who radioed Tinian:

'It's about to drop.'

Precisely at 8.15:17, *Enola Gay*'s bomb-bay doors snapped open, and, without anyone then having to do anything, the world's first atomic bomb dropped clear of its restraining hook.

Simultaneously:

The monitoring cables were pulled from the bomb and the tone signal stopped.

The *Enola Gay* lurched upwards nearly ten feet, suddenly over 9,000 pounds lighter.

Caron, in the tail, gripped the plate camera more tightly and, blinded by the welder's goggles, wondered which way he should point it.

Tibbets began to ram the *Enola Gay* into a diving right-hand turn.

Aboard the *Great Artiste*, Sweeney saw the bomb emerge from the bay of the *Enola Gay*.

Beahan toggled away the blast-measuring equipment.

Aboard *No. 91*, the cameras began turning.

It was 8.15:20 seconds.

In the three seconds which had elapsed, Ferebee shouted 'bomb away', and then turned from his sight to look down, and backwards, through the plexiglass of the *Enola Gay*'s nose.

He saw the bomb drop cleanly out of the bay and the doors slam shut.

For a fleeting eye-blink of time, the weapon appeared to be suspended by some invisible force beneath the bomber. Then Ferebee saw it begin to fall away.

'It wobbled a little until it picked up speed, and then it went right on down just like it was supposed to.'

There were now forty seconds left.

Simultaneously, on the ground:

Lt. Colonel Oya stood at a window of 2nd General Army Headquarters and peered up at the *Enola Gay* and *Great Artiste*. The two bombers seemed to be diving towards the city.

Field Marshal Hata, having tended his 'victory' garden and prayed at his shrine, was now about to dress before going to his communications meeting. He was oblivious of the planes overhead.

Equally oblivious, the Kempei Tai officer, Hiroshi Yanagita, snored insensibly in his bed.

Stripped to the waist in the midsummer heat, Tatsuo Yokoyama was raising a bowl of rice to his mouth, chopsticks poised.

On board the *Enola Gay*, Tibbets continued to hold the bomber in a steep power dive and tight, right turn of 155 degrees. Sweeney's *Great Artiste* was performing an identical manoeuvre to the left.

Inside the bomb, its timer tripped the first switch in the firing circuit, letting the electricity travel a measured distance toward the detonator.

Tibbets asked Caron if he could see anything. Spreadeagled in his turret, the gravitational force draining the blood from his head, the gunner could merely gasp one word.

'Nothing.'

Beser, also trapped by the violence of the manoeuvre, stared fixedly at his instruments and tried to lift his hand to the wire recorder.

Nobody else moved.

There were now twenty seconds left.

Simultaneously, on the ground:

Prince RiGu was cantering his horse on to the Aioi Bridge.

Another senior officer, Colonel Katayama, was mounting his horse after a visit to the dentist in the centre of the city.

The announcer in Radio Hiroshima reached the studio to broadcast the air raid warning.

In the half-underground communications centre at Hiroshima airport, Yasuzawa waited to be told where Hata's meeting was to be held.

On the fire-lanes, supervisors were starting to blow their whistles, the signal for thousands of workers, many of them school-boys and girls, to run to their designated 'safe' areas.

In the grounds of Hiroshima Castle, drill instructors were ordering thousands of soldiers to abandon their morning calisthenics and to form-up into squads to march off the field.

Aboard the *Enola Gay*, Jeppson counted the seconds. Tibbets pulled down his glasses. He could see nothing. He yanked them off.

In the nose, Ferebee had not bothered to put his on.

The *Enola Gay* was coming to the end of its breath-taking turn and was now some five miles from Ferebee's AP, heading away from the city. Tibbets called Caron. Again the tail-gunner reported there was nothing to see.

Lewis involuntarily flexed his fingers over the control column. Beser's hand at last managed to switch on the wire recorder. Nelson stared sightlessly at his radio. Stiborik turned up the brightness on his radar screen so that he could see it through his glasses. Shumard peered blindly out of a blister turret. Duzenbury, his hand on the throttles, worried about what the blast would do to the *Enola Gay*'s engines.

Jeppson continued to count. Five seconds to go.

Simultaneously:

In the bomb, the barometric switch tripped at 5,000 feet above the ground. The shriek of the casing through the air had now increased to a shattering sonic roar, not yet detectable below.

On the ground, Kazumasa Mayurama was walking towards Mayor Senkichi Awaya's house to collect him, as he did every morning before work.

Close by, in the grounds of Hiroshima Castle, a solitary American prisoner of war, blind-folded, was continuing his exercise.

In Radio Hiroshima, the announcer pushed the button that sounded the air raid siren and, out of breath, began to speak into a microphone.

'8.13, Chugoku Regional Army reports . . .'

Jeppson's count reached forty, forty-one, forty-two . . .

The announcer reached: '. . . three large enemy planes spotted, heading . . .'

Simultaneously:

Jeppson reached forty-three.

The bomb's detonator activated 1,890 feet above ground.

At exactly 8.16 a.m., forty-three seconds after falling from the *Enola Gay*, having travelled a distance of nearly six miles, the atomic bomb missed the Aioi Bridge by 800 feet, and exploded directly over Dr. Shima's clinic.

Shockwave

August 6, 1945, 8.16 a.m. to midnight

In the first milli-second after 8.16 a.m.—a time-fraction too small for any watch in Hiroshima to measure—a pinprick of purplish-red light expanded to a glowing fireball hundreds of feet wide. The temperature at its core was 50,000,000 degrees.

Even at 'ground zero', the Shima Clinic, the point on the ground directly beneath the detonation, the temperature reached several thousand degrees centigrade.

The flash heat started fires a mile away, and burnt skin two miles distant.

Of the estimated 320,000 civilians and soldiers in the city, some 80,000 were instantly killed or mortally wounded. About one-third of the casualties were soldiers. Most deaths occurred in the four square miles area around the Aioi Bridge, containing the city's principal residential, commercial and military quarters.

The stone columns flanking the entrance to the Shima Clinic were rammed straight down into the ground. The entire building collapsed. The occupants were vapourised.

Sixty-two thousand other buildings—out of a total of 90,000—were destroyed. All utilities and transportation services were wrecked. Over 70,000 breaks occurred in the water mains. Only sixteen pieces of fire-fighting equipment survived to plug into the ruptured system.

One hundred and eighty of the city's 200 doctors were dead or injured; out of 1,780 nurses, 1,654 were similarly afflicted. Only three of the city's fifty-five hospitals and first-aid centres remained usable.

The largest single group of casualties occurred around Hiroshima Castle, about 900 yards from the epicentre, where, out in the open, several thousand soldiers and one American POW were directly exposed to the spreading blast from the bomb. They were incinerated, their charred bodies burnt into the parade ground. A similar fate befell thousands of others labouring on the fire-lanes.

Hiroshima Castle was totally destroyed.

The mortality rate for its occupants was about ninety percent. Amongst the casualties were the school-girls on duty in the communications centre and most, although apparently not all, of the American POW's.

The radiant heat set alight Radio Hiroshima, and burnt out tram-cars, trucks and railway rolling stock. Stone walls, steel doors and asphalt pavements glowed red hot. The heat burned the black lettering from books and newspapers, and transferred clothing on to skin, fusing them together. More than a mile from the epicentre men had their caps etched on to their scalps, women their kimono patterns imprinted on their bodies, children their socks burned on to their legs.

The blast clogged six of the city's sewer pumping stations and affected the water table beneath the ground. It sent a whirlwind of glass through the area of destruction.

Almost all this happened in the time it took Bob Caron's eyelids to blink shut behind his goggles—his first, uncontrollable response to the flash.

Every man in the *Enola Gay* had seen the light and was overwhelmed by its intensity.

Nobody spoke.

Tibbets could 'taste the brilliance; it tasted like lead'.

An ethereal glow illuminated the instruments in the cockpit, on Duzenbury's panel, on Nelson's radio, on the racks of instruments before Beser.

By the time Caron's eyelids opened, the flash had gone.

Taking its place was something equally stunning. It was, in Caron's words, 'a peep into hell'.

In Hiroshima, a fire-storm raged. From within an area now over a mile wide, a monstrous seething mass of red and purple began to rise into the sky; the column was sucking into its base super-heated air which set fire to everything combustible.

Lt. Colonel Oya recovered consciousness to find himself lying face down on the floor in a devastated 2nd General Army Headquarters. Sand was raining down on him from ruptured sandbags above the broken ceiling. The blast had hurled Oya ten feet from the window and the heat rays had severely burned the back of his head and neck. Blood oozed from his skin where it was punctured by slivers of glass. Colonel Imoto and the other officers in the room were in a similar state. They were just over a mile from ground zero.

On Mount Futaba, slightly further away, 2nd Lieutenant Tatsuo Yokoyama had no conscious recall of the initial flash, the searing blast of heat. His first memory was of being where he now was: standing almost naked outside his quarters, brandishing his ceremonial sword and screaming for his gun-crews to open fire. But there was nothing for them to shoot at. Infuriated by his impotence, Yokoyama turned to look, for the first time, down on Hiroshima. He became aware of 'a strange dense fog beginning to envelop the city'.

In the centre of that fog, his commanding officer, Colonel Abe, and Abe's daughter, were dead. There would be no need for Yokoyama to invent further excuses about not marrying.

Kazumasa Maruyama had been about one mile from ground zero.

He was felled by a stone pillar. By the time he regained consciousness, darkness would be descending on Hiroshima as the great mushroom cloud blotted out the daylight. Staggering to his feet, Maruyama would then stumble back to his home. He would remember nothing of the journey.

Not far from where Maruyama lay was the man he had served so faithfully, Mayor Senkichi Awaya. The mayor's house was wrecked and on fire. Mayor Awaya, his fourteen-year-old son and three-year-old grand-daughter, had been killed instantly. His wife and daughter would die later. The following day, when Maruyama was sufficiently recovered from his injuries, he would go to the still-smouldering ruins of the house and dig out what remained of the mayor's body.

But now, as Maruyama lay unconscious under the pillar, the city he had helped govern was literally disappearing all around him.

From his vantage point in the tail of the *Enola Gay*, still flying away and some ten miles from Hiroshima, Bob Caron was the first to see a frightening phenomenon developing. A great, circular mass of air spread outwards and was rising upwards, travelling at the speed of sound, towards *Enola Gay*. Stupefied, the tail-gunner tried to shout a warning.

His words were unintelligible.

Caron was the first man ever to witness an atomic bomb's shockwave, created by air being so compressed that it seemed to take on a physical form. It looked to Caron like 'the ring around some distant planet had detached itself and was coming up towards us'.

He yelled again.

At the same time, the great circle of air smashed against the wings and fuselage of the *Enola Gay*, bouncing the plane higher. Tibbets grabbed at the controls. But it was the noise that accompanied the shockwave which caused him the greatest concern. Remembering his bombing missions over Europe, he thought 'an 88 mm shell had exploded right beside us'. He immediately shouted, 'Flak!'

Ferebee had the same reaction.

'The sons-of-bitches are shooting at us!'

The two battle-hardened veterans began frantically searching the sky around the plane for smoke-puffs. Pandemonium broke out in the bomber.

In less than four seconds, above the cacophony of voices on the intercom, Caron screamed out again.

'There's another one coming!'

With a spine-jarring crash, the second wall of air hit the *Enola Gay*. Once more the bomber was tossed upwards, tipping Nelson half-out of his seat and sending Beser tumbling.

A voice started to shout in panic. Tibbets silenced it.

Then, as quickly as it had arrived, the shockwave passed. The *Enola Gay* was back in calm air.

Tibbets addressed the crew.

'Okay. That was the reflected shockwave, bounced back from the ground. There won't be any more. It wasn't flak. Stay calm. Now let's get these recordings going. Beser, you set?'

'Yes, Colonel.'

'I want you to go round each of the crew and record their impressions. Keep it short and keep it clean. Bob, start talking.'

'Gee, Colonel. It's just spectacular.'

'Just describe what you can see. Imagine you're doing a radio cast.'

Caron did. With the *Enola Gay* beginning to orbit at 29,200 feet, eleven miles from Hiroshima, the tail-gunner produced a vivid eye-witness account in words he would never forget.

A column of smoke rising fast. It has a fiery red core. A bubbling mass, purple-grey in colour, with that red core. It's all turbulent. Fires are springing up everywhere, like flames shooting out of a huge bed of coals. I am starting to count the fires. One, two, three, four, five, six . . . fourteen, fifteen . . . its impossible. There are too many to count. Here it comes, the mushroom shape that Captain Parsons spoke about. It's coming this way. It's like a mass of bubbling molasses. The mushroom is spreading out. It's maybe a mile or two wide and half a mile high. It's growing up and up and up. It's nearly level with us and climbing. It's very black, but there is a purplish tint to the cloud. The base of the mushroom looks like a heavy undercast that is shot through with flames. The city must be below that. The flames and smoke are billowing out, whirling out into the foothills. The hills are disappearing under the smoke. All I can see now of the city is the main dock and what looks like an airfield. That is still visible. There are planes down there.

In a wide orbit, Tibbets circled the cloud as it climbed towards 60,000 feet.

Waiting to speak on Beser's recorder, Lewis was 'groping for words' to write in his 'log'. There were those on board the plane who would insist his initial reaction to the mushroom cloud was, 'My God, look at that son-of-a-bitch go!' But Lewis later decided to pen, 'My God, what have we done?'

Tibbets was 'surprised, even shocked. I had been expecting to see something big, but what is big? What I saw was of a magnitude and carried with it a connotation of destruction bigger than I had really imagined'.

Beser confined himself to a few words for posterity.

'It's pretty terrific. What a relief it worked.'

Nelson, Shumard and Duzenbury used such words as 'just awesome', 'unbelievable', 'stunning' and 'shattering' to try to convey what they saw. Stiborik thought 'this is the end of the war'. Ferebee and Parsons were too busy preparing the strike report to record their impressions.

In the tail, Caron was beginning to take photographs that would be used around the world.

At 215 miles an hour, at an even 29,000 feet, with an outside temperature of minus 18 degrees Centigrade, the *Enola Gay* completed its first circle around the stricken city.

As it did so, others of the crew could now see Hiroshima airport, its planes almost hidden by the haze.

Second-Lieutenant Matsuo Yasuzawa was running towards one of those planes, the '99 Superior Trainer' which he had landed in Hiroshima less than one hour before. As he ran, he saw that every aircraft he passed had been severely damaged by the blast. Many were on fire.

The airfield was just over two miles from the epicentre and the force of the explosion was largely spent by the time it struck the base. Even so, hardly a window was left intact and many of the buildings suffered structural damage.

After Yasuzawa and his passenger had dug themselves out of the debris of the underground communications centre, they were joined by a number of other officers all of whom had meant to go to Hata's meeting. For a moment they had stared dazedly at the destruction. Then, collecting themselves, the officers jumped on to a truck and headed for the Officers' Club while Yasuzawa began running towards his aircraft.

Yasuzawa wanted to go in pursuit of the bombers. When he first emerged from the shelter he had seen them as three specks in the sky. Now he was 'humiliated and furious' they had not yet been attacked by fighters or anti-aircraft fire.

Weaving his way past burning fuel trucks and aircraft, he continued down the flight line.

His plane was parked at the far end of the field. He reached it, panting, out of breath, and shook his head in wonderment.

The plane was bent like a banana.

It had been broadside to the blast-wave, which had blown out all the glass along one side of the cockpit and re-shaped the fuselage into a shallow figure 'C'.

The tail was swung ten degrees off true, and the nose was similarly bent. It was as if the plane had been warped by some supernatural power. It was the strangest-looking aircraft imaginable, but it was in one piece.

Yasuzawa walked around the aircraft, determined, if at all possible, to fly the plane. He climbed into the cockpit and pressed the starter button. The engine kicked and, incredibly, spluttered into life.

Then, in front of him, Yasuzawa saw a sight that made him shudder. Coming into the airfield was the vanguard of a procession of 'living corpses'. Bleeding and blackened, their skins hanging in shreds, their hair scorched to the roots, the first survivors were seeking sanctuary. Many were totally naked, their clothes burned from their bodies. Some of the women carried babies.

A horified Yasuzawa looked away.

The zombie-like figures shuffled past, oblivious of the engine noise.

There was now a new thought in Yasuzawa's mind: he had to get out and report what had happened to Hiroshima.

He taxied his plane slowly to the runway.

The airport, situated at the bottom of one of Hiroshima's 'fingers' which jutted into the Bay, was upwind of the towering atomic cloud; the wind blew from the harbour, keeping the runway relatively free of the pall.

Yasuzawa pointed his twisted plane away from the cloud, revved the engine, released the brakes, and headed down the runway.

He pulled back the stick and the bent trainer sidled uncertainly into the air. Yasuzawa held it about three feet off the ground for a moment or two, then touched down again.

He now felt confident the plane would fly. He taxied back to the other end of the runway, ready for take-off. Yasuzawa was concentrating so hard on the controls he was hardly aware of the mushroom shape above Hiroshima.

Aboard the *Enola Gay*, Nelson had already sent word that the mission was a success. Now Parsons handed him a second message. It read: '82 V 670. Able, Line 1, Line 2, Line 6, Line 9.'

When it was de-coded it would tell General Farrell, waiting anxiously in the 509th Operations Room on Tinian, the news he had been waiting hours to hear:

Clear cut. Successful in all respects. Visible effects greater than Alamogordo. Conditions normal in airplane following delivery. Proceeding to base.

After a third and final circle around Hiroshima, Tibbets put the *Enola Gay* on course for Tinian. The *Great Artiste* and *No. 91* formed up behind and the three bombers headed down the 'Hirohito Highway' for home.

Some 29,000 feet below and twenty miles away, Matsuo Yasuzawa completed his checks.

He was about to take off when out of the murk stumbled the officer he had earlier flown to Hiroshima. The major reported he had been unable to get to the Officers' Club because the roads were 'filled with fleeing refugees and fallen debris'. The city, he said, 'is a sea of flames'.

When he saw that Yasuzawa intended to take off, he insisted on going as well. The pilot pointed to the precarious state of the plane, but the major would not be put off. He climbed into the seat behind Yasuzawa.

With both men leaning hard to the left, sheltering behind what little glass remained on that side of the cockpit, the misshapen trainer began its journey, crab-like, down the runway. Almost at the end, Yasuzawa pulled back the stick and the plane skewed into the air.

Over Hiroshima Harbour, he turned back towards the city and the smoke.

Yasuzawa did not realise he was about to fly his twisted plane into a cloud caused by an atomic explosion.

Climbing steadily, knowing that if he made one false move on the controls, 'the plane would flip over and that would be the end', the expert flying instructor flew his curved aircraft over the centre of Hiroshima.

The wind howled past the open cockpit. Yasuzawa, concentrating mainly on keeping his distorted plane in the air, was conscious only of 'a thick haze, dust and smoke and flames'.

At 2,000 feet, he levelled out and began to do what Tibbets had done fifteen times higher—circle the city to estimate the damage.

But where the *Enola Gay* had remained well clear of the cloud, Yasuzawa was now flying in and out of the pall, unaware of the risk to which he was subjecting himself and his passenger.

After about five minutes' reconnaissance, he put the crippled plane on course for his Kyushu air base, a hundred miles away.

There, after completing one of the most unusual flights in the history of aviation, he would exchange his extraordinary-looking aircraft for a transport plane, and spend the rest of the day ferrying survivors out of Hiroshima.

On Tinian, preparations were well underway to welcome back the *Enola Gay*.

At 10.30 a.m., when Mess Officer Charles Perry had first heard news that the strike was a success, he turned to his cooks and shouted, 'The party's on!'

The 509th's kitchens became the centre of activity for an event not unprecedented in the annals of warfare, as Perry masterminded a celebration to mark the victors' return. Since dawn, at about the time the *Enola Gay* was passing over Iwo Jima on the way to Hiroshima, Perry had been finalising his plans. By the time the atomic bomb was whistling down on the unsuspecting city, the mess officer was prepared to mark the event with 'a party where nothing would be missing'. Using a mixture of charm and barter, Perry 'scrounged' the ingredients needed for 'everyone in the 509th to have a good time'.

The cooks began preparing the first of hundreds of pies for a pie-eating contest, cooling the first of scores of crates of beer and lemonade, making the first of thousands of hot-dogs, slicing beef and salami for open sandwiches, mixing potato and fruit salads.

Satisfied that the 'biggest blow out' Tinian had ever known was safely under way, Perry sat down at a typewriter and prepared a 'program to mark the occasion'. It read:

509TH
FREE BEER PARTY TODAY 2 P.M.
TODAY—TODAY—TODAY—TODAY—TODAY
PLACE—509TH BALL DIAMOND
FOR ALL MEN OF THE 509TH COMPOSITE GROUP
FOUR(4) BOTTLES OF BEER PER MAN
NO RATION CARD NEEDED
LEMONADE FOR THOSE WHO DO NOT CARE FOR BEER
ALL-STAR SOFT BALL GAME 2 P.M.
JITTER BUG CONTEST
HOT MUSIC
NOVELTY ACTS
SURPRISE CONTEST—YOU'LL FIND OUT
EXTRA—ADDED ATTRACTION, BLONDE, VIVACIOUS, CURVACIOUS, STARLET DIRECT FROM ???????
PRIZES—GOOD ONES TOO
AND RATION FREE BEER
FOOD GALORE BY PERRY & CO. CATERERS
SPECIAL MOVIE WILL FOLLOW AT 1930, 'IT'S A PLEASURE'
IN TECHNICOLOR WITH
SONJA HENIE AND MICHAEL O'SHEA
- - - - - - - - -
CHECK WITH YOUR ORDERLY ROOM
FOR MORE DETAILS
- - - - - - - - -
WEAR OLD CLOTHES   WEAR OLD CLOTHES
6 AUGUST 1945
WELCOME PARTY FOR RETURN OF
ENOLA GAY
FROM
HIROSHIMA MISSION
330

Captain Mitsuo Fuchida, leader of the attack on Pearl Harbor and now flying towards Hiroshima in his navy bomber, wondered what force had created the strange cloud hovering over the city.

He called the airport's control tower.

There was no reply.

As he got closer, Fuchida saw that Hiroshima, the city he had only left the afternoon before, 'was simply not there any more. Huge fires rose up in all quarters. But most of these fires seemed not to be consuming buildings; they were consuming debris'.

Fuchida would have no conscious recall of landing his plane on the runway, the same one from which Yasuzawa had made his epic take-off. His next memory would be of walking towards the airport exit, immaculately dressed in his spotless white uniform, shoes and gloves, and coming face to face 'with a procession of people who seemed to have come out of hell'.

Horrified, not caring about the black blots which were falling on his uniform, Fuchida began to walk into Hiroshima. The dead and the dying clogged the gutters, floated in the rivers, blocked the streets.

The closer he got to the city centre, the more appalled he became. Whole areas had simply disappeared; for at least a square mile, 'nothing remained'. Utterly depressed and exhausted by what he could see, Fuchida, the man who had literally led Japan into World War Two, continued to wander aimlessly through the wasteland which three years, seven months and twenty-nine days later was a grim reminder that surprise in war can be a two-edged sword.

The *Enola Gay* was 363 miles from Hiroshima when Caron finally reported that the mushroom cloud was no longer visible. Only then did Tibbets cat-nap, leaving Lewis to fly the plane.

At 2.20 p.m. Tinian time, Tibbets was awakened by Farrell calling from North Field tower to offer his congratulations.

At 2.30 p.m., refreshed after a tin of fruit juice, Tibbets took over flying the bomber.

At 2.58 p.m., the *Enola Gay* touched down at North Field.

She had been in the air for twelve hours and thirteen minutes. With an empty bomb-bay and having used over 6,000 gallons of fuel, she was 40,000 pounds lighter than at take-off. She had flown 2,960 miles—and into the history books.

Two hundred officers and men were crowded on the apron, ready to greet her. Several thousand more lined the taxi-ways.

They cheered when Tibbets led the crew down through the hatch behind the nose wheel. Then came Parsons, Jeppson and Beser. All were swamped by movie and still camera-men and well-wishers. A brigadier-general ordered the crowds back. Into the space he had cleared stepped General Spaatz. He walked up to Tibbets and pinned the Distinguished Service Cross on the breast of his coveralls. The two men separated, still not having spoken, and saluted each other. Then Spaatz turned and led away a coterie of high-ranking officers. It was the signal for the others on the tarmac to swarm once more around the fliers and ply them with questions.

An officer collected Caron's camera. Another officer took Beser's wire recorder.

The photographs were processed and rushed to Washington for world-wide distribution. The recordings vanished.

The de-briefing was a relaxed, informal affair, helped along by generous shots of bourbon and free cigarettes.

By the time it was over, Perry's party was in full swing.

Somehow, it didn't seem to matter.

All Paul Tibbets and the other men on the *Enola Gay* wanted to do was sleep. They found it easy enough to do so.

Aftermath

August 7, 1945 to mid-day, August 15, 1945

By the morning of August 7, news had trickled through to the Japanese leaders that Hiroshima had been hit by a new kind of bomb. They were told the destruction caused was very great but, in devastated Tokyo, the reports sounded distressingly familiar.

President Truman's statement, describing the weapon in some detail and released to an astounded world and a delirious American public the day before, was then broadcast to Japan. It was dismissed by many politicians as propaganda.

The Japanese public were told nothing by their leaders.

When the Cabinet learned about the bomb, Major-General Seizo Arisue was chosen to head a group of high-ranking officers and scientists to go to Hiroshima to investigate. Among the scientists was Professor Asada, the physicist who had worked on Japan's atomic bomb and who was still busy perfecting his Death Ray.

President Truman's press release warned Japan that unless the country surrendered forthwith, further destruction would follow. Truman now waited in Washington for some response.

On Tinian, crews of the 509th prepared to take part in a mass follow-up attack using conventional bombs. Tibbets ordered Sweeney and the *Great Artiste* to stay behind and prepare to drop the second atomic bomb.

In Hiroshima, with the mayor dead, Field Marshal Hata took over administrative control of the city. He himself had been only superficially injured although his wife was severely burnt. Hata moved his headquarters to the underground bunker cut into the side of Mount Futaba.

Many of his senior officers were dead. Prince RiGu and his white stallion were gone; so too Colonel Katayama whose horse had been found compressed to half its breadth in a crack in the ground. Hata's orders were relayed through Colonel Imoto who, although badly injured, was the Field Marshal's highest-ranking surviving officer.

Relief workers were slow to arrive in Hiroshima. The first help came from the soldiers based at Ujina. The harbour was over two miles from the epicentre and little damage was done to the port. Marines collected the explosive-filled suicide boats, prepared for the American invasion, from the coves around Hiroshima Harbour. The small craft were emptied of their charges, lashed together and covered with planks. Raft-like, they moved slowly up the rivers to Hiroshima's centre, collecting wounded and taking them to the military hospital at Ujina. The boats' passage was hampered by the dead bodies in the rivers; the corpses floated in and out with the tide for days.

The fate of all the American prisoners of war is not certain. Two were reported to have been escorted, wounded but able to walk, to Ujina. One was seen, apparently dying, wearing only a pair of red and white underpants, under a bridge. Two were said to have been battered to death in the Castle grounds by their captors.

Warrant Officer Hiroshi Yanagita, the Kempei Tai leader who had helped collect some of the Americans after they were shot down on July 28, was still suffering from a hangover when the bomb exploded. Less than half a mile from the epicentre, he was thrown naked from his bed in his second-floor room. The house was on fire. He went to the window and jumped—only to find the house had collapsed and his room was at street level. Dressed in a sheet, skirting the edge of the city, Yanagita made his way to Ujina. There he collected some clothes and ten soldiers, and went to the levelled site where Hiroshima Castle once stood. He saw no American POW's. But when he reached his divisional Kempei Tai headquarters in the west of the city, one of his men told him he had tried to bring two prisoners to the headquarters, but finding it impossible, he had left them by the Aioi Bridge. There, one person reported seeing them, hands tied behind their backs, being stoned to death.

American records so far available show that at least the pilot Thomas Cartwright and the tail-gunner William Abel survived the war. Both were awarded the Purple Heart. Cartwright's commission terminated in 1953; Abel retired from the American forces in 1968. It is possible that they, and indeed others of the POW's, had been moved from Hiroshima before the bomb fell.

While everyone in Hiroshima continued to suffer, the politicians talked.

In Moscow, on August 8, late in the afternoon, Naotake Sato, the Japanese ambassador who had tried so hard to make his government surrender before it was too late, was bluntly told by the Foreign Minister Molotov that, as from midnight, the Soviet Union would be at war with Japan.

The following morning, in Tokyo, while the six members of Japan's Inner Cabinet met for the first time since Hiroshima, they learned that Russian troops had marched into Manchuria, and that an atomic bomb had been dropped on Nagasaki. They had now a good indication of what that meant; Arisue and his colleagues had already reported from Hiroshima.

But the Inner Cabinet could not bring themselves to surrender. They talked all morning, afternoon and into the evening. Those in

336

favour of continuing the war pointed out that the millions of Japanese soldiers had hardly yet been tested. They were spoiling for a fight and would probably not surrender even if ordered to.

Premier Suzuki, desperate to break the deadlock, suggested that Emperor Hirohito might graciously agree to listen to their arguments and help them come to a conclusion. The Emperor did so, and at 2 a.m., August 10, Japan's Divine Ruler finally spoke. After gently pointing out past differences between the country's military leaders' promises and their forces' performances, the Emperor stated that he was in complete accord with the view stated by his Foreign Minister. He then left the meeting.

The view of Foreign Minister Togo was that Japan should accept the terms of the Potsdam Proclamation, on the understanding that the Allied demands did not 'prejudice the prerogatives of His Majesty as a Sovereign Ruler'.

When Truman and his advisers learned of this qualification, they too found themselves divided over what they should do. Eventually, Secretary of State Byrnes came up with a compromise formula. While making it clear that the Emperor's authority to rule would at first be subject to that of the Allied Supreme Commander in Japan, it reiterated that eventually the Japanese people would be free to choose whatever form of government they wished.

Britain suggested, and Truman agreed, that the American reply should not insist that Emperor Hirohito himself suffer the ignominy of having to sign the surrender document.

When the Japanese hierarchy received America's reply, they still could not agree to capitulate. They talked through August 12, 13, and into August 14. Then Emperor Hirohito acted again. After discussing the situation with various of his most trusted confidants, including Field Marshal Hata who had just flown from Hiroshima, he called a conference and told the military and civil leaders that they should 'bear the unbearable and accept the Allied reply'. He agreed personally to inform his people by radio of the decision the next day.

It was Emperor Hirohito's finest hour.

The Japanese surrender was made known to the American public late in the afternoon of August 14. They were left in little doubt that the atomic bomb had ended the war.

The Russian public were told the Red Army had forced Japan to submit.

In truth, it was probably the fact of the bomb plus the fear of the Russians that caused—or made it possible for—Japan to give up.

On August 15, just before noon, all over Japan people waited to hear their Emperor speak. They had been told in the past, and most

337

still believed, they were winning the war. They had no understanding yet of what had happened to Hiroshima and Nagasaki.

In Hiroshima, a crowd gathered by the demolished railway station where a loudspeaker had been fixed so that they could listen to the sacred words of their Divine Monarch.

Emperor Hirohito used such formal and oblique phrases—the word 'surrender' was never uttered—that it was almost impossible for the average person to grasp what he meant.

But a great number no longer thought they were winning the war. They believed they had *won*. For, as one of those in the crowd at Hiroshima station later recalled, 'We thought there was no other way the war could end.'

EPILOGUE

Early in September 1945, Tibbets, Ferebee and van Kirk flew to Japan to inspect Nagasaki. By then, there were 'no burnt people to see, only human beings going about their business trying to pick up the pieces'. After touring the city, a walk which had little emotional impact on Tibbets, he 'wound up shopping. I bought rice bowls and wooden carved hand trays, so did Ferebee, and we became typical American tourists'.

Tibbets took back his souvenirs to America and found himself a controversial figure. Unlike some members of the crew, he hated the publicity. He was glad to be sent to the Air War College in Alabama, where he could pursue the only life he knew—studying the tactics for waging successful war. He wrote a thesis on 'the employment of atomic bombs', used by the Strategic Air Command, America's answer to Russia's world-wide manoeuvring.

In the immediate post-war years, Tibbets' career followed an uneventful path. In the late 1950s, he served as a senior officer with NATO in France. He returned to the States to run the national military command defence system for the Joint Chiefs of Staff.

By then he had largely perfected his own defence mechanism, allowing him to effectively cloak his feelings. Tibbets was determined he 'didn't want anybody to read me. I didn't have to explain anything I didn't want to explain'.

He re-married, this time successfully.

In May 1965, at the age of fifty, a brigadier-general, Tibbets was appointed deputy director of the United States Military Supply Mission to India. Almost twenty years had passed since he had destroyed Hiroshima, but within a week of his arrival in New Delhi, Tibbets was greeted by virulent headlines in the pro-Communist press who labelled him 'the world's greatest killer'.

He was given a Gurkha bodyguard. But nobody could protect him from the continued newspaper harassment. An embarrassed State Department recalled Tibbets and closed down the Mission. Back in Washington, Tibbets was given a desk job.

He believed his career in the Air Force was over. After thirty years in the service he retired, convinced he was an 'expendable victim' of a changing public attitude towards what he had been ordered to do over Hiroshima.

Withdrawn, even within his family circle, he has stayed close to his first love—aeroplanes. He is president of an executive jet company in the Mid-West and still regularly flies Lear jets, and, when the rare occasion arises, a B-29. He has arranged that, when he dies, his ashes will be scattered in the sky.

Claude Eatherly created his own memorial. To millions of people, particularly in Communist countries, he is the pilot who 'led the Hiroshima raid' and was 'imprisoned in a military mental hospital in Waco, Texas because he repented the crime of Hiroshima'. He is the man who 'turned to ordinary crime seeking punishment for a greater crime'. He is 'the martyr who became the American Dreyfus'.

Bertrand Russell said, 'He has been punished solely because he repented of his comparatively innocent participation in a wanton act of mass murder.' In passionate, purplish prose, Robert Jungk, author of two other books on Hiroshima, stated in a foreword to a polemical collection of Eatherly's letters that, 'The Eatherly Case is only a fresh manifestation of that ever recurring process in human affairs, in which some saintly fool, different from those around him, throws out a challenge to the ruling class of the moment and by so doing exposes the decadence of their code of ethics'.

High-flown sentiments—but hardly applicable to the publicity-seeking Eatherly, who became the subject of books and an astonishing number of newspaper and magazine articles.

Eatherly left the Air Force in 1947 with the reputation of being a gambler and a drunk among those who knew him well. He bounced from one job to another, saw his marriage break up. He staged a robbery with a toy pistol and fled without the cash. Finally he was sent to a veterans' mental hospital—and sowed the seeds for a legend when he started to correspond with the German philosopher Gunther Anders, who produced a book called *Burning Conscience*.

The blurb for that book stated that 'Eatherly was a typical "uncomplicated" young American when he volunteered for service in the Air Force in 1939. In 1943 he was treated for battle fatigue after thirteen months of duty in the Pacific but recovered after a fortnight's treatment and was appointed Commander of the bomber group responsible for the Hiroshima and Nagasaki raids'.

It was shameless exploitation and an incredible distortion of the facts. But it was believed.

Gunther Anders and his publishers had between them—no doubt unwittingly—laid the foundation for extremely successful anti-American Communist propaganda; Eatherly also became almost overnight a hero for the 'Ban the Bomb' groups.

Even a sobering expose of the Eatherly mythology by that fine reporter, William Huie, has failed to stem the flow of Communist-inspired lies. Huie's book, *The Hiroshima Pilot*, is a brave attempt to turn the tide of fiction that Eatherly continues to generate.

Eatherly's wish for fame was amply fulfilled. In 1974, a throat malignancy robbed him of his voice but, in 1976, at the age of fifty-seven, re-married, the father of two young daughters, he seemed to have found his idea of serenity. He lived on social security and a disability pension in a modest cottage near Houston, Texas. He liked to watch television, fish and play pool; a greying man in a straw hat and cowboy boots, fatalistic about facing the cancer to which he succumbed on July 1, 1978

The crew of the *Enola Gay* go their separate ways. Beser still regrets 'that I didn't get to drop the bomb on Berlin because of what the Germans did to the Jews'. He spends a good deal of his time organising the 509th reunions which are held every three years.

Lewis auctioned his 'log' in 1971 for $37,000. It helped him buy marble from which he nowadays enjoys sculpting religious motifs. And thirty years after Hiroshima, in 1976, he still felt it was 'my plane' and 'my crew' that flew the mission.

Van Kirk returned to college and got a degree in Chemical Engineering, with honours. In 1950 he joined DuPont, continuing with that firm for decades.

Nelson was living in California. Caron continued to collect memorabilia of the atomic missions, but for many years failed to make any real money from selling colour prints of the *Enola Gay*.

Duzenbury and Stiborik live quietly and have long put the mission behind them. Shumard died in April 1967.

Parsons became a Rear Admiral. He died on December 5, 1953.

His assistant over Hiroshima, Morris Jeppson, remained the same modest, articulate man he was then, subsequently selling out his business, and becoming a consultant.

Ferebee remained in the Air Force and, after a stint in Vietnam, he retired. He divides his time between selling real estate, cultivating his one-acre flower and vegetable garden and occasionally camping out. Although he found his visit with Tibbets to Nagasaki 'horrible', he also remembers the hundreds of kamikaze planes he saw hidden in camouflaged hangars. He looks back on his experience as the world's first A-bombardier without regret, believing it 'was a job that had to be done'.

After the war, Field Marshal Hata was tried as one of the twenty-five major Japanese war criminals. He was found guilty in 1948 and sentenced to imprisonment for life. He died in 1962.

Commander Hashimoto, too, found himself involved in a trial, the court-martial of his former adversary and captain of the

Indianapolis, Charles McVay. Hashimoto's impending arrival in the United States was announced by the Navy on December 8, 1945, the day after the anniversary of Pearl Harbor. The reception the barrel-chested submarine commander received was cool. He understood a little English and did not like what he heard. During the trial, he often felt his evidence was being incorrectly translated. He thought it likely the *Indianapolis* had been making a zig-zag course but, when asked to draw the course on a blackboard, he drew a straight line, 'because I was confused and uncertain'. McVay was found guilty of negligence and was demoted, although his sentence was later remitted. Hashimoto became a merchant ship's captain, often calling at U.S. and British ports. Retired, he became Head Priest at a Shinto Shrine in Kyoto.

Lieutenant-Colonel Oya was interrogated by the Americans about the way he had treated prisoners of war. He tried to conceal the fact that ten POW's were murdered after the war's end at Fukuoka on Kyushu; he told his interrogaters the prisoners had died in Hiroshima along with the others held there. When the questions became difficult, Oya simply 'pointed at my injured neck and said, "ever since the bomb my memory has gone"'. In 1977 Oya was alive and well, a frequent visitor to the United States.

After the war, the hero of Pearl Harbor, Mitsuo Fuchida, was converted from Buddhism to Christianity. He toured the U.S. as a 'flying missionary' and was not always welcomed by his audiences. He wrote a booklet entitled *No More Pearl Harbors,* and was annoyed by the military medals and citations he continued to receive. Fuchida died May 30, 1976.

The flying instructor Matsuo Yasuzawa, who had flown his bent plane from Hiroshima, was, after the war, barred by the occupying forces from flying again until 1952. By then his eyesight had begun to deteriorate and he was afflicted by a constant cough. He was unable to fulfil his life-long dream of becoming a civilian airline pilot, and in 1977, constantly fearing death from the 'A-bomb disease', he lived frugally on the small disability pension he had just begun to receive.

Chief Warrant Officer Imai, having been in hiding on Tinian for well over a year, finally gave himself up in September 1945, the last man in his cave to do so. He subsequently became president of a large builders' association in Tokyo.

Today, Tinian has Commonwealth status within the U.S.—administered Trust Territories of the Pacific. The jungle has obliterated almost all signs of its wartime role. Some 700 Tinianese live in tin shanties in San Jose, the island's only village. A white-robed and hooded Capuchin priest takes care of their spiritual needs in an imposing pink-coloured Catholic Church. Its tabernacle and baptismal font are US Navy World War II thirty-gallon smoke tanks. Inside, the upper walls of the church are of plasterboard taken from the 509th Tech. Area.

On December 14, 1970, General Curtis LeMay was given a citation from the grateful people of Tinian for the 'outstanding service' he had rendered them, 'working untiringly to improve the welfare and living standards'.

Six years before, LeMay had been decorated by the Japanese Government with the First Class Order of the Grand Cordon of the Rising Sun, for helping them build their post-war air self-defence force. The award was criticised in the Diet, but Minoru Genda, the man who had masterminded the Pearl Harbor raid, defended the decision.

Genda himself received in 1969 the coveted U.S. Legion of Merit, conferred on him by President Kennedy. Genda later became a Senator in the Japanese Parliament.

Among all the medals he has received, LeMay, living quietly in California, is most proud of the Distinguished Flying Cross pinned on him personally by Winston Churchill.

Hiroshima today is a bustling hodge-podge of a city with a population nearing 900,000, almost three times its pre-atomic bomb figure. The citizens seldom talk of August 6, 1945. Those who still show signs of their injuries tend to keep to themselves, often suffering guilt that they lived while so many died. The A-bomb dome has been left standing as it was, in all its gruesomeness, as a terrible reminder. Seeing it, sightseers shudder, avert their eyes, and pass on.

In October 1976, Paul Tibbets again hit the international headlines. He had eagerly accepted the invitation to fly a restored B-29 at an Air Show in Texas featuring vintage aircraft. The highlight of the display was a simulated atom bomb drop from the plane Tibbets was flying. U.S. Army engineers provided the explosives to make the mushroom-shaped cloud.

Many people were appalled. The Japanese Government protested and the United States Government apologised.

Tibbets thinks the fuss was 'ridiculous'. He, along with the organisers of the display, maintains that 'the demonstration was simply a re-enactment of history, similar to many such events held regularly all over the world'.

In 1990, the *Enola Gay*, half way through its restoration was on public view at the Smithsonian's Silver Hill, Maryland, facility, pending completion of the task and removal four years hence to a planned extension of the Air and Space Museum.

CHAPTER NOTES

As befits the subject of this book, we have striven throughout to be objective, factual and impartial, allowing only our conscience and the facts as we have discovered them to be our guide. The responsibility, therefore, for the story as we have told it is ours alone.

The source material we have used consists principally of extensive interviews which we conducted personally in Japan and the United States in 1975 and 1976 with participants in the events described and of documentary evidence from both countries, much of which was originally classified as Top Secret and has only recently been released. Apart from the intrinsic importance of each of these two prime sources, we have used them as a means of providing checks and balances one against the other, so enabling us to present the story as authentically and as true to the historical record as possible.

When dealing with the Japanese language, we were very much aware that it seldom allowed a literal translation into English; with the help of our interpreters, to whom we owe special thanks, we tried to take every care to preserve in the translation the meaning and tone of the original.

In the detailed source notes which follow, documents and reports to the best of our knowledge unpublished at the time of writing are so indicated; *Private Papers*, a third valuable source of research material, comprise personal diaries, aide-mémoires, letters, manuscripts; *Transcripts* refers to interviews conducted by others or to documentary broadcasts; finally, a number of published books, magazine and newspaper articles proved useful and are acknowledged.

The form of identification used is:

AI = Authors' Interviews
B = Books
C = Correspondence
D = Documents and Reports
M = Magazines, Periodicals and Booklets
N = Newspapers
PP = Private Papers
T = Transcripts

A combined list of all written material consulted may be found in the Bibliography; interviewees in the Special Thanks section.

September 1, 1944
AI: Tibbets, LeMay.
B: *The Birth of the Bomb* (Clark); *Victor's Justice* (Minear); *No High Ground* (Knebel/Bailey); *The Great Decision* (Amrine); *Now It Can*

Be Told (Groves); *The New World* (Hewlett/Anderson); *Britain and Atomic Energy* (Gowing); *Manhattan Project* (Groueff).
C: Montgomery.
D: Letter, Einstein to Roosevelt, August 2, 1939; record of meeting September 23, 1942, in office of Secretary of War (unpublished); letter, Groves to Dill, January 17, 1944 (unpublished); letter, Stimson to Truman, August 13, 1944 (unpublished); memo, Derry to Groves, August 29, 1944 (unpublished).
M: *Air Force Magazine*, August, 1973: Training the 509th for Hiroshima (Tibbets).
N: *Chicago Tribune* interviews with Tibbets, March 10–22, 1968 (Thomis); *The Register*, Newport Beach, Calif., August 3, 1975.
PP: Tibbets (notes made subsequent to events described here).
T: Ashworth; *The Building of the Bomb* (BBC-TV).

September 6, 1944
AI: Tibbets, Beser, Jeppson, Brode.
D: Letter, undated, written in April 1943, from Condon to Oppenheimer; White House Appointments Register, August 26, 1944; memo, Somervell to Chief of Engineers, USA, September 17, 1944; Harrison-Bundy Files.
M: *Bulletin of the Atomic Scientists*, June, 1970; April, 1975; May, 1975.
T: Groves.

September 8, 1944
AI: Tibbets.

September 9, 1944
AI: Yokoyama, Kaizuka, Kosakai, Genda, Fuchida.
B: *Hiroshima in Memoriam* (Takayama); *A History of Modern Japan* (Storry); *Hiroshima* (Hersey); *The Fall of Japan* (Craig); *Death in Life* (Lipton); *Japan Subdued* (Feis); *Hirohito* (Mosley); *The Glory and The Dream* (Manchester); *The Hiroshima Memoirs* (Hiroshima City).
D: U.S. Strategic Bombing Surveys (USSBS); *Mission Accomplished.*
PP: Notes made by Yokoyama in 1944/5.

September 12, 1944
AI: Tibbetts, Ferebee, Beser, King, Slusky, Grennan, Gackenbach, Perry, Caron, Strudwick, Biel, Jernigan.
B: *The Hiroshima Pilot* (Huie).
D: Roster of Officers, 393rd Squadron (unpublished); 509th Pictorial Album; Short Narrative History, 509th Group (unpublished); Historical report, medical activity 509th (unpublished); History 509th/20th Air Force (unpublished).
PP: Beser, Tibbets, Perry, Gackenbach.
T: Interview with Tibbets, USAF 5-4410-90 (unpublished); interview with Tibbets, Air Historical Branch, USAF, September, 1966 (unpublished).

September 17, 1944:
AI: Hashimoto.
B: *Sunk* (Hashimoto); *Abandon Ship* (Newcomb).

September 19, 1944:
AI: Tibbets, Beser, Brode, Jeppson.
B: *Dawn Over Zero* (Laurence); *Brighter Than 1000 Suns* (Jungk); *Now It Can Be Told* (Groves); *Atomic Quest* (Compton); *A Peril and a Hope* (Smith); *The Great Decision* (Amrine).
D: United States Atomic Energy Commission, In the Matter of J. Robert Oppenheimer; United States Atomic Energy Commission, *Historical Document No. 279*; Harrison-Bundy Files.
M: *Bulletin of the Atomic Scientists*, October, 1958; *Look*, August 13, 1963; *American Historical Review*, October, 1973; *Journal of American History*, March, 1974.
T: Ashworth, Birch, Burroughs, Groves, Hayward.

October 1, 1944:
Osaka:
AI: Asada, Suzuki, Nizuma.
B: *Imperial Tragedy* (Coffey).
D: Asada manuscript on Japanese Navy and atomic energy, May 12, 1965 (unpublished); Asada research document 19176-2-18 (unpublished).
PP: Asada (notes made subsequent to events described).

Tokyo:
AI: Arisue, Oya.
D: Office of Strategic Services: reports and intelligence data (unpublished); U.S. Army, Supreme Commander of the Allied Powers, Counter Intelligence Section: reports and intelligence data.
PP: Oya (notes made subsequent to events described).

Hiroshima:
AI: Yokoyama.

October 21, 1944:
AI: Tibbets, Lewis, Beser, van Kirk, Duzenbury, Caron, Perry, King, Slusky, Jernigan, Biel, Grennan.
B: *No High Ground* (Knebel/Bailey); *The Hiroshima Pilot* (Huie); *Seven Hours to Zero* (Marx).
D: B-29 Familiarisation File, marked 'Enola Gay', serial No: 15 (unpublished); Short narrative History, 509th Group (unpublished).
PP: Notes kept by Tibbets, Beser, Perry, van Kirk; letters written by Lewis.

October 25, 1944:
AI: Arisue, Sakai.
B: *The Fall of Japan* (Craig); *Imperial Tragedy* (Coffey); *The Nobility of Failure* (Morris); *Samurai* (Sakai).
D: Intelligence summary No. 17 (vol. 2) HQ, 7th Air Force, Central Pacific area; analysis of Japanese radio broadcasts; 20th Air Force Intelligence report ACESEA-WIS, No. 87 (unpublished); Japanese Research Division (ATIS) monographs nos. 45, 53, 83.
N: *Sunday Times*, London, November 23, 1975.

November 24, 1944:
AI: Tibbets, Lewis, King, van Kirk, Ferebee, Olivi, Sweeney, Beser, Grennan, Jernigan, Perry.
B: *Seven Hours to Zero* (Marx); *The Hiroshima Pilot* (Huie).
D: Short Narrative History, 509th Group (unpublished).
PP: Tibbets, Beser, Lewis, van Kirk.

December 6, 1944:
AI: Yokoyama, Maruyama, Kosakai.
B: *Imperial Tragedy* (Coffey); *The Fall of Japan* (Craig); *No High Ground* (Knebel/Bailey); *The Hiroshima Memoirs.*
D: USSBS.

December 7, 1944:
B: *The Glory and the Dream* (Manchester); *Now It Can Be Told* (Groves).
D: Sach's memo to Roosevelt, December 8, 1944.
N: *New York Times, Washington Post, Los Angeles Times, San Francisco Chronicle, Denver Post, Chicago Tribune,* all of this date.

December 12, 1944:
AI: Arisue, Oya.
B: *The Fall of Japan* (Craig); *Hiroshima Decision* (Baldwin) *In Hiroshima Plus 20* (*New York Times*).
D: Office of Strategic Services: reports and intelligence data (unpublished).

December 14, 1944:
AI: Asada.
D: Asada manuscript on Japanese Navy and atomic energy, May 12, 1965 (unpublished); *Asada research document 19176-2-18* (unpublished).
PP: Asada.

December 17, 1944:
AI: Tibbets, Sweeney, Beser, Lewis, Ferebee, van Kirk, Grennan, Caron, Duzenbury, Stiborik.
D: General Order No. 6 USAAF (unpublished).
PP: Beser, Lewis, Tibbets.

December 25, 1944:
AI: Perry, Tibbets, Beser, Downey, van Kirk, Ferebee.
PP: Beser (letters); van Kirk (notes).

December 29, 1944:
AI: Hashimoto.
B: *Sunk* (Hashimoto).

December 30, 1944:
AI: Tibbets.
D: Memo, written by Groves of meeting at White House between Stimson and Roosevelt (unpublished); memo, Groves to Marshall (unpublished); memo, Groves to file (unpublished), all of this date.
T: Groves.

January 6, 1945:
AI: Tibbets, Lewis, Slusky, Grennan, Caron, Ferebee, van Kirk, Perry, Beser, Sweeney, LeMay.
PP: Perry (menus); Lewis (letters).

January 16, 1945:
AI: Hashimoto.
B: *Sunk* (Hashimoto); *Abandon Ship* (Newcomb).

January 17, 1945:
AI: Tibbets.
B: *The Glory and The Dream* (Manchester); *Now It Can Be Told* (Groves).
D: Troop movement order 6105 (unpublished); memo, Groves to file, January 6 (unpublished); memo, Derry to Goves, January 6 (unpublished).

January 20, 1945:
AI: LeMay, Tibbets, Lewis, Sweeney.
B: *The Fall of Japan* (Craig); *Mission With LeMay* (LeMay).
D: USSBS.

January 27, 1945:
D: Letter, King to Nimitz; memo, Derry to Groves February 10, 1945 (unpublished).
T: Groves, Ashworth.

January 28, 1945:
AI: Tibbets, King, Lewis, Duzenbury.

February 1, 1945:
AI: Yokoyama.
B: *The Hiroshima Memoirs.*
PP: Yokoyama.

February 2, 1945:
AI: Beser, Perry, Duzenbury.
D: Short Narrative History of 509th Group (unpublished); historical report, medical activity 509th Group (unpublished); 509th Pictorial album; History 509th/20th Air Force (unpublished).
PP: Beser, Perry.

March 2, 1945:
B: *The Glory and The Dream* (Manchester); *Brighter than 1000 Suns* (Jungk); *On Active Service in Peace and War* (Stimson/Bundy).
D: Memo from Patterson to Styer, February 15, 1945 (unpublished).
M: *Harper's Magazine*, February, 1947.
PP: Stimson.

March 3, 1945:
AI: Shima.
B: *The Hiroshima Memoirs*
D: USSBS; Mission Accomplished.

March 4, 1945:
Los Alamos:
AI: Beser, Tibbets.
B: *Brighter than 1000 Suns* (Jungk).
M: *Bulletin of the Atomic Scientists,* June 1970, April 1975, May 1975.
T: Groves, Ashworth.

Washington, D.C.:
B: *Now It Can Be Told* (Groves); *The Great Decision* (Amrine); *Brighter than 1000 Suns* (Jungk); *Speaking Frankly* (Byrnes).
D: Memo, Byrnes to Roosevelt, March 3, 1945 (unpublished); memo, Groves to file, March 3, 1945 (unpublished).
T: Groves.

March 7, 1945:
AI: Tibbets, Jeppson, Beser, van Kirk, Jernigan, Caron, Perry, Grennan, Lewis, Gackenbach.
D: Short Narrative History of 509th Group (unpublished); 509th Pictorial Album; History 509th/20th Air Force (unpublished).
PP: Beser, Lewis.

March 8, 1945:
B: *Now It Can Be Told* (Groves); *On Active Service in Peace and War* (Stimson/Bundy).
D: Memo, Groves to Stimson, March 8, 1945 (unpublished).
T: Groves.

March 9, 1945:
AI: LeMay.
B: *The Army Air Forces in World War Two,* Vol. V, *The Pacific: Matterhorn to Nagasaki,* June 1944 to August, 1945 (Craven/Cate); *The Fall of Japan* (Craig).

March 10, 1945:
AI: Lewis, Ferebee, Jeppson, Slusky, Duzenbury.

March 11, 1945:
AI: Arisue.
B: *The Fall of Japan* (Craig); *Imperial Tragedy* (Coffey).
D: Office of Strategic Services: reports and Intelligence data; U.S. Department of Defense: military plans (1941–1945) for the entry of the Soviet Union into the war against Japan; USSBS.

March 12, 1945:
AI: Maruyama.
B: *The Hiroshima Memoirs.*

March 22, 1945:
AI: Tibbets, Jeppson, Slusky, Brode, Ferebee.
C: Alvarez.

April 1, 1945:
AI: Yokoyama, Maruyama, Kosakai.

B: *The Hiroshima Memoirs.*
D: USSBS.

April 12, 1945:
Early afternoon:
B: *The Glory and the Dream* (Manchester); *Japan's Decision to Surrender* (Butow); *I was Roosevelt's Shadow* (Reilly); *F.D.R. My Boss* (Tully); *Thank You, Mr. President* (Smith); *When F.D.R. Died* (Asbell); *F.D.R.'s Last Year* (Bishop).
N: *New York Times,* April 13, 1945.

Late afternoon:
B: *Year of Decisions* (Truman); *Plain Speaking* (Miller).
N: *New York Times,* April 13, 1945.
PP: Truman.

Early evening:
AI: Tibbets, Lewis, Beser, King, Gackenbach, Grennan, Perry, Caron.

Late evening:
B: *Now It Can Be Told* (Groves).
D: Report, prepared by Groves, titled 'Atomic Bombs', serial no. NND 750152 (unpublished).

April 13, 1945:
B: *The Glory and The Dream* (Manchester); *The Great Decision* (Amrine); *Speaking Frankly* (Byrnes); *Year of Decisions* (Truman).
PP: Truman.

April 15, 1945:
AI: Arisue, Oya.
B: *The Fall of Japan* (Craig); *Hirohito* (Mosley); *Japan Subdued* (Feis).
D: USSBS.

April 19, 1945:
AI: Tibbets, Sweeney, Lewis, Spitzer, Olivi.
PP: Spitzer's diary.

April 21, 1945:
AI: Yokoyama.

April 23, 1945:
AI: Tibbets, Lewis, King, Strudwick, Biel.
B: *We Dropped The A-Bomb* (Miller/Spitzer).
D: Letters, quoted by Huie from Bowen and Thornhill, in *The Hiroshima Pilot.*
PP: Spitzer's diary.

April 24, 1945:
AI: Asada.
D: USSBS.
N: *New York Times,* August 8, 1976.
PP: Asada.

April 25, 1945:
B: *Now It Can Be Told* (Groves); *Brighter than 1000 Suns* (Jungk); *The Great Decision* (Amrine); *On Active Service in Peace and War* (Stimson/Bundy).
D: Memo, Groves to Stimson, April 23, 1945 (unpublished); memo, Groves to file, April 25, 1945 (unpublished); memo, Stimson to Truman, April 25, 1945 (unpublished); letter, Stimson to Truman, April 24, 1945.

April 26, 1945:
AI: Arisue.
B: *The Fall of Japan* (Craig).

April 28, 1945:
AI: Yokoyama, Maruyama, Yasuzawa.
D: USSBS.

April 29, 1945:
AI: Lewis, Nelson, Beser, Duzenbury, Caron, Stiborik, Grennan.
B: *The Hiroshima Pilot* (Huie).

April 30, 1945:
Kure:
AI: Hashimoto.
B: *Sunk* (Hashimoto).

Hiroshima:
AI: Shima, Kosakai.
B: *The Hiroshima Memoirs.*
D: USSBS.

May 8, 1945:
B: *The Fall of Japan* (Craig); *Hirohito* (Mosley); *Japan Subdued* (Feis); *Japan's Decision to Surrender* (Butow); *Year of Decisions* (Truman).
D: USSBS.

May 9, 1945:
AI: Tibbets.

May 27, 1945:
AI: Arisue.
B: *The Fall of Japan* (Craig).
D: Japanese Defense Agency, Historical Division, Tokyo: selection of documents relating to military and naval activities, March–September, 1945 (unpublished); Office of Strategic Services; reports and Intelligence data.

May 28, 1945:
AI: Tibbets, Beser.
D: Report of Target Committee, May 12, 1945 (unpublished).
PP: Beser.

May 30, 1945:
AI: Maruyama, Oya, Yanagita.

B: *The Knights of Bushido* (Russell); *History of the U.N. War Crimes Commission* (HMSO, 1948); *Imperial Tragedy* (Coffey).
D: Notes for the Interrogation of Prisoners of War, IJA, issued on August 6, 1943; reports from the International Military Tribunal for the Far East, May 1946 thru to November 1948; reports from the United Nations Commission for the Investigation of War Crimes 1946; USSBS.

June 1, 1945:
B: *On Active Service in Peace and War* (Stimson/Bundy); *The Great Decision* (Amrine); *The Fall of Japan* (Craig); *Atomic Quest* (Compton); *A History of the U.S. Atomic Energy Commission* (Hewlett/Anderson); *Speaking Frankly* (Byrnes).
D: Memo, Samford to Chief of Staff, 20th Air Force, May 5, 1945 (unpublished); Interim Committee Notes and Minutes, May 1, May 4, May 9, May 15, May 18, May 31, June 1, 1945 (all unpublished); The Decision to Use the Atomic Bomb, extracted from *Command Decisions*, published by the Office of the Chief of Military History, Department of the Army, 1971.
M: *Harper's Magazine*, vol. 194 (No. 1161), February 1947; *U.S. News & World Report*, vol. 1 (49), August 15, 1960; *Bulletin of the Atomic Scientists*, vol. 26, June 1970 and vol. 31, February 1975.
T: Groves.

June 12, 1945:
B: *Now It Can Be Told* (Groves); *On Active Service in Peace and War* (Stimson/Bundy).
D: Memo Groves to Marshall (unpublished).
T: Groves.

June 14, 1945:
AI: Lewis, Duzenbury, Stiborik, Nelson, Caron.
PP: Lewis (documents and letters); Caron (notes).

June 15, 1945:
AI: Arisue.
B: *The Fall of Japan* (Craig).

June 18, 1945:
B: *No High Ground* (Knebel/Bailey); *The Great Decision* (Amrine); *The Fall of Japan* (Craig); *On Active Service in Peace and War* (Stimson/Bundy); *The Glory and the Dream* (Manchester); *The Challenge to American Foreign Policy* (McCloy).
D: Memo, Chief of Staff, of Olympic invasion plan for Japan, (June 1945) and staff study, Coronet invasion plan of same month (both unpublished); Recommended Bombing Program Study, May, 1945 (unpublished); the Decision to use the Atomic Bomb, extracted from *Command Decisions*.
T: Eric Sevareid in conversation with John J. McCloy (CBS News Special, July 20, 1975).

June 19, 1945:
AI: Yokoyama, Imoto, Oya, Endo, Kosakai, Genda, Miura.
B: *The Hiroshima Memoirs.*
D: Reports from the Interntional Military Tribunal for the Far East, May 1946 thru to November 1948 in relation to Hata; USSBS.

June 23, 1945:
AI: Tibbets, LeMay.
B: *Now It Can Be Told* (Groves).
D: Preliminary report on operational procedures by D. M. Dennison, May 5, 1945 (unpublished); notes on initial meeting of Target Committee, April 27, 1945 (unpublished); 20th Air Force target reports and summaries (unpublished); USAAF target photographs (unpublished).

June 27, 1945:
AI: Lewis, Caron, Nelson, Duzenbury, Stiborik.
PP: Lewis (letters); Caron (notes).

June 28, 1945:
AI: Imai, Saito, Beser, Perry, Tibbets, Gackenbach, Caron, King, LeMay.
B: *US Marines and Amphibious Warfare* (Isley); *History of the United States Naval Operations in World War Two* (Morison); *The Two-Ocean War* (Morison).
D: Memos, June 10 and July 21, Kirkpatrick to Groves (both unpublished); CINPAC analysis of air operations, July, 1944 (unpublished); VII AAF Intelligence Summary, No. 43 (unpublished); USSBS interrogations of Fuchida; Report on N.A.B. Tinian (unpublished).
M: *Saturday Evening Post,* December 23, 1944.

July 1, 1945:
AI: Arisue, Oya.
B: *Japan's Decision to Surrender* (Butow); *The Fall of Japan* (Craig); *No High Ground* (Knebel/Bailey); *Imperial Tragedy* (Coffey); *Hirohito* (Mosley).

July 2, 1945:
AI: Lewis, Stiborik, Caron, Nelson, Duzenbury.
D: Map of Tinian, sixth Naval Construction Brigade (unpublished); Short Narrative History of the 509th Group (unpublished); 509th Pictorial Album.
PP: Lewis (letters); Caron and Nelson (notes).

July 6, 1945:
AI: Elsey.
B: *Between War and Peace* (Feis); *Year of Decisions* (Truman); *The Glory and The Dream* (Manchester).
D: Memo, Stimson to Truman, July 2, 1945; log of the President's trip to Berlin Conference, July 6 thru to August 7, 1945 (unpublished).

July 9, 1945:
AI: Oya, Arisue.

July 12, 1945:
AI: Perry, Beser, Lewis, Jeppson, van Kirk, Duzenbury, Nelson.
D: Ballad, *Nobody Knows,* Short Narrative History of the 509th Group (unpublished); 509th Pictorial Album.

July 13, 1945:
B: *A Peril and a Hope* (Smith) for complete text of the 'Franck Report'; *Now It Can Be Told* (Groves); *Command Decisions* (Morton); *Speaking Frankly* (Byrnes).
D: Harrison-Bundy Files; Memo, Groves to Secretary of War on Szilard, 29 Oct, 1945 (unpublished): MED TS Files (unpublished).
M: *Bulletin of the Atomic Scientists,* vol. 26, June 1970; vol. 31, No. 2 February, 1975; *U.S. News and World Report,* vol. 49, August 15, 1960.
T: Groves.

July 14, 1945:
B: *No High Ground* (Knebel/Bailey); *The Great Decision* (Amrine); *Now It Can Be Told* (Groves); *Abandon Ship* (Newcomb).
D: Memos, Parsons to Tibbets, June 30, 1945 (unpublished); Oppenheimer and Parsons to Groves, June 29, 1945 (unpublished).

July 15, 1945:
Wiesbaden:
AI: Arisue.
B: *No High Ground* (Knebel/Bailey); *Fall of Japan* (Craig).

Wendover:
AI: Tibbets, Ferebee.
D: Memo, Parsons to Tibbets, July 15, 1945 (unpublished); memo, Parsons and Oppenheimer to Groves, June 29, 1945 (unpublished); memo, Parsons to Tibbets, June 30, 1945 (unpublished).
T: Ashworth.

July 16, 1945:
Alamogordo:
AI: Tibbets.
B: *Dawn Over Zero* (Laurence); *The Glory and The Dream* (Manchester); *All in Our Time* (Wilson); *Now It Can Be Told* (Groves).
D: Report on Test II at Trinity, 16, July 1945, Warren to Groves (unpublished); memo, Groves to Chief of Staff, July 30, 1945 (unpublished).
M: *Bulletins of the Atomic Scientists:* vol. 31, April 1975, *Prelude to Trinity,* vol. 31, May, 1975, *A Foul and Awesome Display* (both by Bainbridge); vol. 26, June 1970, *Some Recollections of July 16, 1945* (Groves).
N: The *New York Times,* articles in issues between September 9 and October 9, 1945 by William Lawrence.
T: *The Day The Sun Blew Up* (BBC-TV); *The Building of The Bomb* (BBC-TV): Groves.

San Francisco:
AI: Hashimoto.

B: *Abandon Ship* (Newcomb); *History of the United States Naval Operations in World War Two* (Morison); *Sunk* (Hashimoto); *No High Ground* (Knebel/Bailey).
T: Ashworth.

July 17, 1945:
AI: Elsey.
B: *Between War and Peace* (Feis); *Japan Subdued* (Feis); *Year of Decisions* (Truman); *Triumph and Tragedy* (Churchill); *On Active Service in Peace and War* (Stimson); *Japan's Decision to Surrender* (Butow).
D: Telegrams, Harrison to Stimson and Stimson to Harrison, July 16, and 17, 1945; Log of The President's Trip (unpublished).
N: *New York Times*, 18 July, 1945; *Daily Mirror*, London, August 2, 1945.
PP: Diaries, Stimson, Truman.

July 18, 1945:
AI: Tibbets, Ferebee, Lewis, Caron, Beser, Duzenbury, Nelson, van Kirk, Perry, LeMay, Spitzer, Grennan, Gackenbach, Jernigan, Sweeney, Arisue.
B: *Japan Subdued* (Feis); *We Dropped The A-Bomb* (Miller/Spitzer). *Hirohito* (Mosley); *Japan's Decision to Surrender* (Butow).
D: Memos, Kirkpatrick to Groves, June 10 and July 21, 1945 (unpublished).
PP: Spitzer's diary.

July 19, 1945:
AI: Tibbets, LeMay, Ferebee, van Kirk, Hashimoto.
B: *Sunk* (Hashimoto); *Abandon Ship* (Newcomb).

July 20, 1945:
AI: Arisue, Imai, Lewis, Tibbets, Caron, Beser, Grennan, Duzenbury.
B: *Japan Subdued* (Feis); *The Hiroshima Pilot* (Huie); *The Fall of Japan* (Craig); *Between War and Peace* (Feis); *Japan's Decision to Surrender* (Butow); *No High Ground* (Knebel/Bailey); *Seven Hours to Zero* (Marx).
D: History of the 509th (unpublished); 509th Pictorial Album; report of Combined Intelligence Committee, July, 1945.
PP: Stimson.

July 21, 1945:
AI: Imoto, Endo, Oya, Maruyama, Yanagita, Kaizuka, Yokoyama, Tibbets, Lewis.
D: USSBS Interrogations of Hata (unpublished); reports from the International Military Tribunal for the Far East, May 1946 thru to November, 1948, in relation to Hata.

July 22, 1945:
AI: Arisue, Oya.
B: *On Active Service in Peace and War* (Stimson); *Japan Subdued* (Feis); *Between War and Peace* (Feis); *Japan's Decision to Surrender* (Butow); *Year of Decisions* (Truman); *Triumph and Tragedy* (Churchill).

D: Memo, Groves to Stimson, July 18, 1945; Log of the President's Trip
      (unpublished).

July 23, 1945:
AI: Beser, Imai, Tibbets, Ferebee, Van Kirk, Duzenbury.

July 27, 1945:
AI: Arisue, Oya.
B: *Hirohito* (Mosley); *The New World* (Hewlett); *Ten Years In Japan*
      (Grew); *Imperial Tragedy* (Coffey); *The Fall of Japan* (Craig); *Japan
      Subdued* (Feis); *Japan's Decision to Surrender* (Butow); *On Active
      Service in Peace and War* (Stimson).
N: *Nippon Times*, July 29, 30, August 1, 1945; *Asahi Shimbun*, July 28,
      1945.

July 28, 1945:
Tinian:
AI: Tibbets, Beser, Lewis, Jernigan, Grennan, King, van Kirk, Downey,
      Duzenbury, Caron, Nelson, Jeppson, Stiborik, Biel, Cheshire.
B: *No High Ground* (Knebel/Bailey).
D: History of 509th Group (unpublished); 509th Pictorial Album.

Hiroshima:
AI: Yanagita, Shima, Maruyama, Matsuoka, Kosakai, Hiroto, Yoko-
      yama, Imoto, Endo.
B: *The Hiroshima Memoirs; Hirohito* (Mosley); *The Fall of Japan*
      (Craig).
D: Crews' Records (unpublished); two Missing Air Crew reports, 866
      Bombardment Squadron (H), 494th Bombardment Group (H), July
      30, 1945 (unpublished); Reports, CINCAFPAC, September 23,
      October 9, 18, 1945 (unpublished); mission orders, VII Bomber
      Command, 494th Bomb Group, Field Order 45–92, July 27, 1945
      (unpublished); mission report, 494th Bomb Group (unpublished).
PP: Yokoyama (notes), Hiroto, Matsuoka.

July 29, 30, 1945:
Tinian, Guam:
AI: Tibbets, Lewis, LeMay, Sweeney.
B: *Now It Can Be Told* (Groves); *No High Ground* (Knebel/Bailey); *The
      Hiroshima Pilot* (Huie).
D: Memo, Oppenheimer to Parsons, July 23, 1945 (unpublished); memo,
      Groves to Marshall, July 18, 1945 (unpublished); History of the
      509th Group (unpublished).
S.W. of Tinian:
AI: Hashimoto, Beser.
B: *Sunk* (Hashimoto); *Abandon Ship* (Newcomb); *Now It Can Be Told*
      (Groves).
D: Memo, Groves to Chief of Staff, July 30, 1945 (unpublished).

Hiroshima:
AI: Matsuoka, Oya, Kosakai, Yanagita.
B: *The Hiroshima Memoirs.*

July 31, 1945:
Washington:
B: *Now It Can Be Told* (Groves).
D: Cable no. 1005, Spaatz to War Department, July 31, 1945 (unpublished); cable no. 10027, Spaatz to War Department, 31 July 1945 (unpublished); cable Handy to Spaatz, no. 3542, July 31, 1945 (unpublished); memo Groves to Chief of Staff July 30, 1945 (unpublished).

Tinian:
AI: Beser, Cheshire, Ferebee, van Kirk, Tibbets.
B: *No High Ground* (Knebel/Bailey); *Now It Can Be Told* (Groves).
C: Lord.
D: Daily Intelligence summaries, 20th Air Force, Guam, July 1945 (unpublished).
PP: Beser.

August 1, 1945:
Tinian:
AI: Tibbets, Ferebee, Perry, LeMay.
D: Field Order No. 13, 20th Air Force (unpublished).

Manila:
B: *Now It Can Be Told* (Groves); *No High Ground* (Knebel/Bailey).

Tinian:
AI: Tibbets.

Guam:
AI: LeMay.
D: Cables, Groves to Farrell and Farrell to Groves, July 30, 1945 (unpublished).

Tinian:
AI: Tibbets, Sweeney, Perry, Lewis.

Washington, D.C.:
B: *Now It Can Be Told* (Groves).
D: Cable, Farrell to Groves, July 30, 1945 (unpublished).

August 2, 1945:
AI: LeMay, Ferebee, Tibbets.

August 3, 1945:
AI: Matsuoka, Maruyama, Kosakai, Kaizuka, Shima, LeMay, Ferebee, Tibbets, van Kirk.
B: *The Hiroshima Memoirs; No High Ground* (Knebel/Bailey).
D: Field Order No. 13, 20th Air Force (unpublished); USSBS.

August 4, 1945:
AI: Tibbets, Lewis, Beser, Jeppson, Jernigan, Caron, Duzenbury, Nelson, Stiborik, Slusky, Gackenbach, Grennan, Ferebee, van Kirk, King, Spitzer, Sweeney, Cheshire, LeMay, Brode, Strudwick.
B: *We Dropped The A-Bomb* (Miller/Spitzer).

C: Alvarez.
PP: Spitzer's diary.

August 5, 1945:
Tinian:
AI: Tibbets, LeMay, Lewis, Beser, Jeppson, Caron, Duzenbury, Brode, Sweeney, van Kirk, Perry, Downey, Nelson, Stiborik, Ferebee, King, Jernigan.
B: *Now It Can Be Told* (Groves).
C: Alvarez.
D: Operations Order No. 35, 509th Group (unpublished); telecom message, LeMay to 509th, August 5, 1945 (unpublished); telegram, Doll to Oppenheimer, August 5, 1945 (unpublished).
T: Ashworth.

Hiroshima:
AI: Maruyama, Oya, Imoto, Shima, Matsuoka, Kosakai.
B: *The Hiroshima Memoirs.*
PP: Oya, Maruyama.

Midnight to 8.16 a.m.
August 6, 1945:
Tinian:
AI: Tibbets, Lewis, Jeppson, Duzenbury, Nelson, Stiborik, Caron, Beser, Ferebee, van Kirk, Imai, Downey, Spitzer, Sweeney, Grennan, King, Jernigan.
B: *Now It Can Be Told* (Groves).
M: *Time Out* (Downey's prayer); *Yank*, September 7, 1945.
T: Ashworth.

Hiroshima:
AI: Yasuzawa, Oya, Kosakai, Yokoyama.
B: *The Hiroshima Memoirs.*
D: Daily Intelligence Summaries, August, 1945 (unpublished).

Aboard the Enola Gay:
AI: Tibbets, Lewis, Jeppson, Duzenbury, Nelson, Stiborik, Caron, Beser, Ferebee, van Kirk; plus Sweeney, Spitzer, Gackenbach, Grennan, King, Brode.
B: *We Dropped The A-Bomb* (Miller/Spitzer); *Seven Hours to Zero* (Marx).
C: Alvarez.
D: Mission reports, August 1945, (unpublished); Parsons' check list (unpublished); navigator's log prepared by van Kirk; Twentieth Air Force Intelligence summary for August 6, 1945 (unpublished); B-29 crew instruction manual.
PP: Spitzer's diary, Lewis' 'log'.
T: Ashworth, Groves.

Hiroshima:
AI: Maruyama, Oya, Shima, Yasuzawa, Fuchida, Imoto, Endo, Kosakai, Kaizuka, Yanagita.

358

B: *The Hiroshima Memoirs.*
D: USSBS interrogations of Oya, Hata, Fuchida.
M: Philosophical Transactions of the Royal Society, London, vol. 266, no. 1177, June 1970.
PP: Imoto, Oya, Endo (notes made subsequent to events described).

8.16 a.m. to midnight, August 6, 1945:
AI: Tibbets, Ferebee, Lewis, van Kirk, Beser, Stiborik, Caron, Jeppson, Nelson, Duzenbury, Sweeney, Spitzer, Grennan, Perry, Maruyama, Oya, Imoto, Endo, Yanagita, Hiroto, Matsuoka, Shima, Kosakai, Yokoyama, Yasuzawa, Fuchida, Kaizuka, King, Downey, Matsushige, Hatsuko, Cheshire.
B: *The Hiroshima Memoirs; Imperial Tragedy* (Coffey); *Hiroshima in Memoriam and Today* (Takayama); *No High Ground* (Knebel/Bailey).
D: Report, Manhattan Engineering District, 'The Atomic Bombing of Hiroshima and Nagasaki'; Final Report, Mission No. 13, HQ, 509th Composite Group, dated August 6, 1945, prepared by Stevenson (unpublished); report to COMGENUSTAF, Guam, on Mission No. 13 (unpublished); USSBS.
M: Booklets: *A Bomb, A City Tells its Story* (compiled by Kosakai); *Hiroshima* (foreword by Araki).
PP: Oya, Endo, Imoto, Perry, Matsuoka, Hiroto, Maruyama.
T: *Hot to Handle* (BBC-TV): Groves, Ashworth.

August 7—August 15:
AI: Miura, Endo, Imoto, Oya, Tibbets, Sweeney, Yanagita, Hatsuko, Arisue, Asada, Nizuma, Suzuki, Matsushige.
D: USSBS; Reports: CINCAFPAC to COMGEN Sixth Army, 23 September, 1945 (unpublished); CG 6th Army to CINCAFPAC, 9 October, 1945 (unpublished); crews' records (unpublished).
B: *Japan Subdued* (Feis); *Hirohito* (Mosley); *Year of Decisions* (Truman); *Japan's Decision to Surrender* (Butow); *Hiroshima, 1945* (Ichiro Osako); *The Hiroshima Memoirs.*
M: *Time*, August 9, 1971.
PP: Asada, Hiroto, Oya, Imoto, Endo, Matsuoka.

Epilogue:
AI: Tibbets, Beser, Ferebee, van Kirk, Beser, Jeppson, Stiborik, Nelson, Grennan, Caron, Duzenbury, Lewis, King, Hashimoto, Oya, Fuchida, Yasuzawa, Imai, LeMay, Genda.
B: *The Hiroshima Pilot* (Huie); *Burning Conscience* (Anders); *Abandon Ship* (Newcomb).
D: Reports from the International Military Tribunal for the Far East, May 1946 thru November, 1948, in relation to Hata; news release, Confederate Air Force, October, 1976.
N: *Los Angeles Times*, June 15, 1969; *The Japan Times*, February 26, 1976; *The Washington Post*, October 14, 1976; *The New York Times*, May 17, 1965.
M: *People Magazine*, August 11, 1975.

SPECIAL THANKS

Authors' Interviews

Arisue, Seizo
Asada, Tsunesaburo

Beser, Jacob
Biel, Raymond
Bock, Frederick
Brode, Robert

Caron, George
Casey, John
Cheshire, Leonard
Cole, Leon
Costa, Thomas
Costello, Edward

Downey, William
Duzenbury, Wyatt

Elsey, George
Endo, Shin

Ferebee, Tom
Fuchida, Kitaoka

Gackenbach, Russell
Genda, Minoru
Grennan, Thomas
Gruning, Wayne

Hashimoto, Mochitsura
Hatanaka, Kuniso
Hatsuko, Tominaga
Hiroto, Kanai

Iki, Haruki
Imai, Kizo
Imoto, Kumao

Jeppson, Morris
Jernigan, Norris

Kaizuka, Yoshiro
King, John
Kosakai, Yoshiteru

LeMay, Curtis
Lewis, Robert

Maruyama, Kazumasa
Matsuoka, Masaru
Matsushige, Yoshito
Matubara, Miyoko
McKnight, Charles
Miura, Hiroshi
Moritaki, Ichiro

Nasu, Yoshio
Nelson, Richard
Nizuma, Seichi

Olivi, Frederick
Osako, Ichiro
Oya, Kakuzo

Perry, Charles

Saito, Masatoshi
Sakai, Saburo
Shima, Kaoru
Slusky, Joseph
Spitzer, Abe
Stiborik, Joseph
Strudwick, James
Suzuki, Tatsusaburo
Sweeney, Charles

Takahashi, Akahiro
Takai, Sadao
Tibbets, Paul

van Kirk, Theodore

Yanagita, Hiroshi
Yasuzawa, Matsuo
Yokoyama, Tatsuo

(and in correspondence)
Alvarez, Luis
Lord, Edmund
Montgomery, J. B.

Translators

As indicated earlier, we owe a special debt to our translators.

In Japan, John Silver worked the impossible, always finding an acceptable way of putting our questions which in the circumstances were sometimes delicate and awkward in the extreme. He was simply invaluable.

Shizuko Pritchard, a native of Hiroshima, has been exceedingly helpful in maintaining through correspondence certain of our contacts there since we left that city. She has also translated many documents in meticulous fashion.

Others

In Tokyo, Sen Matsuda and Ko Shioya, Editor-in-Chief and Deputy Editor respectively at the *Reader's Digest*, were willing and able to provide expert help and advice whenever we asked; and, unlike certain others in the field of communications, they never attempted to impress upon us their personal views on the war and the Bomb. We also much appreciated the help of two of their staff, Miss Katsuko Konno and Mr. Sekiya Hashimoto.

In Hiroshima, two reporters, Kawamoto and Kaneguchi, from the *Chugoku Shimbun* were particularly co-operative; Yoshiteru Kosakai, Chief, Historical Division, Hiroshima Library, supplied a wealth of important background information; Hideo Sasaki, Director, Hiroshima Peace Culture Centre, generously provided us with one of the last remaining complete sets of *Hiroshima Genbaku Sensai Shi*, a five-volume reference work of fundamental importance.

In Washington, as with our previous books, we benefited from the specialist guidance and information received from John Taylor at the National Archives; from Sheila McGouch at the Carnegie Institution; from Dr. Allard at the Naval Historical Center; and from Air Force Archivist Gail Guido.

In New York, Bill Maxwell gave us unquestioned help at times when it was most needed.

In Dublin, as in the past, Bill Moloney aided us on the technical aspects of bombing.

And in London, as always, Michael Weigall was there to give us his own special kind of assistance.

Acknowledgements

A-Bomb Survivor's Relief Organisation, Hiroshima (K. Shimuza).
Albert F. Simpson Historical Research Center, Maxwell, Alabama (Gloria Atkinson and Allen Striepe).
American Embassy, London.
American National Red Cross, Washington, (George Elsey, Mac Slee).
Atomic Bomb Hospital, Hiroshima (I. Sadama).
Atomic Energy Commission, Historical Office, Washington.
British Embassy, Washington (Peter Bond).
British Library, Reference, Division, London; Newspaper Library Colindale.
Chugoku Shimbun, Hiroshima (Akira Matsuura).
Hiroshima Peace Culture Centre (K. Kiyama).

Imperial Army Officer's Club, Tokyo (Mr. Senno).
Japanese Defense Agency, Historical Division, Tokyo.
National Archives, Washington; Modern Military Section (John Taylor); Historical Office State Dept., Bureau of Public Affairs; General Archives Division (Janet Hargett).
National Personnel Records Center, St. Louis.
Naval Historical Center, Washington (D. C. Allard).
Naval Weapons Center, China Lake (A. B. Christman).
New York Public Library.
Franklin D. Roosevelt Library, Hyde Park, N.Y. (W. R. Emerson).
Town Hall, Hiroshima (A. Takahashi).
Harry S. Truman Library, Independence (P. H. Lagerquist).

BIBLIOGRAPHY

Books
These, as with other published material related to the subject of this book, should be consulted with caution; the scorched earth of Hiroshima has proved fertile ground for propagandists.

For readers interested in the after-effects of the bomb, in human terms, we recommend the documentary novel *Black Rain* by Masuji Ibuse.

Alperovitz, Gar. *Atomic Diplomacy—Hiroshima and Potsdam*. Simon & Schuster, New York, 1965.

Amrine, Michael. *The Great Decision*. G. P. Putnam's Sons, New York, 1959.

Anders, Gunther (with Eatherly, Claude). *Burning Conscience*. Monthly Review Press, New York, 1962.

Arisue, Seizo. *Memoirs*. Fuyo Shobo, Tokyo, 1974.

Arnold, Henry H. *A Global Mission*. Harper & Bros., New York, 1949.

Asahi Shimbun, *A-Bomb*. Hiroshima Peace Culture Centre, 1972.— (foreword E. O. Reischauer). *The Pacific Rivals*. Tokyo, 1972.

Asbell, Bernard. *When F.D.R. Died*. Holt, Rinehart and Winston, New York, 1961.

Baldwin, Hanson W. *Great Mistakes of the War*. Harper & Bros., New York, 1950.

Batchelder, Robert C. *The Irreversible Decision*. Houghton Mifflin, Boston, 1962.

Bateson, Charles. *The War With Japan*. Ure Smith Pty. Ltd., Sydney, 1968.

Bishop, Jim. *F.D.R.'s Last Year*. Wm. Morrow & Co., New York, 1974.

Blackett, P. M. S. *Fear, War and the Bomb*. Whittlesey House, New York, 1948.

Boyle, Andrew. *No Passing Glory*. Collins, London, 1955.

Braddon, Russell. *Cheshire V.C.* Evans Bros. Ltd., London, 1965.

Bush, Vannevar. *Pieces of the Action*. Wm. Morrow & Co., New York, 1970.

Butow, Robert J. C. *Japan's Decision to Surrender*. Stanford University Press, 1954.

— *Tojo and the Coming of the War*. Princeton University Press, 1961.

Byrnes, James F. *Speaking Frankly*. Harper & Bros., New York, 1947.

Campbell, J. W. *The Atomic Story*. Henry Holt & Co., New York, 1947.

Churchill, Winston S. *The Second World War* (esp. vol. 6). Bantam Books Inc., New York, 1962.

Clark, R.W. *The Birth of the Bomb*. Horizon Press, New York, 1961.

Coffey, Thomas M. *Imperial Tragedy*. World Publishing Co., New York, 1970.

Compton, Arthur Holly. *Atomic Quest*. Oxford University Press, New York. 1956.

Craig, William. *The Fall of Japan*. Dial Press, New York, 1967.

Craigie, Sir Robert. *Behind the Japanese Mask*. Hutchinson & Co., London, 1945.

Craven, W. F. & Cate, J. L. (Eds.) *The Army Air Forces in World War II* (esp. vol. 5). University of Chicago Press, 1953.

Crowl, Philip A. *U.S. Army in World War II, The War In The Pacific, Campaign in the Marianas*. Dept. of the Army, Washington D.C., 1960.

Eatherly, Claude R. (with Anders, Gunther). *Burning Conscience*. Monthly Review Press, New York, 1962.

Feis, Herbert. *The Road to Pearl Harbor*. Princeton University Press, 1950.
— *Between War and Peace*. Oxford University Press, 1960.
— *Japan Subdued*. Princeton University Press, 1961.
— *The Atomic Bomb and the End of World War II*. Princeton University Press, 1966.

Fuchida, Mitsuo and Okumiya, Masatake. *Midway, the Battle that Doomed Japan*. U.S. Naval Institute, Annapolis, 1955.

Gigon, Fernand (Trans. Constantine FitzGibbon). *Formula For Death*. Roy Publishers, New York, 1959.

Giovannitti, Len and Freed, Fred. *The Decision to Drop the Bomb*. Coward-McCann Inc., New York, 1965.

Gowing, Margaret. *Britain and Atomic Energy 1939–1945*. St. Martin's Press, New York, 1964.

Grew, J. C. *Ten Years in Japan*. Simon & Shuster Inc., New York, 1944.

Groueff, Stephane. *Manhattan Project*. Little, Brown, Boston, 1967.

Groves, Leslie R. *Now It Can Be Told*. reprint, Da Capo Press, New York, 1975.

Hachiya, Michihiko (transl. Wells W.). *Hiroshima Diary*. University of North Carolina Press, Chapel Hill, 1955.

Hasimoto, Mochitsura. *Sunk, The Story of the Japanse Submarine Fleet, 1942-45*. Henry Holt, New York, 1954.

Hewlett, Richard G. and Anderson, Oscar E. *A History of the United States Atomic Energy Commission* (esp. vol. 1). The Pennsylvania State University Press, University Park, 1962.

Hillman, William. *Mr. President*. Farrar, Straus & Young, New York, 1952.

Hines, Neal O. *Proving Ground*. University of Washington Press, Seattle, 1962.

Hiroshima City. Hiroshima City Hall, 1971.

Hirschfeld, Burt. *A Cloud Over Hiroshima*. Julian Messner, New York, 1967.

History of the U.N. War Crimes Commission, H.M.S.O. London, 1948.

Huie, William Bradford. *The Hiroshima Pilot*. G.P. Putnam's Sons, New York, 1964.

Hull, Cordell. *The Memoirs of Cordell Hull* (esp. vol. 2). The Macmillan Co., New York, 1948.

Inoguchi, Rikihei and Nakajima, Tadashi. *The Divine Wind*. U.S. Naval Institute, Annapolis, 1958.

Irving, David. *German Atomic Bomb,* (orig. title, *The Virus House*) Simon and Schuster, New York, 1968.

Isely, J. A. and Crowl, P. A. *The U.S. Marines and Amphibious Warfare*. Princeton University Press, 1951.

James, David H. *The Rise and Fall of the Japanese Empire*. Macmillan, New York, 1951.

Jungk, Robert. *Brighter than 1000 Suns.* Harcourt Brace Jovanovich, New York, 1970.

— *Children of the Ashes*. Harcourt, Brace & World, New York, 1961.

Knebel, Fletcher and Bailey, Charles W. *No High Ground*. Harper & Row, New York, 1960.

Konoye, Fumimaro. *Memoirs*. Asahi Shimbun, Tokyo, 1946.

Lansing, Lamont, *Day of Trinity*. Atheneum Publishers, New York, 1965.

Lapp, Ralph E. *Kill and Overkill*. Basic Books, New York, 1962.

Laurence, William L. *Dawn Over Zero*. Knopf, New York, 1947.

Leahy, William D. *I Was There*. Whittlesey House, New York, 1950.

LeMay, Curtis E. (with Kantor, M.). *Mission With LeMay*. Doubleday & Co. Inc., New York, 1965.

Lipton, Robert J. *Death in Life*. Random House, New York, 1967.

Lord, Walter. *Day of Infamy*. Holt, Rinehart & Winston, New York, 1957.

MacArthur, Douglas. *Reminiscences*. McGraw-Hill Inc., New York, 1964.

Major, John. *The Oppenheimer Hearing*. Stein & Day, New York, 1971.

Manchester, William. *The Glory and the Dream*. Little, Brown, Boston, 1974.

Marx, Joseph L. *Seven Hours to Zero*. G. P. Putnam's Sons, New York, 1967.

McCloy, John J. *The Challenge to American Foreign Policy*. Harvard University Press, 1953.

Miller, Merle, *Plain Speaking*. G.P. Putnam's Sons, New York, 1974.

— and Spitzer, Abe. *We Dropped the A-Bomb*. Thos. Y. Crowell Co., New York, 1946.

Millis, Walter. *This is Pearl!* Wm. Morrow & Co. Inc., New York, 1947.

Minear, Richard H. *Victor's Justice*. Princeton University Press, 1971.

Morison, Samuel Eliot. *History of the United States Naval Operations in World War II* (esp. vols. 3, 8 and 14). Little, Brown & Co., Boston 1947–1962.

— *The Two-Ocean War*. Little, Brown & Co., Boston, 1963.

Morris, Ivan. *The Nobility of Failure*. New American Library, New York, 1976.

Morton, Louis. *Command Decisions,* Dept. of the Army, Washington D.C., 1971.

Mosley, Leonard. *Hirohito*. Weidenfeld & Nicolson, London, 1966.

Moss, Norman. *Men Who Play God*. Harper & Row, New York, 1969.

Nakamoto, Hiroko and Pace, M. M. *My Japan 1930–51*. McGraw Hill, New York, 1970.

Newcomb, Richard F. *Abandon Ship!* Reprint of 1958 edn., Indiana Univ. Press, Bloomington, 1976.

New York Times. *Hiroshima Plus 20*. Delacorte Press, New York, 1965. (Baldwin, H. W. *Hiroshima Decision;* Lapp, R.E. *The Einstein Letter*).

Osada, A. *Children of the A-Bomb*. Putnam's, New York, 1963.
Osako, Ichiro. *Hiroshima 1945*. Chuko Shinsho, Tokyo, 1975.
Ota, Y. *Shikabane no Machi (Town of Corpses)*. Kawade Shobo, Tokyo, 1955.
Oughterson, A. W. and Warren, S. *Medical Effects of the Atomic Bomb in Japan*. McGraw-Hill, New York, 1956.

Reilly, Michael F. *I Was Roosevelt's Shadow*. W. Foulsham & Co., London, 1946.
Russell, Lord, of Liverpool. *The Knights of Bushido*. E.P. Dutton, New York, 1958.
Ryder, Sue. *And The Tomorrow is Theirs*. Burleigh Press, Bristol, 1975.

Sakai, Saburo. *Samurai*. E. P. Dutton and Co., New York, 1957.
Shoenberger, Walter S. *Decision of Destiny*. Ohio University Press, Athens, 1969.
Shigemitsu, Mamoru. *Japan and Her Destiny*. E. P. Dutton & Co., New York, 1958.
Smith, Alice Kimball. *A Peril and a Hope*. University of Chicago Press, 1965.
Smith, Merriman. *Thank You, Mr. President*. Harper & Brothers, New York, 1946.
Stimson, Henry Lewis and Bundy, McGeorge. *On Active Service in Peace and War*. Harper & Row, New York, 1947.
Storry, Richard A. *A History of Modern Japan*. Penguin Books Ltd., London, 1960.

Takayama, Hitoshi (Ed.) *Hiroshima in Memoriam and Today*. Hiroshima Peace Culture Centre, 1973.
Taylor, A. J. P. *The Origins of the Second World War*. Atheneum, New York, 1962.
Teller, Edward with Brown, Allen. *The Legacy of Hiroshima*. Doubleday, Garden City, N.Y., 1962.
Togo, Shigenori. *The Cause of Japan*. Simon & Shuster, New York, 1956.
Toland, John. *The Rising Sun*. Random House, New York, 1970.
Truman, Harry S. *Year of Decisions, 1945*. Doubleday, Garden City, N.Y., 1955.
— *Mr. Citizen*. Bernard Geis, New York, 1960.
Trumbull, Robert. *Nine Who Survived Hiroshima and Nagasaki*. E. P. Dutton & Co., New York, 1957.
Tully, Grace. *F.D.R. My Boss*. Charles Scribner's Sons, New York, 1949.

Wilson, Jane (Ed.). *All in Our Time*. The Bulletin of the Atomic Scientists, Chicago, 1975.

Zacharias, Ellis M. *Secret Missions*. G. P. Putnam's Sons, New York, 1946.

Documents/Reports

Individual items, too numerous to mention, many recently declassified, may be found at:

The National Archives, Washington: *Record Group No. 77: MED Top*

Secret Files, MED H & B Files, Top Secret Files of Special Interest To General Groves; Record Group No. 165: OPD Project Decimal Files, OPD Olympic; U.S. Strategic Bombing Surveys etc.

Albert F. Simpson Historical Research Center, Maxwell AFB: *Record Groups: GP-509-SU, HI, RE (Comp), HI (Comp), OP-5, Oral interviews.*

Historical Office, State Dept., Bureau of Public Affairs, Washington: *Interim Committee etc.*

Naval Historical Center, Washington: *Tinian NAB, USS Indianapolis, Oral Interviews etc.*

American National Red Cross, Washington: *Tinian, medical and social.*

Atomic Energy Commission, Historical Office, Washington: *Oppenheimer, Research and Development etc.*

Japanese Defence Agency, Historical Section, Tokyo: *General and Specific Naval and Army activities during World War II.*

B-29 Flight Manual (Familiarisation File, USAAF).

Dull, Paul S. and Umemura, Michael T. *The Tokyo Trials.* University of Michigan Press, Ann Arbor, 1957.

Franck, James. *Report of the Committee on Social and Political Implications, June 1945* ('The Franck Report', complete text in *A Peril and a Hope*).

History of the 509th Composite Group, 313 Bombardment Wing, Twentieth Air Force—Activation to 15 August, 1945. *Official Historian,* Tinian, 31 August 1945.

International Military Tribunal For the Far East (Nat. Archives, esp. vols. 60, 61, 64, 65, 74).

Log of the President's Trip to the Berlin Conference, July 6, 1945 to August 7, 1945. Written and compiled by Wm. M. Rigdon, USN, 1946, with a foreword by Lieut. George M. Elsey, USNR.

Manhattan Engineer District. *The Atomic Bombings of Hiroshima and Nagasaki.* Washington, D.C., 1957.

Ossip, Jerome J. (Ed.) *509th Pictorial Album, Tinian, 1945.*

Report of the British Mission to Japan. The Effects of the Atomic Bombs at Hiroshima and Nagasaki. H.M. Stationery Office, London, 1946.

Short History of the 509th Group. Roswell, N.M., 1947.

Smyth, H. D. *A General Account of the Development of the Methods of Using Atomic Energy for Military Purposes under the Auspices of the United States Government, 1940–1945.* Government Printing Office, Washington, D.C., 1946.

US Army Air Forces. *Mission Accomplished* (Interrogation of Japanese Industrial, Military and Civil Leaders of WW II). U.S. Government Printing Office, Washington, D.C., 1955.

US Strategic Bombing Surveys: *Interrogations; The Effects of Strategic Bombing on Japan's War Economy; Japan's Struggle to End the War; The Effects of the Atomic Bombs on Hiroshima and Nagasaki; The Effects of Strategic Bombing on Japanese Morale; Effects of Air Attack on the City of Hiroshima; Effects of the Atomic Bomb on Hiroshima, Japan.* All published by US Government Printing Office, Washington, 1945–1947.

Magazines/Periodicals/Booklets.

Araki, Takeshi (Foreword). *Hiroshima*. Hiroshima Peace Culture Centre, 1975.

Bainbridge, Kenneth T. *Prelude To Trinity, in Bulletin of the Atomic Scientists, vol. 31, No. 4.* April 1975; *A Foul and Awesome Display in vol. 31, No. 5,* May 1975.

Batchelor, John (Ed.) *Battle of the Pacific.* Purnell, London, 1975.

Bishop, John. *The Trick That Was a Steppingstone to Japan,* in the *Saturday Evening Post,* December 23, 1944.

Caron, George R. *Mission Destruction,* in *Veterans of Foreign Wars Magazine,* November, 1959.

Compton, Karl T. *If the Atomic Bomb Had Not Been Used,* in *Atlantic Monthly,* December, 1946.

Coronet Magazine. Fifteen Years Later—The Men Who Bombed Hiroshima. Vol. 48, No. 4, August, 1960.

Frisch, David H. *Scientists and the Decision to Bomb Japan,* in *Bulletin of the Atomic Scientists,* Vol. 26, June, 1970.

Groves, Leslie R. *Some Recollections of July 16, 1945,* in *Bulletin of the Atomic Scientists,* vol. 26, 1970.

Kosakai, Yoshiteru (Compiler). *A-Bomb: A City Tells its Story.* Hiroshima Peace Culture Centre, 1972.

Laurence, William L. *The Story of the Atomic Bomb.* The *New York Times,* 1946.

Leighton, Alexander H. *That Day at Hiroshima,* in *Atlantic Monthly,* October 1946.

Lewis, Robert A. *How We Dropped the Bomb,* in *Popular Science,* vol. 171, No. 2, August 1957.

New Yorker Magazine, issue of August 31, 1946 contains the original work by John Hersey: *Hiroshima.*

People Magazine. Memories of Hiroshima, in vol. 4, No. 6, August 11, 1975.

Philosophical Transactions of the Royal Society. *The Nuclear Yields at Hiroshima and Nagasaki,* in Vol. 266, No. 1177. June 11, 1970, by Lord Penney, D. E. J. Samuels and G. C. Scorgie.

Ransom, Jay Ellis, *Wendover, Home of the Atomic Bomb,* in Code 41, November, 1973, Ely, Nevada.

Schwartz, Robert L. *Atomic Bomb Away,* in *Yank Magazine,* Sept. 7, 1945; *The Week the War Ended,* in *Life Magazine,* July 17, 1950.

Siemes, P. T. *The Atomic Bomb on Hiroshima,* in the *Irish Monthly,* March and April, 1946.

Smith, Alice Kimball. *Los Alamos: Focus of an Age,* in *Bulletin of the Scientists,* vol. 26, June 1970.

Small, Collie. *The Biggest Blast,* in *Colliers Magazine,* August 13, 1949.

Steiner, Arthur. *Baptism of the Atomic Scientists,* in *Bulletin of the Atomic Scientists,* Vol. 31, No. 2, February 1945.

Stimson, Henry L. *The Decision to Use the Atomic Bomb,* in *Harper's Magazine,* Vol. 194, No. 1161, February, 1947.

Tibbets, Paul W. *Ten p.m. August 5—and After,* in *Survey Graphic Magazine,* Vol. 35, January 1946; *How to Drop An Atom Bomb,* in the

Saturday Evening Post, June 8, 1946 (with Wesley Price); *Training the 509th for Hiroshima*, in *Air Force Magazine*, August, 1973.

Time Magazine. The Unmentioned Victims, in issue of August 9, 1971.

Time Out. Prayer or Curse? (Downey's prayer) in Vol. 1, No. 4, April, 1961, Luther League of America, Philadelphia, Penn.

U.S. News & World Report. *Was A-Bomb on Japan a Mistake?*, in Vol. 49, August 15, 1960.

Newspapers

The following lists those found most useful.

Asahi Simbun, Chicago Tribune, Chugoku Shimbun, Los Angeles Times, Mainichi Shimbun, The New York Times, San Francisco Chronicle, The Times of London, *Washington Post, Japan Times and Advertiser*, and the July and August 1945, editions of the *Daily Mission*, published by the 313th Bombardment Wing Information Office, Tinian, Marianas.

Private Papers

Tsunesaburo Asada	Kumao Imoto	Abe Spitzer
Jacob Beser	Robert Lewis	Henry L. Stimson
George Caron	Kazumasa Maruyama	Paul Tibbets
Shin Endo	Masaru Matsuoka	Harry S. Truman
Russell Gackenbach	Richard Nelson	Theodore van Kirk
Leslie Groves	Kakuzo Oya	Tatsuo Yokoyama
Kanai Hiroto	Charles Perry	

Transcripts

Official interviews conducted by A. B. Christman, NOTS, China Lake:
Vice Admiral F. L. Ashworth, April, 1969.
Dr. A. Francis Birch, February, 1971.
Mrs. Robert Burroughs (formerly Mrs. W. S. Parsons), April 1966.
Lieutenant General Leslie R. Groves, May 1967.
Vice Admiral John T. Hayward, May 1966.
Others:
Brigadier General Paul W. Tibbets, December 1960 (Kenneth Leish); September 1966 (Arthur Marmor)
General Nathan F. Twining, November 1965 (Arthur Marmor)
And television documentaries:
The Building of the Bomb, BBC-TV., March 1975.
Hot to Handle, BBC-TV., September 1966.
Eric Sevareid in Conversation with John J. McCloy, CBS News Special in two parts, July 1975.
The Day the Sun Blew Up, BBC-TV., October 1976.

INDEX

Abe, Colonel, 127–9, 137, 139, 161, 229–30; killed by bomb, 324

Abel, William, 336

Abwehr, 42, 44

Adachi, Dr. Sakyo, and balloon bombs, 132

Alamogordo firing range, 76, 95, 153, 179, 188, 197; first firing of plutonium bomb, 202–6, 209–11, 217, 231–2, 254, 328; Site S (Jornada del muerto), 203; Ground Zero, 203; film of test, 278, 282

Albuquerque, New Mexico, 33, 54, 146, 198; shuttle service to Wendover, 101

Albury, Don, pilot, 30

Alvarez, Luis, 285–6; and release mechanism, 286

Apra Harbour, shipping attacked by *kaiten* pilots, 80

Arisue, Major-General Seizo, head of Imperial Army Intelligence, 42–4, 65–8, 191, 223; weekly summaries of U.S. Press, 42; overseas agents, 42–4, 65; fails to get spy into U.S.A., 43, 44, 65; and possibility of negotiated peace, 66–8, 108, 124, 183, 184, 199; and air raid on Tokyo, 108; news of Roosevelt's death, 124; profile of Truman, 124; information from Berne, 124–5, 136, 159, 184, 199; and Emperor's desire for approach to Moscow, 217; on defences of Hiroshima and Tokyo area, 235–6; and Potsdam Proclamation, 236, 238; investigation in Hiroshima after bomb, 335, 336

Army Academy for Officers, Tokyo, 14, 16

Arnold, General Henry, chief of Army Air Force, 12, 165, 166, 211; and use of atomic bomb, 232–3

Asada, Dr. Tsunesaburo, 29–41, 131–2, 251, 335; career, 40; atomic research, 40; Projects A and B, 40–1; Death Ray project, 41, 68, 132, 251, 335; proximity fuse, 132

Ashworth, Commander Frederic L., 85–6, 201; and choice of overseas base for 509th Group, 86, 96; tells Nimitz of the bomb, 96; at briefing session, 279

Augusta, cruiser, 188

Awaya, Senkichi, Mayor of Hiroshima, 59–61, 109, 112, 114, 138, 151, 246, 247, 275, 276, 314, 319; and creation of fire-breaks, 59–60; devout Christian, 60; anti-militarist, 60–1, wife and family, 138, 151, 325; problems in Hiroshima, 229, 275, 276, 290, 291; killed, 325, 335

B-24 aircraft: bomb Kure, 246; two planes shot down over Hiroshima, 247–9; their crews as prisoners, 250, 262–3

B-29 Superfortresses, 3, 12, 20, 25, 28–30, 45, 48, 53, 55, 56, 78, 79, 83, 85, 90, 105, 107, 110, 125–7, 137, 140, 142, 143, 180, 181, 192, 194, 201, 214, 216, 220, 251, 266, 269, 281, 287, 288, 340, 343; first one delivered to Wendover, 46–7;

371

Fulton, Robert, 6–7
Furman, Major Robert, and transport of bomb's inner cannon to Tinian, 197–8, 206–7

Gackenbach, Navigator Russell, 27, 181, 216
Genda, Minoru, assistant Japanese naval attaché in London, 14; and planning for Pearl Harbour, 14, 16, 164; commands fighter group on Kyushu, 164; post-war career, 343
Germany, 16; agreement with Japan, 14; atomic research, 40, 63; spy network in South America, 43
Gestapo, the, 114
Giles, General, 5
Ginga bomber: attacks Saipan, 131–2; fitted with proximity fuse, 132
Goering, Hermann, xviii; personal squadron, 29
Goldwyn, Sam, xviii
Goto Islands, 163
Great Artiste, Sweeney's plane, 251, 252, 285, 307–9, 316–18, 328, 335; as flying laboratory, 269, 280, 281, 296; takes off, 303
Greenglass, David, espionage activities, 38
Grennan, 2nd Lieutenant Eugene, 27, 216, 313
Gromyko, Andrei, 133
Groves, Brigadier-General Leslie Richard, chief of Manhattan Project, 9–12, 28, 65, 74–6, 95, 101, 131, 146, 177, 197, 198, 201, 209–211, 213, 217, 245, 268–9, 278, 279; and Bohr, 9–11, 38; career, 11; characteristics, 11; and Tibbets, 12, 28, 55, 70; and Oppenheimer, 34–5; discussions on target selection, 75; gives Marshall date for first bomb, 76, 93; and transport for 509th Group, 86; and MacArthur, 86; and expenditure on secret project, 92; ques-

tion of time and place of bombing, 96–8, 103, 155–7; and Marshall, 96–8; against collaboration with Britain on atomic research, 96–7; and Byrnes' intervention, 97–8, 102, 117; Marshall makes him responsible for choice of target, 98; memorandum to Stimson, 102–3; and visits for Congressmen, 102–3, 117; and Roosevelt's death, 122; impatience with scientists, 130–1; talks on bomb with Truman and Stimson, 134–5; at Pentagon Conference, 149, 151; and Interim Committee, 153; discussions with Stimson on target for bomb, 155–7, 265, 270; aspects of launching atomic strike, 166; policy of silence, 195; at Alamogordo, 203–6; report on test, 231–2; anxiety over expected loss of life, 253; drafts document on bomb for Handy, 253; and delivery of bomb by ship, 261–2; and U.S. prisoners of war in Nagasaki district, 263–5; learns that bomb is ready, 269–70; opposes 'arming' of bomb in flight, 281, 289; orders camera crews to Tinian, 297
Guam, 13, 79–82, 103, 104, 165, 179, 180, 190, 206, 256, 258, 263, 268–271, 278, 286; aircraft carrier engagement, 63; Headquarters of XXI Bomber Command, 83–5; as possible base for 509th Group, 86; proves unsuitable, 96; meeting on use of bomb, 253–5

Hack, Dr. Frederick, 159; and Japanese Intelligence, 66–7; advises Japan to negotiate peace, 67; meeting with Americans, 136
Hahn, Otto, 40
Handy, General Thomas T., acting Chief of Staff: gives Spaatz document on use of bomb, 253–4; anxiety over expected loss of life,

380

memorandum from Oppenheimer, 254–5; at briefing session, 278–83; decides to arm bomb after take-off, 281, 289; check list, 304–5; completes loading of charge, 306; reports success of mission, 328; Rear-Admiral, 341; death, 341

Patterson, Robert, Under-Secretary of War, and expenditure on secret project, 91–3, 102

Patton, General George, 11, 63

Payette, Lt.-Colonel Hazen, Intelligence Officer, 23, 213, 251, 268, 278, 280–3

Pearl Harbor, 7, 14, 16, 22, 31, 40, 43, 51, 57, 62, 63, 82, 121, 132, 138, 144, 164, 206, 217, 218, 227, 240, 241, 311, 331, 342, 343

Pedersen, Roy, navigator of *Lonesome Lady*, 249

Penney, William (Lord Penney), British observer on Tinian, 243, 266, 278–9; on Target Committee, 243, 266; excluded from atomic mission, 279

Pentagon, the, 232, 253; conferences at, 149–51, 164–8

Perry, Lieutenant Charles, Mess Officer, 24, 53, 55, 71, 77, 79, 121; on Tinian, 192, 214, 216, 244, 265–7, 269, 292; party after mission, 329–30, 332

Philippine Islands, 256, 258, 268

Plutonium bomb, 38, 76, 95, 153, 179, 201; test firing, 202–6

Potsdam Conference, 184, 187–9, 200, 201, 208–11, 220–4, 231–3, 241, 253, 264

Potsdam Proclamation, 236–8, 246, 337; Japanese reaction, 238–41, 270; rejected by Japanese Government, 241

Power, General Tom, 104

Prince of Wales, loss of, 57; Japanese divers remove radar equipment, 41

Project A., Japanese atomic research, 40, 41

Project B., Japanese development of radar, etc., 41

Proximity fuses, 36, 41, 127, 132

Radar, 37, 41, 48

Radio Guam, 143

Radio Hiroshima, 245, 291, 314, 318, 319, 323

Radio Japan, *see* Japan Radio

Ramsey, Professor Norman, 5, 6, 8, 12, 23, 33, 35, 95; and security, 34; and role of radar officer, 37; at briefing session, 278

Rayburn, Sam, Speaker of the Senate, 118

Red Cross Hospital, Hiroshima, 94

Repulse, loss of, 57; Japanese divers remove radar equipment, 41

Ri Gu, Lt.-Colonel, Korean prince, 228–9, 291, 311, 314, 318; killed, 335

Roosevelt, Eleanor, 118, 120, 123

Roosevelt, President Franklin D., xviii, 9–11, 19, 38, 40, 64–5, 67, 92–3, 102, 112, 114, 115, 118, 119, 123, 188, 200, 201; Einstein's warning, 6–7; calls for action, 7; authorises substantial sums, 7; attitude towards project, 8; passion for secrecy, 8, 65; and Groves, 10–11; ill-health, 93; and collaboration with Britain on atomic research, 97; memorandum from Byrnes, 97–8, 116–17; at Warm Springs, 115–17; and Russia, 115–16; sudden death, 117, 118, 120–2, 124

Rota: Japanese garrison cut off, 178; bombs dropped on island as practice, 178, 186, 192, 193, 214, 218, 219, 279

Royal Air Force, 22, 55, 97, 228, 243

Russell, Bertrand, 340

Russia, 16, 97, 115–16, 133, 337; espionage activities, 38; Red Army, 63; will not renew Neutrality Pact with Japan, 124, 183; influence in Far East, 144, 148,

bomb, 119–20; talks with Truman and Groves on bomb, 133–5; memorandum to Truman, 134–135; chairman of Interim Committee, 135, 153–4; and question of demonstration bomb, 154; on target for bomb, 155–7; and plans to invade Japan, 160; memorandum to Truman on giving Japan final warning, 188–189; at Potsdam, 208, 209, 220, 221; and Alamogordo test, 220–221; sees Allen Dulles, 220–3; and use of atomic bomb, 232–3

Stone, Harlan, Chief Justice, 119

Straight Flush, Eatherly's aircraft, 216, 224–5, 281, 296, 312, 313

Strassmann, Fritz, 40

Strategic Air Forces (U.S.), 233, 253, 270

Strudwick, Captain James, 24

Styer, General W. D., 92

Superdumbos, 283, 309

Suzuki, Admiral Kantaro: appointed Japanese Prime Minister, 124, 163; and finding means to end war, 124; militant speech to Diet, 144–5; calls meeting of Inner Cabinet, 182; urged by Emperor to approach Moscow, 217; and Potsdam Proclamation, 240–1; rejection (*mokusatsu*) of Proclamation, 241; and question of surrender, 337

Sweeney, Charles, pilot, 30, 69, 79, 125–7, 215, 251, 269, 291, 306, 308, 317; and Lewis, 126; and premature detonation of dummy, 127, 132; in command of 393rd Squadron, 214; at briefing session, 280; conducts fusing test, 285–6; and preparations for second bomb, 335

Szilard, Leo, 63–4, 92, 116, 153, 196

Taloa (B-24), 246–8, 250; shot down over Hiroshima, 248; crew bale out and are captured, 249–250

Target Committee, 130–1, 149–51, 243

Taylor, Major Ralph, pilot, 281

Teheran Conference, 188

Teller, Edward, 8

1027th Air Materiel Squadron, 56

1395th Military Police Company, 56

Thornhill, Francis, navigator, 224

315th Bombardment Wing, 69

320th Troop Carrier Squadron, 56

390th Air Service Group, 56

393rd Heavy Bombardment Squadron, 24, 26–8, 87, 126, 186, 212, 214, 268, 269; assigned to Tibbets, 9; at Wendover, 19–30, 52–57; security measures, 27–8; at full strength, 52

Tibbets, Enola Gay, mother of Paul Tibbets, 4, 26, 267

Tibbets, Lucie, wife of Paul Tibbets, 71–3, 87–8, 146

Tibbets, Paul Warfield, 3–6, 12–13, 19, 33, 46–50, 52–7, 69–73, 79–91, 101, 111, 126, 130, 131, 158, 192, 201, 203, 219–21, 230, 266–7, 271–2, 277, 279, 285, 286, 289, 290, 292, 296, 331; birth and upbringing, 3–4; enlists in U.S. Air Corps, 4; successful bomber pilot, 3; leads first U.S. raid on North Africa, 3; flight tests new Superfortress, 3; vetted by Intelligence, 3–5; told that he is to drop atom bomb, 6; to command and train atomic strike force, 8–9

sets up office, 12; search for men, 12; at Wendover, 23–30; dual command with Classen, 23; and Eatherly, 24, 56–7; and Groves, 12, 28, 55, 70; and Ferebee, 28–30; recruitment of experienced men, 29–30; in Los Alamos, 33–9; and Oppenheimer, 34–7, 39; bomb explained to him, 35–7; tactical requirements for delivering bomb 49–50; use of stripped down bombers, 50; enlargement of command, 56; his squadron unified as 509th Com-

Tibbetts, Paul Warfield—*contd.*
posite Group, 69; bomb-sight problem and answer, 69–70, 76; wife and children, 71–3, 87–8

talks with Groves on target selection, 75; and special training in Cuba, 77–9; promoted full Colonel, 77; favours Tinian as overseas base, 86; training of crews not sent to Cuba, 86–7; and 1st Ordnance Squadron, 96, 98–100; and replacement machines, 105; and security breaches, 109–12; on Truman, 121; impatience with scientists, 130; decides not to transfer Eatherly, 141; selects best aircraft at Omaha, 146–7, 157

at Pentagon Conferences, 149–151; photographs of Hiroshima, 164; on its suitability as target, 165; and approach to Hiroshima, 166; meteorological problems, 166–7; inspection of Tinian, 177–179; and LeMay, 178–9, 211–12; instructions not to fly over Japan, 179, 214, 251; flies to Tinian, 202; at Tinian, 211–16; and attempt to break up Group, 212; learns of Alamogordo test, 217; confrontation with LeMay, 217–218; authorises Group's first mission over Japan, 224; prefers Hiroshima as target, 235; orders psychological observations by flight surgeon, 242, 245; and British observers, 243; and well-being of Group, 243–4; personal strain, 244–5; and Eatherly, 245, 268; at meeting in Guam, 253, 255; misunderstanding with Lewis, 255–6; drafts order for first atomic attack, 267, 268; gives briefings, 268–9, 276–7; finalising details with LeMay, 270–1; Hiroshima as primary target, 270; strike set for August 6 (1945), 277; last flight to Rota, 279; at briefing session, 280–3;

names his aircraft *Enola Gay*, 287–9; final briefing, 292–4; concern about Japanese intelligence, 294; and camera crews, 297–301; and cyanide capsules, 300

boards *Enola Gay*, 300; reaches take-off position, 301; takes off, 303; on the flight, 304–10, 312, 315; rendezvous at Iwo Jima, 308; bomb ready for dropping, 310; confirms Hiroshima as target, 313; reaches target, 316, 317; dropping of bomb, 318, 319, 323; and shockwaves, 326; recording of crews' impressions, 326

lands on Tinian, 331; awarded Distinguished Service Cross, 332; preparations for second bomb, 335; inspects Nagasaki, 339, 342; post-war career, 339–40; thesis on use of atom bomb, 339; attacked by pro-Communist press in India, 339; flies B-29 at Air Show when simulated atom bomb is dropped, 343

Tinian, 16, 99, 173–81, 211–17, 225–227, 230, 233–5, 242–5, 251–2, 255–6, 265–9, 276–90, 292–4, 296–305, 313, 317, 328, 331, 342–343; as possible base for 509th Group, 13, 86; North Field chosen as base, 96, 105, 131, 146, 169, 170, 184; Japanese bombing of airfield, 176; U.S. artillery bombardment, 176; siege of island, 176; U.S. Marines storm and capture island, 176, 186; Japanese troops in hiding, 173–7, 216, 225–6, 233–5, 342; deployment of U.S. forces, 173–4; naval anchorage, 174; Tinian Town, 174–6, 186

compound for 509th Group, 177; arrival of the special bomber, 184–6; life on Tinian, 192–5, 216; bomb parts carried there, 201–2, 206; scientists arrive, 214; hunts for Japanese troops, 233–5; British observers, 243, 278–9;

384

briefing session for Mission, 278–284; planes take off, 296, 303; welcome to *Enola Gay* on return, 328–30; preparations for second bomb, 335; Commonwealth status within U.S. Trust Territories, 342

Togo, Shigenori, Japanese Foreign Minister, 222–3; and Potsdam Proclamation, 238–40; and acceptance of its terms, 337

Tojo, General Hideki, 163; Minister of War, 16; Prime Minister, 16; forced to resign, 16, 44, 124

Tokyo, 19, 113, 128, 129, 137–9, 152, 160, 235–40, 291; in reach of bombers based on Marianas, 63; as possible target for atom bomb, 75; heavy raid on northeastern sector, 103–4, 107–9; devastation by bombs, 139, 236, 239; Emperor's Palace as possible target, 149; bomb aimed at Imperial Palace, 224–8; defences of Tokyo area, 236; and Potsdam Proclamation, 236–41; bombs near Palace, 239

Tokyo Rose, 63, 152, 225–7; mentions 509th Group, 194

Top Secret (B-29) secondary role at Iwo Jima, 281, 296, 309, 317

Toyo Industries, Hiroshima, 17, 275

Toyoda, Admiral, Japanese Navy Chief of Staff, 108, 132–3, 148

Truman, Bess, 118, 123, 187, 208

Truman, Harry S., xvii, 117–20, 123, 128, 135, 153–5, 159–61, 187–90, 196, 200, 204, 236, 254, 269–70; becomes Vice-President, 92, 118; asks questions about project, 92–3; told of Roosevelt's death, 118; takes oath as President, 119; learns of atom bomb, 119–20, 123; talks with Stimson and Groves on the bomb, 133–5; bluntness with the Russians, 133–134; agrees with necessity for project, 135; broadcasts on VE Day, 144; on unconditional surrender by Japan, 144, 145, 152; opposes Kyoto as site for bomb, 157; meeting on plans to invade Japan, 160–1, 182; concern about casualties, 161

and Potsdam Conference, 187–189; and Stalin, 188, 208–10, 231; and Churchill, 188, 210, 231–3; at Potsdam, 208–11, 231–3; in ruins of Berlin, 208; review of military strategy in light of bomb, 211; and how much to tell the Russians, 220, 323; and Groves' report on Alamogordo test, 231–232; and readiness of uranium bomb, 232–3; agrees to presence of British representatives, 243; statement on the bomb, 335; warns of further destruction, 335; and terms of Japanese surrender, 337

Truman, Margaret, 123, 187

20th Air Force, 85

XXI Bomber Command, 179

Uanna, Major William L. ('Bud') supervises security of Squadron and Group, 23, 26, 27, 52, 56, 78, 98–100, 109–10, 141, 243, 267, 287, 309, 313, 317

Ube, bombing of, 251, 295

Ujina, 94, 164, 190, 335, 336

United Nations, 133–5

Uranium bomb, 111, 154, 201, 203; building of, 35; its mechanism, 36, 75, 96; modifications, 55; date for its availability, 96; core, 111; tamper, 111; 'bullet', 111; details of bomb, 153; its readiness, 232–3; dropped on Hiroshima, 317–19

U.S. Marines, 12, 206, 234–5; storm Tinian, 176, 186

U.S. Military Supply Mission to India, 339

Van Kirk, Theodore ('Dutch'), navigator, 29, 30, 45, 46, 53, 54, 71, 72, 110, 128, 218, 219, 251,

385